Shojo Beat

ANONYMOUS NOISE

Ryoko Fukuyama

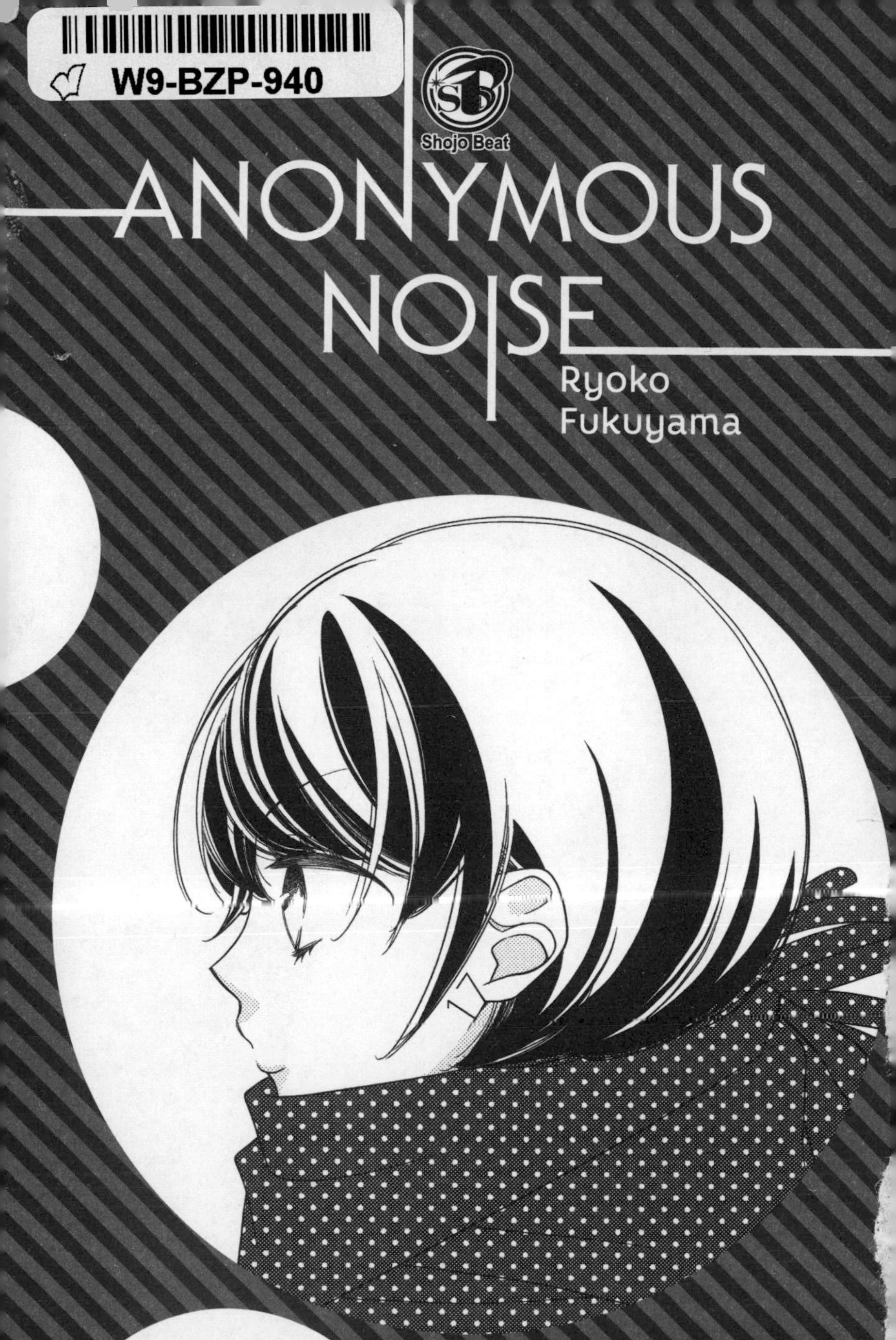

Anonymous Noise

Volume 17

CONTENTS

Song 94...............3
Song 95...............33
Song 96...............63
Song 97...............91
Song 98..............121

Song 64: Side B...151
Melody 1.............157
Melody 2.............165

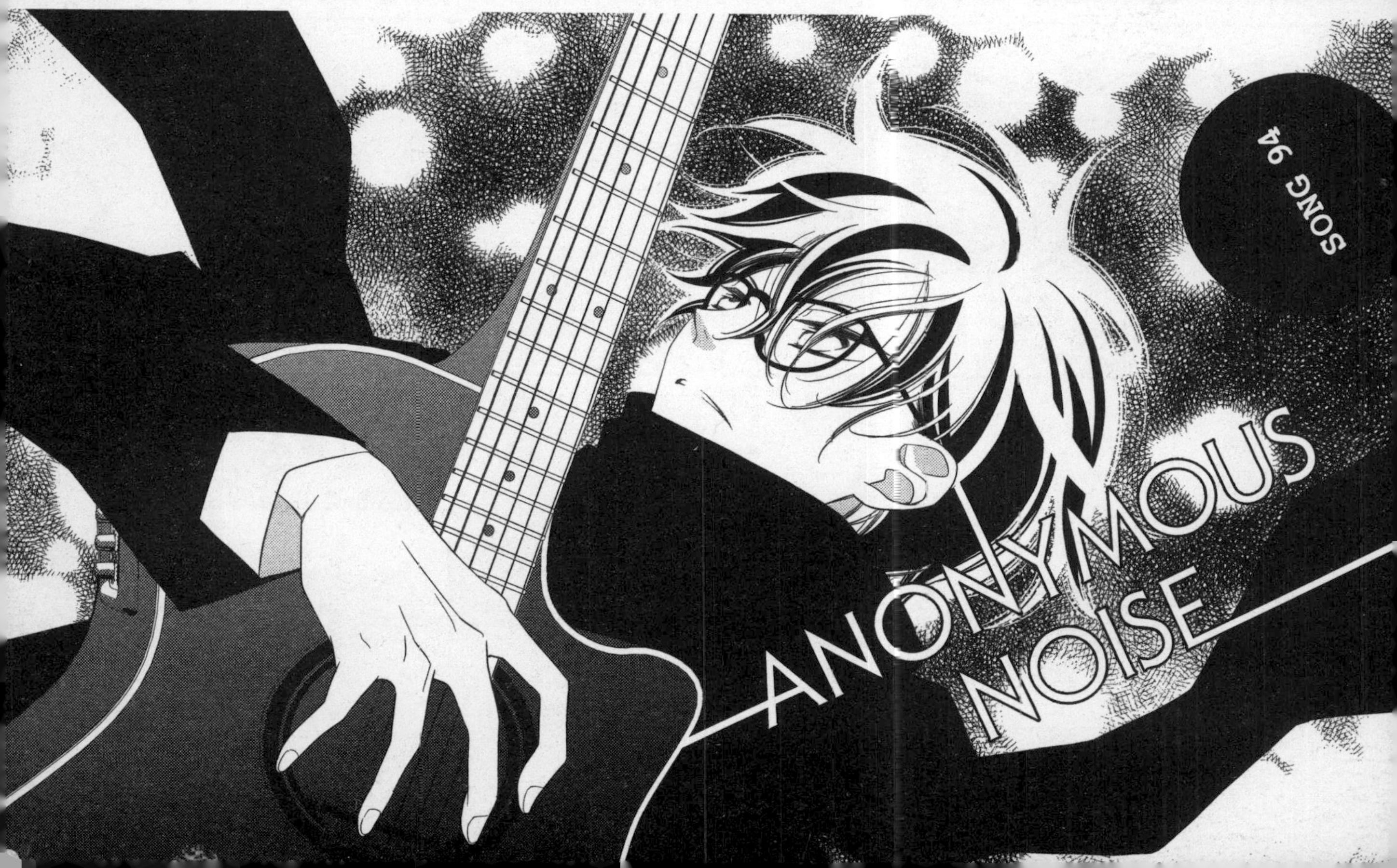
SONG 94
ANONYMOUS NOISE

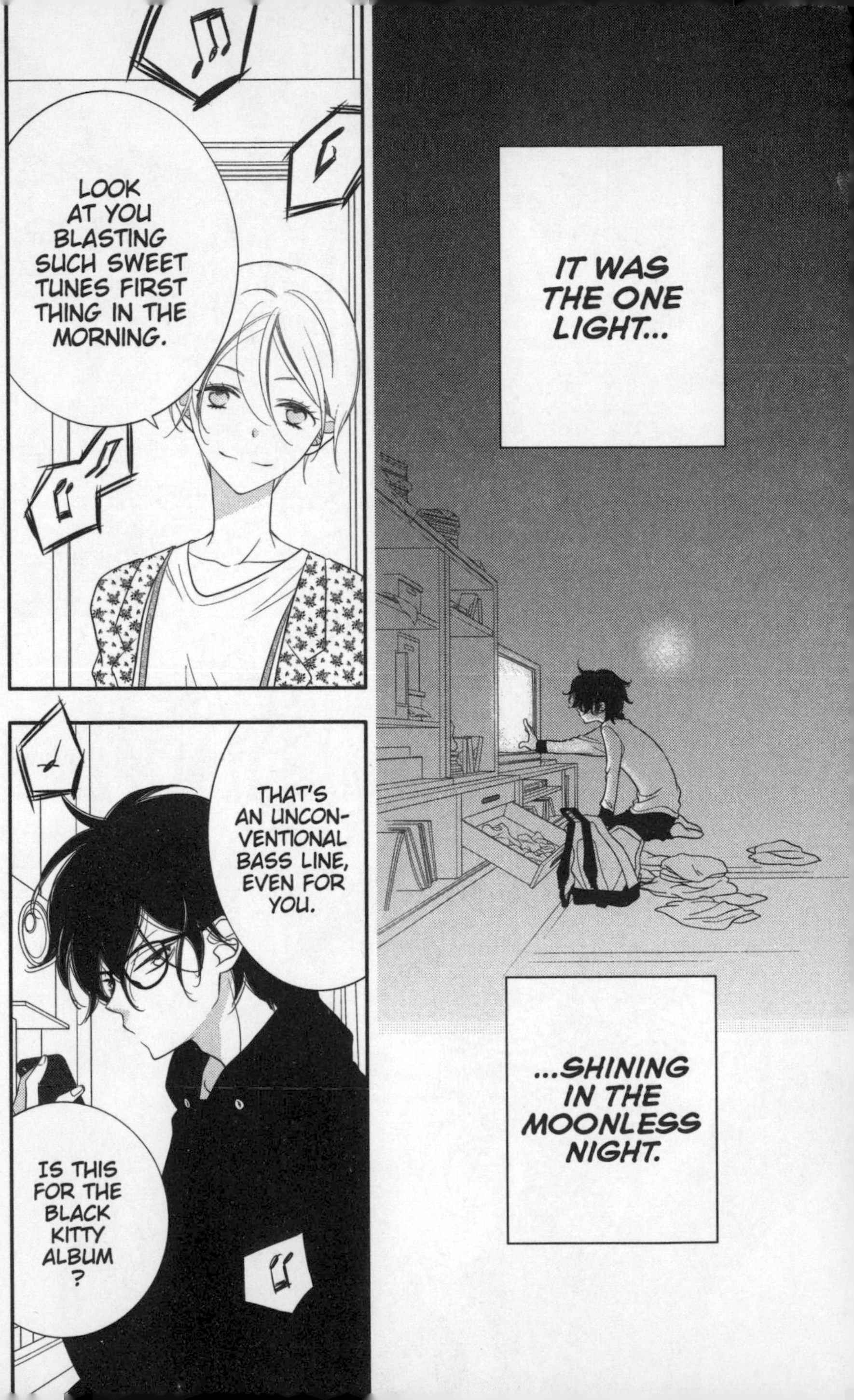
IT WAS THE ONE LIGHT...
...SHINING IN THE MOONLESS NIGHT.
LOOK AT YOU BLASTING SUCH SWEET TUNES FIRST THING IN THE MORNING.
THAT'S AN UNCON-VENTIONAL BASS LINE, EVEN FOR YOU.
IS THIS FOR THE BLACK KITTY ALBUM?

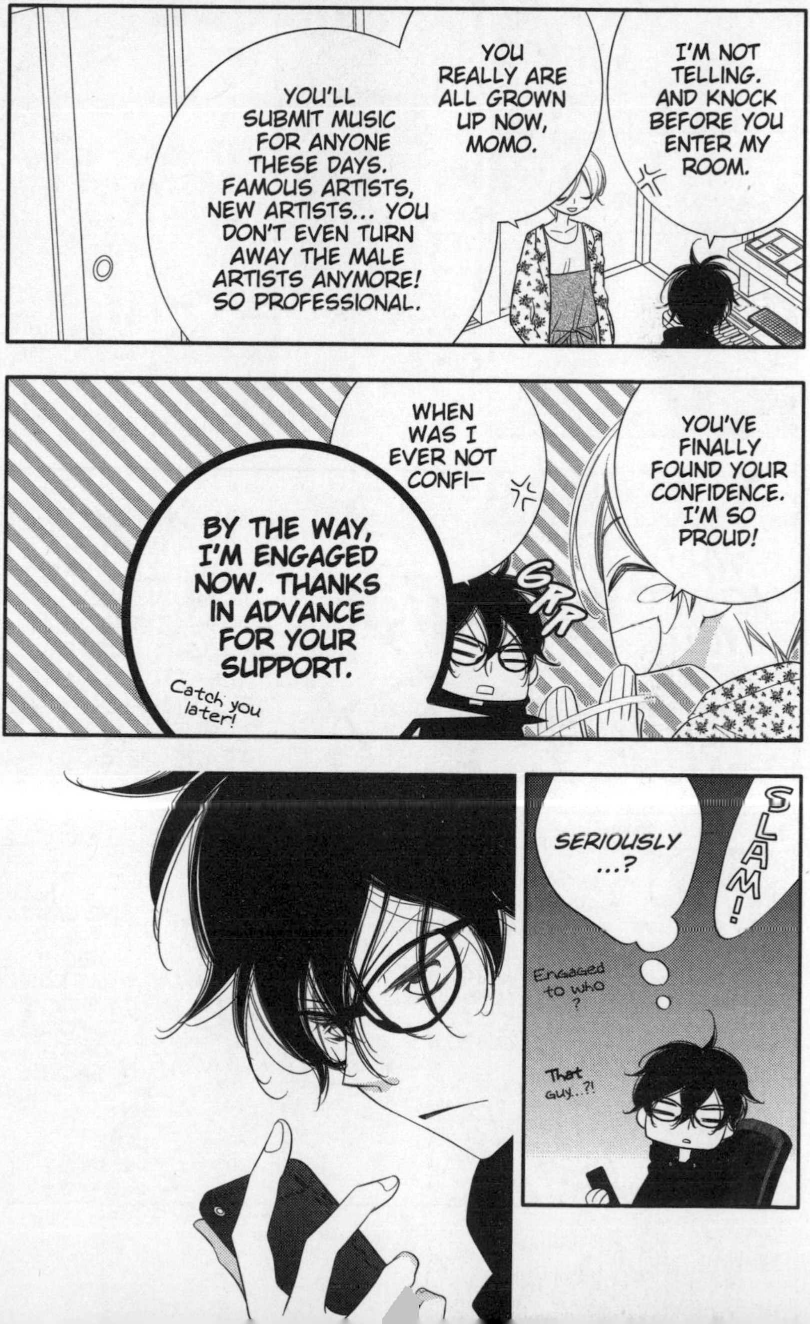
I'M NOT TELLING. AND KNOCK BEFORE YOU ENTER MY ROOM.
YOU REALLY ARE ALL GROWN UP NOW, MOMO.
YOU'LL SUBMIT MUSIC FOR ANYONE THESE DAYS. FAMOUS ARTISTS, NEW ARTISTS... YOU DON'T EVEN TURN AWAY THE MALE ARTISTS ANYMORE! SO PROFESSIONAL.
YOU'VE FINALLY FOUND YOUR CONFIDENCE. I'M SO PROUD!
WHEN WAS I EVER NOT CONFI—
GRR
BY THE WAY, I'M ENGAGED NOW. THANKS IN ADVANCE FOR YOUR SUPPORT.
Catch you later!
SLAM!
SERIOUSLY ...?
Engaged to who?
That guy...?!

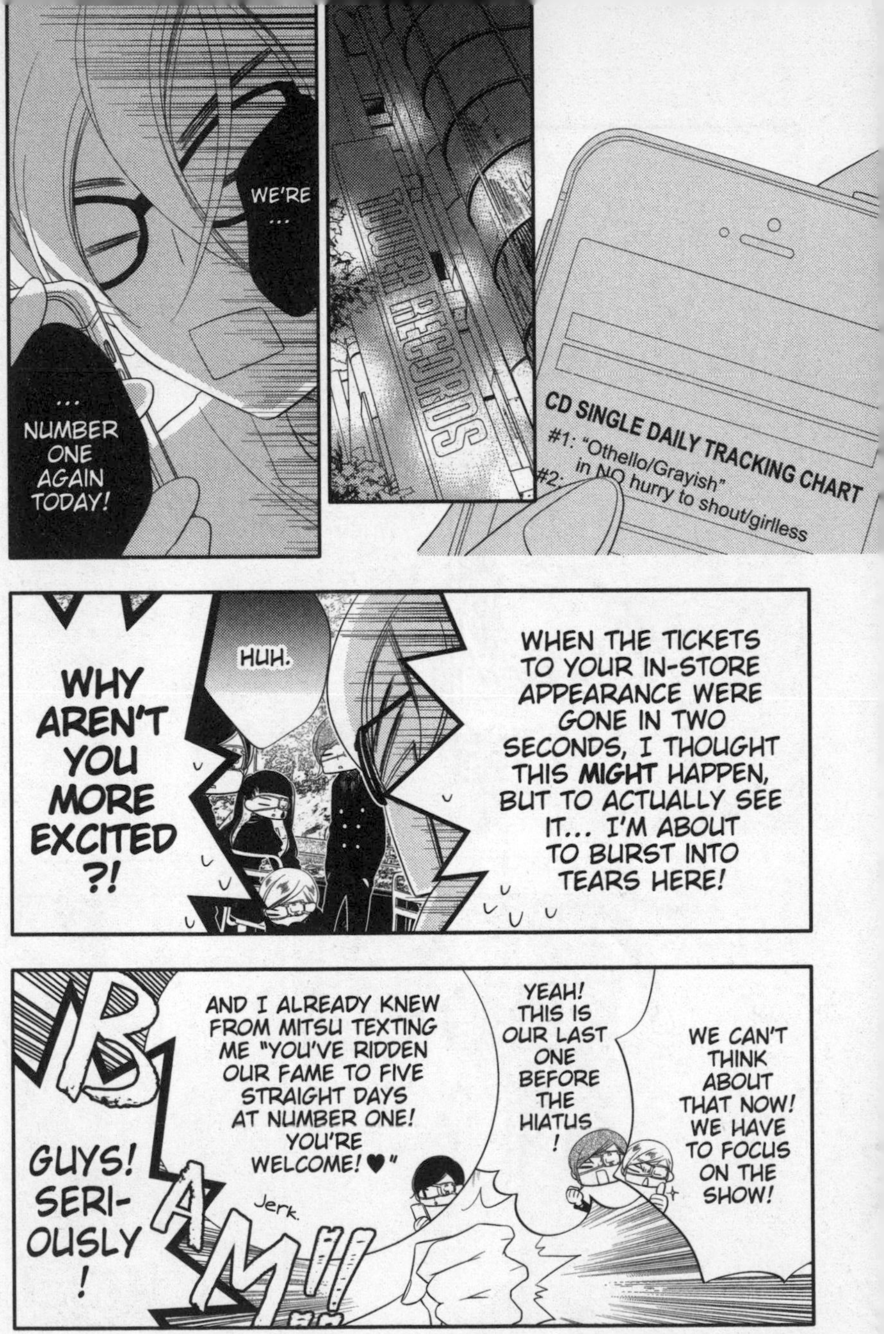
CD SINGLE DAILY TRACKING CHART
#1: "Othello/Grayish"
in NO hurry to shout/girlless
#2:
RECORDS
WE'RE ...
... NUMBER ONE AGAIN TODAY!
WHEN THE TICKETS TO YOUR IN-STORE APPEARANCE WERE GONE IN TWO SECONDS, I THOUGHT THIS MIGHT HAPPEN, BUT TO ACTUALLY SEE IT... I'M ABOUT TO BURST INTO TEARS HERE!
HUH.
WHY AREN'T YOU MORE EXCITED?!
WE CAN'T THINK ABOUT THAT NOW! WE HAVE TO FOCUS ON THE SHOW!
YEAH! THIS IS OUR LAST ONE BEFORE THE HIATUS!
AND I ALREADY KNEW FROM MITSU TEXTING ME "YOU'VE RIDDEN OUR FAME TO FIVE STRAIGHT DAYS AT NUMBER ONE! YOU'RE WELCOME! ♥"
Jerk.
BLAM!!
GUYS! SERI-OUSLY!

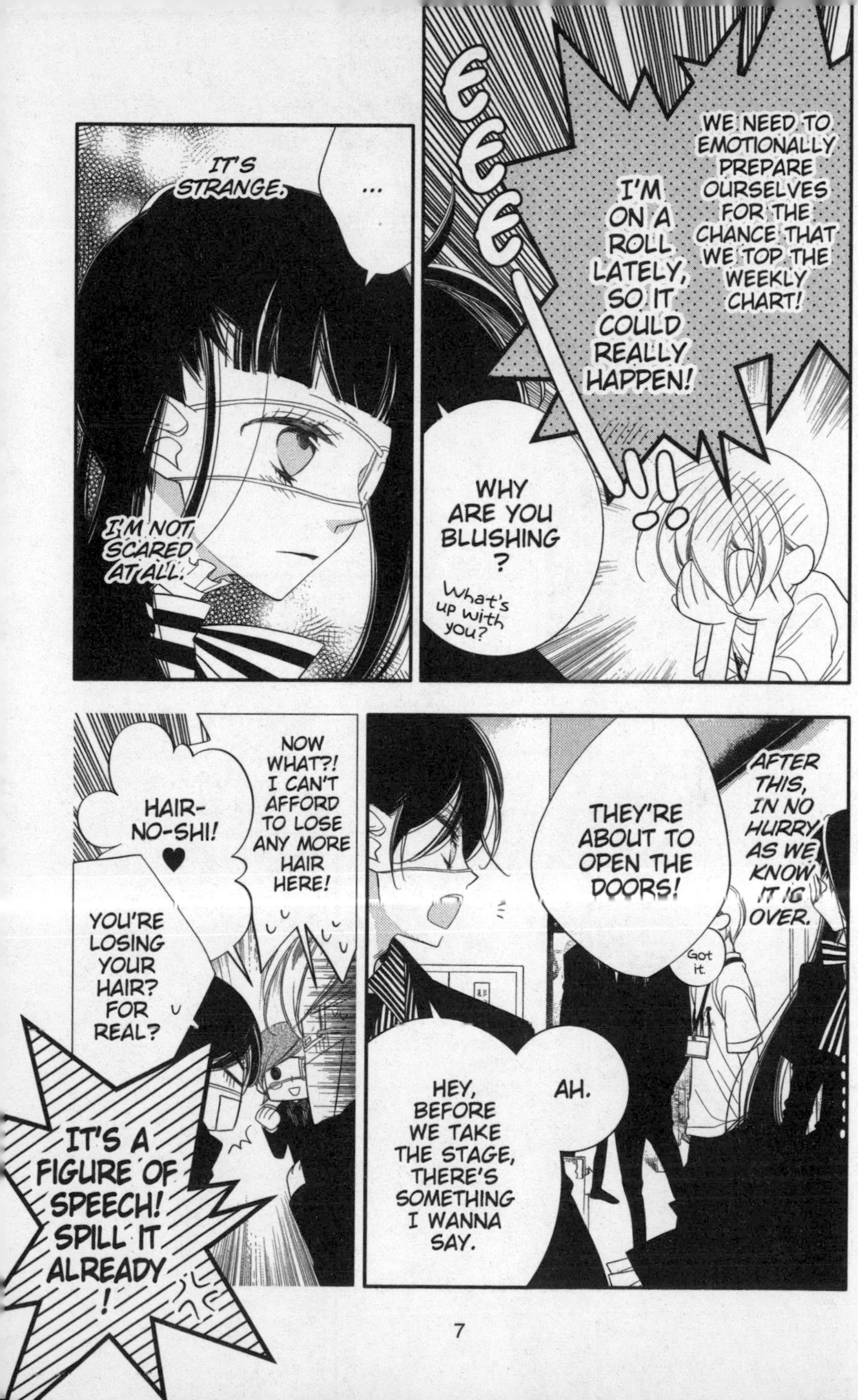
EEEE
WE NEED TO EMOTIONALLY PREPARE OURSELVES FOR THE CHANCE THAT WE TOP THE WEEKLY CHART!
I'M ON A ROLL LATELY, SO IT COULD REALLY HAPPEN!
WHY ARE YOU BLUSHING?
What's up with you?
...
IT'S STRANGE.
I'M NOT SCARED AT ALL.
AFTER THIS, IN NO HURRY AS WE KNOW IT IS OVER.
THEY'RE ABOUT TO OPEN THE DOORS!
Got it.
AH.
HEY, BEFORE WE TAKE THE STAGE, THERE'S SOMETHING I WANNA SAY.
NOW WHAT?! I CAN'T AFFORD TO LOSE ANY MORE HAIR HERE!
HAIR-NO-SHI! ♥
YOU'RE LOSING YOUR HAIR? FOR REAL?
IT'S A FIGURE OF SPEECH! SPILL IT ALREADY!

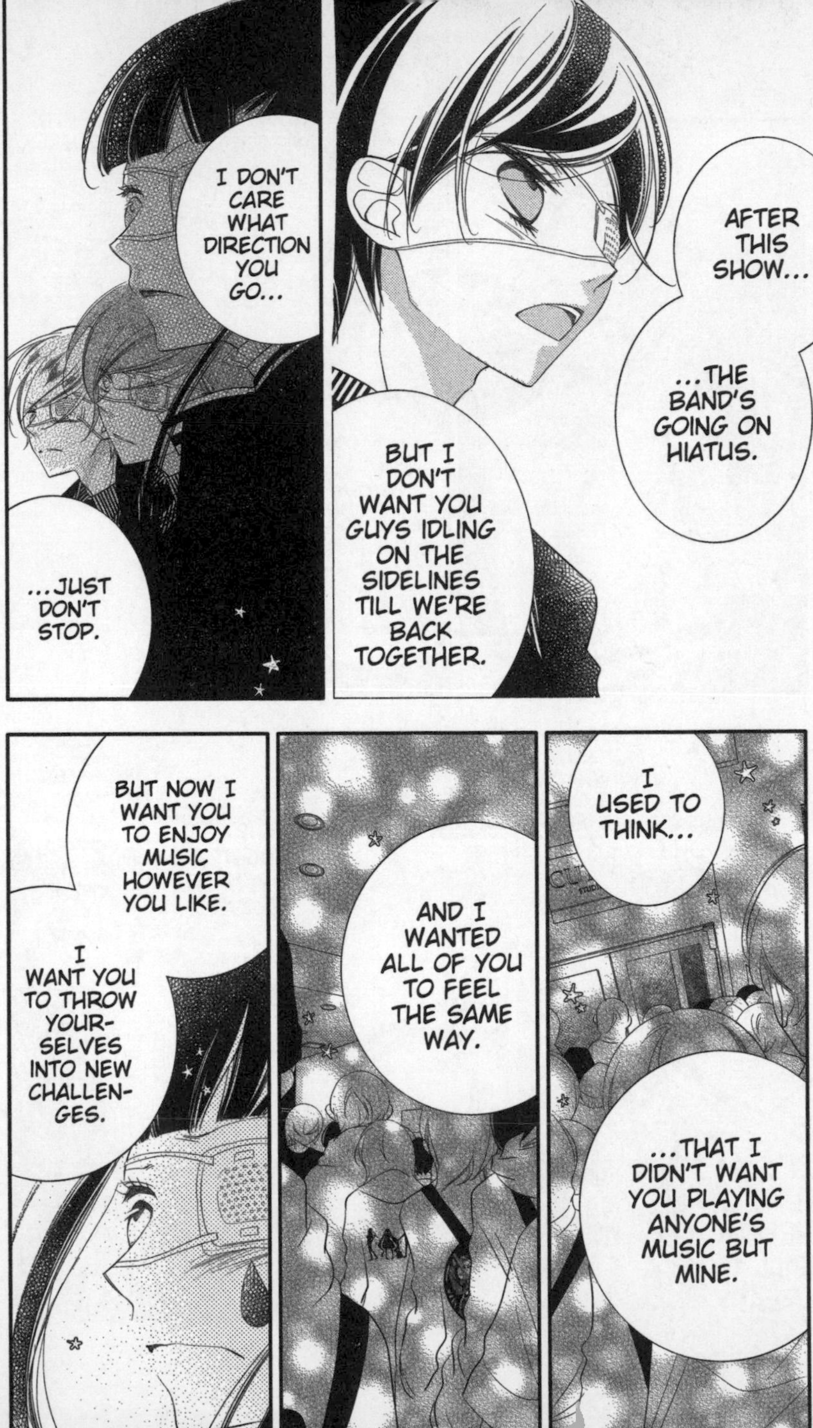
AFTER THIS SHOW...
...THE BAND'S GOING ON HIATUS.
BUT I DON'T WANT YOU GUYS IDLING ON THE SIDELINES TILL WE'RE BACK TOGETHER.
I DON'T CARE WHAT DIRECTION YOU GO...
...JUST DON'T STOP.
I USED TO THINK...
...THAT I DIDN'T WANT YOU PLAYING ANYONE'S MUSIC BUT MINE.
AND I WANTED ALL OF YOU TO FEEL THE SAME WAY.
BUT NOW I WANT YOU TO ENJOY MUSIC HOWEVER YOU LIKE.
I WANT YOU TO THROW YOUR-SELVES INTO NEW CHALLEN-GES.

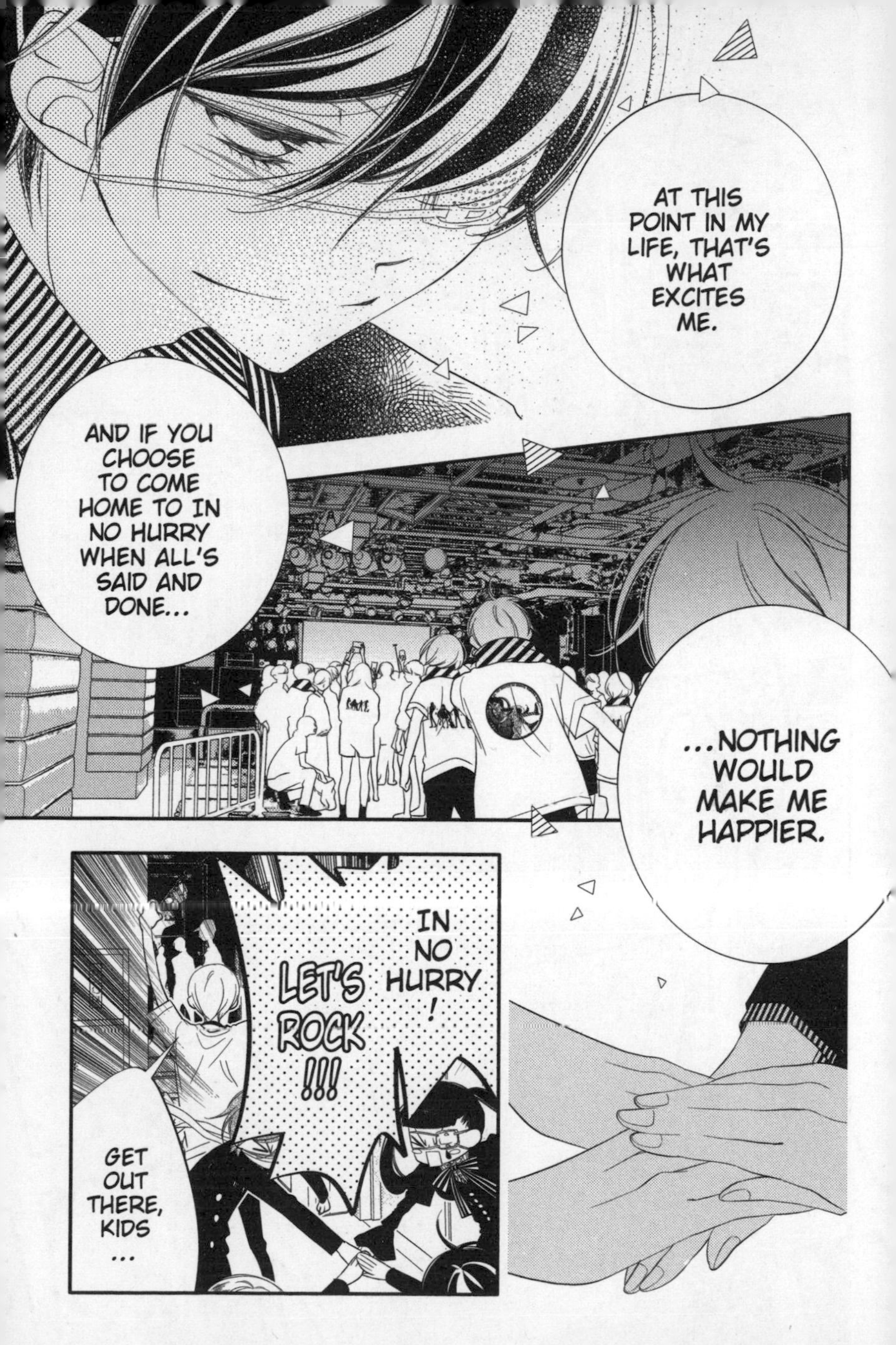
AT THIS POINT IN MY LIFE, THAT'S WHAT EXCITES ME.
AND IF YOU CHOOSE TO COME HOME TO IN NO HURRY WHEN ALL'S SAID AND DONE...
...NOTHING WOULD MAKE ME HAPPIER.
IN NO HURRY!
LET'S ROCK!!!
GET OUT THERE, KIDS...

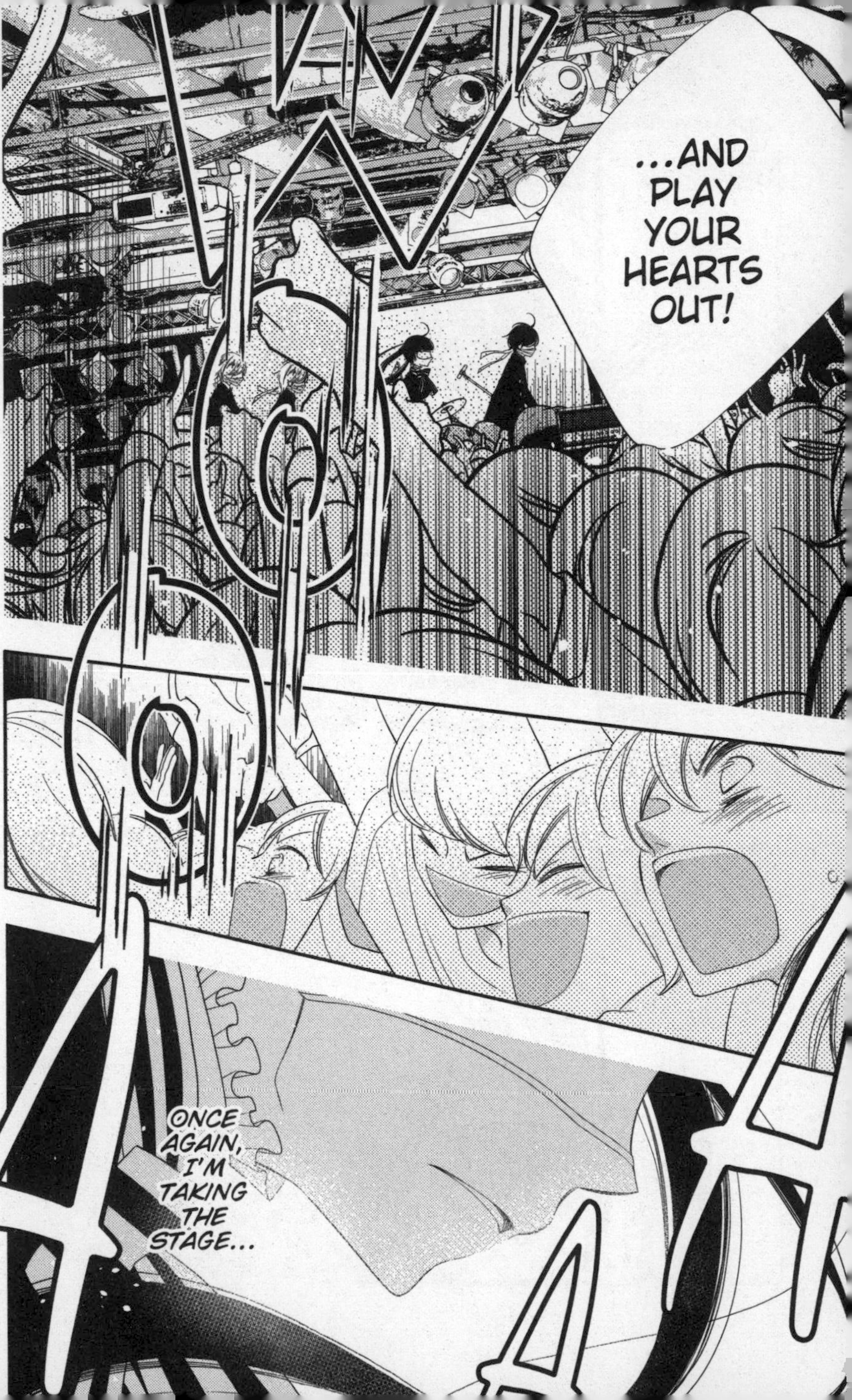
...AND PLAY YOUR HEARTS OUT!
ONCE AGAIN, I'M TAKING THE STAGE...

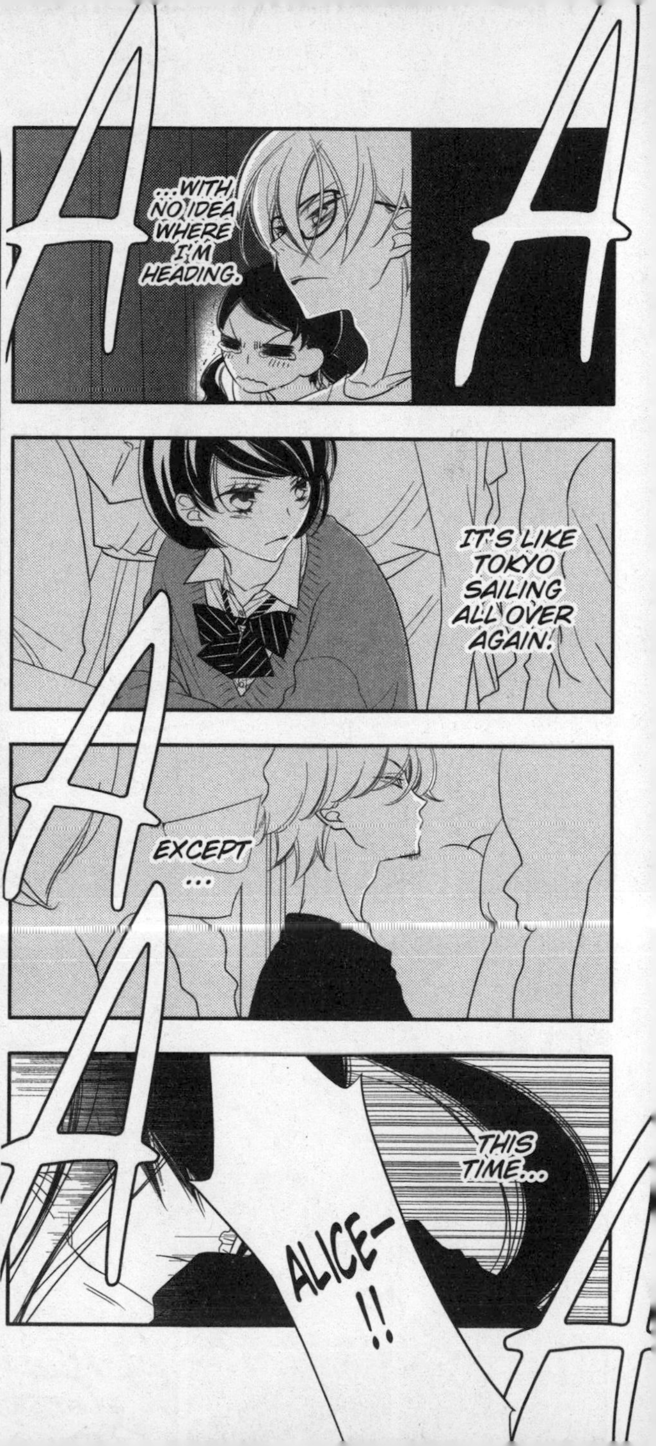
...WITH NO IDEA WHERE I'M HEADING.
IT'S LIKE TOKYO SAILING ALL OVER AGAIN!
EXCEPT...
THIS TIME...
ALICE—!!

1

Hello, how are you doing? It's me, Ryoko Fukuyama!

I hope you've been well. Thank you so much for picking up volume 17 of Anonymous Noise

Look, I'm hand-writing my columns again! I'm digging deep to remember everything I learned about proper penmanship in my youth, so I bet it looks super weird this time, right? Ugh, I'm already exhausted.

Miou graces this volume's cover. It feels like it's been a long time since I did a full-color illustration of a female character, so it was a lot of fun for me to draw. I really hope you enjoy volume 17!

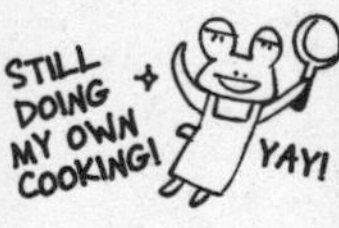
STILL DOING MY OWN COOKING!
YAY!

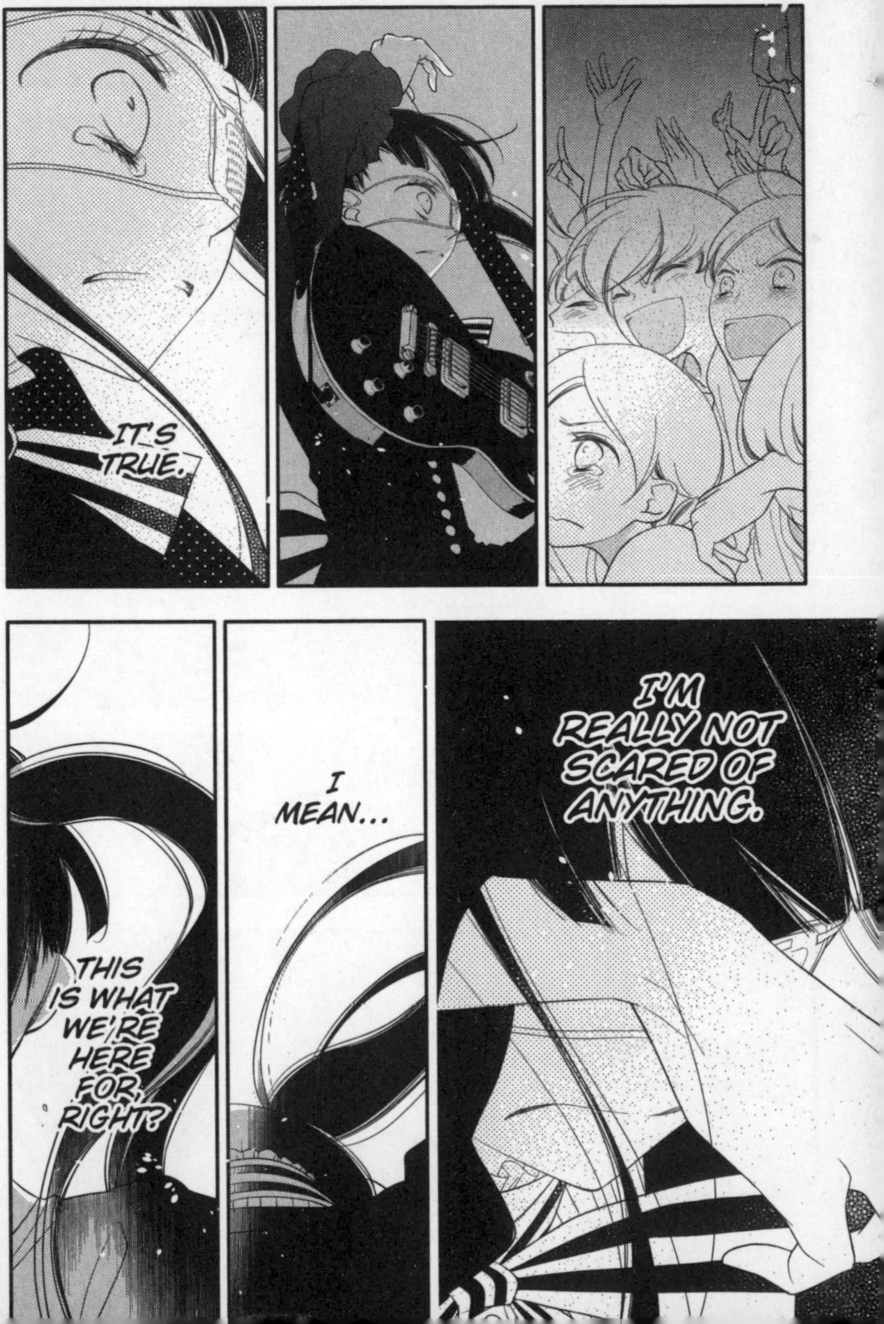
IT'S TRUE.
I'M REALLY NOT SCARED OF ANYTHING.
I MEAN...
THIS IS WHAT WE'RE HERE FOR, RIGHT?

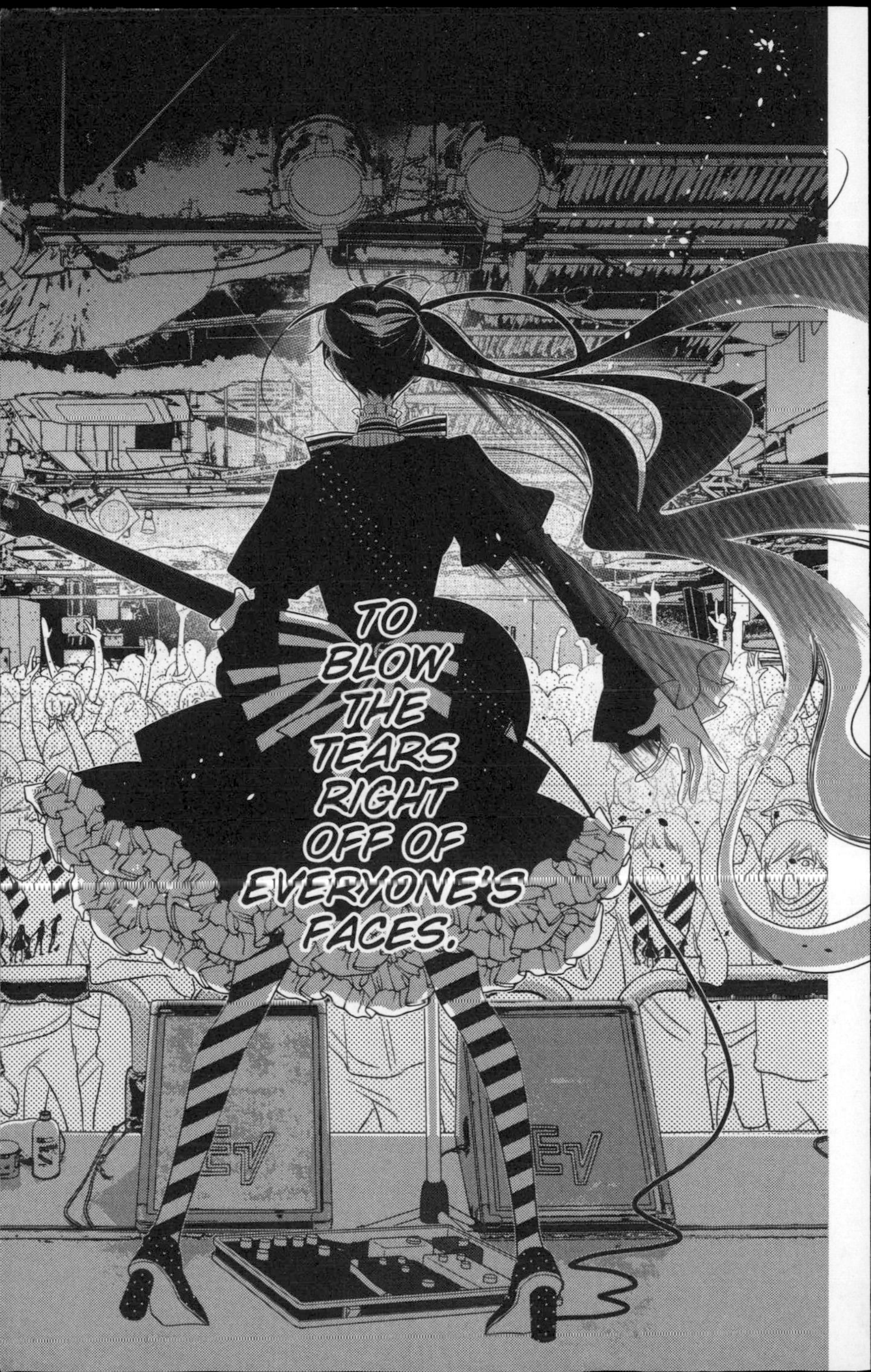
TO BLOW THE TEARS RIGHT OFF OF EVERYONE'S FACES.

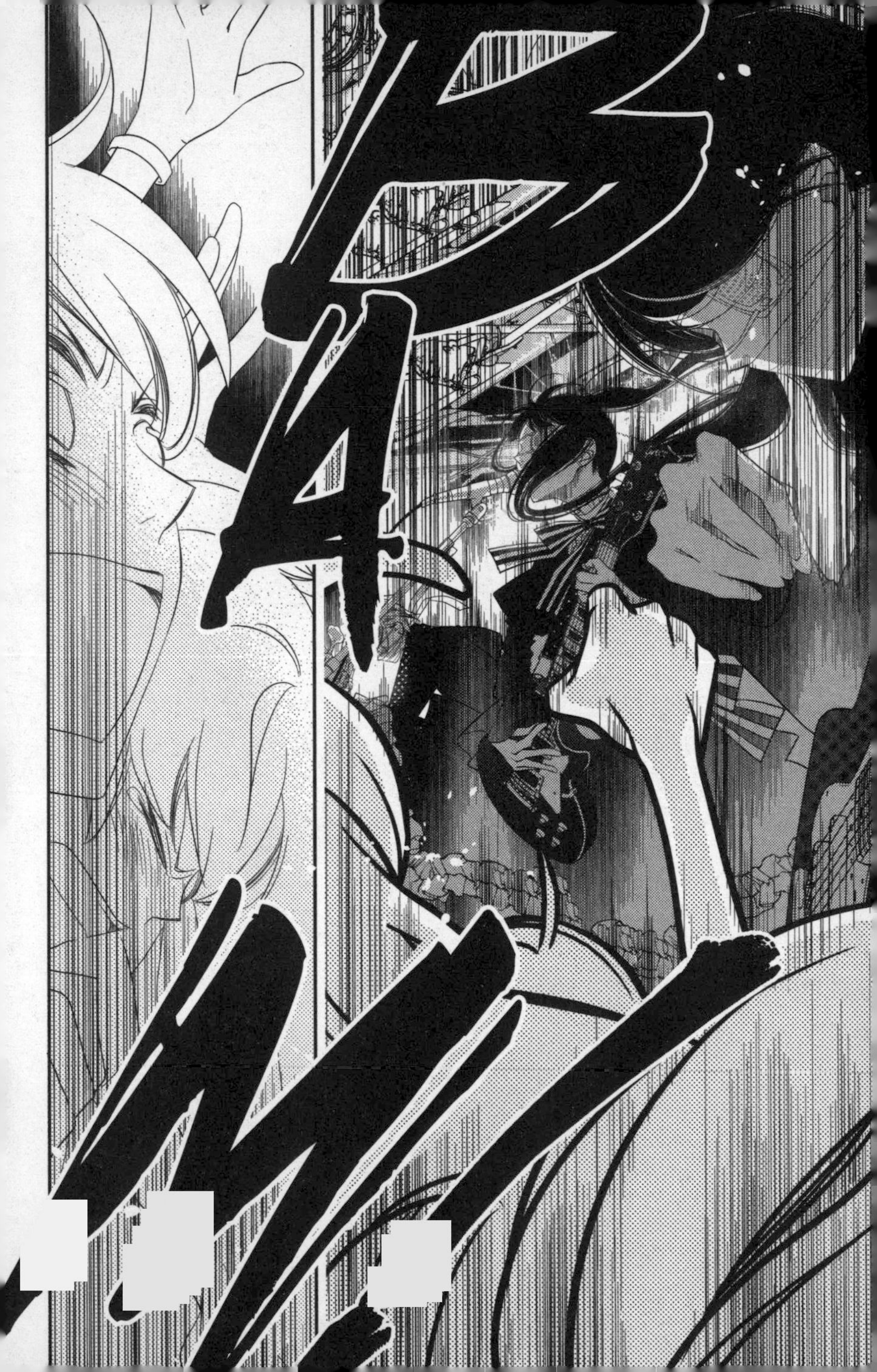

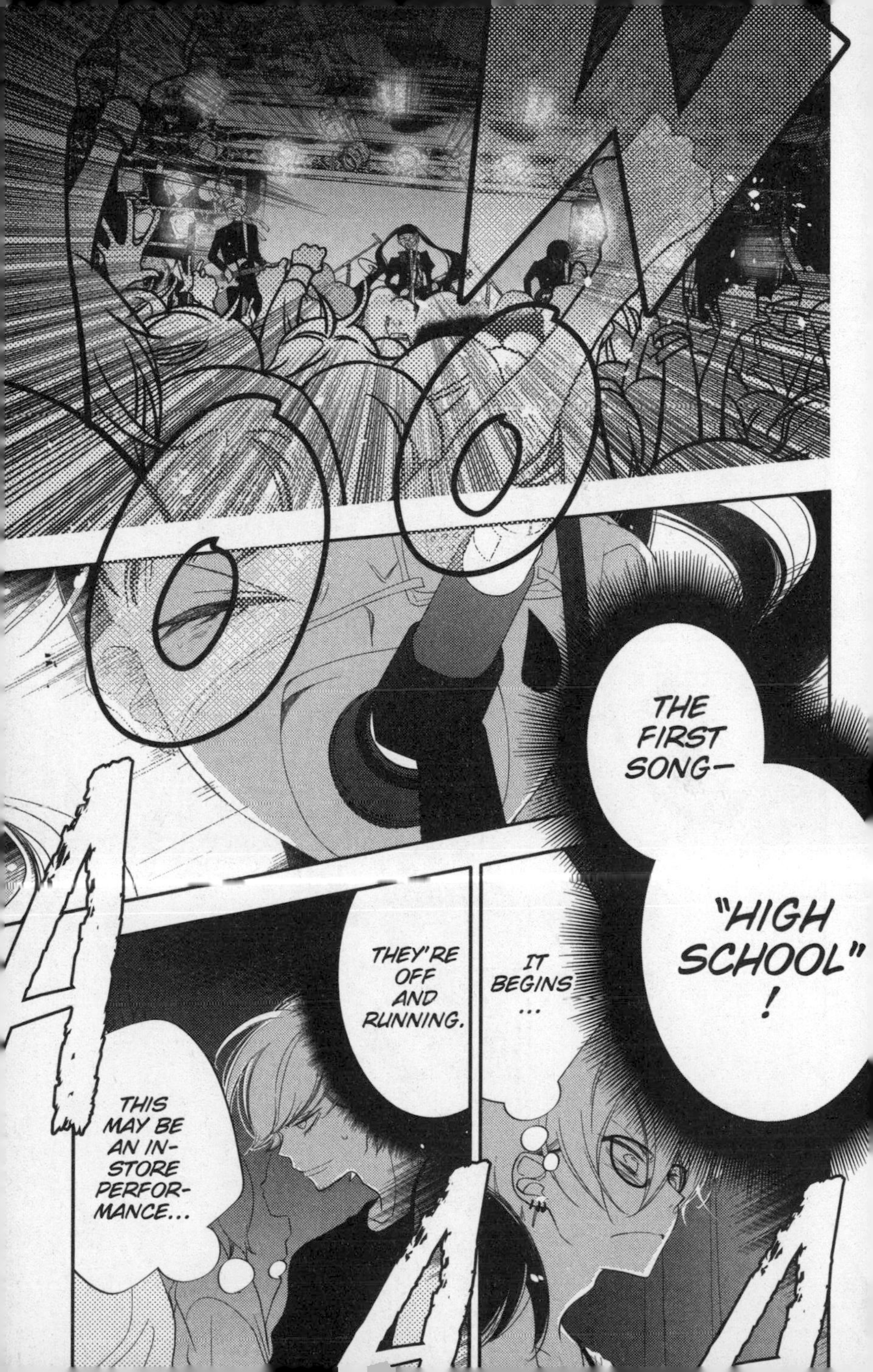
THE FIRST SONG—
"HIGH SCHOOL"!
IT BEGINS...
THEY'RE OFF AND RUNNING.
THIS MAY BE AN IN-STORE PERFORMANCE...

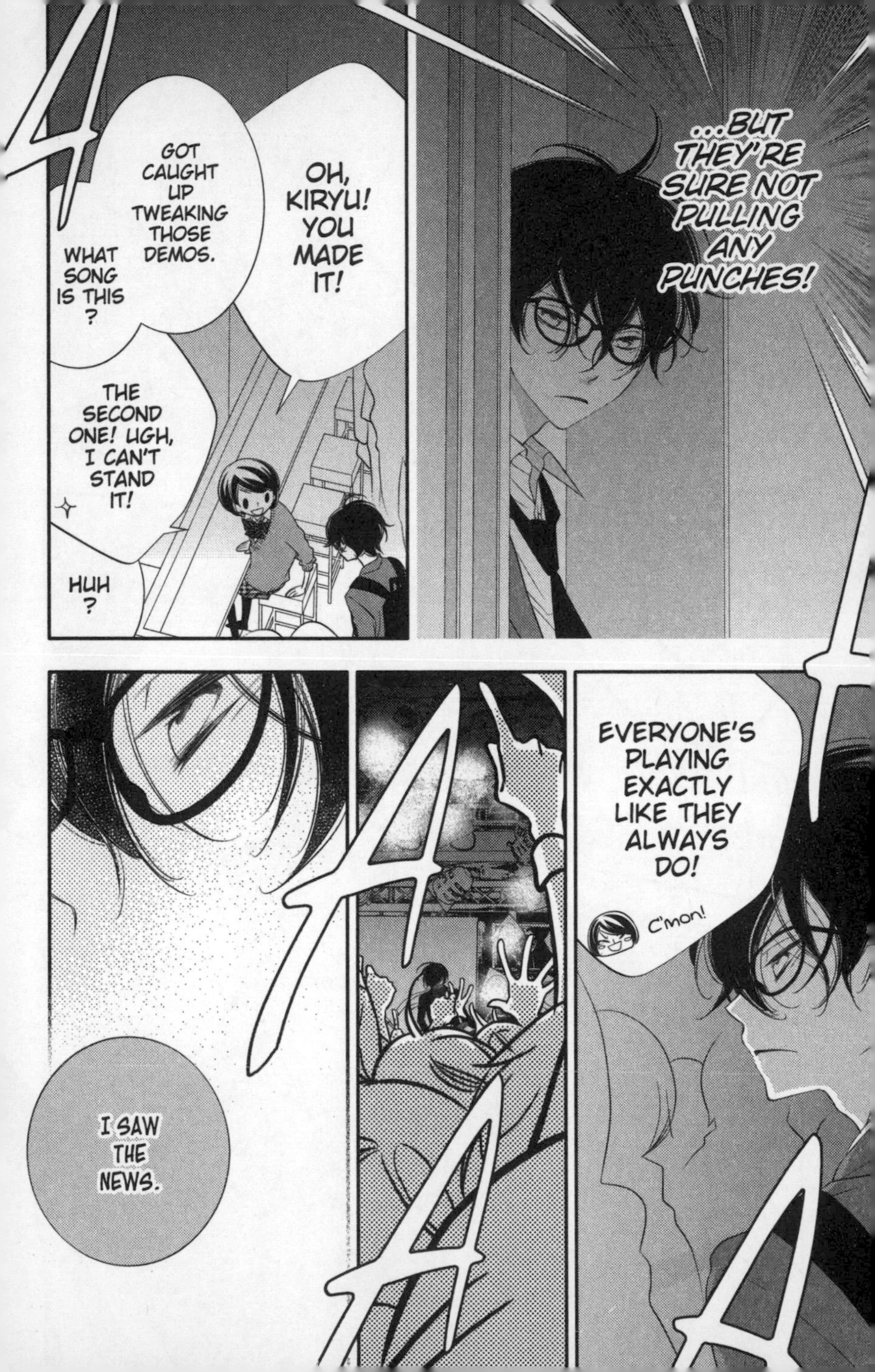
...BUT THEY'RE SURE NOT PULLING ANY PUNCHES!
OH, KIRYU! YOU MADE IT!
GOT CAUGHT UP TWEAKING THOSE DEMOS.
WHAT SONG IS THIS?
THE SECOND ONE! UGH, I CAN'T STAND IT!
HUH?
EVERYONE'S PLAYING EXACTLY LIKE THEY ALWAYS DO!
C'mon!
I SAW THE NEWS.

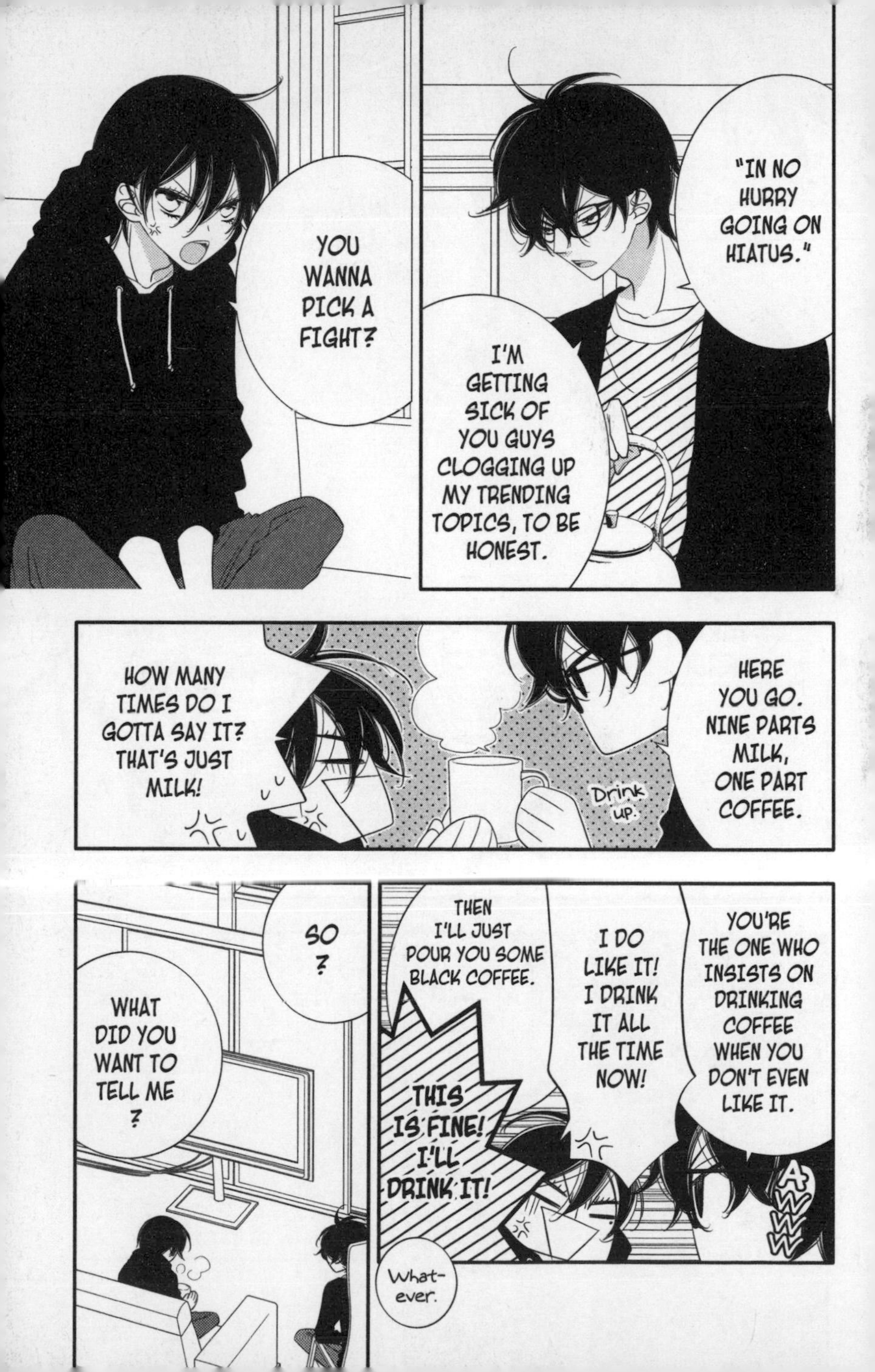
"IN NO HURRY GOING ON HIATUS."
I'M GETTING SICK OF YOU GUYS CLOGGING UP MY TRENDING TOPICS, TO BE HONEST.
YOU WANNA PICK A FIGHT?
HERE YOU GO. NINE PARTS MILK, ONE PART COFFEE.
Drink up.
HOW MANY TIMES DO I GOTTA SAY IT? THAT'S JUST MILK!
YOU'RE THE ONE WHO INSISTS ON DRINKING COFFEE WHEN YOU DON'T EVEN LIKE IT.
AWWW
I DO LIKE IT! I DRINK IT ALL THE TIME NOW!
THEN I'LL JUST POUR YOU SOME BLACK COFFEE.
THIS IS FINE! I'LL DRINK IT!
What-ever.
SO?
WHAT DID YOU WANT TO TELL ME?

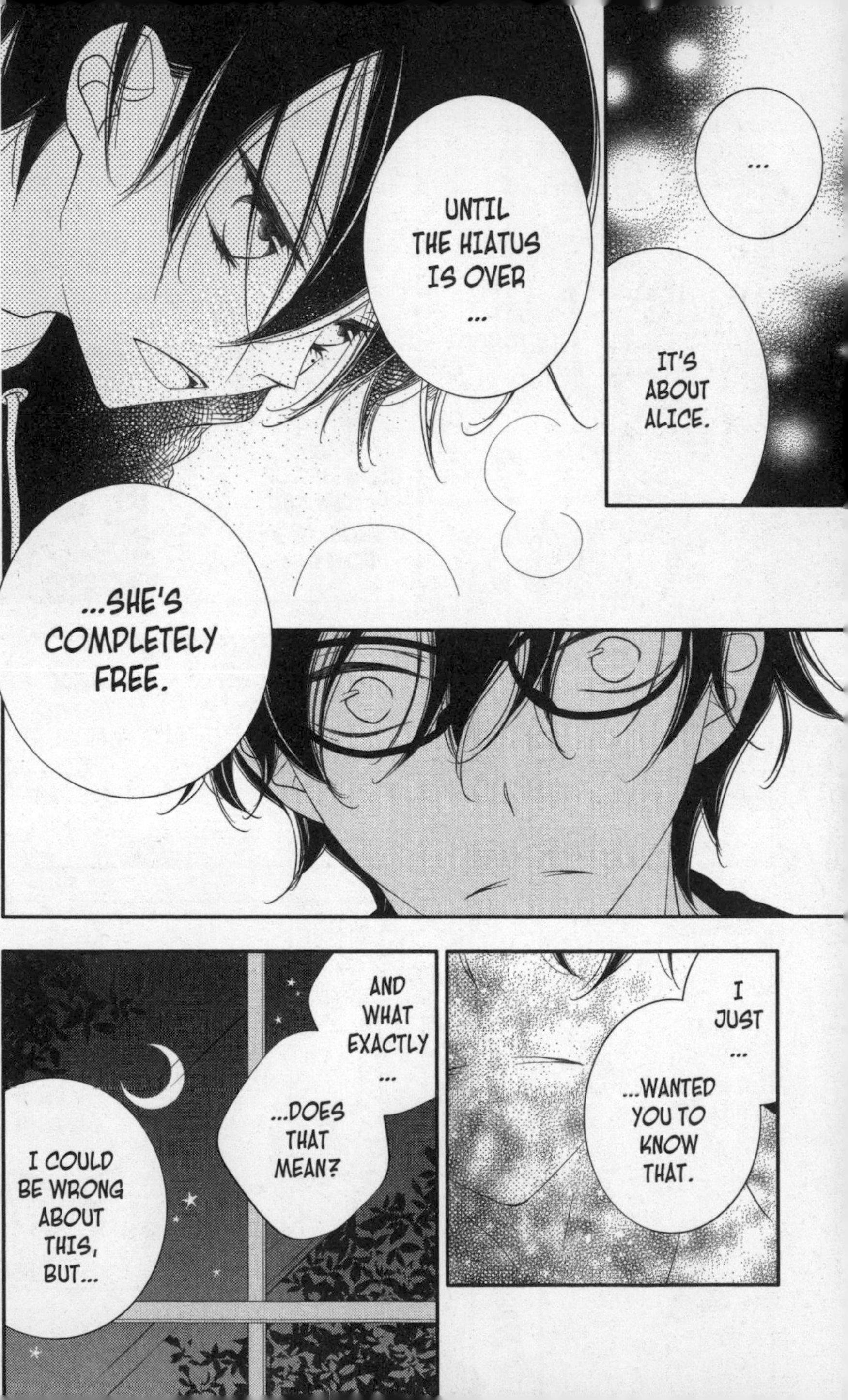
...
IT'S ABOUT ALICE.
UNTIL THE HIATUS IS OVER ...
...SHE'S COMPLETELY FREE.
I JUST ...
...WANTED YOU TO KNOW THAT.
AND WHAT EXACTLY ...
...DOES THAT MEAN?
I COULD BE WRONG ABOUT THIS, BUT...

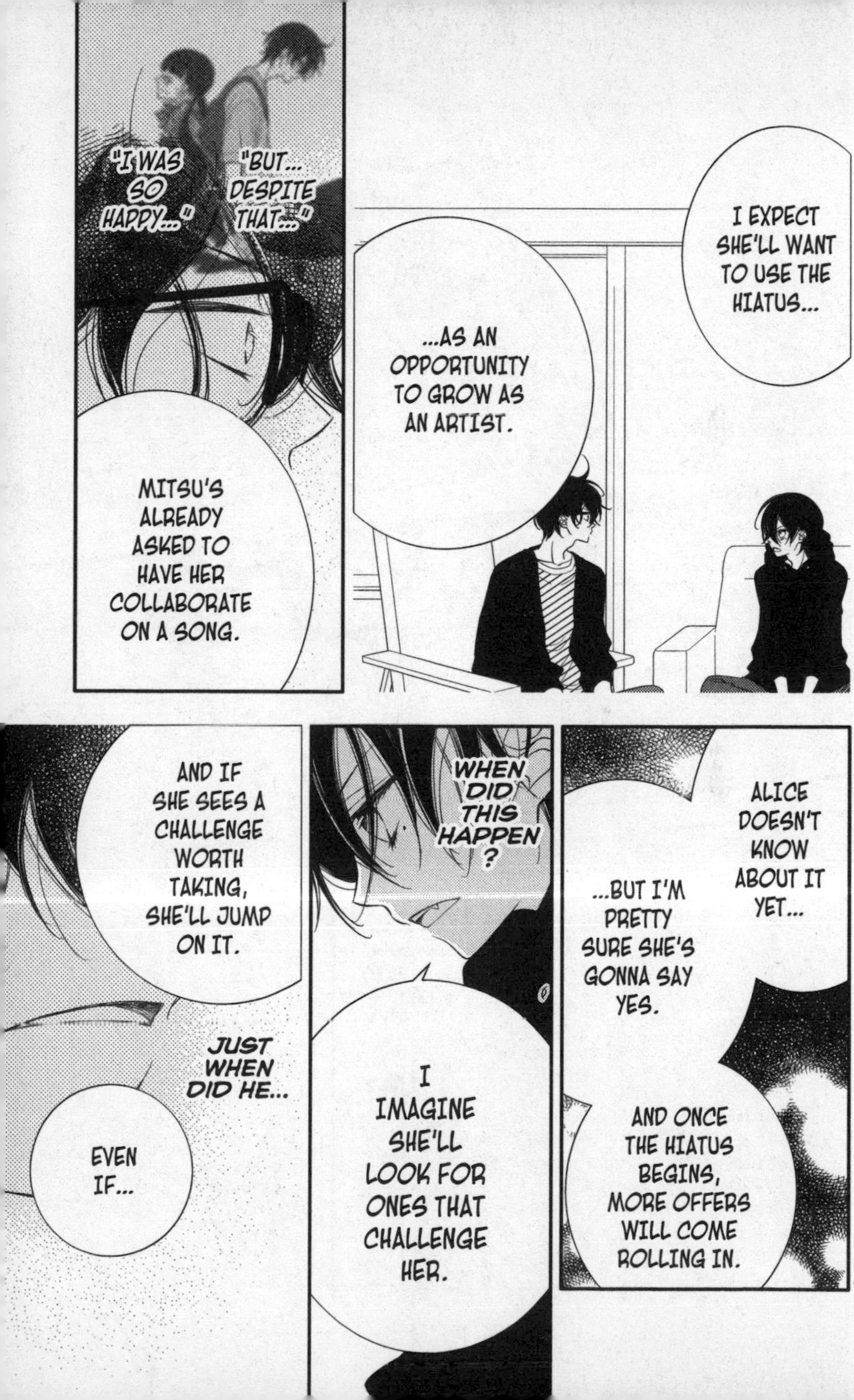
I EXPECT SHE'LL WANT TO USE THE HIATUS...
...AS AN OPPORTUNITY TO GROW AS AN ARTIST.
"BUT... DESPITE THAT..."
"I WAS SO HAPPY..."
MITSU'S ALREADY ASKED TO HAVE HER COLLABORATE ON A SONG.
ALICE DOESN'T KNOW ABOUT IT YET...
...BUT I'M PRETTY SURE SHE'S GONNA SAY YES.
AND ONCE THE HIATUS BEGINS, MORE OFFERS WILL COME ROLLING IN.
WHEN DID THIS HAPPEN?
I IMAGINE SHE'LL LOOK FOR ONES THAT CHALLENGE HER.
AND IF SHE SEES A CHALLENGE WORTH TAKING, SHE'LL JUMP ON IT.
JUST WHEN DID HE...
EVEN IF...

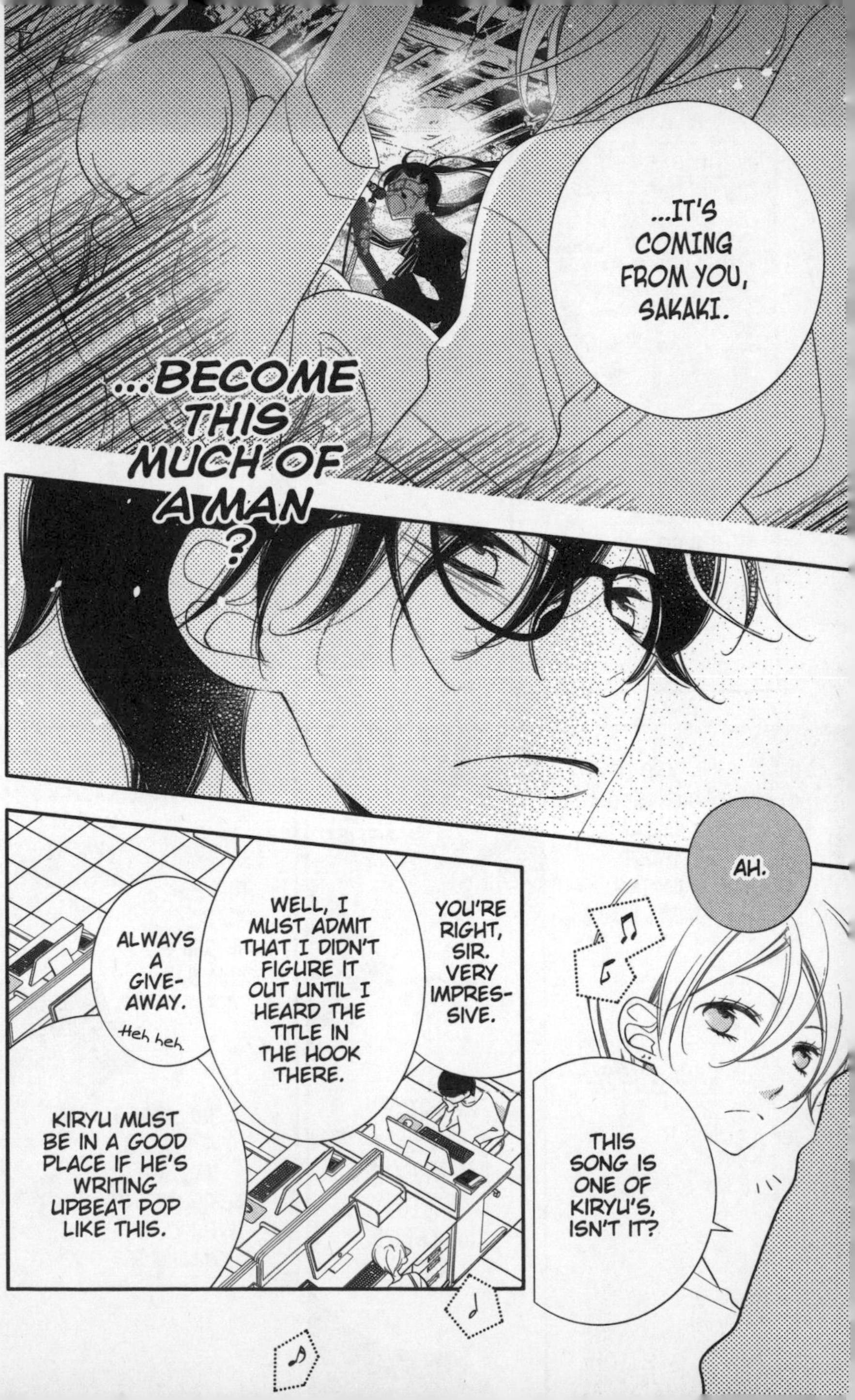
...IT'S COMING FROM YOU, SAKAKI.
...BECOME THIS MUCH OF A MAN?
AH.
THIS SONG IS ONE OF KIRYU'S, ISN'T IT?
YOU'RE RIGHT, SIR. VERY IMPRESSIVE.
WELL, I MUST ADMIT THAT I DIDN'T FIGURE IT OUT UNTIL I HEARD THE TITLE IN THE HOOK THERE.
ALWAYS A GIVE-AWAY.
Heh heh.
KIRYU MUST BE IN A GOOD PLACE IF HE'S WRITING UPBEAT POP LIKE THIS.

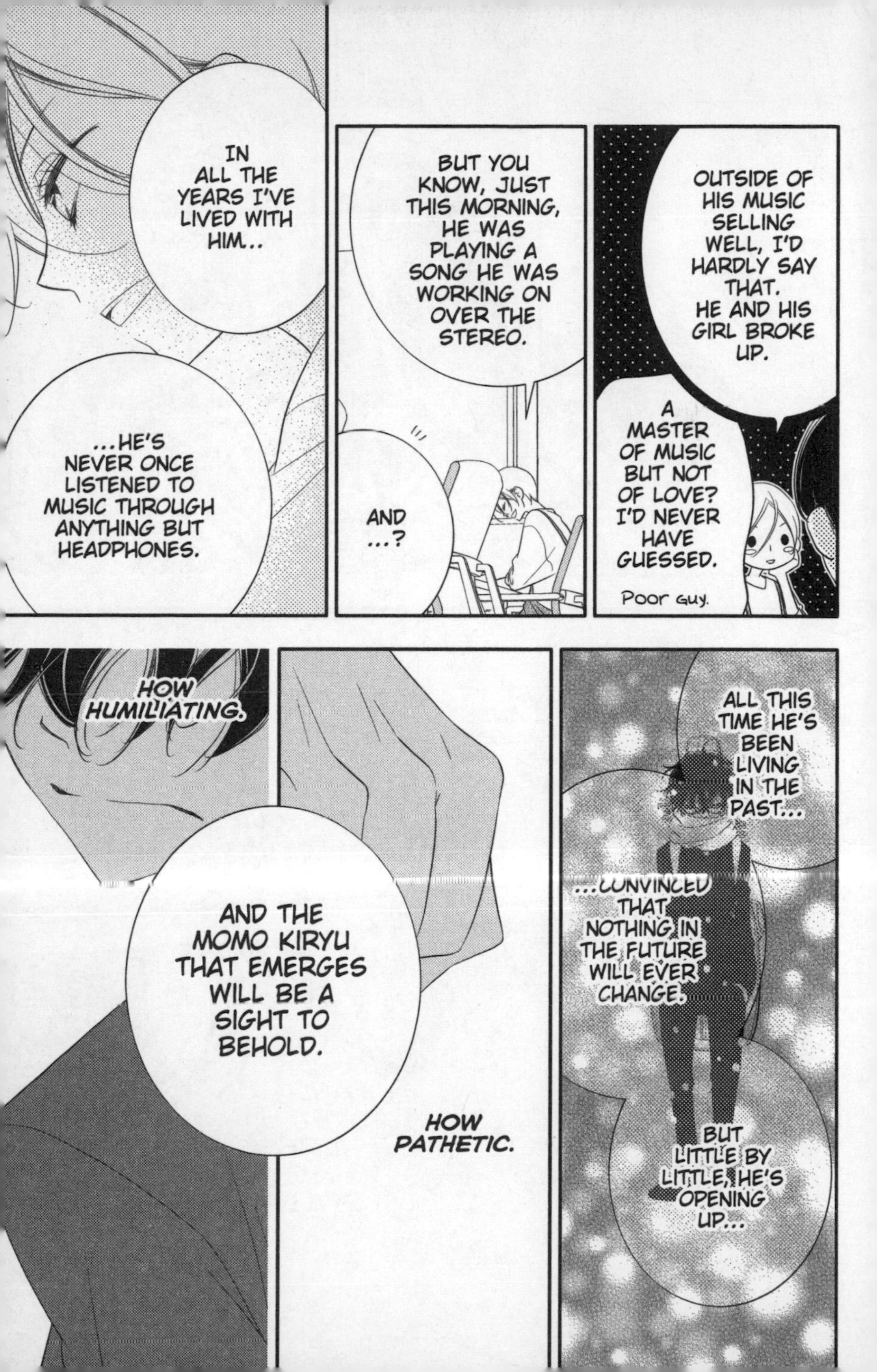
OUTSIDE OF HIS MUSIC SELLING WELL, I'D HARDLY SAY THAT. HE AND HIS GIRL BROKE UP.
A MASTER OF MUSIC BUT NOT OF LOVE? I'D NEVER HAVE GUESSED.
Poor guy.
BUT YOU KNOW, JUST THIS MORNING, HE WAS PLAYING A SONG HE WAS WORKING ON OVER THE STEREO.
AND ...?
IN ALL THE YEARS I'VE LIVED WITH HIM...
...HE'S NEVER ONCE LISTENED TO MUSIC THROUGH ANYTHING BUT HEADPHONES.
ALL THIS TIME HE'S BEEN LIVING IN THE PAST...
...CONVINCED THAT NOTHING IN THE FUTURE WILL EVER CHANGE.
BUT LITTLE BY LITTLE, HE'S OPENING UP...
AND THE MOMO KIRYU THAT EMERGES WILL BE A SIGHT TO BEHOLD.
HOW PATHETIC.
HOW HUMILIATING.

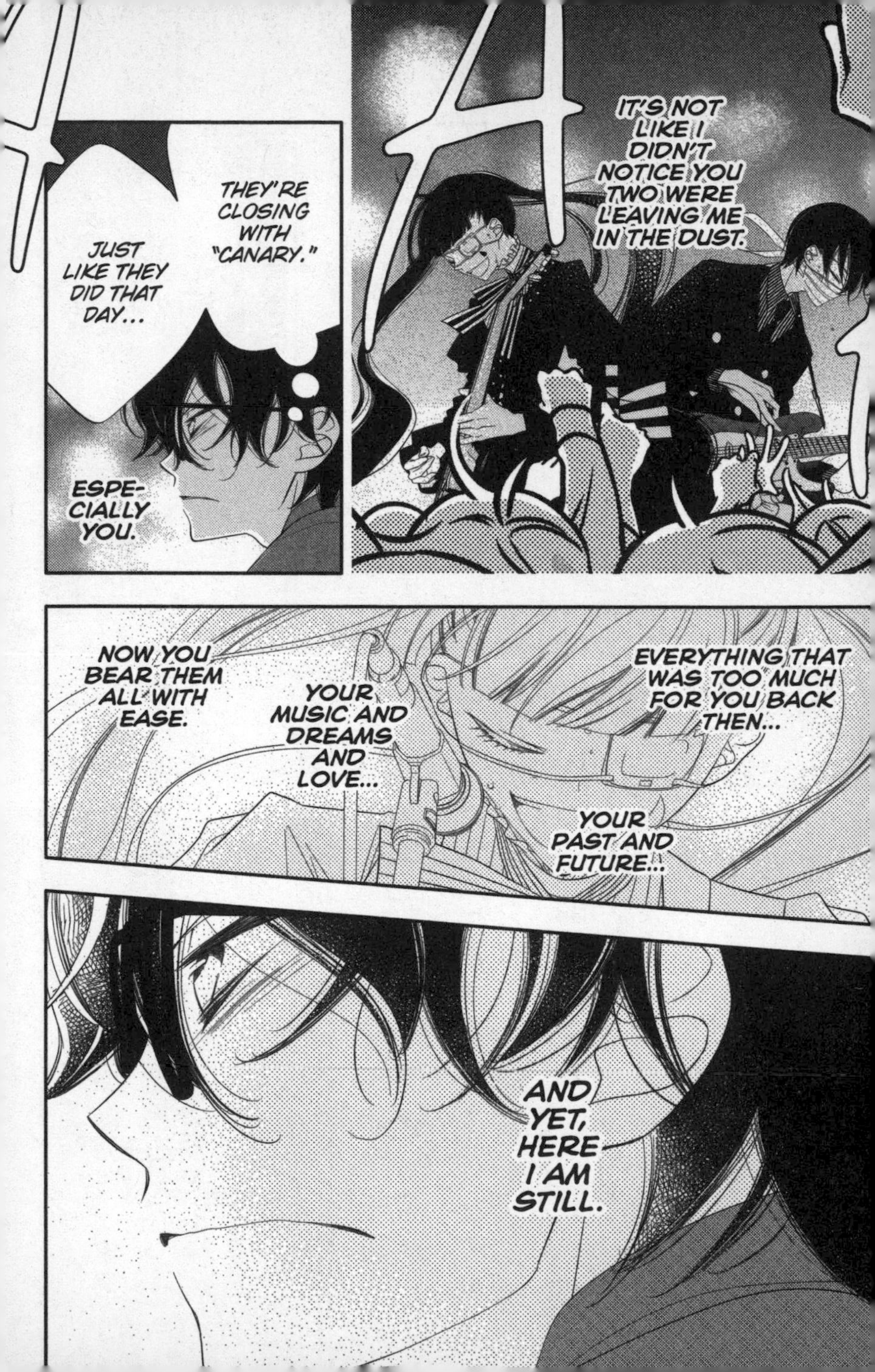
IT'S NOT LIKE I DIDN'T NOTICE YOU TWO WERE LEAVING ME IN THE DUST.
THEY'RE CLOSING WITH "CANARY."
JUST LIKE THEY DID THAT DAY...
ESPE-CIALLY YOU.
EVERYTHING THAT WAS TOO MUCH FOR YOU BACK THEN...
YOUR MUSIC AND DREAMS AND LOVE...
YOUR PAST AND FUTURE...
NOW YOU BEAR THEM ALL WITH EASE.
AND YET, HERE I AM STILL.

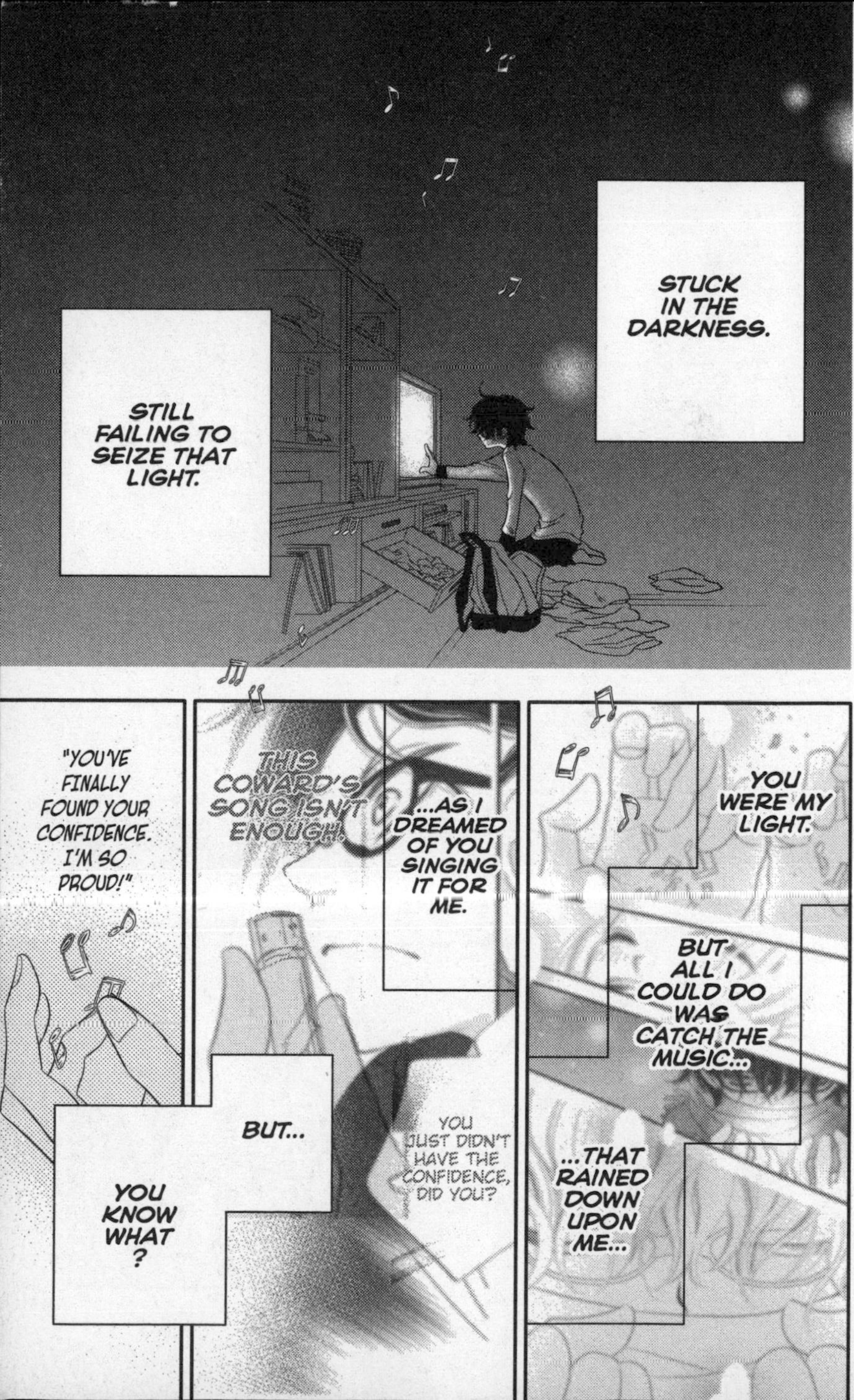
STUCK IN THE DARKNESS.
STILL FAILING TO SEIZE THAT LIGHT.
YOU WERE MY LIGHT.
BUT ALL I COULD DO WAS CATCH THE MUSIC...
...THAT RAINED DOWN UPON ME...
...AS I DREAMED OF YOU SINGING IT FOR ME.
THIS COWARD'S SONG ISN'T ENOUGH!
YOU JUST DIDN'T HAVE THE CONFIDENCE, DID YOU?
"YOU'VE FINALLY FOUND YOUR CONFIDENCE. I'M SO PROUD!"
BUT...
YOU KNOW WHAT?

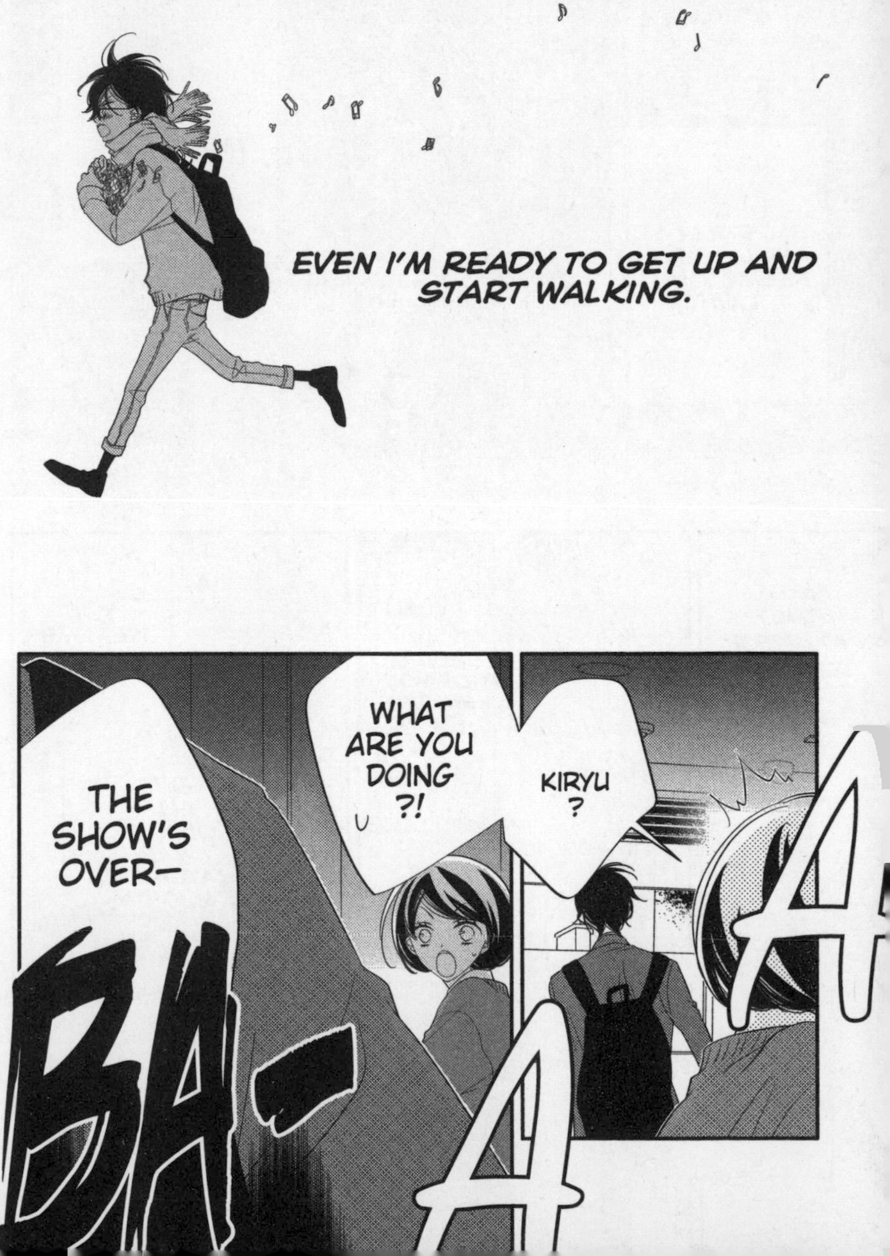
EVEN I'M READY TO GET UP AND START WALKING.
KIRYU ?
WHAT ARE YOU DOING ?!
THE SHOW'S OVER—
BA-A-A

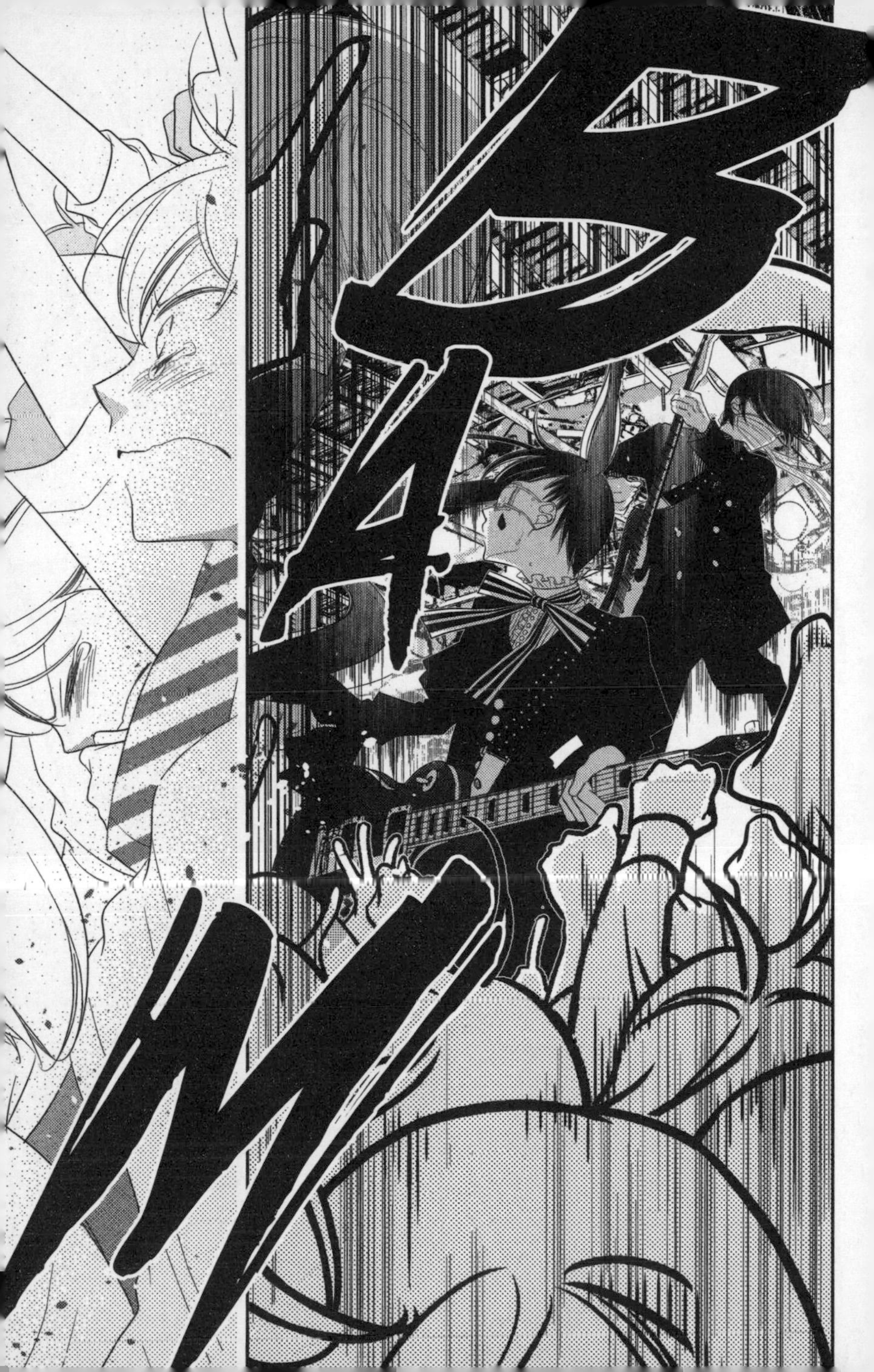
BAM

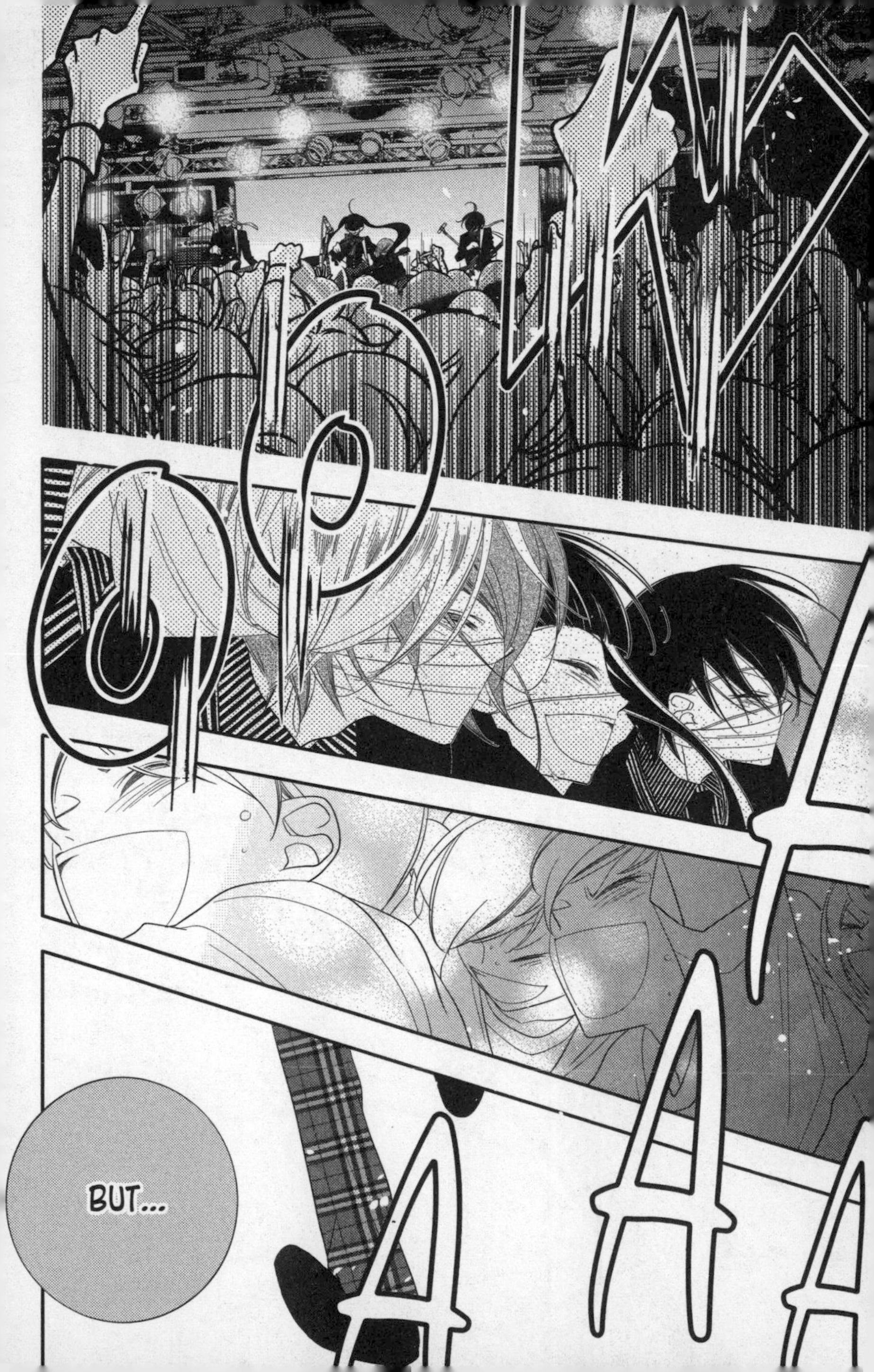
BUT...

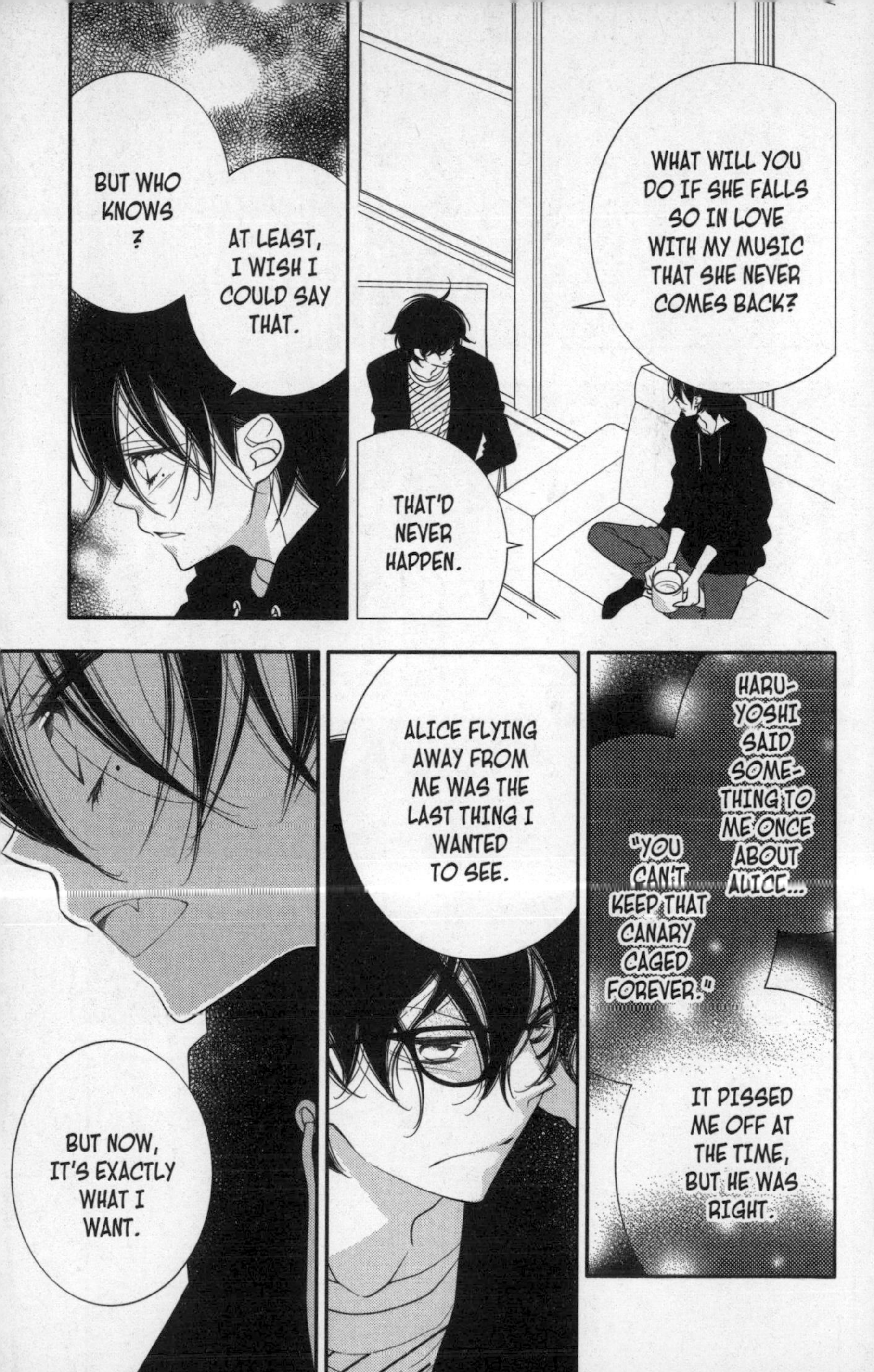
WHAT WILL YOU DO IF SHE FALLS SO IN LOVE WITH MY MUSIC THAT SHE NEVER COMES BACK?
THAT'D NEVER HAPPEN.
AT LEAST, I WISH I COULD SAY THAT.
BUT WHO KNOWS?
HARU-YOSHI SAID SOME-THING TO ME ONCE ABOUT ALICE...
"YOU CAN'T KEEP THAT CANARY CAGED FOREVER."
IT PISSED ME OFF AT THE TIME, BUT HE WAS RIGHT.
ALICE FLYING AWAY FROM ME WAS THE LAST THING I WANTED TO SEE.
BUT NOW, IT'S EXACTLY WHAT I WANT.

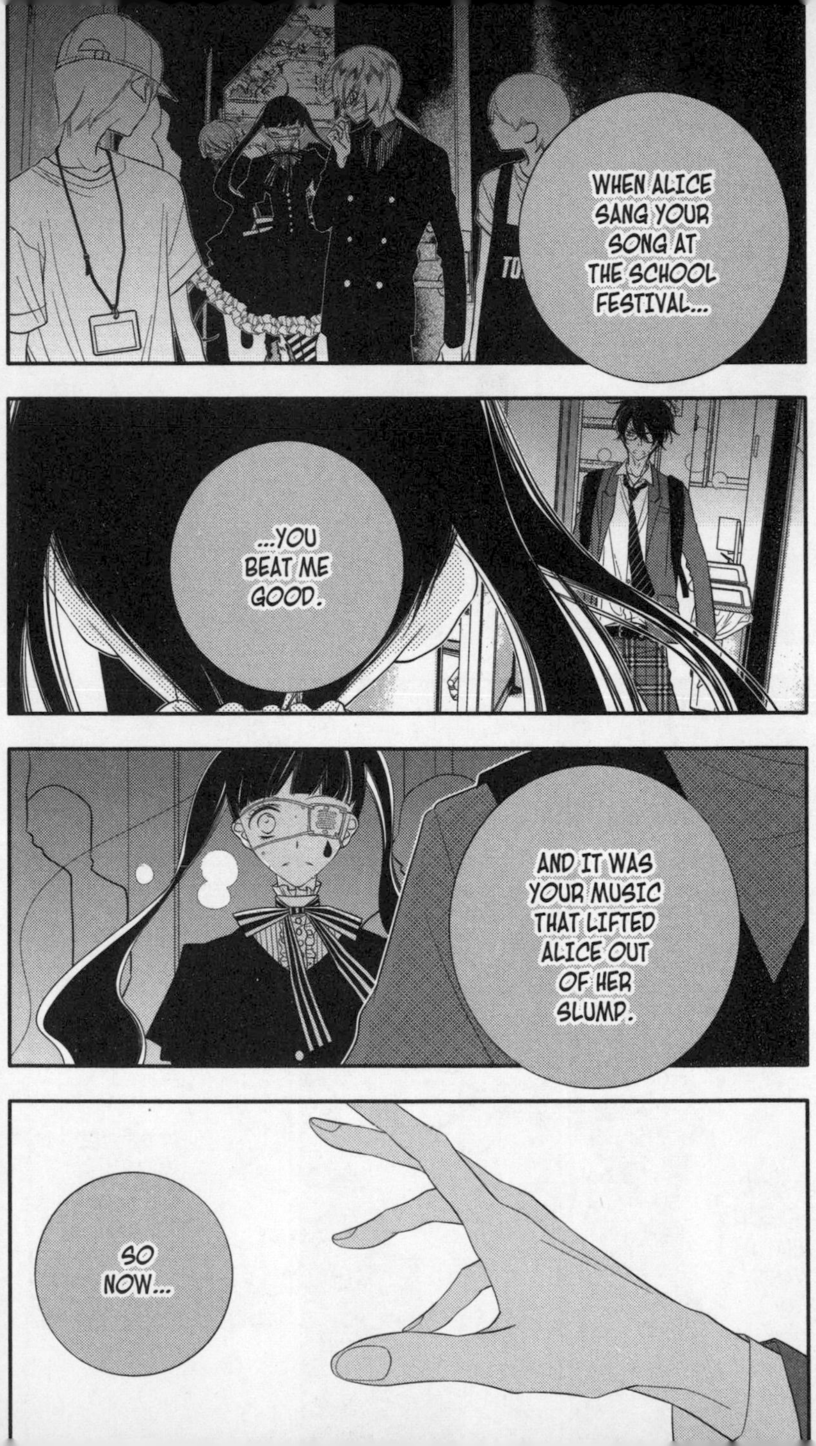
WHEN ALICE SANG YOUR SONG AT THE SCHOOL FESTIVAL...
...YOU BEAT ME GOOD.
AND IT WAS YOUR MUSIC THAT LIFTED ALICE OUT OF HER SLUMP.
SO NOW...

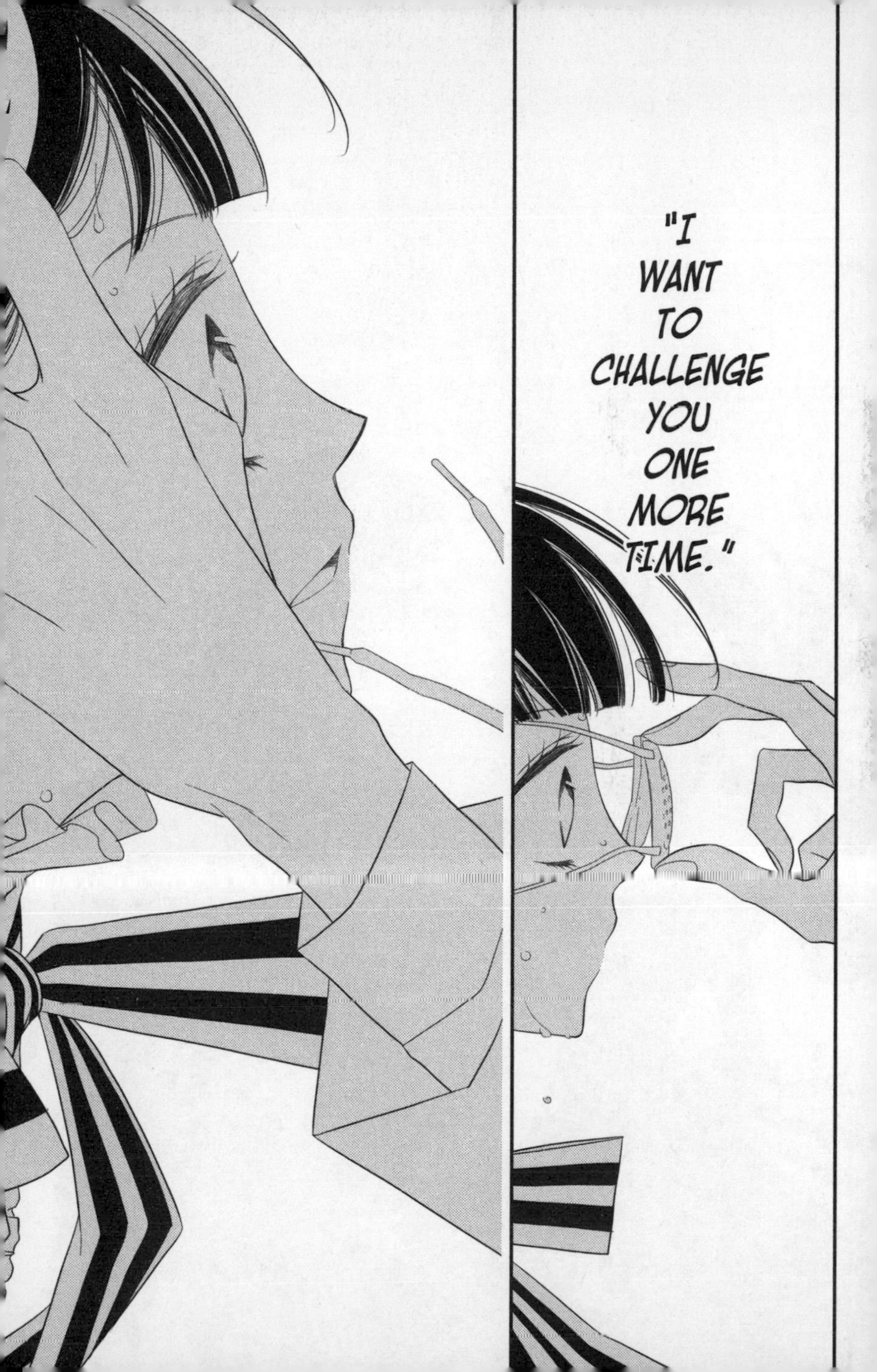
"I WANT TO CHALLENGE YOU ONE MORE TIME."

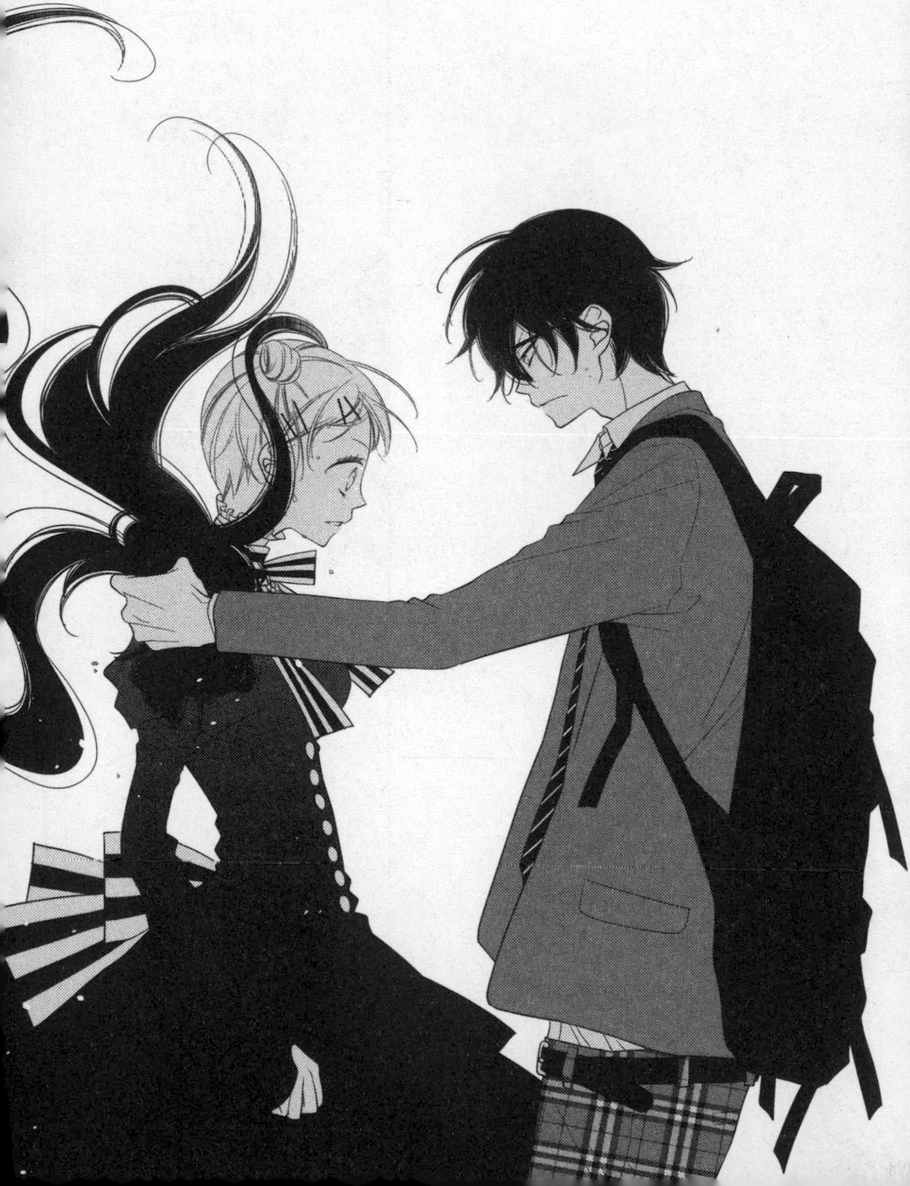

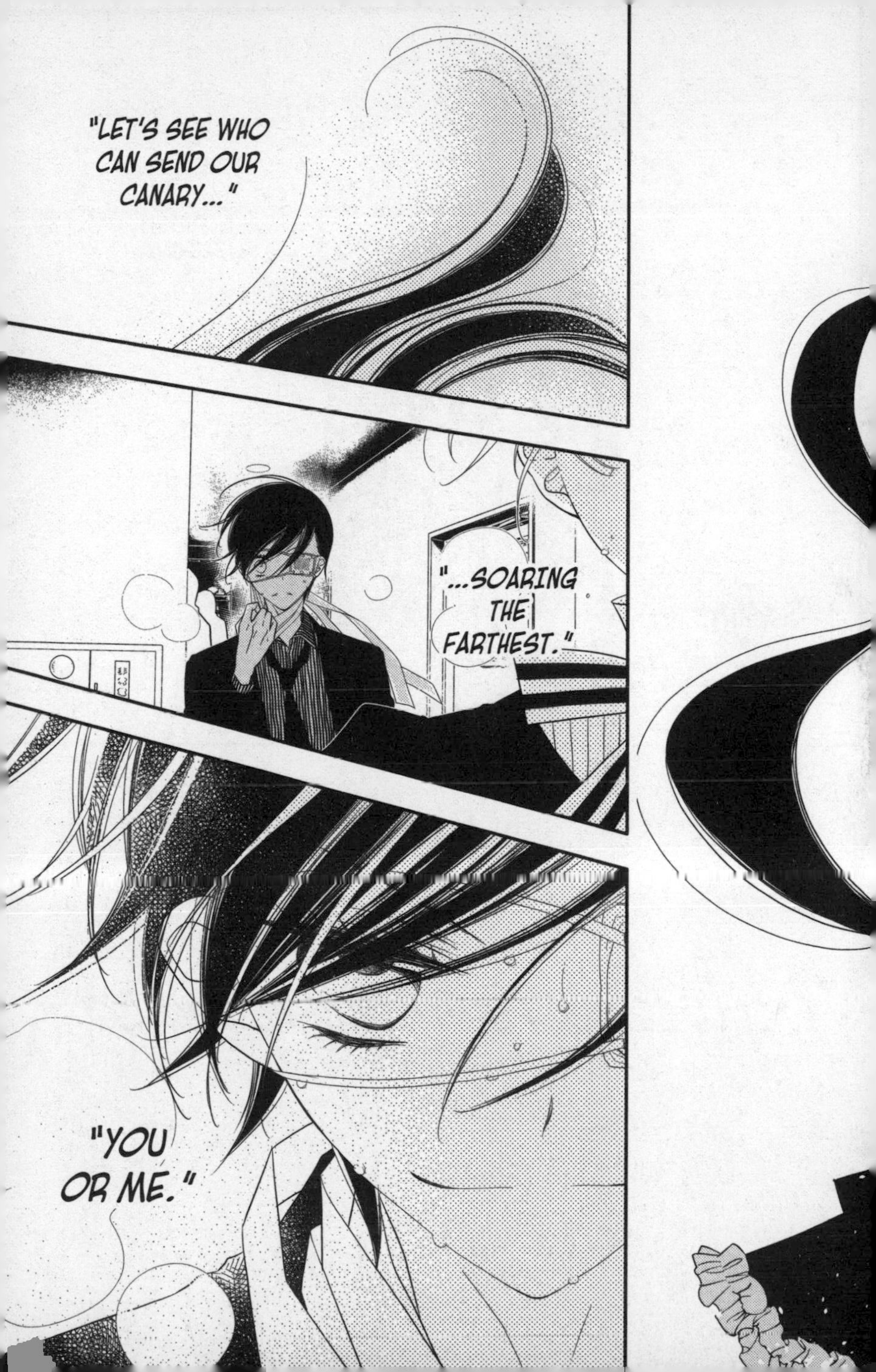
"LET'S SEE WHO CAN SEND OUR CANARY..."
"...SOARING THE FARTHEST."
"YOU OR ME."

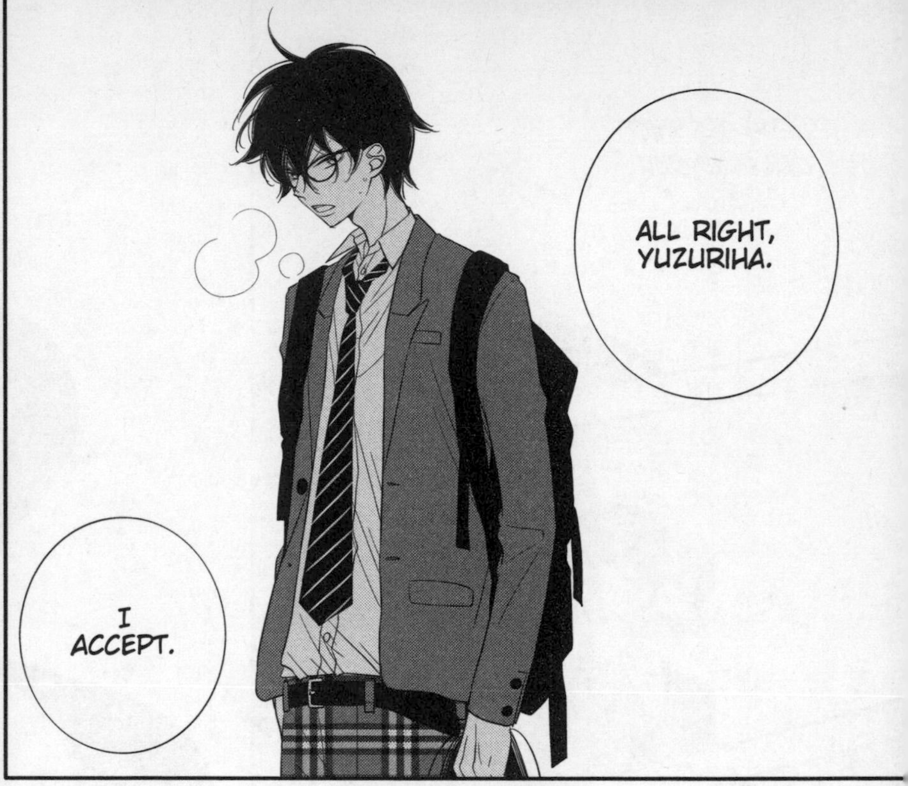
ALL RIGHT, YUZURIHA.
I ACCEPT.

"IT'LL BE OUR FINAL CONTEST, SAKAKI."

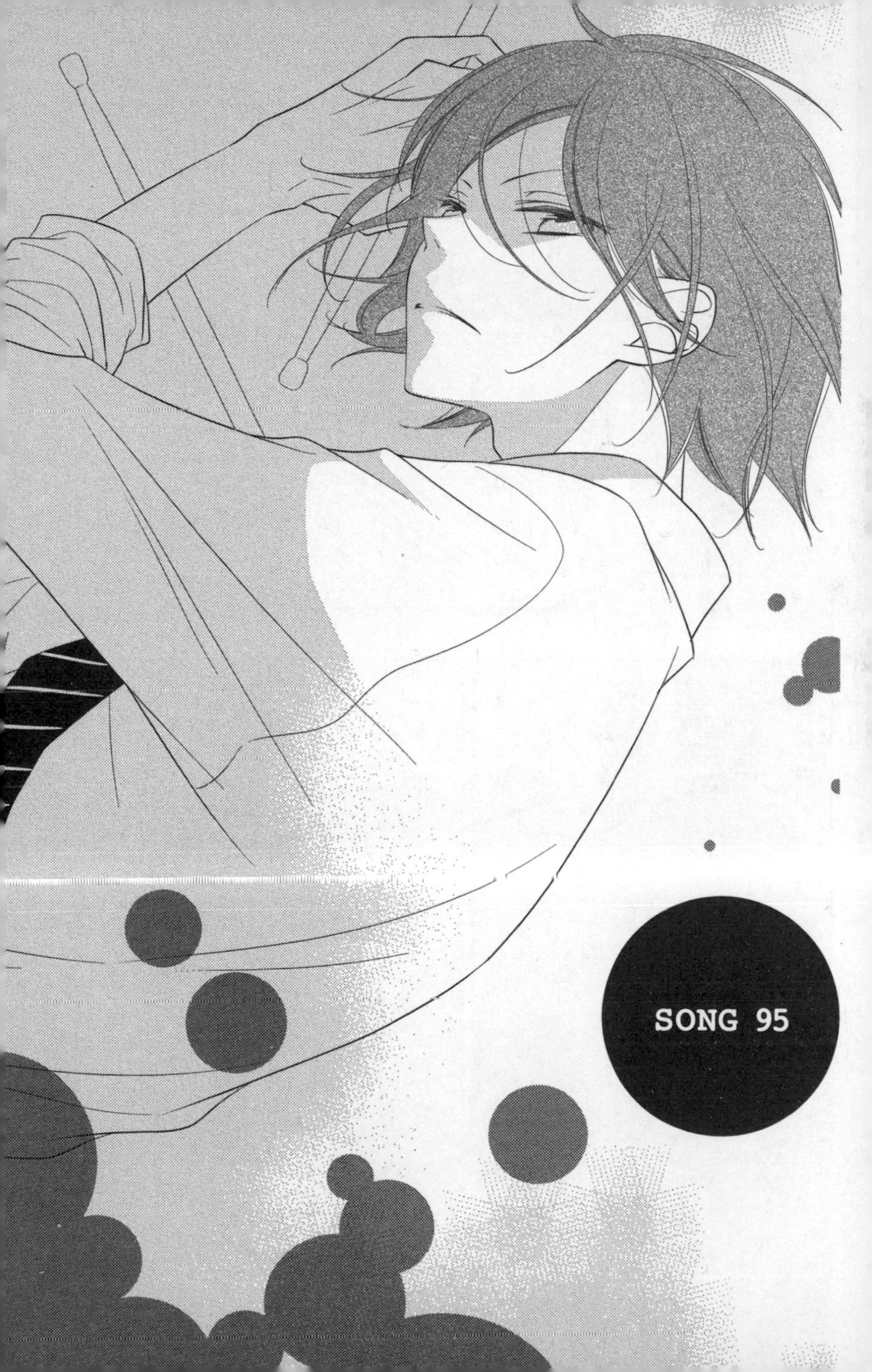
SONG 95

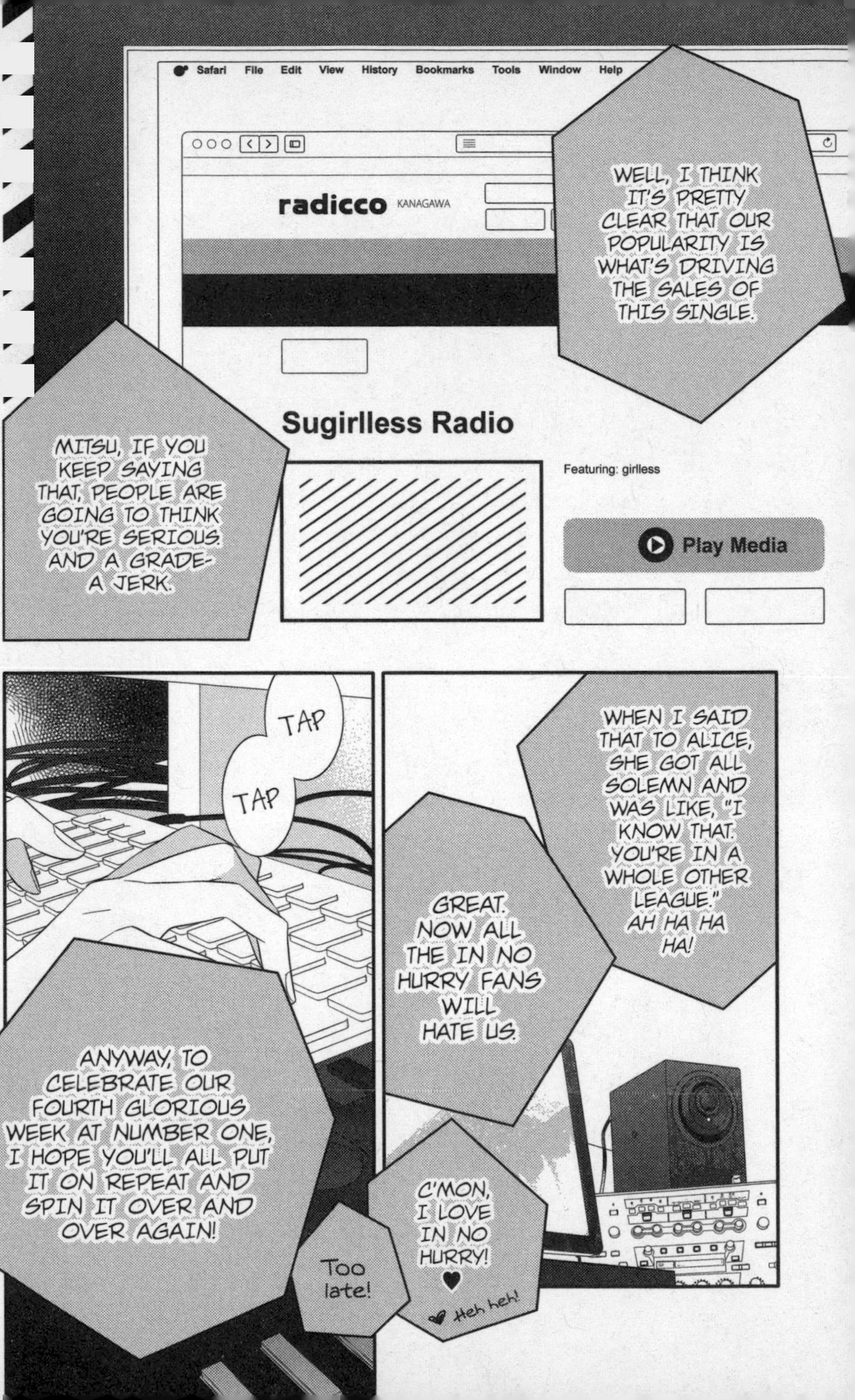
Safari File Edit View History Bookmarks Tools Window Help
radicco KANAGAWA
Sugirlless Radio
Featuring: girlless
Play Media
WELL, I THINK IT'S PRETTY CLEAR THAT OUR POPULARITY IS WHAT'S DRIVING THE SALES OF THIS SINGLE.
MITSU, IF YOU KEEP SAYING THAT, PEOPLE ARE GOING TO THINK YOU'RE SERIOUS. AND A GRADE-A JERK.
WHEN I SAID THAT TO ALICE, SHE GOT ALL SOLEMN AND WAS LIKE, "I KNOW THAT. YOU'RE IN A WHOLE OTHER LEAGUE." AH HA HA HA!
GREAT. NOW ALL THE IN NO HURRY FANS WILL HATE US.
C'MON, I LOVE IN NO HURRY! ♥
Heh heh!
TAP
TAP
ANYWAY, TO CELEBRATE OUR FOURTH GLORIOUS WEEK AT NUMBER ONE, I HOPE YOU'LL ALL PUT IT ON REPEAT AND SPIN IT OVER AND OVER AGAIN!
Too late!

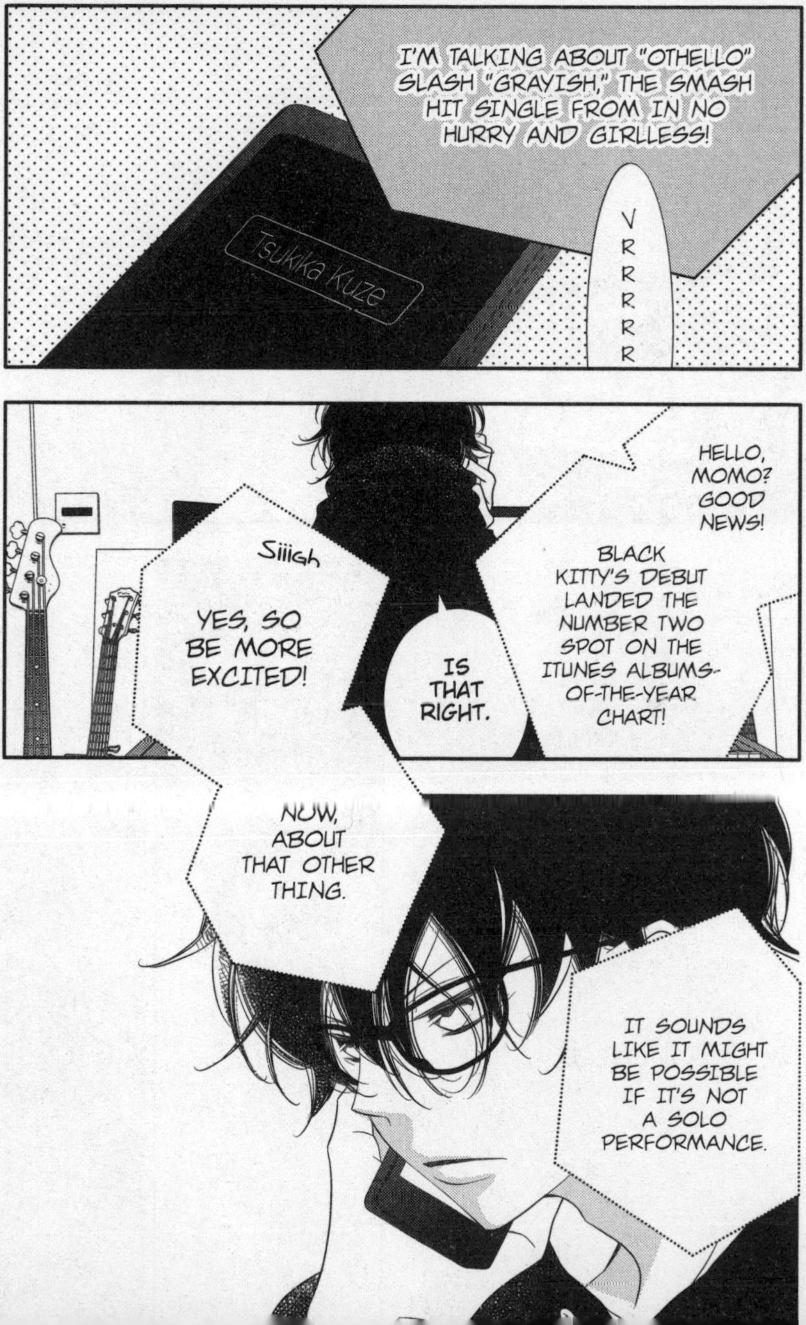
I'M TALKING ABOUT "OTHELLO" SLASH "GRAYISH," THE SMASH HIT SINGLE FROM IN NO HURRY AND GIRLLESS!
VRRRRR
Tsukika Kuze
HELLO, MOMO? GOOD NEWS!
BLACK KITTY'S DEBUT LANDED THE NUMBER TWO SPOT ON THE ITUNES ALBUMS-OF-THE-YEAR CHART!
IS THAT RIGHT.
Siiigh
YES, SO BE MORE EXCITED!
NOW, ABOUT THAT OTHER THING.
IT SOUNDS LIKE IT MIGHT BE POSSIBLE IF IT'S NOT A SOLO PERFORMANCE.

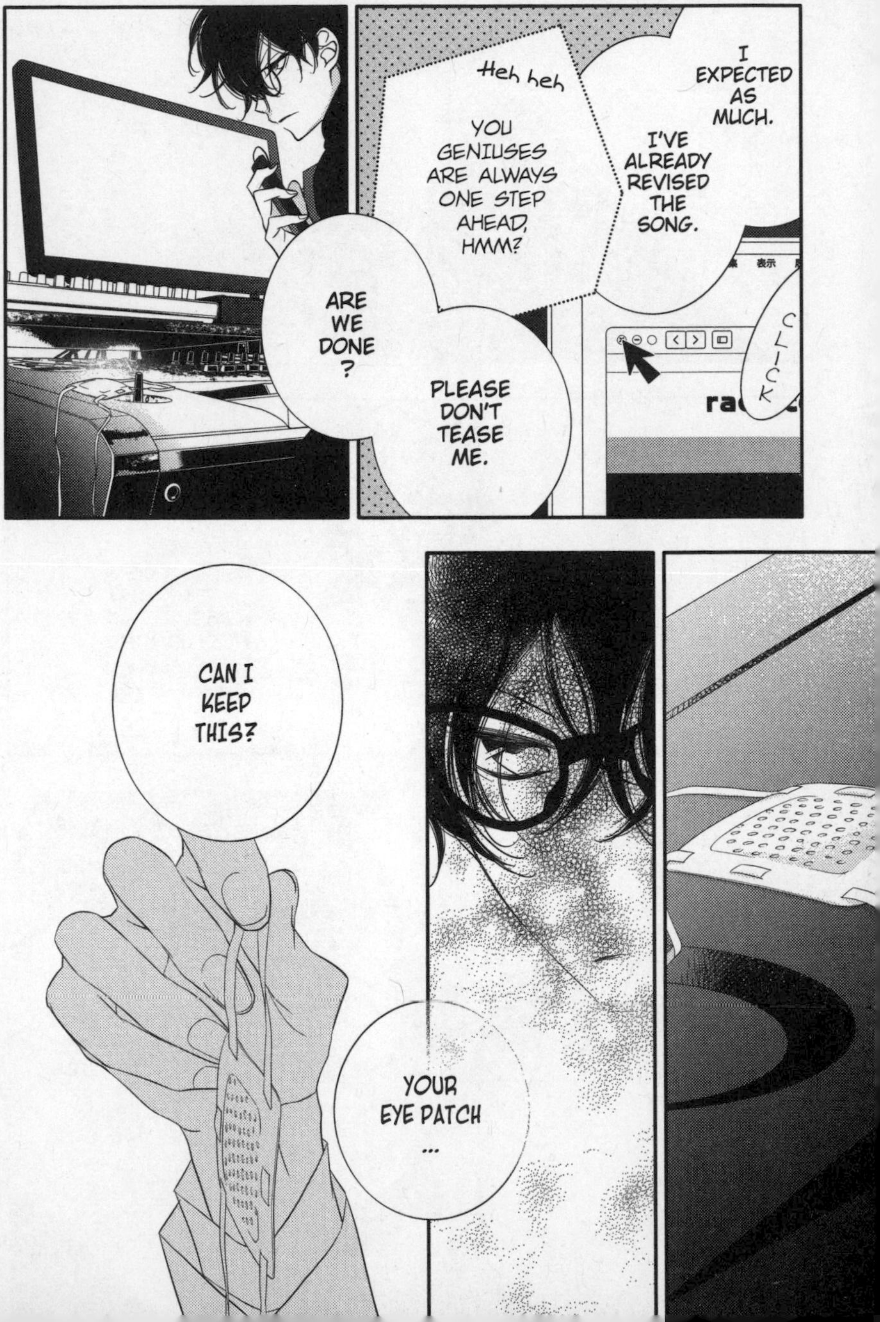
I EXPECTED AS MUCH.
I'VE ALREADY REVISED THE SONG.
Heh heh
YOU GENIUSES ARE ALWAYS ONE STEP AHEAD, HMM?
CLICK
PLEASE DON'T TEASE ME.
ARE WE DONE?
YOUR EYE PATCH...
CAN I KEEP THIS?

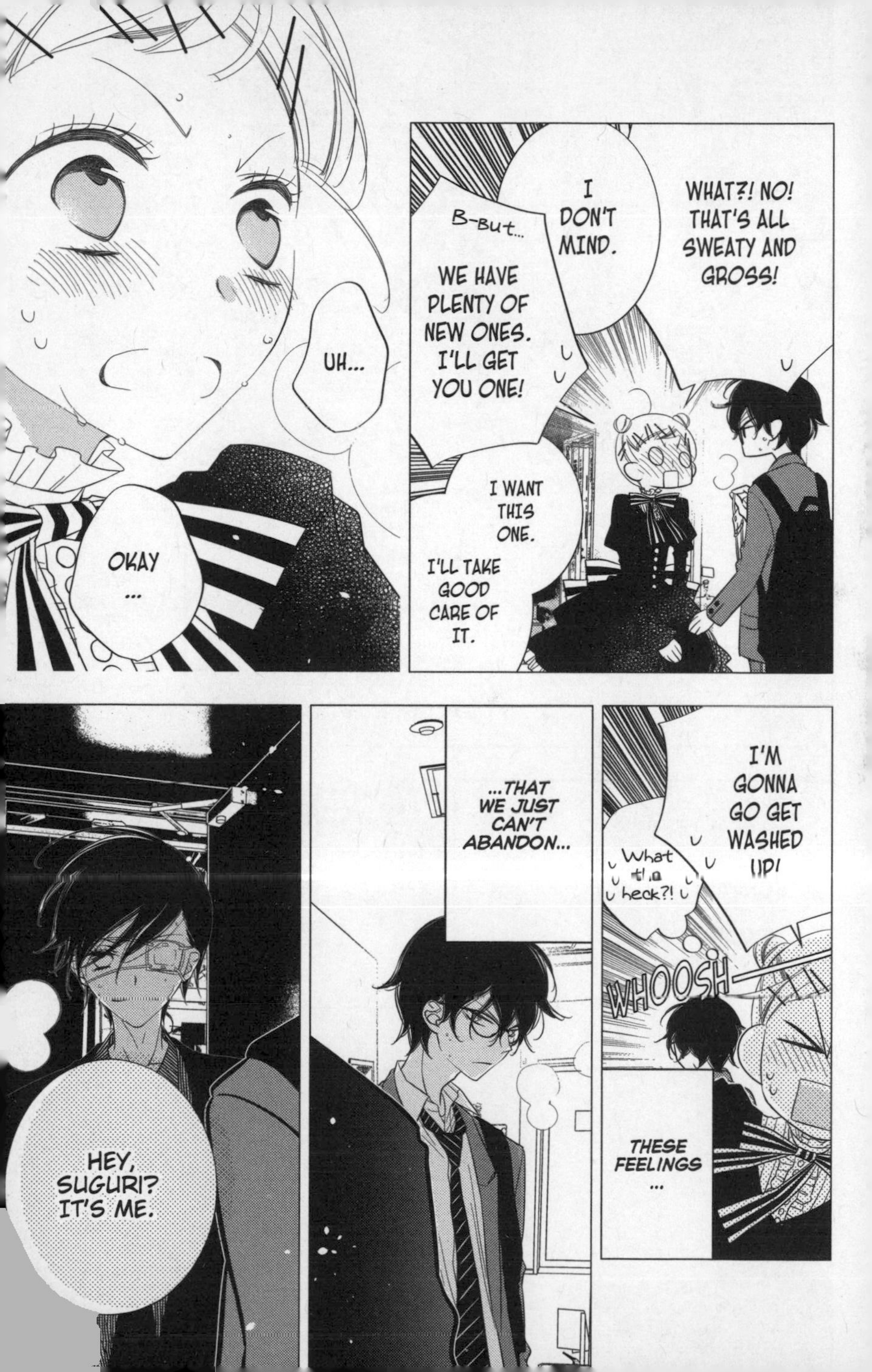
WHAT?! NO! THAT'S ALL SWEATY AND GROSS!
I DON'T MIND.
B-but...
WE HAVE PLENTY OF NEW ONES. I'LL GET YOU ONE!
I WANT THIS ONE.
I'LL TAKE GOOD CARE OF IT.
UH...
OKAY ...
I'M GONNA GO GET WASHED UP!
What the heck?!
WHOOSH
THESE FEELINGS ...
...THAT WE JUST CAN'T ABANDON...
HEY, SUGURI? IT'S ME.

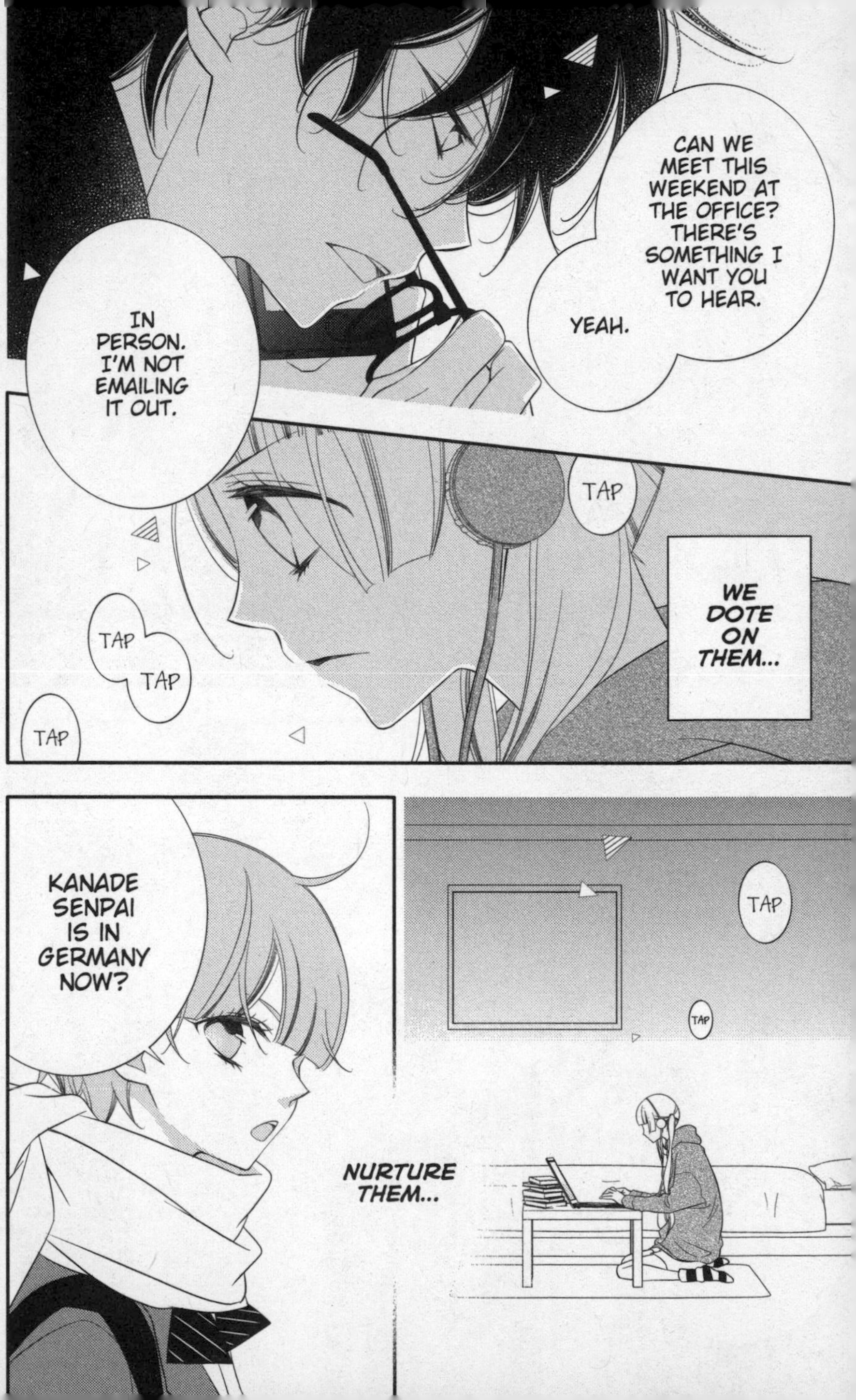
CAN WE MEET THIS WEEKEND AT THE OFFICE? THERE'S SOMETHING I WANT YOU TO HEAR.
YEAH.
IN PERSON. I'M NOT EMAILING IT OUT.
TAP
WE DOTE ON THEM...
TAP
TAP
TAP
TAP
TAP
NURTURE THEM...
KANADE SENPAI IS IN GERMANY NOW?

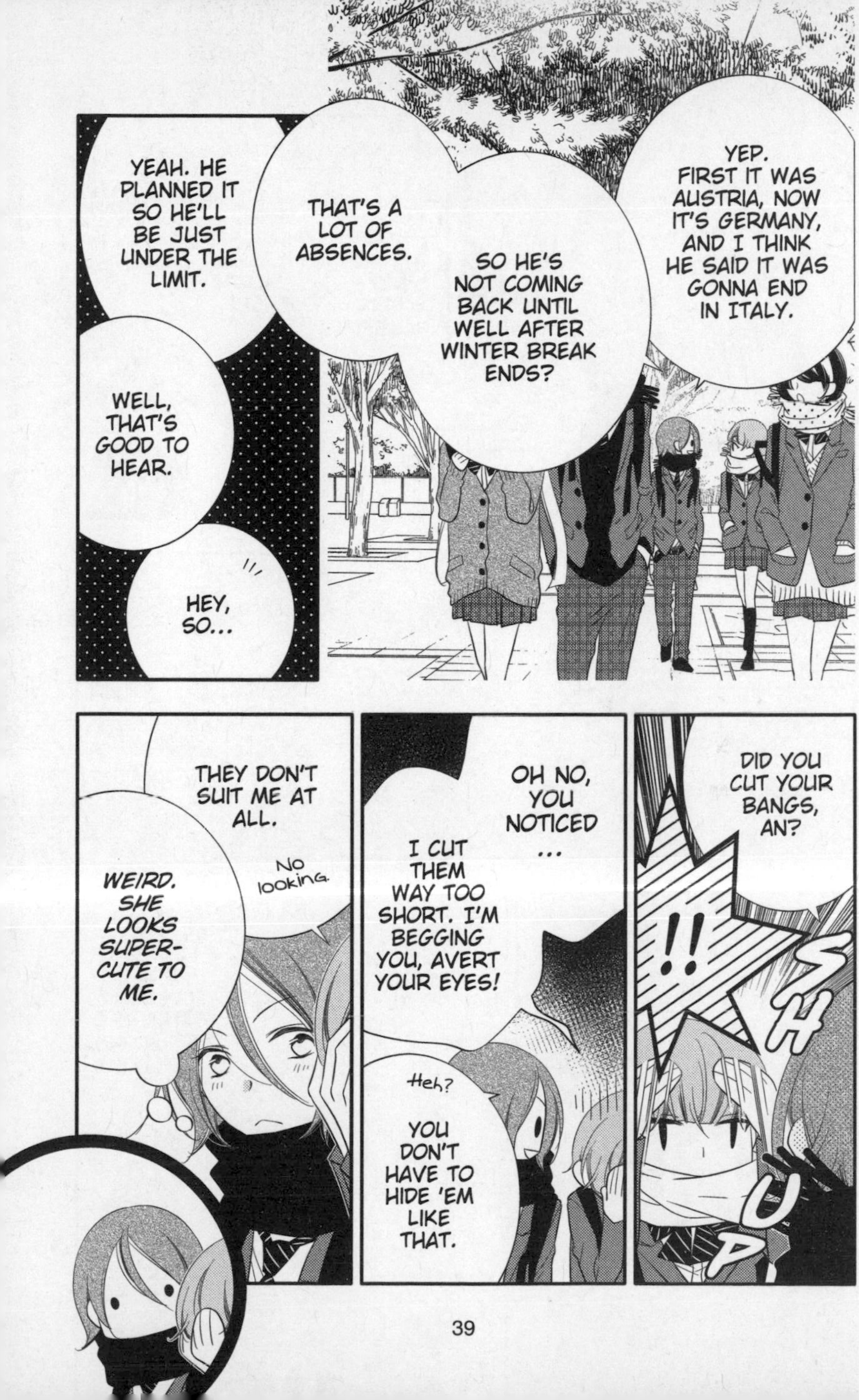
YEP. FIRST IT WAS AUSTRIA, NOW IT'S GERMANY, AND I THINK HE SAID IT WAS GONNA END IN ITALY.
SO HE'S NOT COMING BACK UNTIL WELL AFTER WINTER BREAK ENDS?
THAT'S A LOT OF ABSENCES.
YEAH. HE PLANNED IT SO HE'LL BE JUST UNDER THE LIMIT.
WELL, THAT'S GOOD TO HEAR.
HEY, SO...
DID YOU CUT YOUR BANGS, AN?
!!
SHUP
OH NO, YOU NOTICED...
I CUT THEM WAY TOO SHORT. I'M BEGGING YOU, AVERT YOUR EYES!
Heh?
YOU DON'T HAVE TO HIDE 'EM LIKE THAT.
THEY DON'T SUIT ME AT ALL.
No looking.
WEIRD. SHE LOOKS SUPER-CUTE TO ME.

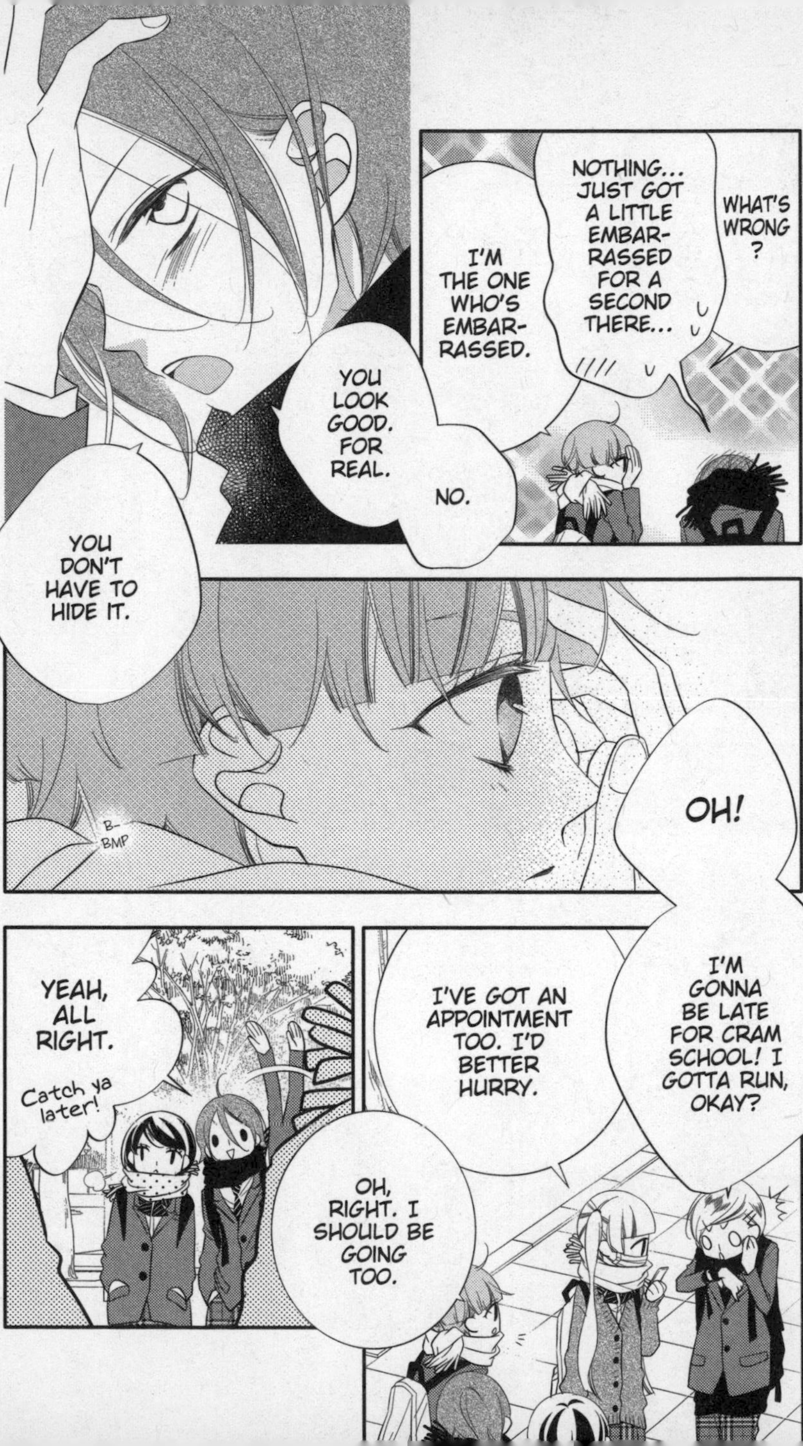
WHAT'S WRONG?
NOTHING... JUST GOT A LITTLE EMBARRASSED FOR A SECOND THERE...
I'M THE ONE WHO'S EMBARRASSED.
YOU LOOK GOOD. FOR REAL.
NO.
YOU DON'T HAVE TO HIDE IT.
B-BMP
OH!
I'M GONNA BE LATE FOR CRAM SCHOOL! I GOTTA RUN, OKAY?
I'VE GOT AN APPOINTMENT TOO. I'D BETTER HURRY.
OH, RIGHT. I SHOULD BE GOING TOO.
YEAH, ALL RIGHT.
Catch ya later!

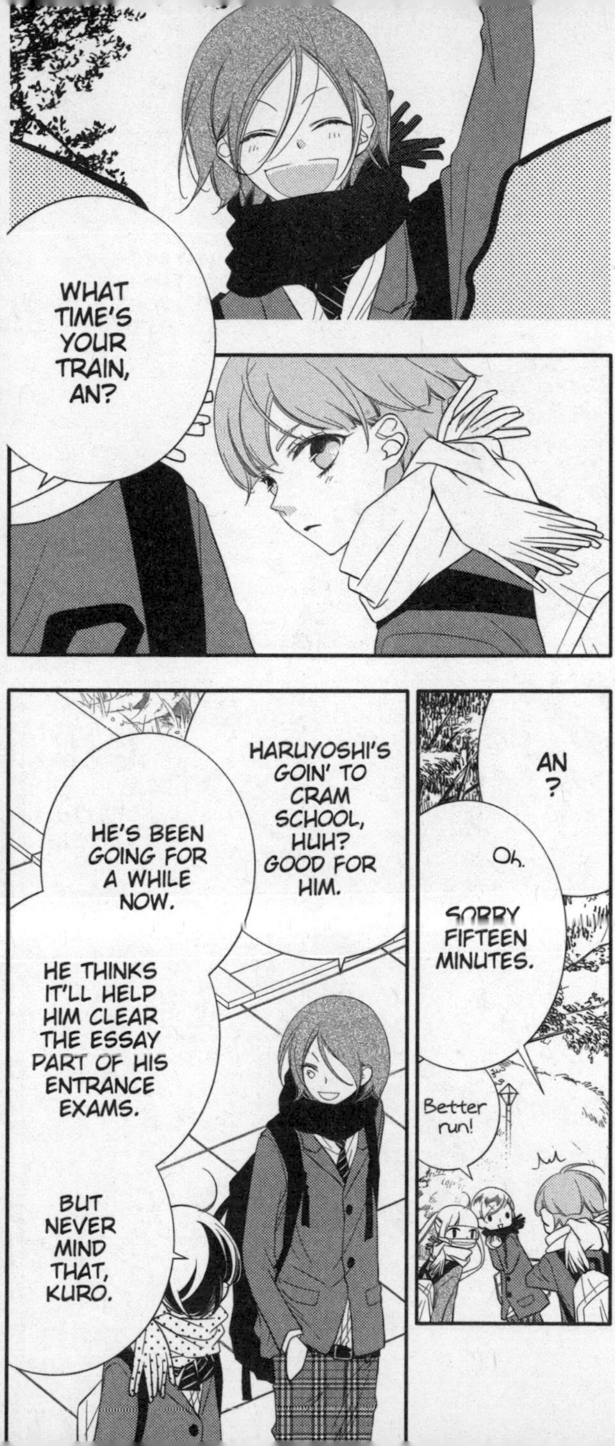
WHAT TIME'S YOUR TRAIN, AN?
AN?
Oh.
SORRY FIFTEEN MINUTES.
Better run!
HARUYOSHI'S GOIN' TO CRAM SCHOOL, HUH? GOOD FOR HIM.
HE'S BEEN GOING FOR A WHILE NOW.
HE THINKS IT'LL HELP HIM CLEAR THE ESSAY PART OF HIS ENTRANCE EXAMS.
BUT NEVER MIND THAT, KURO.

2

I'm sorry. I can't do the proper penmanship thing anymore. It requires so much focus that I can't write anything interesting! How am I supposed to write hilarious anecdotes under these circumstances?!

Oh, right! This is volume 17, huh. Can you believe it? I had to make a lot of revisions in this volume, so it might be interesting for you to compare it to the versions published in the Japanese magazine. Now that we're at the climax of the story, it's getting very emotional for me. It's embarrassing to admit this, but I burst into tears several times during the process of plotting and storyboarding these final chapters! And of course, actually writing and drawing them out is even harder, so this volume took a lot more time to put together than usual.

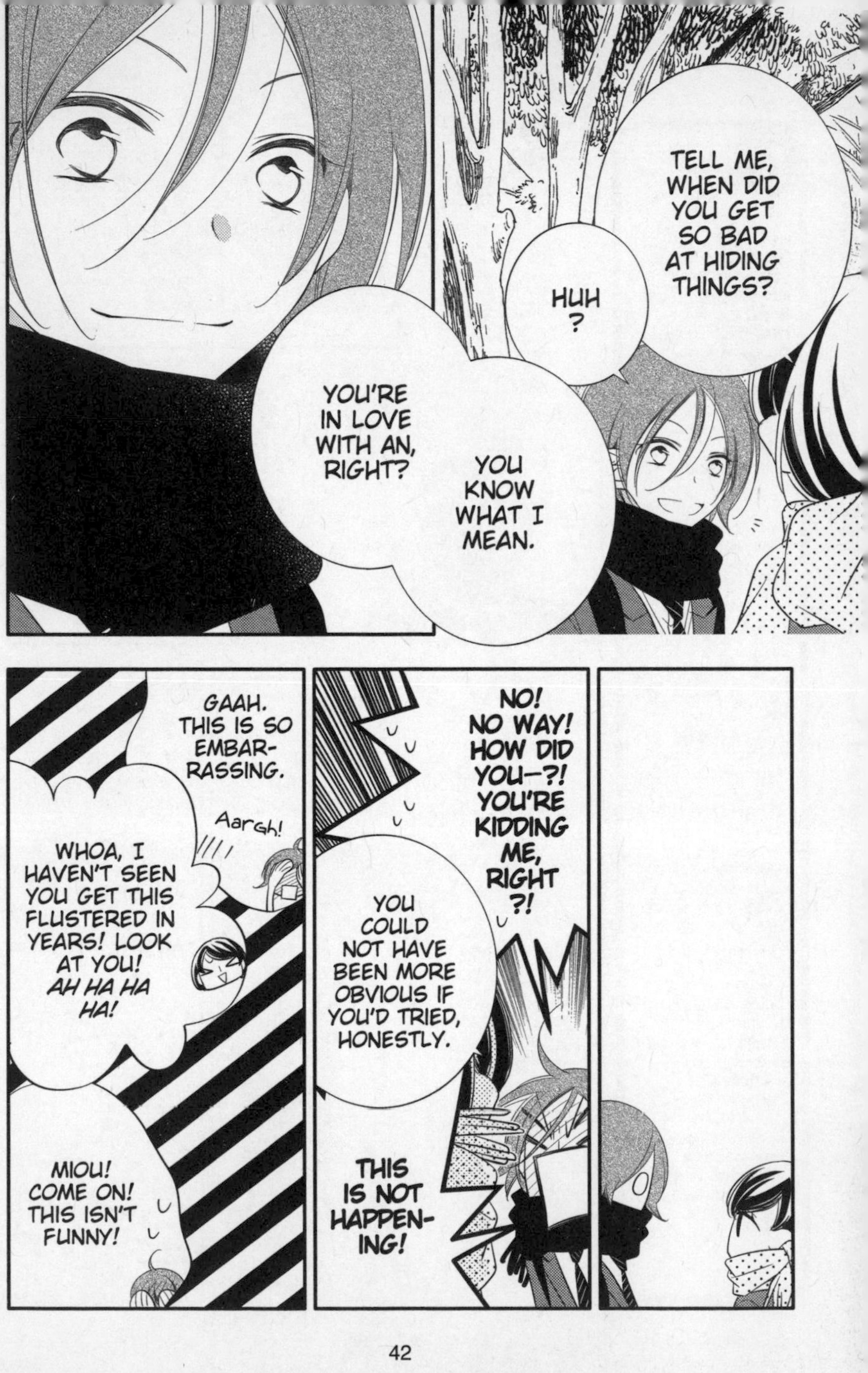
TELL ME, WHEN DID YOU GET SO BAD AT HIDING THINGS?
HUH?
YOU'RE IN LOVE WITH AN, RIGHT?
YOU KNOW WHAT I MEAN.
NO! NO WAY! HOW DID YOU—?! YOU'RE KIDDING ME, RIGHT?!
YOU COULD NOT HAVE BEEN MORE OBVIOUS IF YOU'D TRIED, HONESTLY.
THIS IS NOT HAPPEN-ING!
GAAH. THIS IS SO EMBAR-RASSING.
Aargh!
WHOA, I HAVEN'T SEEN YOU GET THIS FLUSTERED IN YEARS! LOOK AT YOU! AH HA HA HA!
MIOU! COME ON! THIS ISN'T FUNNY!

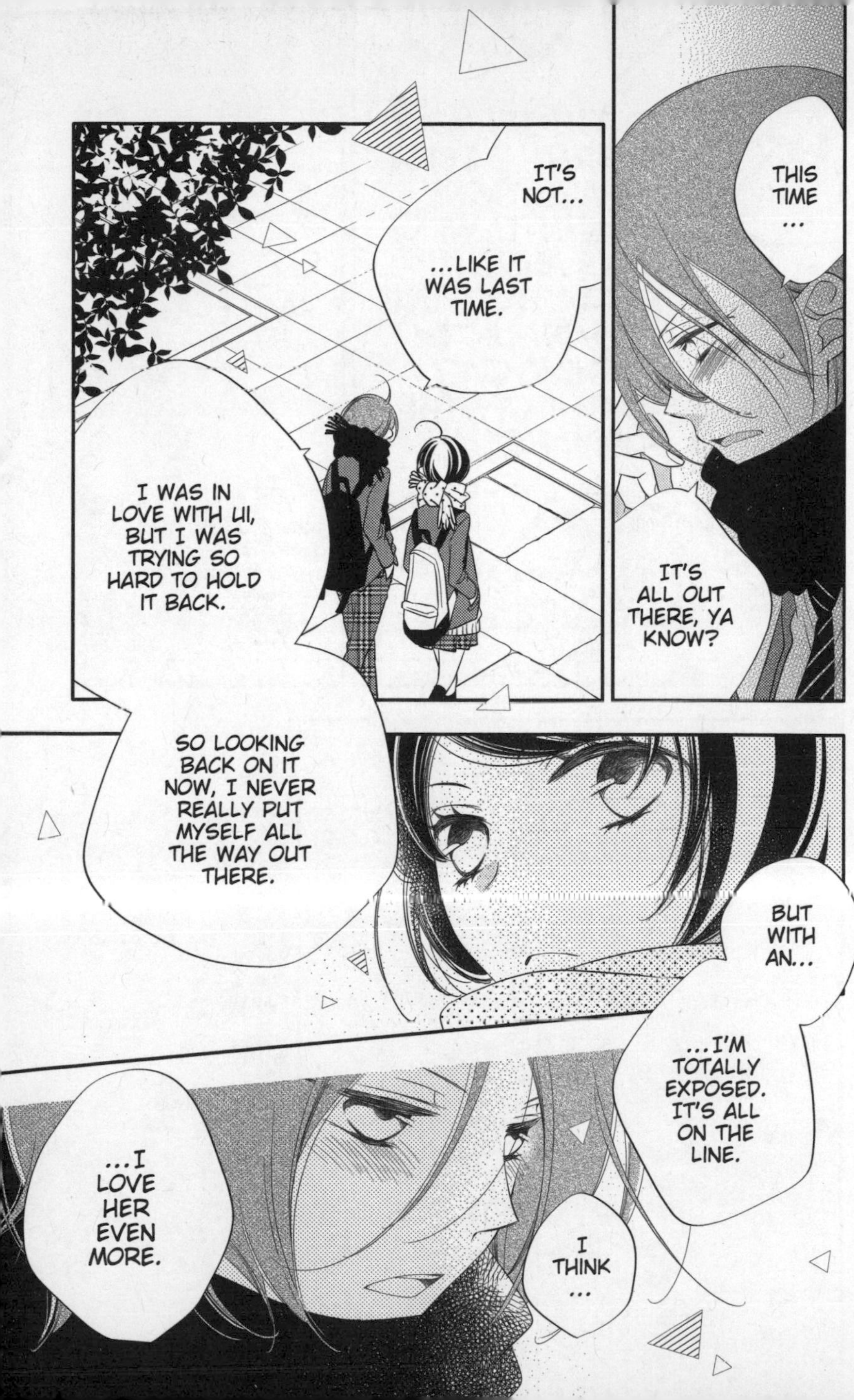
THIS TIME...
IT'S ALL OUT THERE, YA KNOW?
IT'S NOT...
...LIKE IT WAS LAST TIME.
I WAS IN LOVE WITH UI, BUT I WAS TRYING SO HARD TO HOLD IT BACK.
SO LOOKING BACK ON IT NOW, I NEVER REALLY PUT MYSELF ALL THE WAY OUT THERE.
BUT WITH AN...
...I'M TOTALLY EXPOSED. IT'S ALL ON THE LINE.
I THINK...
...I LOVE HER EVEN MORE.

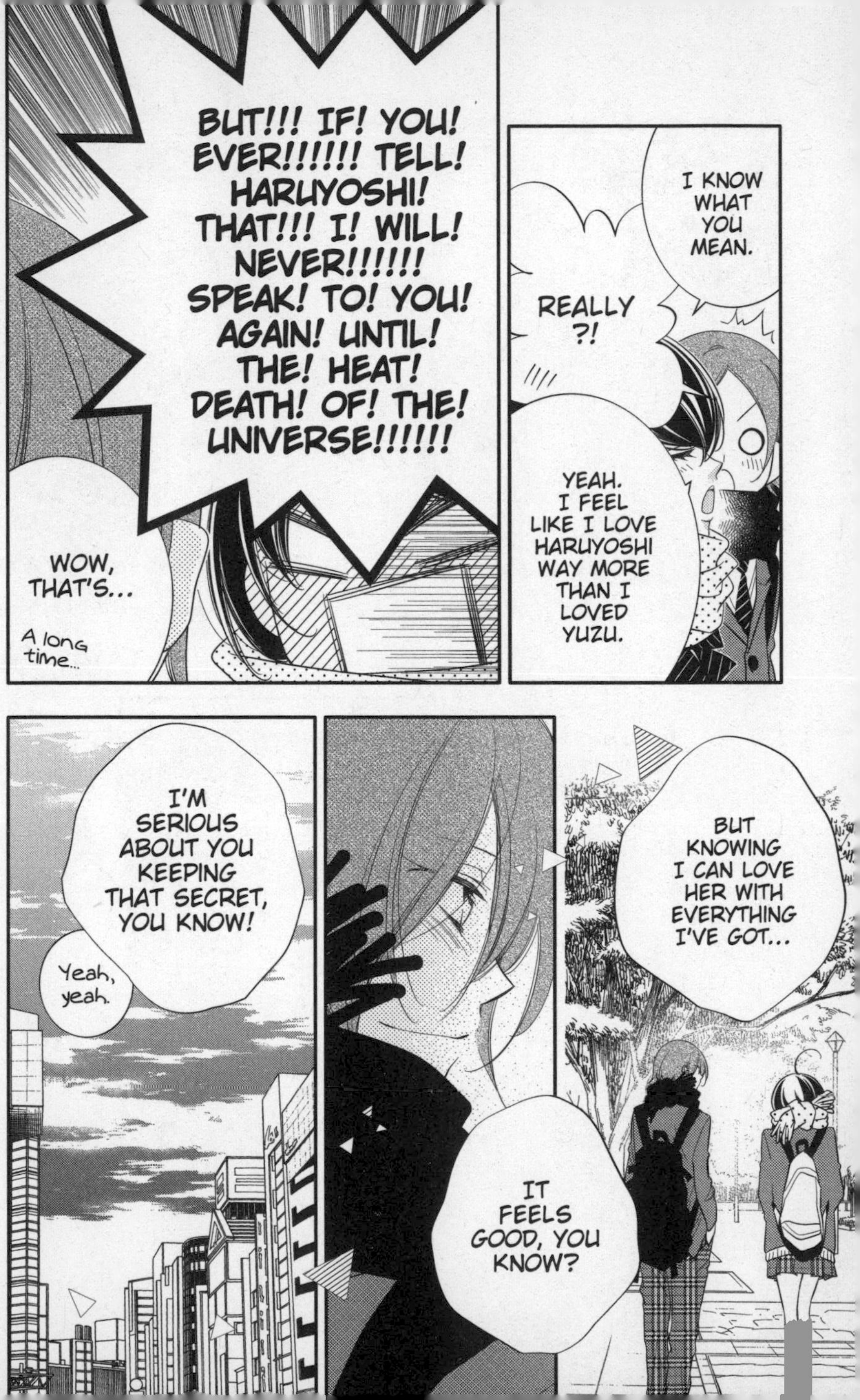
I KNOW WHAT YOU MEAN.
REALLY ?!
YEAH. I FEEL LIKE I LOVE HARUYOSHI WAY MORE THAN I LOVED YUZU.
BUT!!! IF! YOU! EVER!!!!!! TELL! HARUYOSHI! THAT!!! I! WILL! NEVER!!!!!! SPEAK! TO! YOU! AGAIN! UNTIL! THE! HEAT! DEATH! OF! THE! UNIVERSE!!!!!!
WOW, THAT'S...
A long time...
BUT KNOWING I CAN LOVE HER WITH EVERYTHING I'VE GOT...
IT FEELS GOOD, YOU KNOW?
I'M SERIOUS ABOUT YOU KEEPING THAT SECRET, YOU KNOW!
Yeah, yeah.

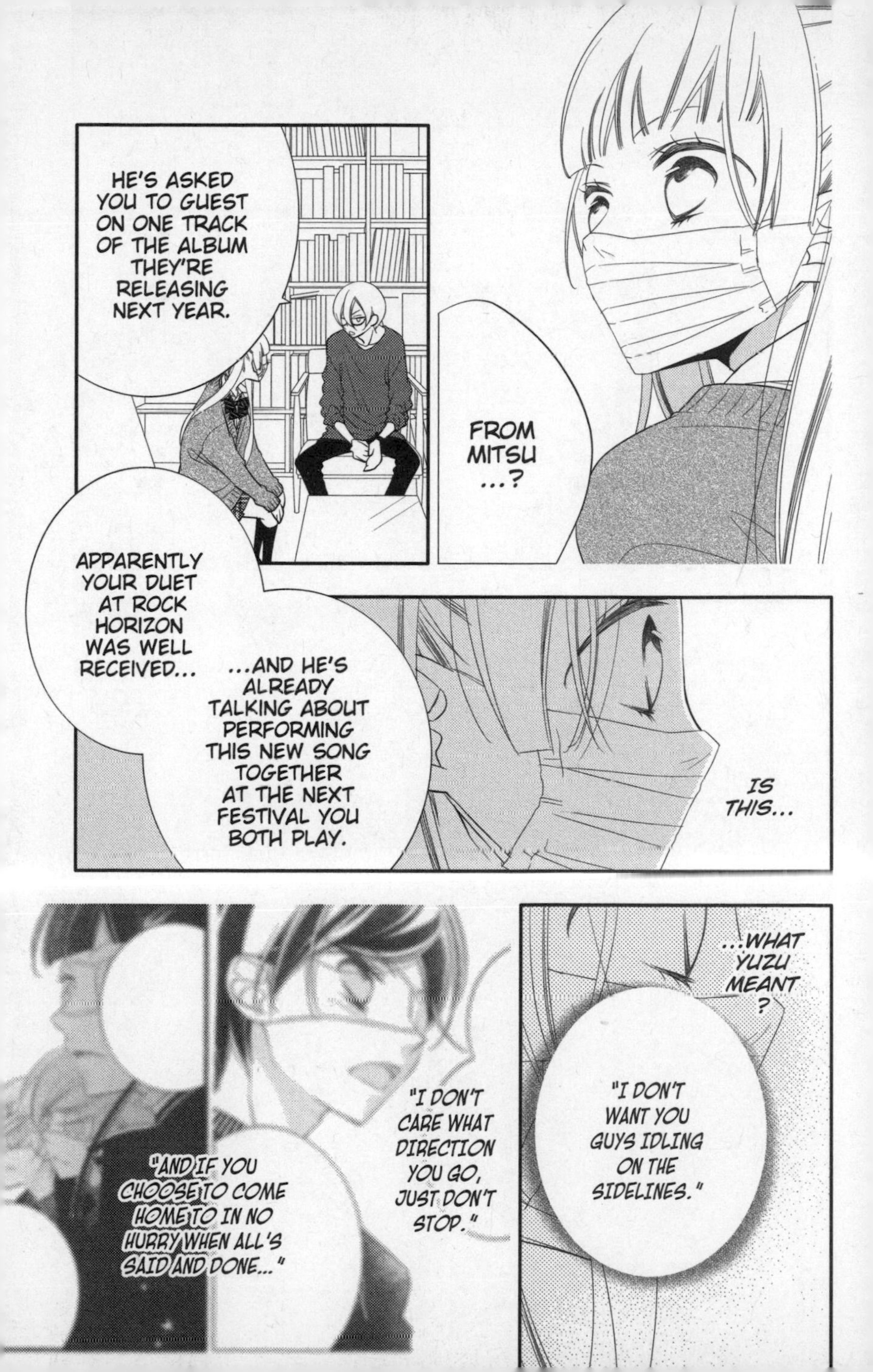
FROM MITSU ...?
HE'S ASKED YOU TO GUEST ON ONE TRACK OF THE ALBUM THEY'RE RELEASING NEXT YEAR.
APPARENTLY YOUR DUET AT ROCK HORIZON WAS WELL RECEIVED...
...AND HE'S ALREADY TALKING ABOUT PERFORMING THIS NEW SONG TOGETHER AT THE NEXT FESTIVAL YOU BOTH PLAY.
IS THIS...
...WHAT YUZU MEANT ?
"I DON'T WANT YOU GUYS IDLING ON THE SIDELINES."
"I DON'T CARE WHAT DIRECTION YOU GO, JUST DON'T STOP."
"AND IF YOU CHOOSE TO COME HOME TO IN NO HURRY WHEN ALL'S SAID AND DONE..."

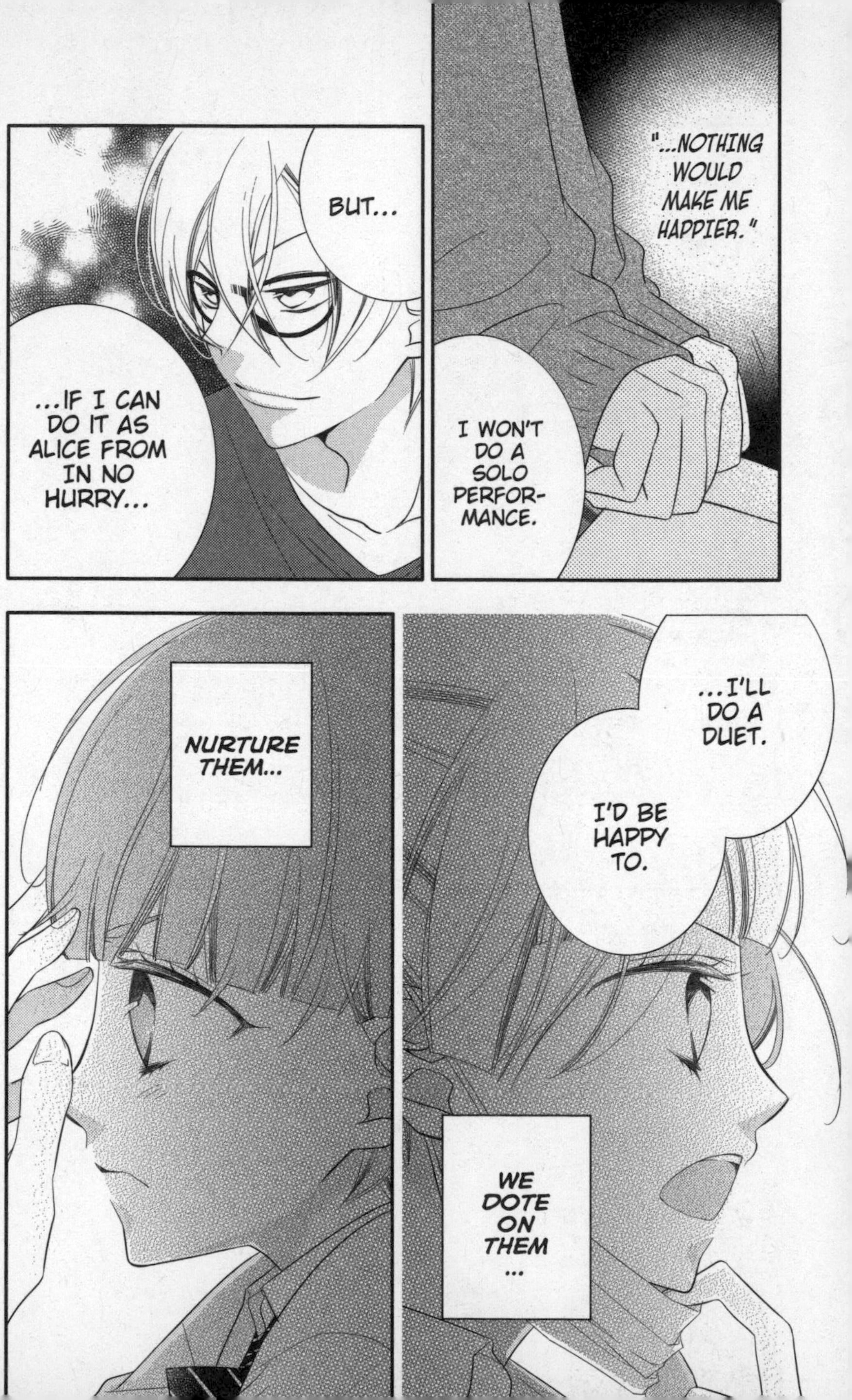
"...NOTHING WOULD MAKE ME HAPPIER."
I WON'T DO A SOLO PERFORMANCE.
BUT...
...IF I CAN DO IT AS ALICE FROM IN NO HURRY...
...I'LL DO A DUET.
I'D BE HAPPY TO.
WE DOTE ON THEM...
NURTURE THEM...

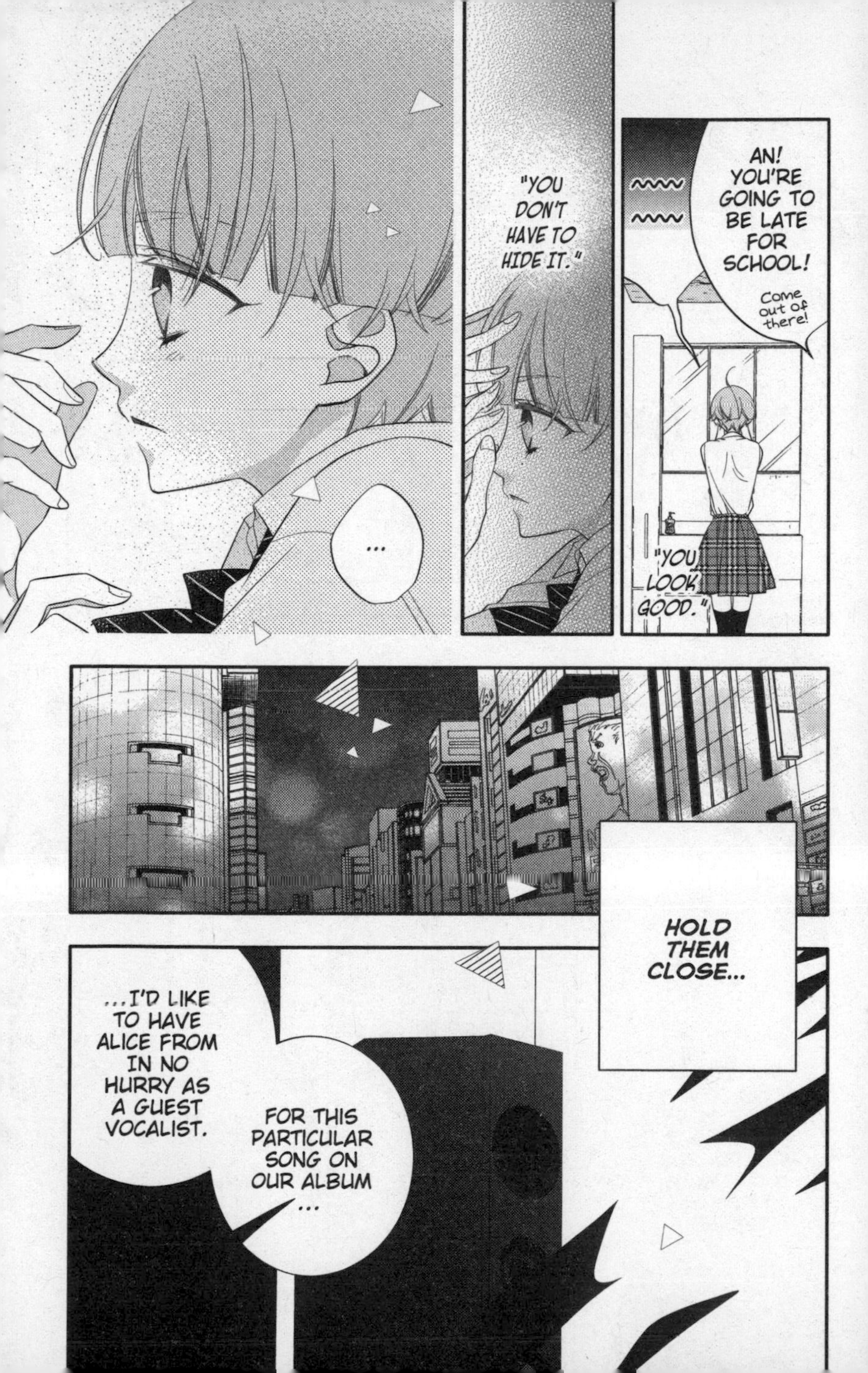

AN! YOU'RE GOING TO BE LATE FOR SCHOOL!
Come out of there!
"YOU LOOK GOOD."
"YOU DON'T HAVE TO HIDE IT."
...
HOLD THEM CLOSE...
FOR THIS PARTICULAR SONG ON OUR ALBUM...
...I'D LIKE TO HAVE ALICE FROM IN NO HURRY AS A GUEST VOCALIST.

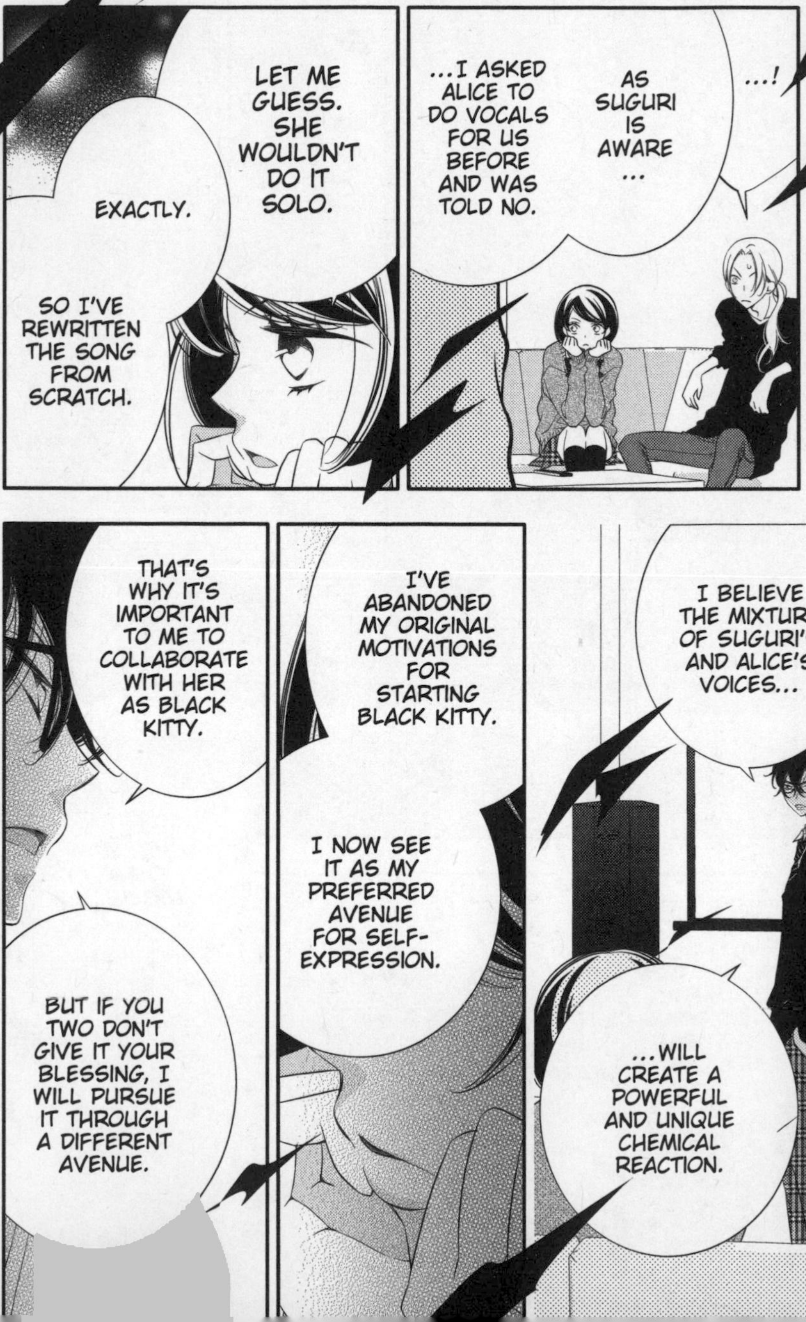
...!
AS SUGURI IS AWARE...
...I ASKED ALICE TO DO VOCALS FOR US BEFORE AND WAS TOLD NO.
LET ME GUESS. SHE WOULDN'T DO IT SOLO.
EXACTLY.
SO I'VE REWRITTEN THE SONG FROM SCRATCH.
I BELIEVE THE MIXTURE OF SUGURI'S AND ALICE'S VOICES...
...WILL CREATE A POWERFUL AND UNIQUE CHEMICAL REACTION.
I'VE ABANDONED MY ORIGINAL MOTIVATIONS FOR STARTING BLACK KITTY.
I NOW SEE IT AS MY PREFERRED AVENUE FOR SELF-EXPRESSION.
THAT'S WHY IT'S IMPORTANT TO ME TO COLLABORATE WITH HER AS BLACK KITTY.
BUT IF YOU TWO DON'T GIVE IT YOUR BLESSING, I WILL PURSUE IT THROUGH A DIFFERENT AVENUE.

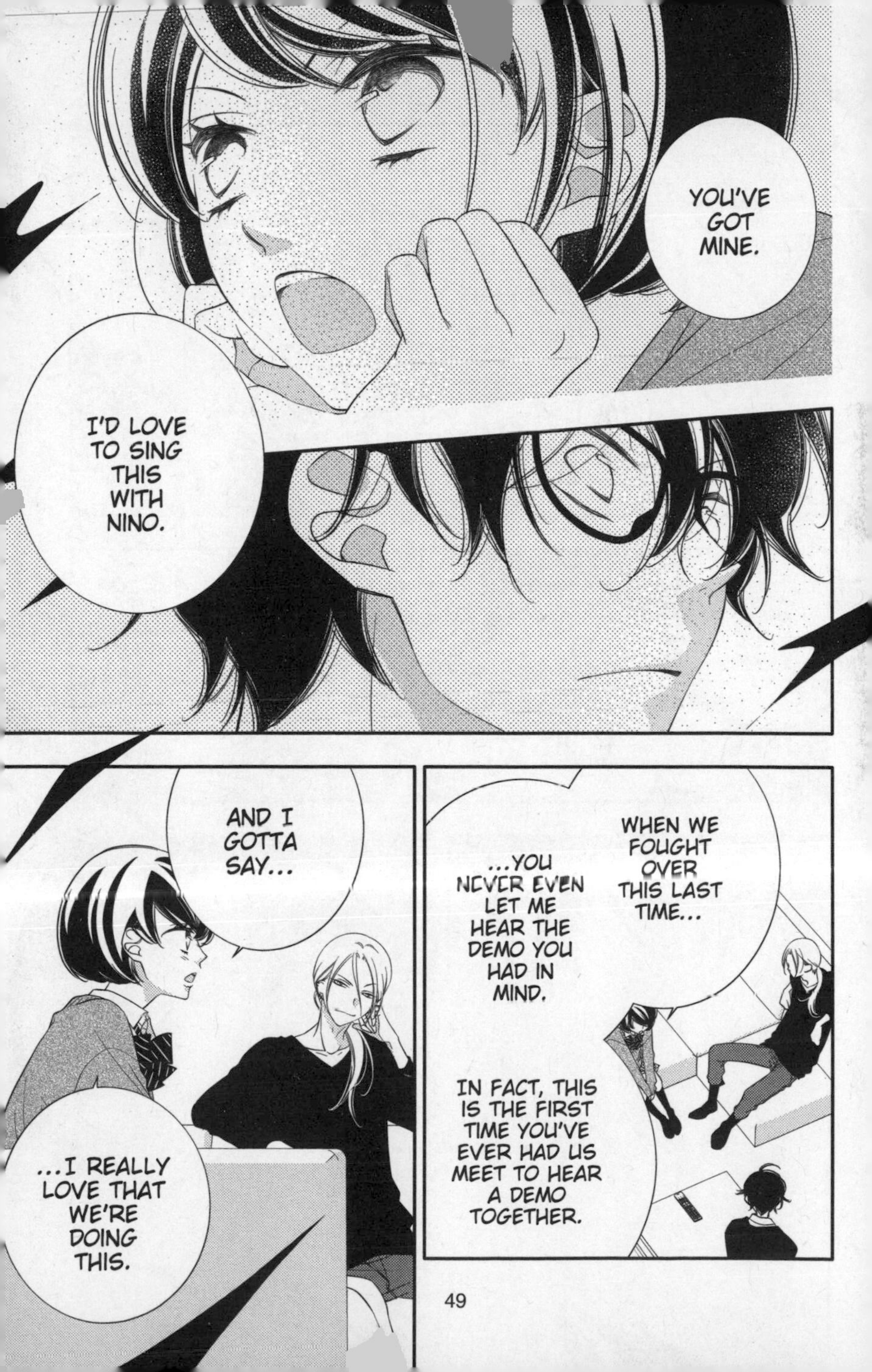
YOU'VE GOT MINE.
I'D LOVE TO SING THIS WITH NINO.
WHEN WE FOUGHT OVER THIS LAST TIME...
...YOU NEVER EVEN LET ME HEAR THE DEMO YOU HAD IN MIND.
IN FACT, THIS IS THE FIRST TIME YOU'VE EVER HAD US MEET TO HEAR A DEMO TOGETHER.
AND I GOTTA SAY...
...I REALLY LOVE THAT WE'RE DOING THIS.

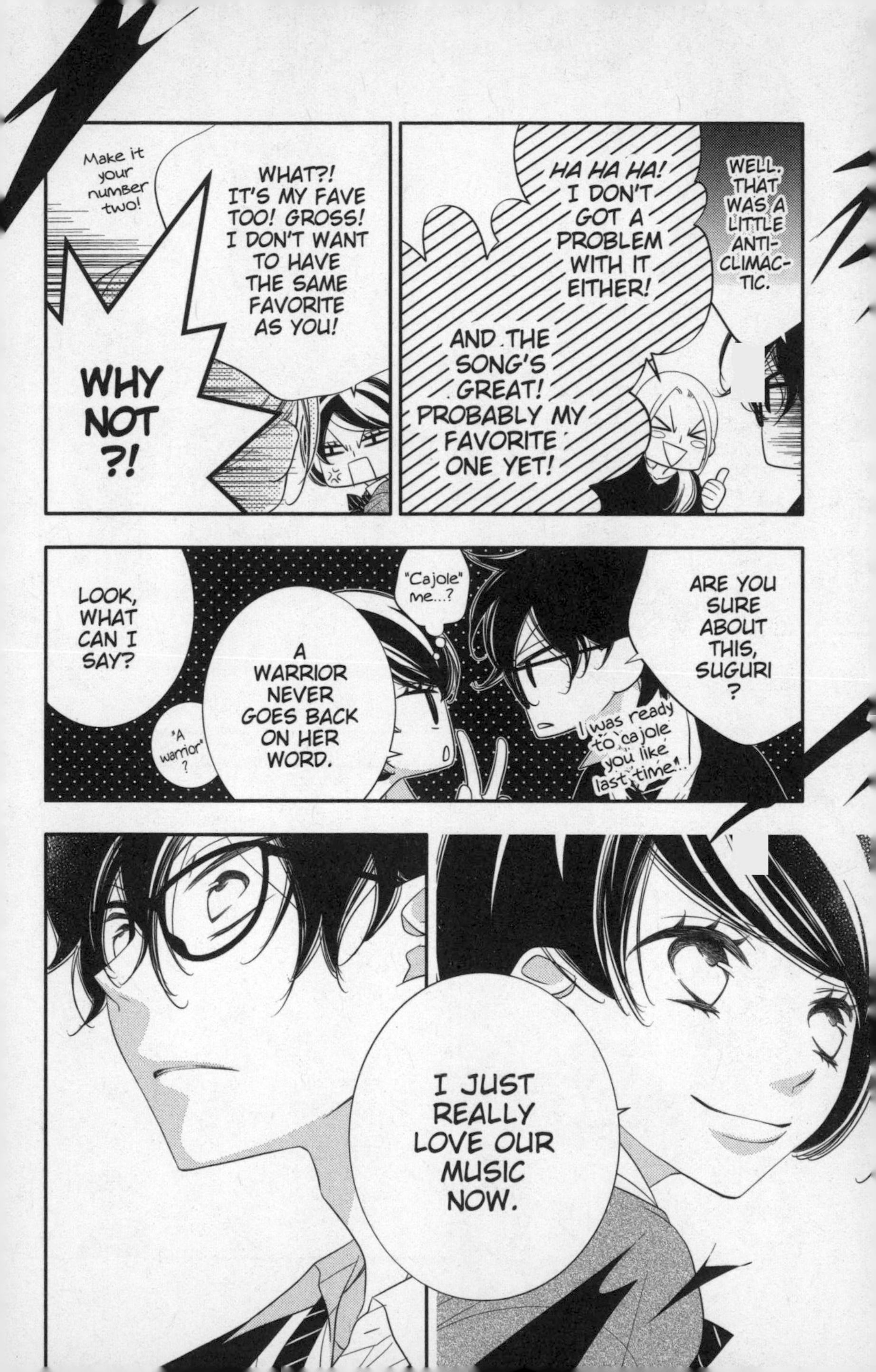
WELL, THAT WAS A LITTLE ANTI-CLIMACTIC.
HA HA HA! I DON'T GOT A PROBLEM WITH IT EITHER!
AND THE SONG'S GREAT! PROBABLY MY FAVORITE ONE YET!
WHAT?! IT'S MY FAVE TOO! GROSS! I DON'T WANT TO HAVE THE SAME FAVORITE AS YOU!
Make it your number two!
WHY NOT?!
ARE YOU SURE ABOUT THIS, SUGURI?
I was ready to cajole you like last time!..
"Cajole" me...?
A WARRIOR NEVER GOES BACK ON HER WORD.
LOOK, WHAT CAN I SAY?
"A warrior"?
I JUST REALLY LOVE OUR MUSIC NOW.

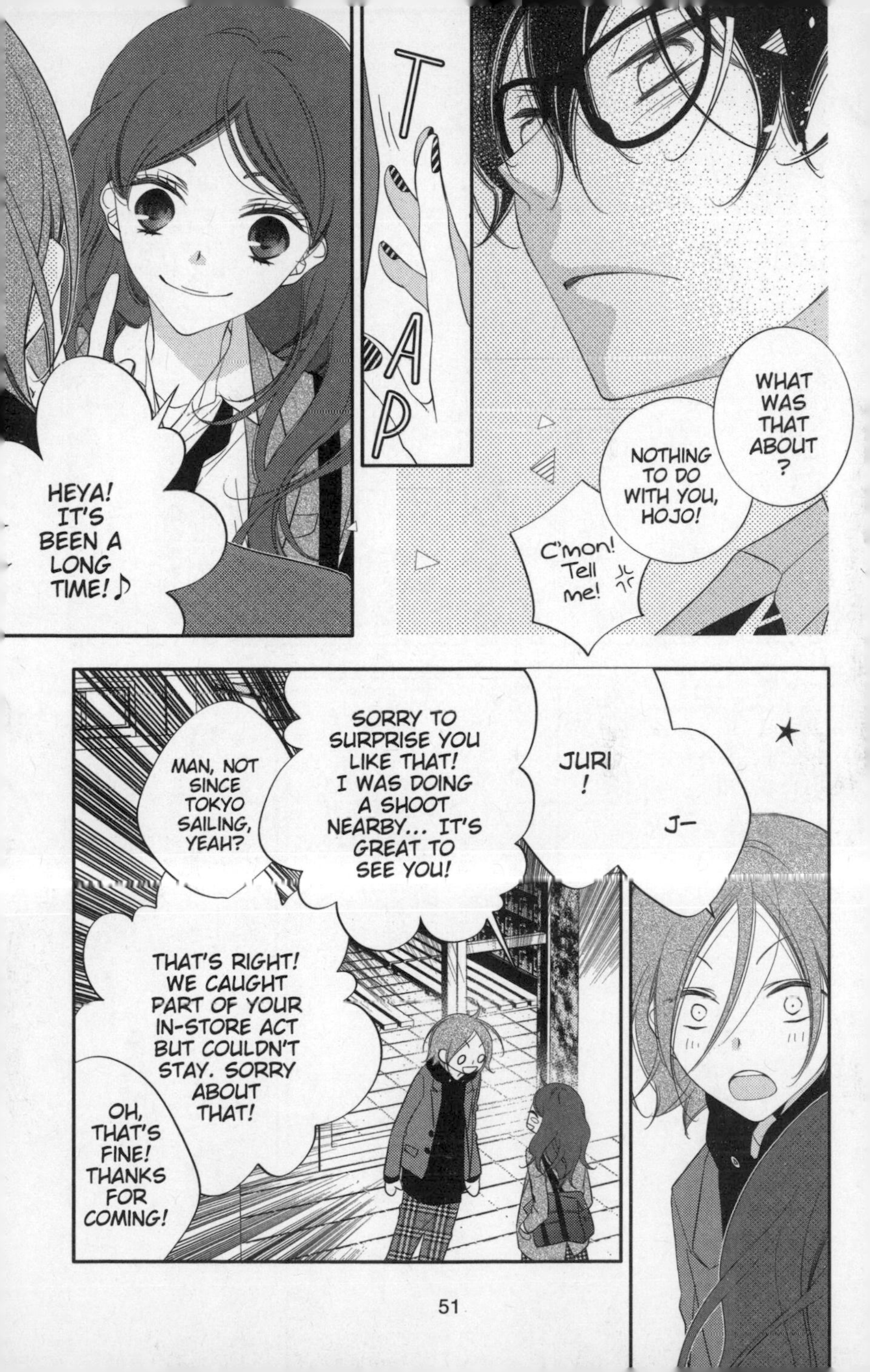
WHAT WAS THAT ABOUT?
NOTHING TO DO WITH YOU, HOJO!
C'mon! Tell me!
TAP
HEYA! IT'S BEEN A LONG TIME!♪
J—
JURI!
SORRY TO SURPRISE YOU LIKE THAT! I WAS DOING A SHOOT NEARBY... IT'S GREAT TO SEE YOU!
MAN, NOT SINCE TOKYO SAILING, YEAH?
THAT'S RIGHT! WE CAUGHT PART OF YOUR IN-STORE ACT BUT COULDN'T STAY. SORRY ABOUT THAT!
OH, THAT'S FINE! THANKS FOR COMING!

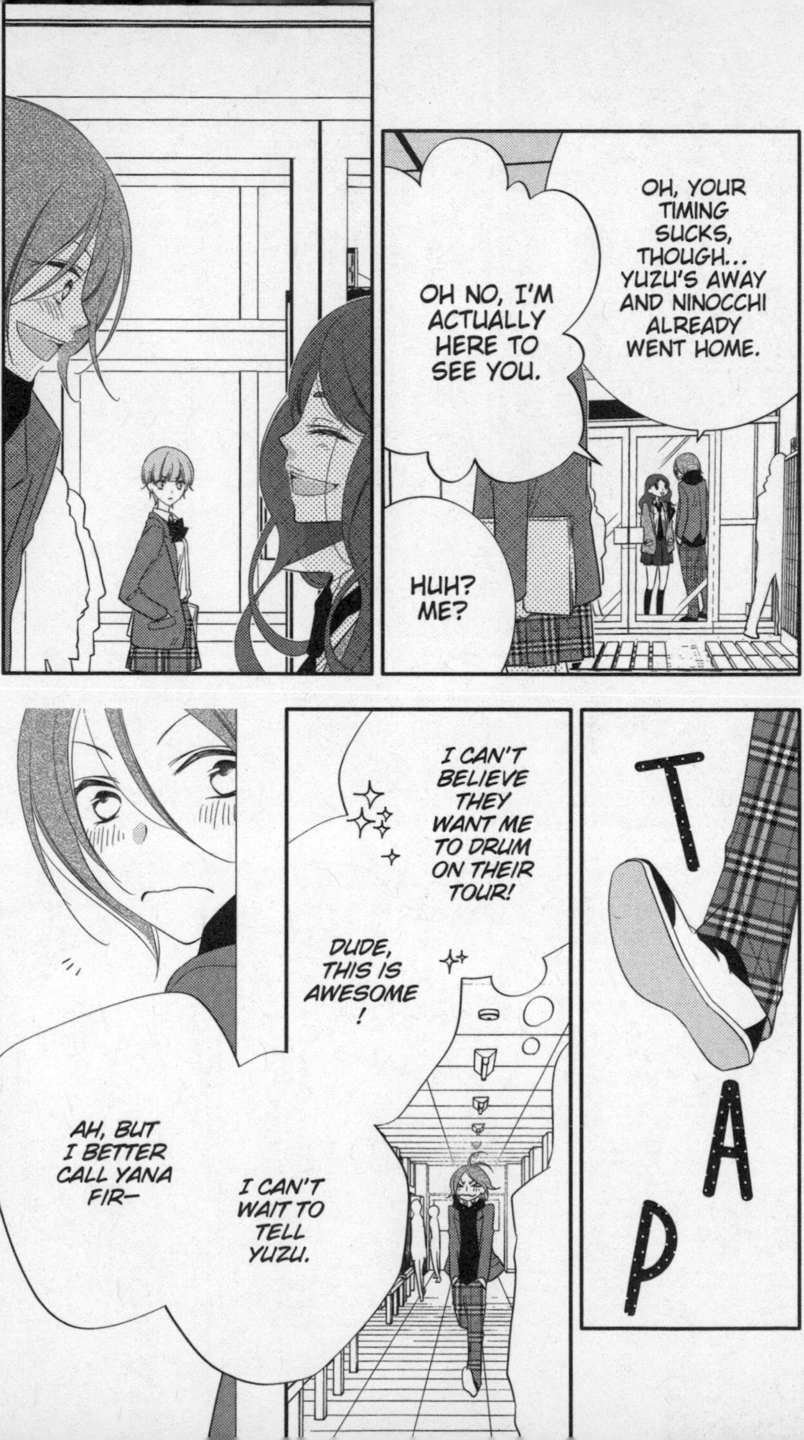
OH, YOUR TIMING SUCKS, THOUGH... YUZU'S AWAY AND NINOCCHI ALREADY WENT HOME.
OH NO, I'M ACTUALLY HERE TO SEE YOU.
HUH? ME?
TAP
I CAN'T BELIEVE THEY WANT ME TO DRUM ON THEIR TOUR!
DUDE, THIS IS AWESOME!
I CAN'T WAIT TO TELL YUZU.
AH, BUT I BETTER CALL YANA FIR–

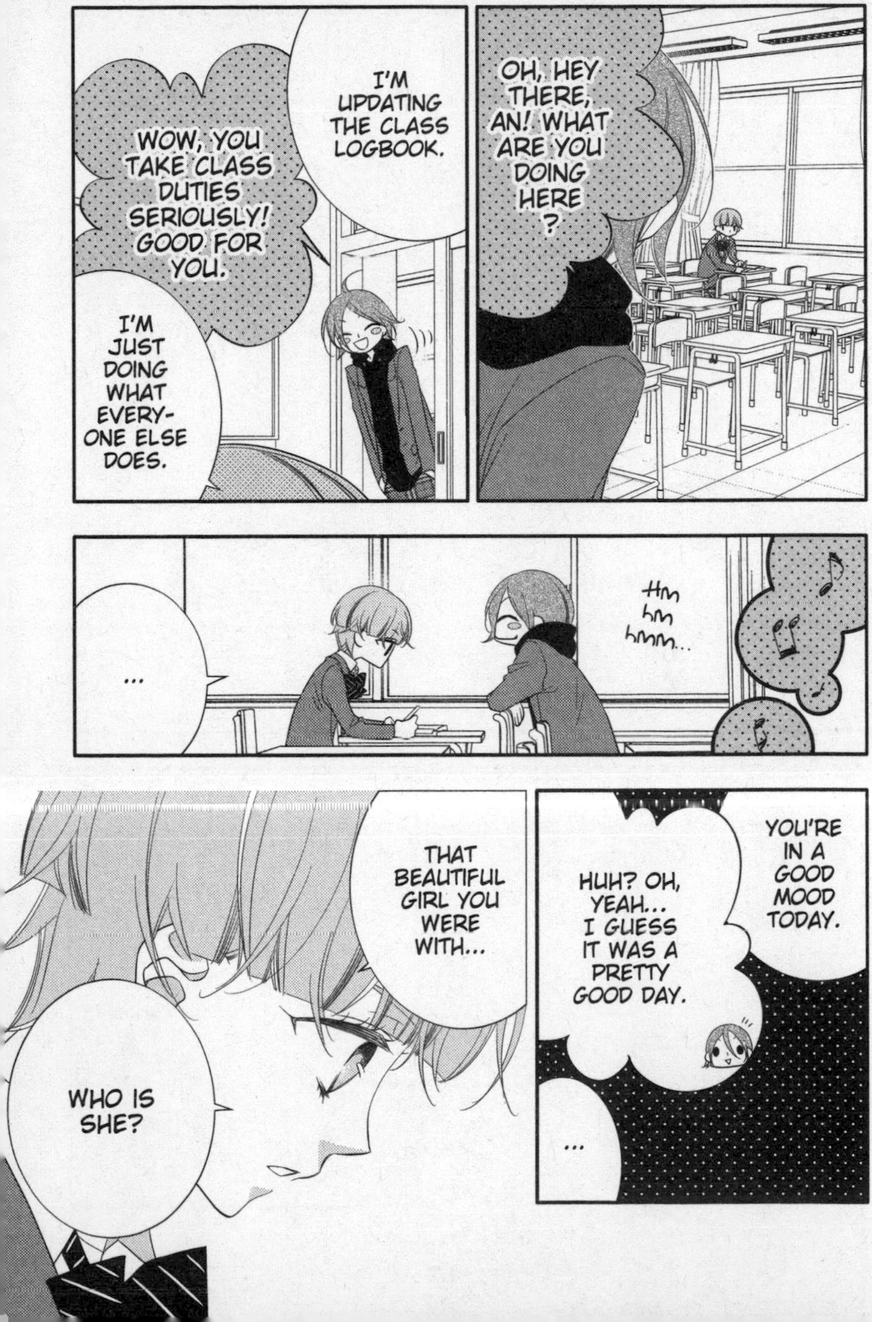
OH, HEY THERE, AN! WHAT ARE YOU DOING HERE?
I'M UPDATING THE CLASS LOGBOOK.
WOW, YOU TAKE CLASS DUTIES SERIOUSLY! GOOD FOR YOU.
I'M JUST DOING WHAT EVERY-ONE ELSE DOES.
Hm hm hmm...
...
YOU'RE IN A GOOD MOOD TODAY.
HUH? OH, YEAH... I GUESS IT WAS A PRETTY GOOD DAY.
...
THAT BEAUTIFUL GIRL YOU WERE WITH...
WHO IS SHE?

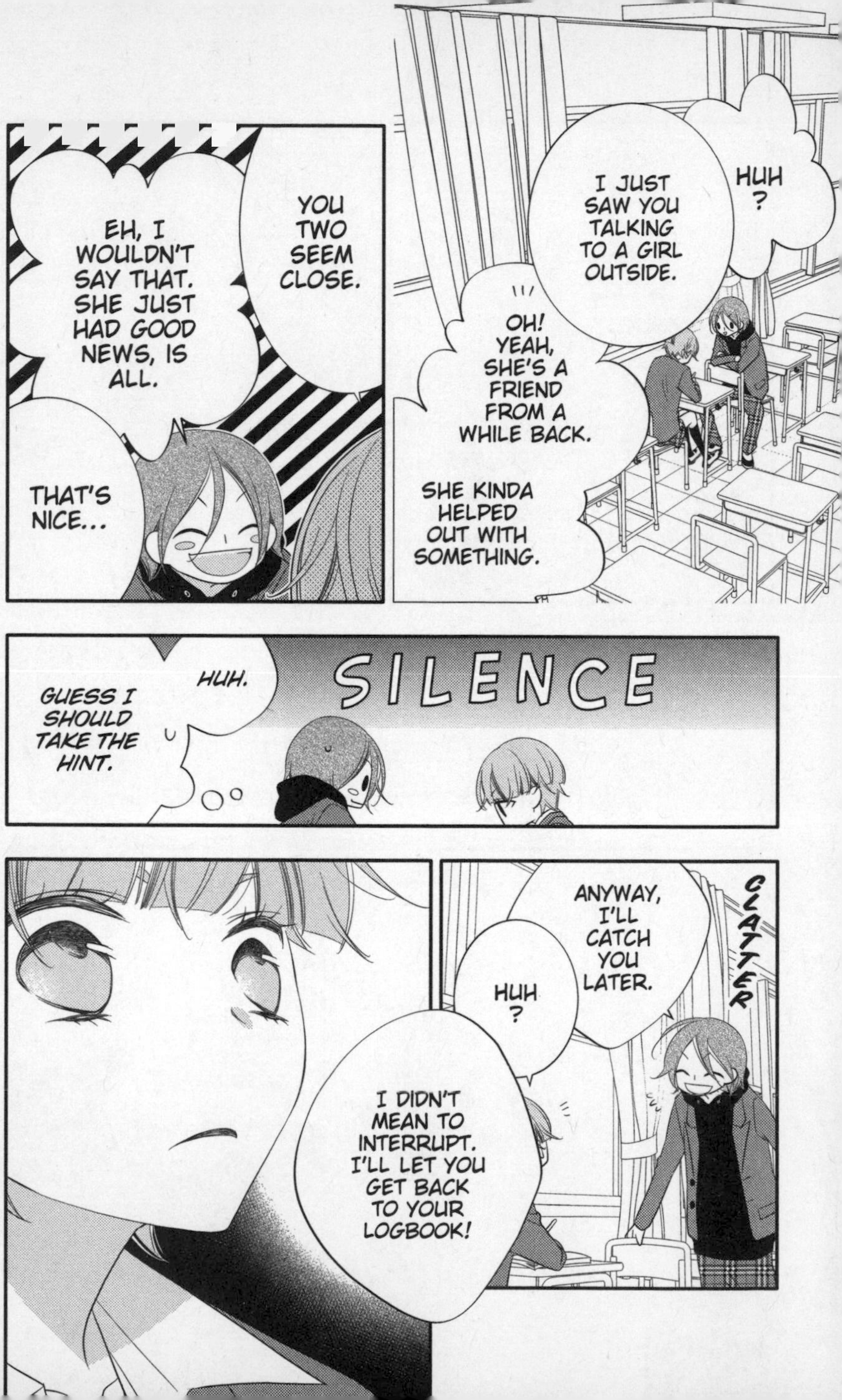
HUH?
I JUST SAW YOU TALKING TO A GIRL OUTSIDE.
OH! YEAH, SHE'S A FRIEND FROM A WHILE BACK.
SHE KINDA HELPED OUT WITH SOMETHING.
YOU TWO SEEM CLOSE.
EH, I WOULDN'T SAY THAT. SHE JUST HAD GOOD NEWS, IS ALL.
THAT'S NICE...
SILENCE
HUH.
GUESS I SHOULD TAKE THE HINT.
CLATTER
ANYWAY, I'LL CATCH YOU LATER.
HUH?
I DIDN'T MEAN TO INTERRUPT. I'LL LET YOU GET BACK TO YOUR LOGBOOK!

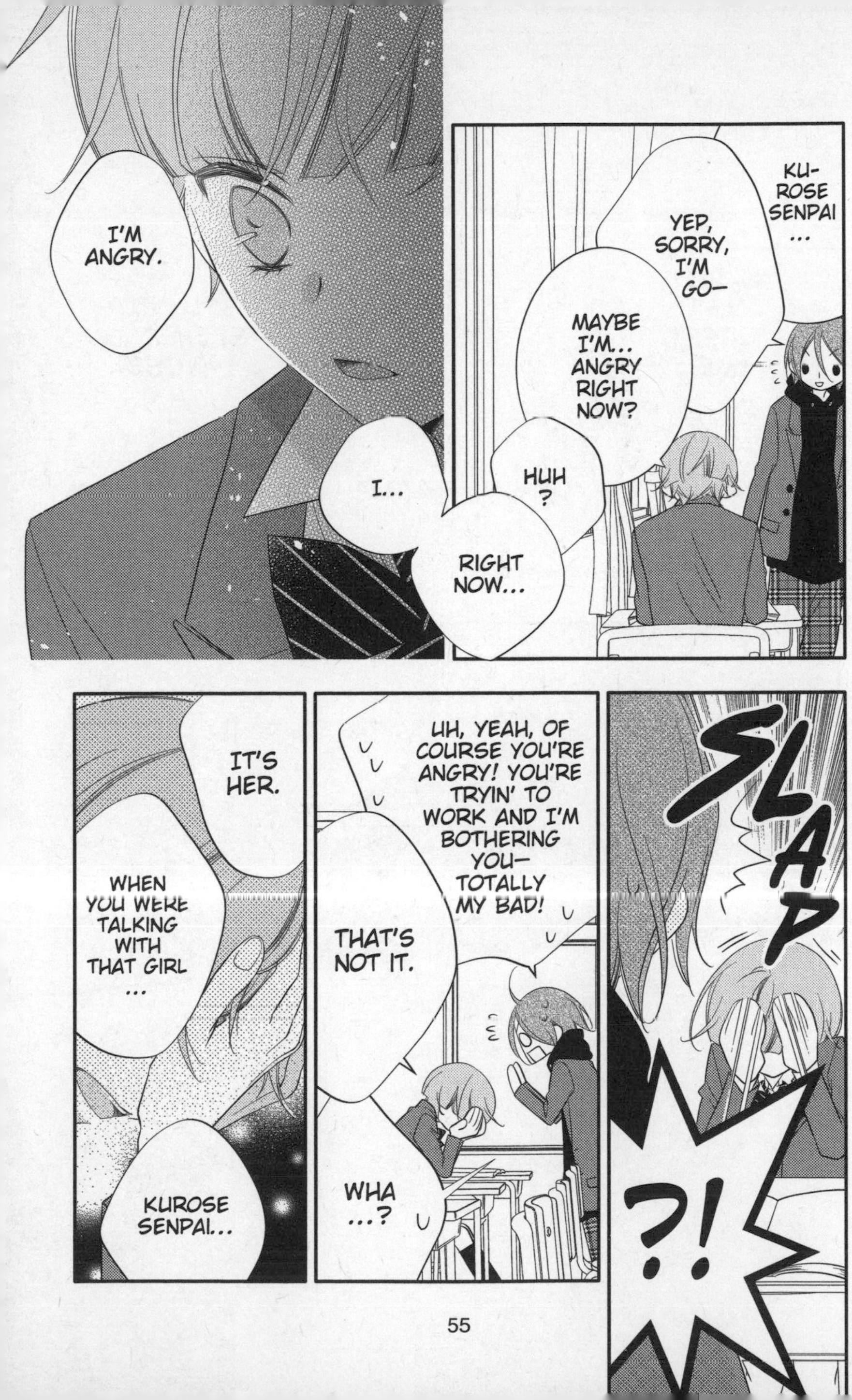
KU-ROSE SENPAI...
YEP, SORRY, I'M GO—
MAYBE I'M... ANGRY RIGHT NOW?
HUH?
I...
RIGHT NOW...
I'M ANGRY.
SLAP
?!
UH, YEAH, OF COURSE YOU'RE ANGRY! YOU'RE TRYIN' TO WORK AND I'M BOTHERING YOU—TOTALLY MY BAD!
THAT'S NOT IT.
WHA...?
IT'S HER.
WHEN YOU WERE TALKING WITH THAT GIRL...
KUROSE SENPAI...

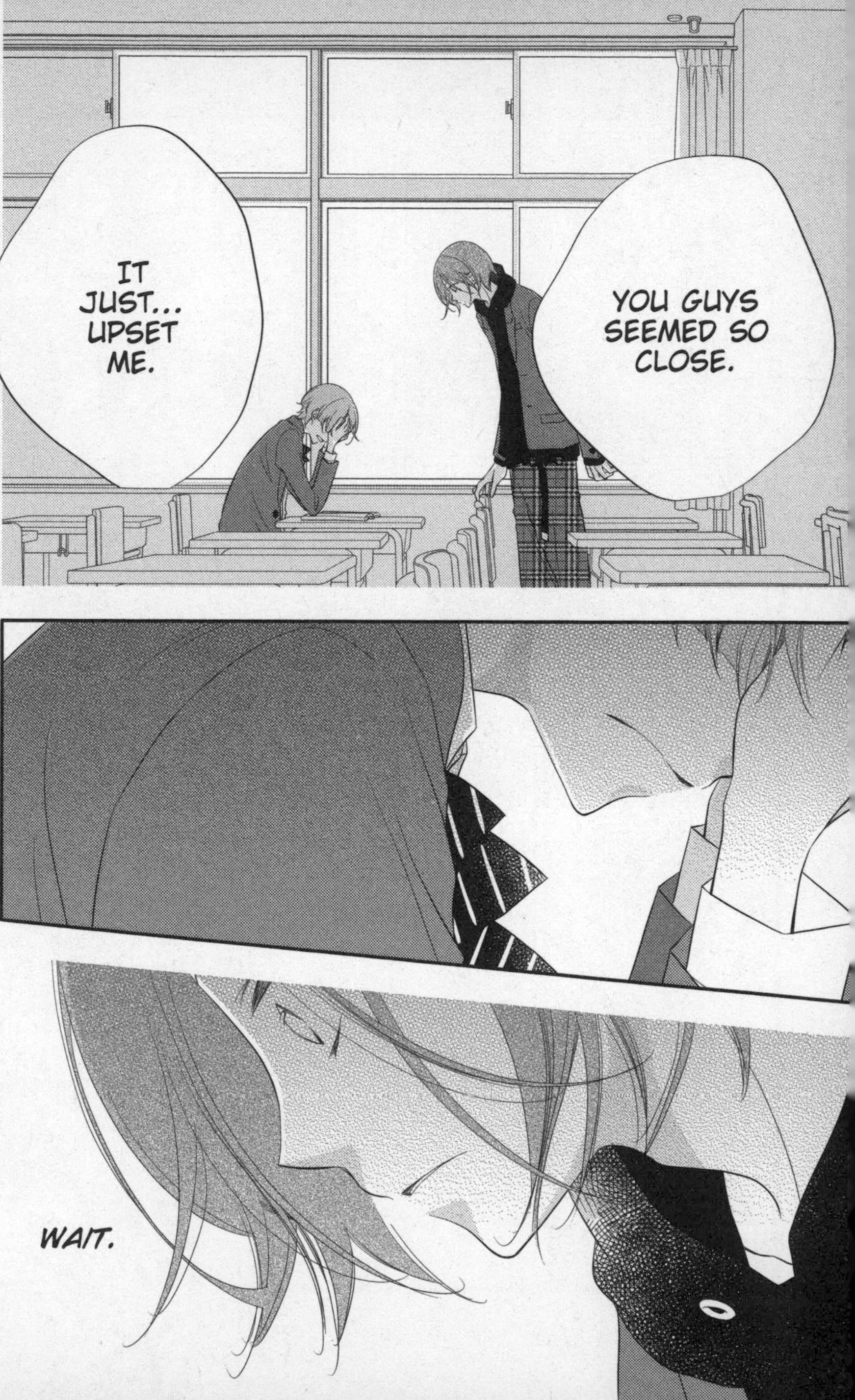
YOU GUYS SEEMED SO CLOSE.
IT JUST... UPSET ME.
WAIT.

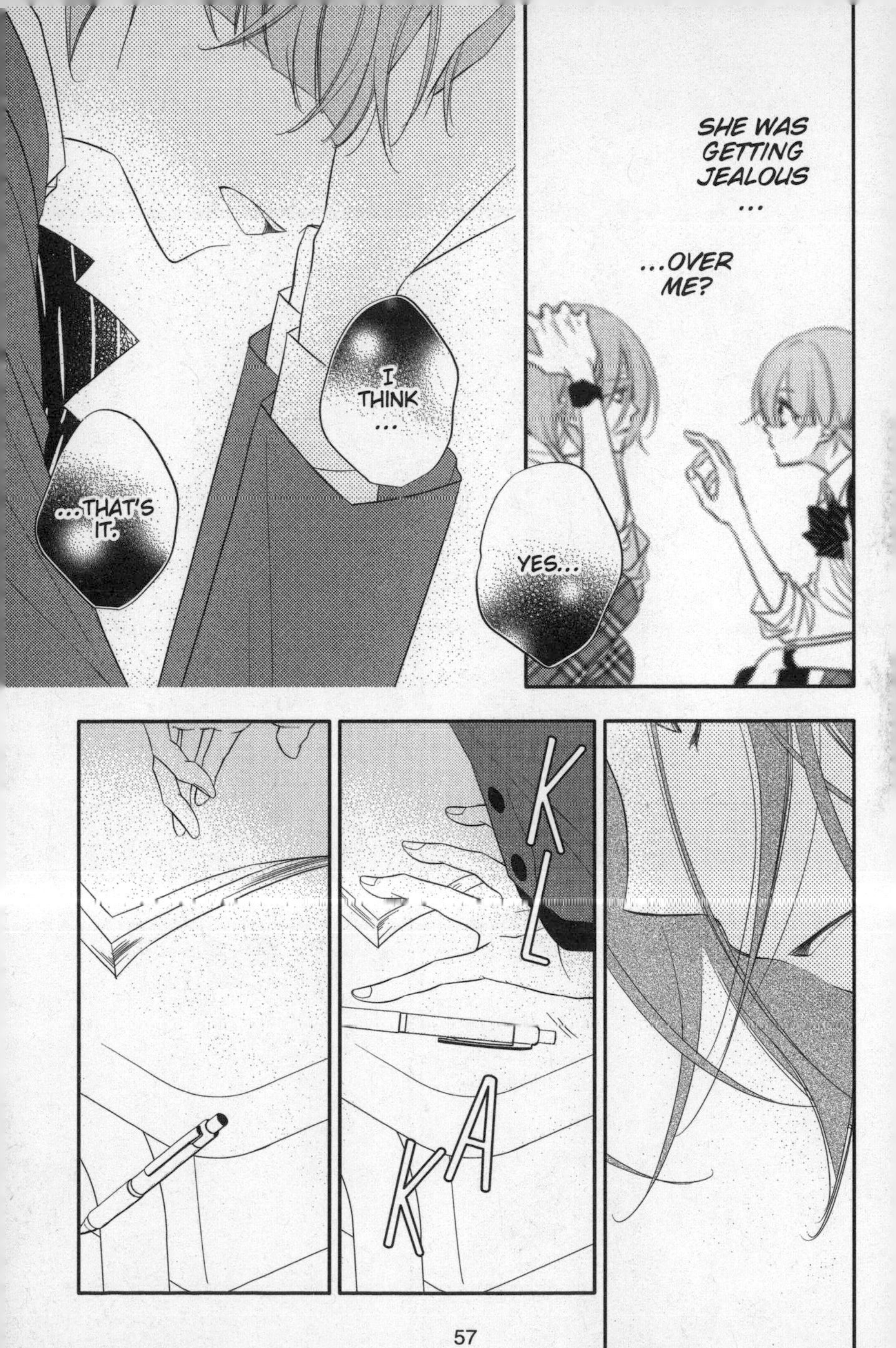
SHE WAS GETTING JEALOUS ...
...OVER ME?
YES...
I THINK ...
...THAT'S IT.
KLAKA

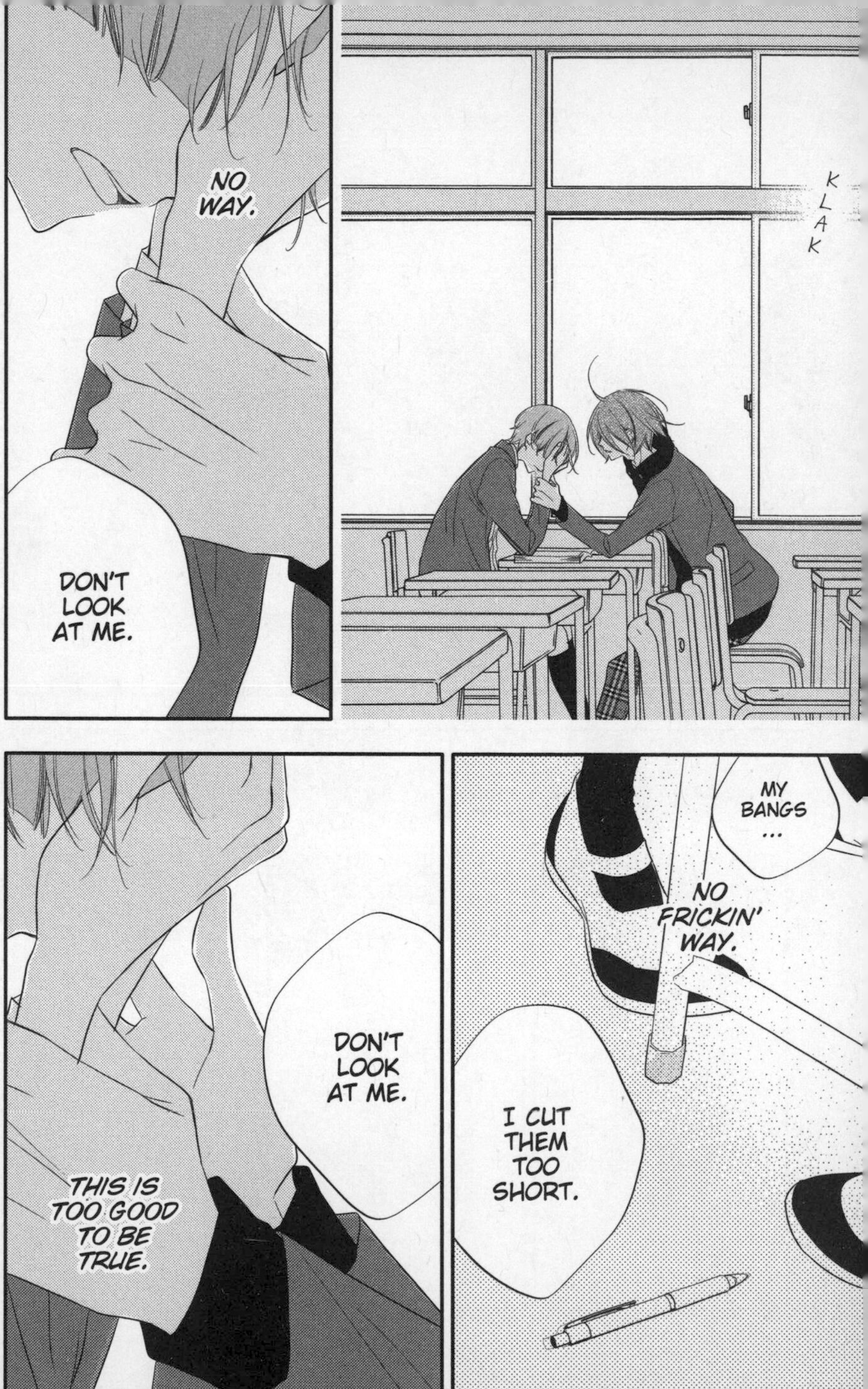
KLAK
NO WAY.
DON'T LOOK AT ME.
MY BANGS ...
NO FRICKIN' WAY.
I CUT THEM TOO SHORT.
DON'T LOOK AT ME.
THIS IS TOO GOOD TO BE TRUE.

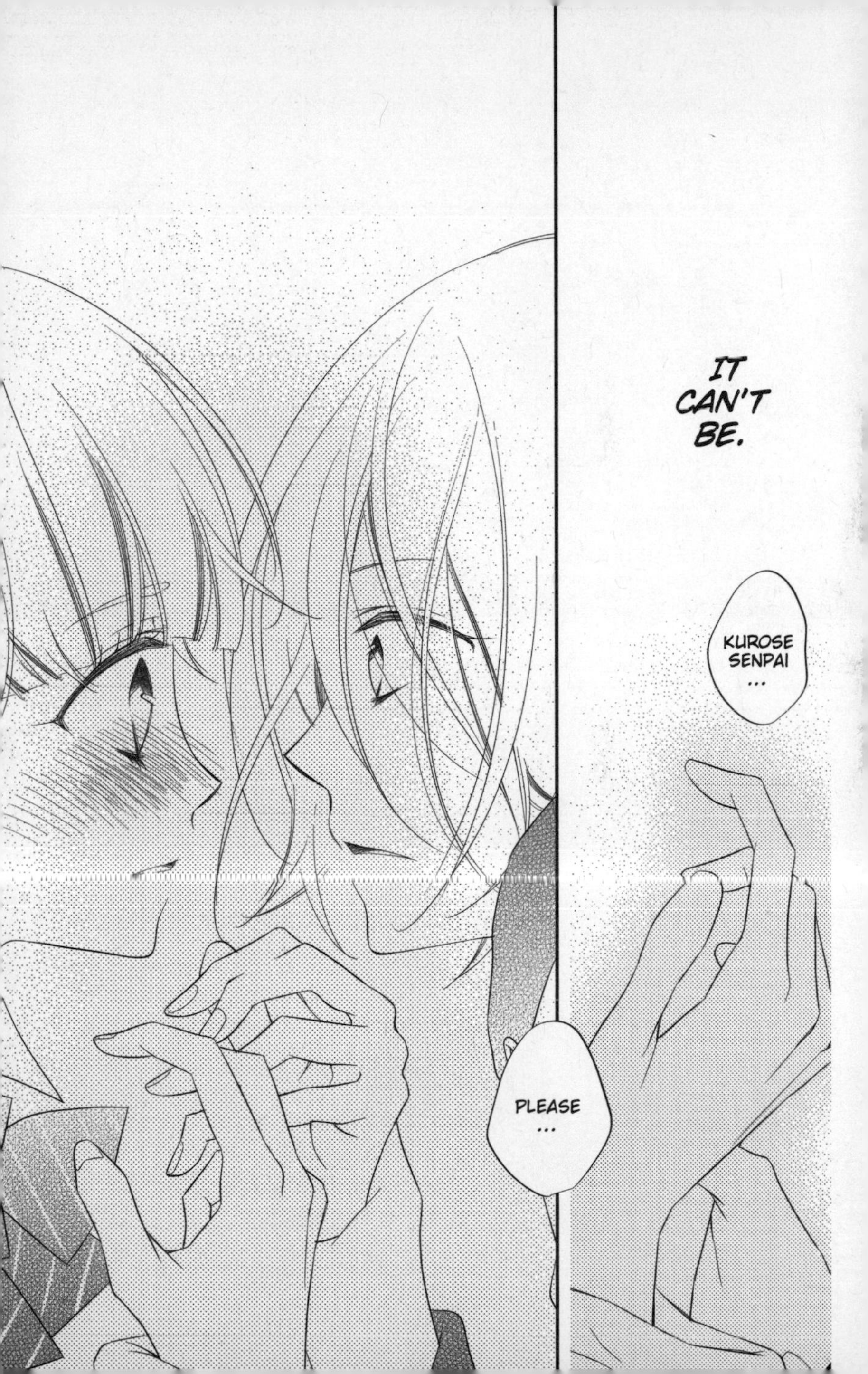
IT CAN'T BE.
KUROSE SENPAI ...
PLEASE ...

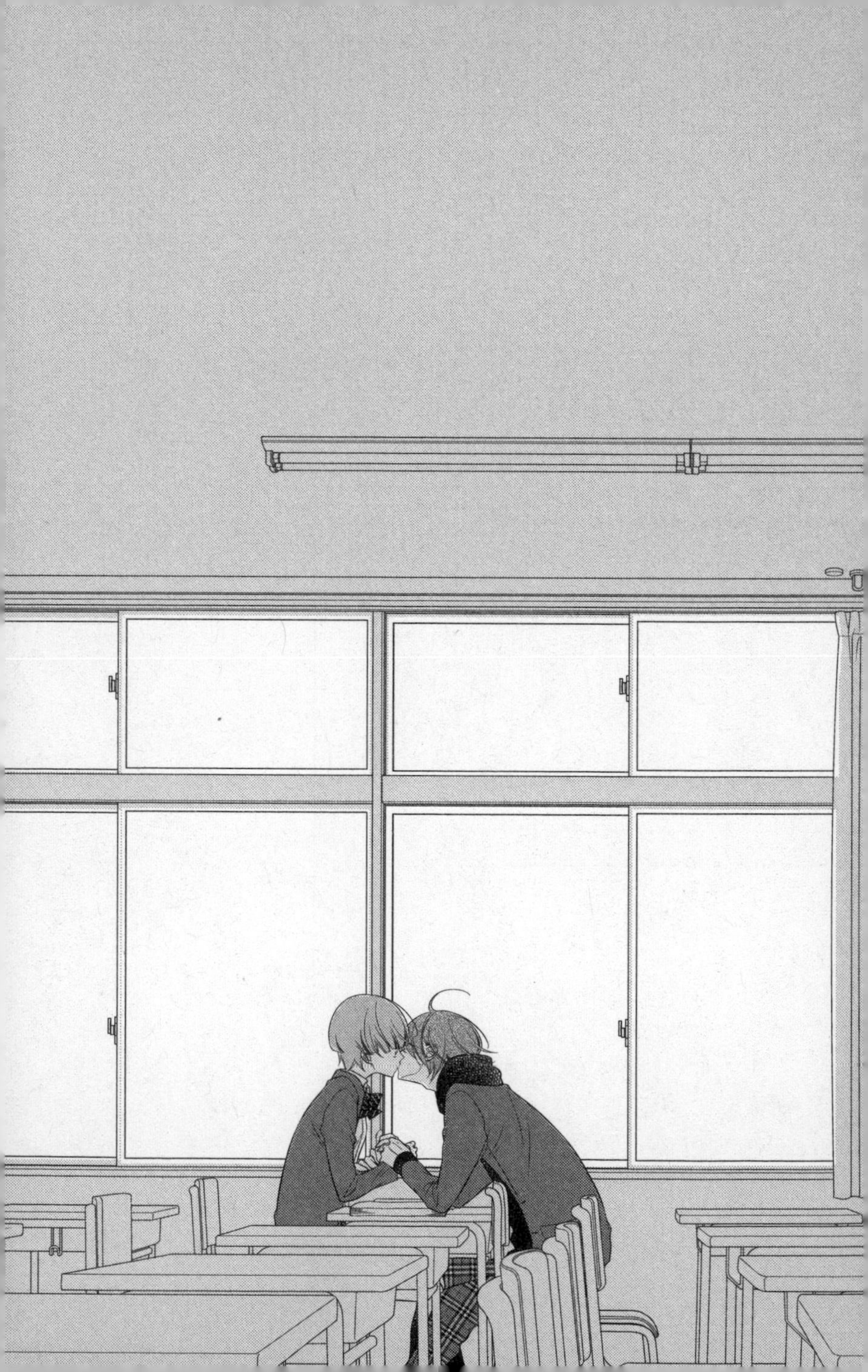

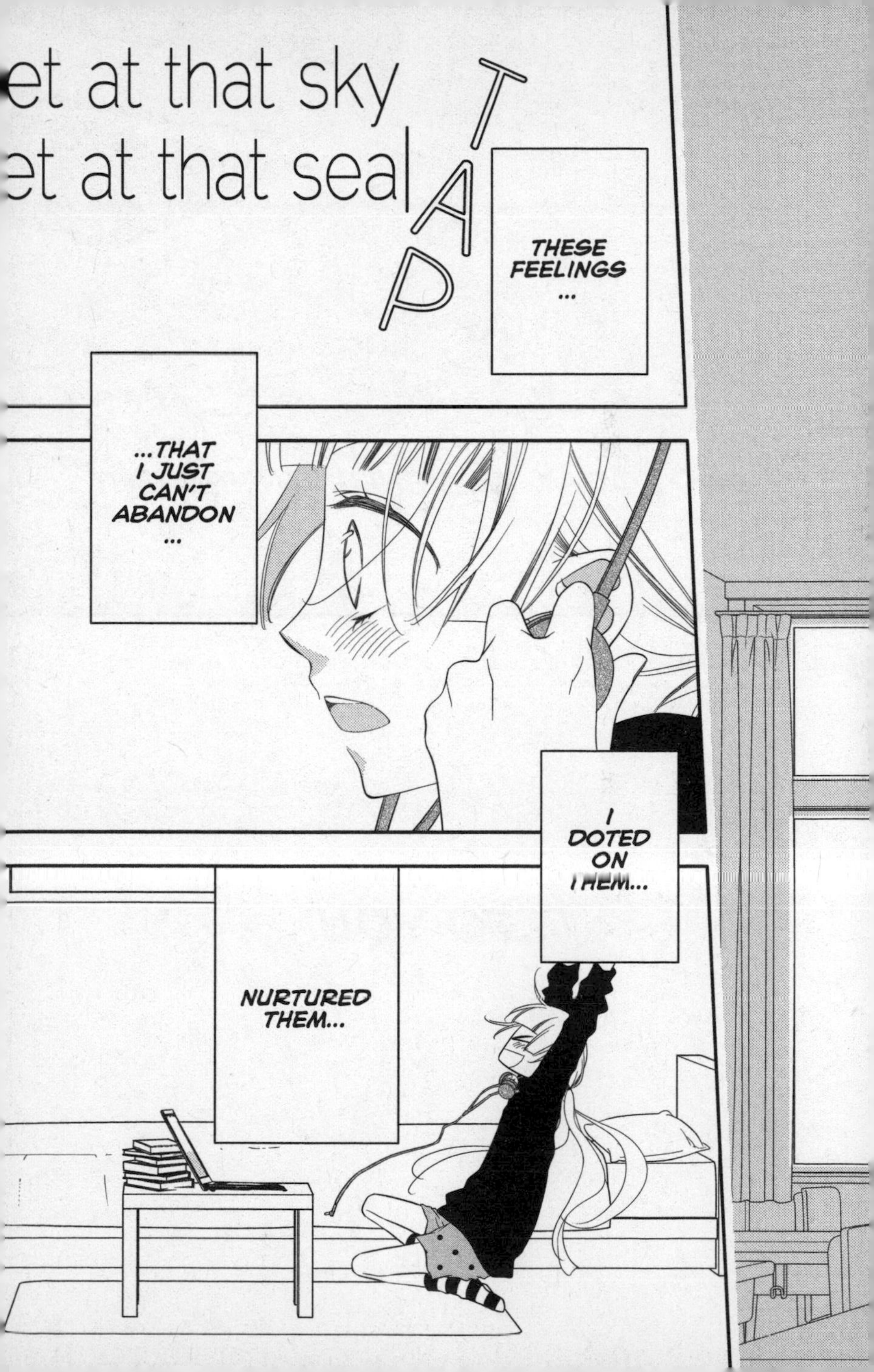
THESE FEELINGS ...
TAP
et at that sky
et at that sea
...THAT I JUST CAN'T ABANDON ...
I DOTED ON THEM...
NURTURED THEM...

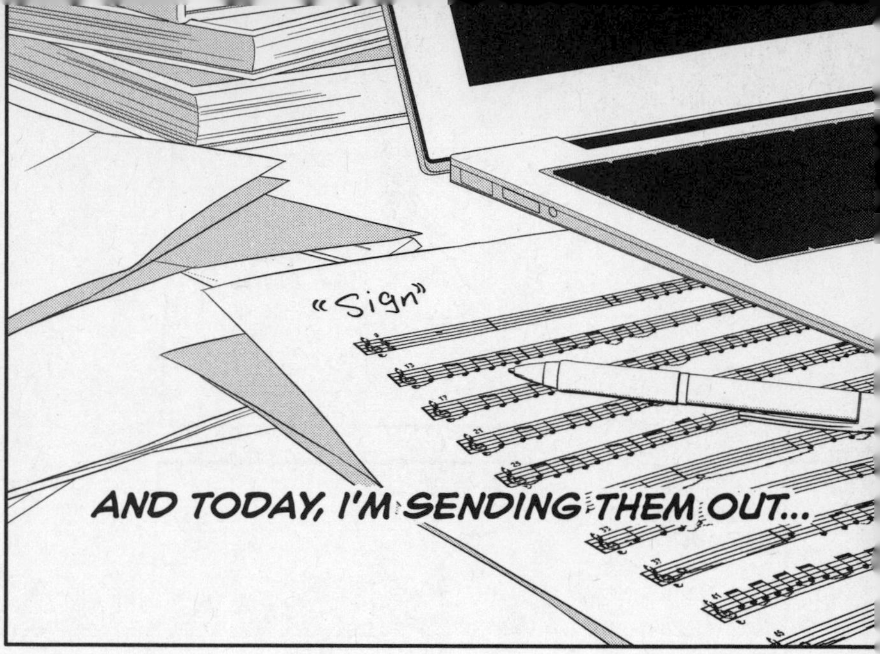
"Sign"
AND TODAY, I'M SENDING THEM OUT...

...TO YOU.

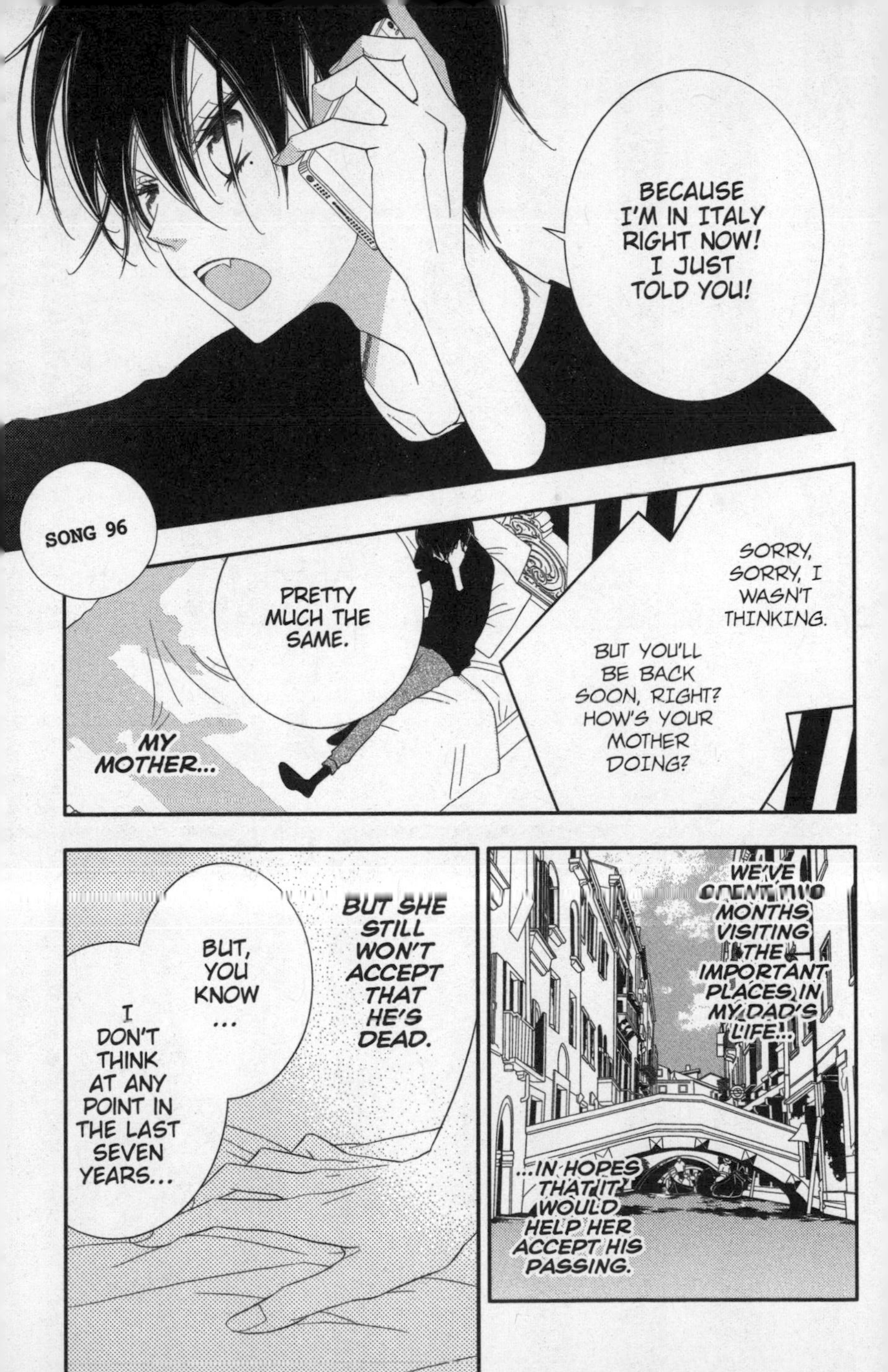
BECAUSE I'M IN ITALY RIGHT NOW! I JUST TOLD YOU!
SONG 96
SORRY, SORRY, I WASN'T THINKING.
BUT YOU'LL BE BACK SOON, RIGHT? HOW'S YOUR MOTHER DOING?
PRETTY MUCH THE SAME.
MY MOTHER...
WE'VE
MONTHS VISITING THE IMPORTANT PLACES IN MY DAD'S LIFE...
...IN HOPES THAT IT WOULD HELP HER ACCEPT HIS PASSING.
BUT SHE STILL WON'T ACCEPT THAT HE'S DEAD.
BUT, YOU KNOW ...
I DON'T THINK AT ANY POINT IN THE LAST SEVEN YEARS...

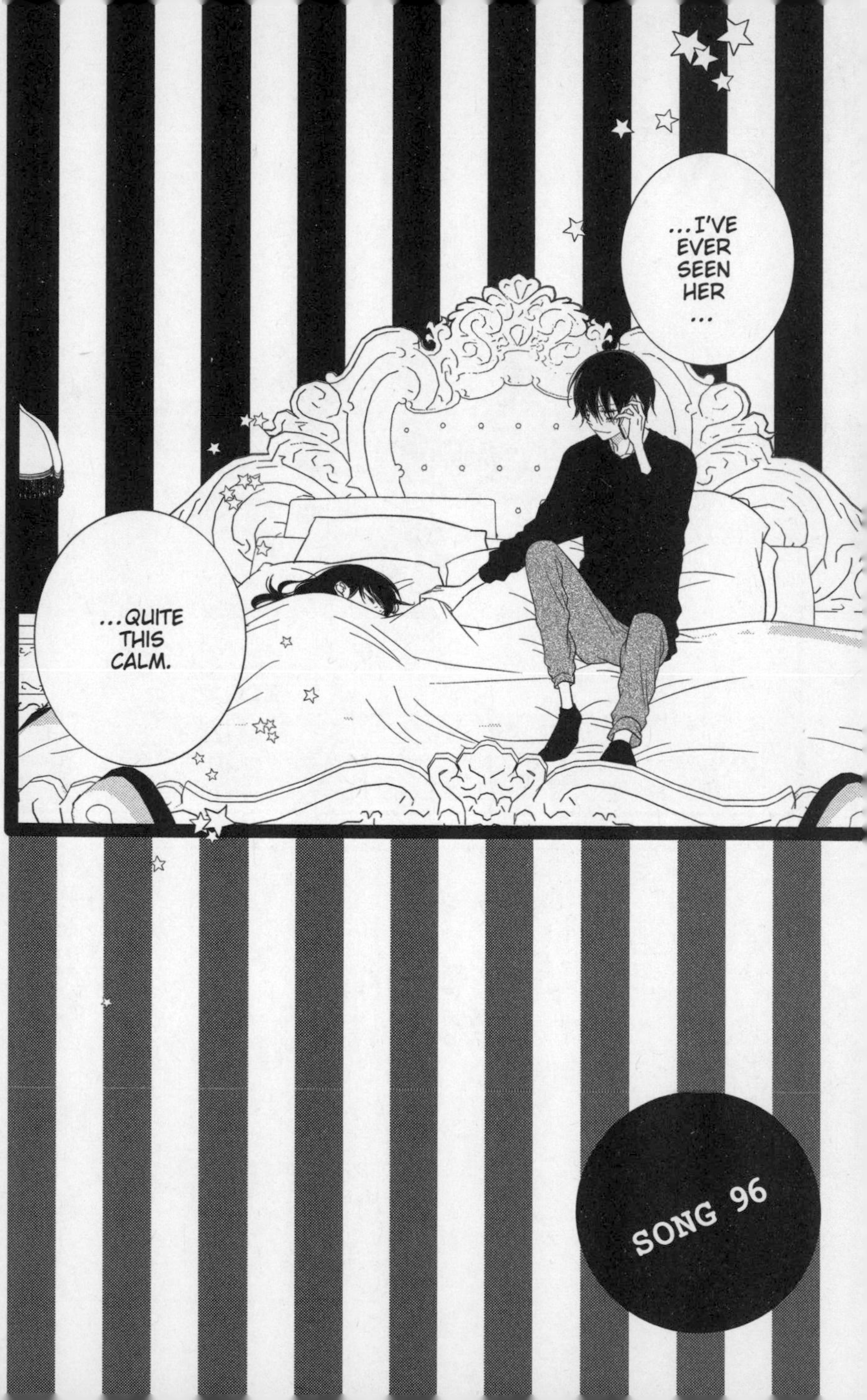
...I'VE EVER SEEN HER ...
...QUITE THIS CALM.
SONG 96

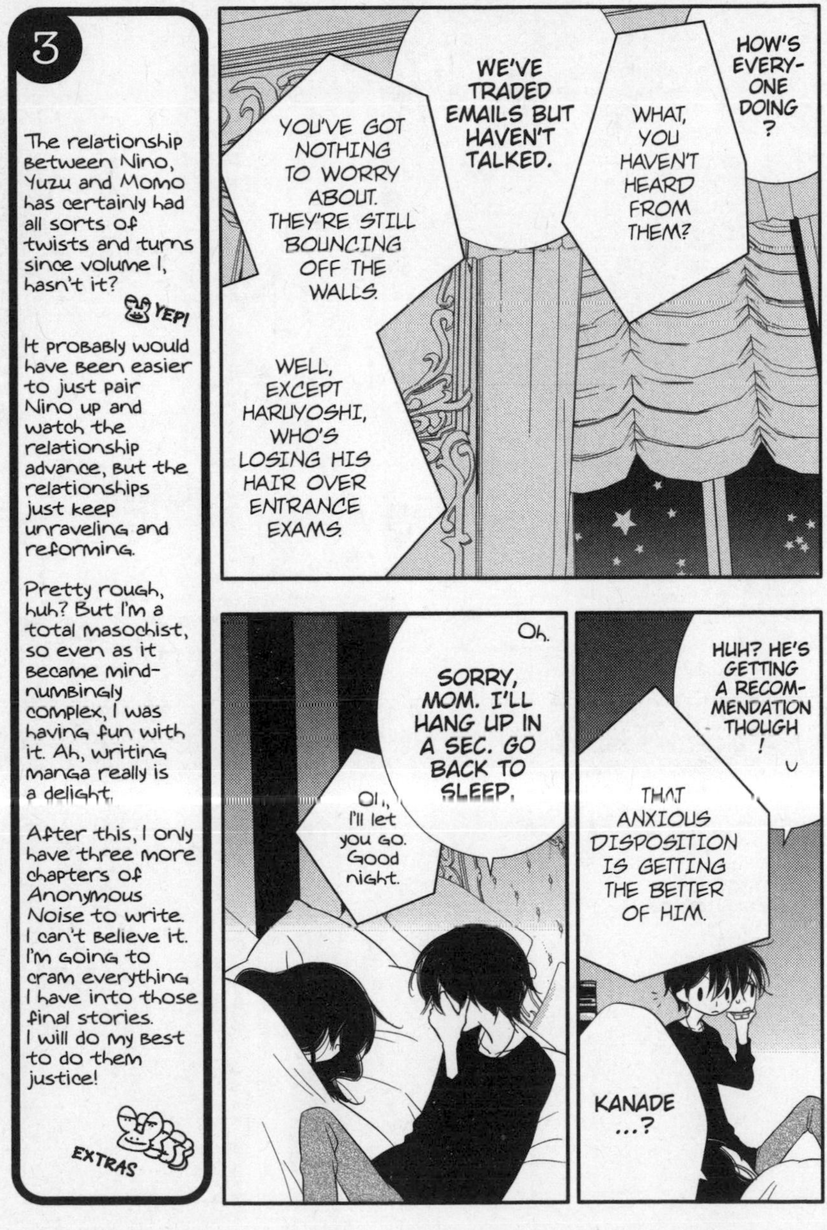
HOW'S EVERYONE DOING?
WHAT, YOU HAVEN'T HEARD FROM THEM?
WE'VE TRADED EMAILS BUT HAVEN'T TALKED.
YOU'VE GOT NOTHING TO WORRY ABOUT. THEY'RE STILL BOUNCING OFF THE WALLS.
WELL, EXCEPT HARUYOSHI, WHO'S LOSING HIS HAIR OVER ENTRANCE EXAMS.
HUH? HE'S GETTING A RECOMMENDATION THOUGH!
THAT ANXIOUS DISPOSITION IS GETTING THE BETTER OF HIM.
KANADE ...?
Oh.
SORRY, MOM. I'LL HANG UP IN A SEC. GO BACK TO SLEEP.
I'll let you go. Good night.

3

The relationship between Nino, Yuzu and Momo has certainly had all sorts of twists and turns since volume 1, hasn't it?

YEP!

It probably would have been easier to just pair Nino up and watch the relationship advance, but the relationships just keep unraveling and reforming.

Pretty rough, huh? But I'm a total masochist, so even as it became mind-numbingly complex, I was having fun with it. Ah, writing manga really is a delight.

After this, I only have three more chapters of Anonymous Noise to write. I can't believe it. I'm going to cram everything I have into those final stories. I will do my best to do them justice!

EXTRAS

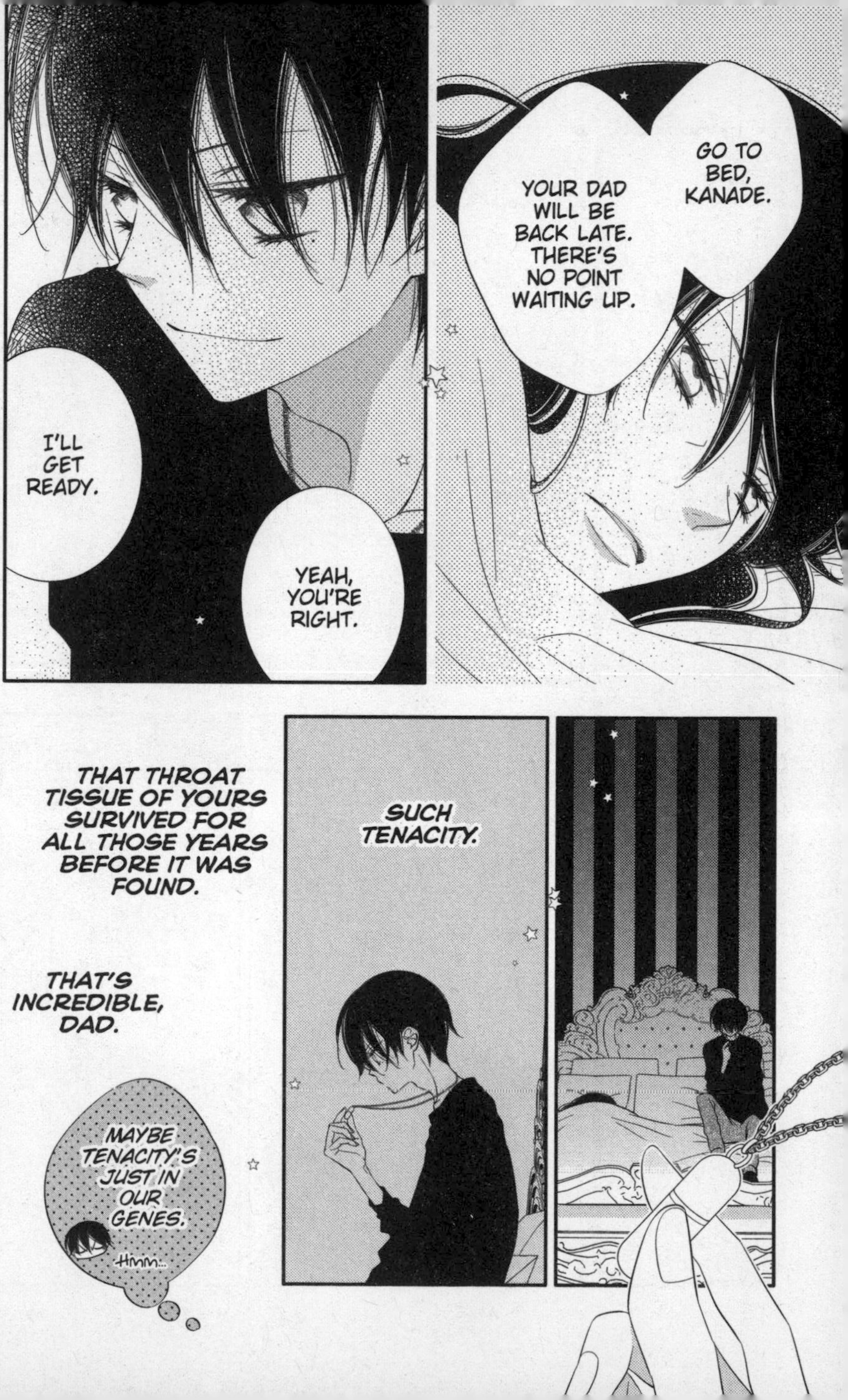
GO TO BED, KANADE.
YOUR DAD WILL BE BACK LATE. THERE'S NO POINT WAITING UP.
YEAH, YOU'RE RIGHT.
I'LL GET READY.
SUCH TENACITY.
THAT THROAT TISSUE OF YOURS SURVIVED FOR ALL THOSE YEARS BEFORE IT WAS FOUND.
THAT'S INCREDIBLE, DAD.
MAYBE TENACITY'S JUST IN OUR GENES.
Hmm...

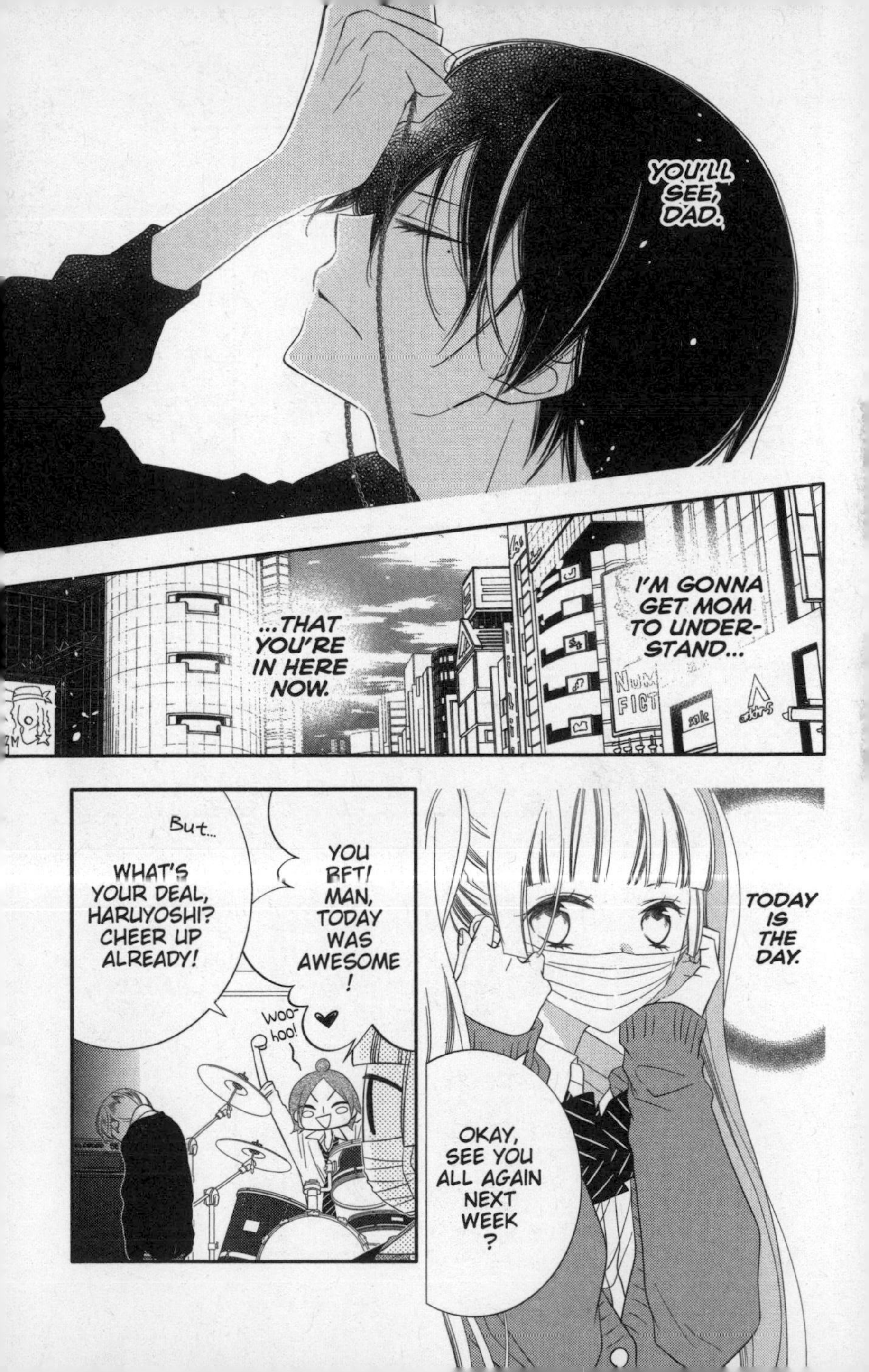
YOU'LL SEE, DAD.
I'M GONNA GET MOM TO UNDER-STAND...
...THAT YOU'RE IN HERE NOW.
TODAY IS THE DAY.
OKAY, SEE YOU ALL AGAIN NEXT WEEK?
YOU BFT! MAN, TODAY WAS AWESOME!
But...
WHAT'S YOUR DEAL, HARUYOSHI? CHEER UP ALREADY!
Woo-hoo!

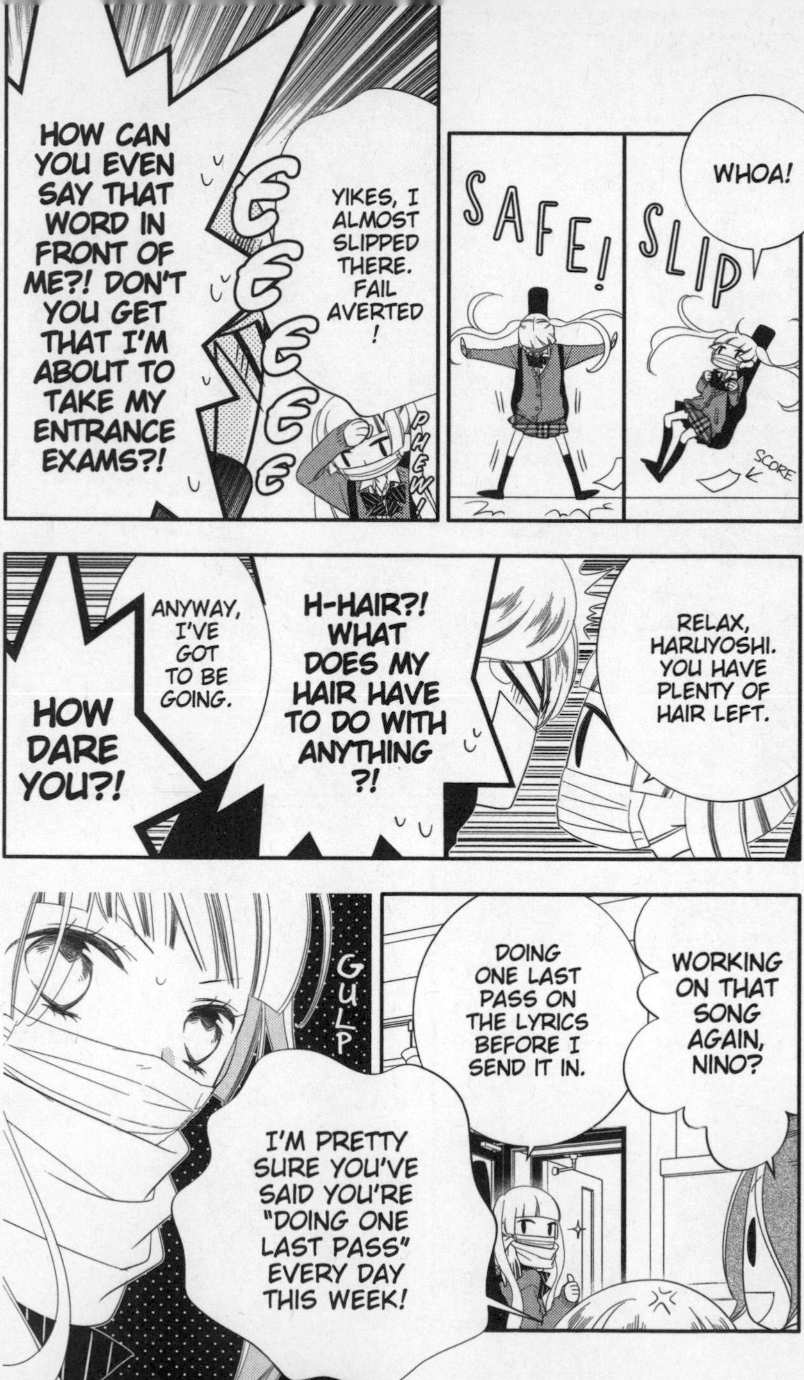
WHOA!
SLIP
SCORE
SAFE!
HOW CAN YOU EVEN SAY THAT WORD IN FRONT OF ME?! DON'T YOU GET THAT I'M ABOUT TO TAKE MY ENTRANCE EXAMS?!
YIKES, I ALMOST SLIPPED THERE. FAIL AVERTED!
PHEW
RELAX, HARUYOSHI. YOU HAVE PLENTY OF HAIR LEFT.
H-HAIR?! WHAT DOES MY HAIR HAVE TO DO WITH ANYTHING?!
ANYWAY, I'VE GOT TO BE GOING.
HOW DARE YOU?!
WORKING ON THAT SONG AGAIN, NINO?
DOING ONE LAST PASS ON THE LYRICS BEFORE I SEND IT IN.
GULP
I'M PRETTY SURE YOU'VE SAID YOU'RE "DOING ONE LAST PASS" EVERY DAY THIS WEEK!

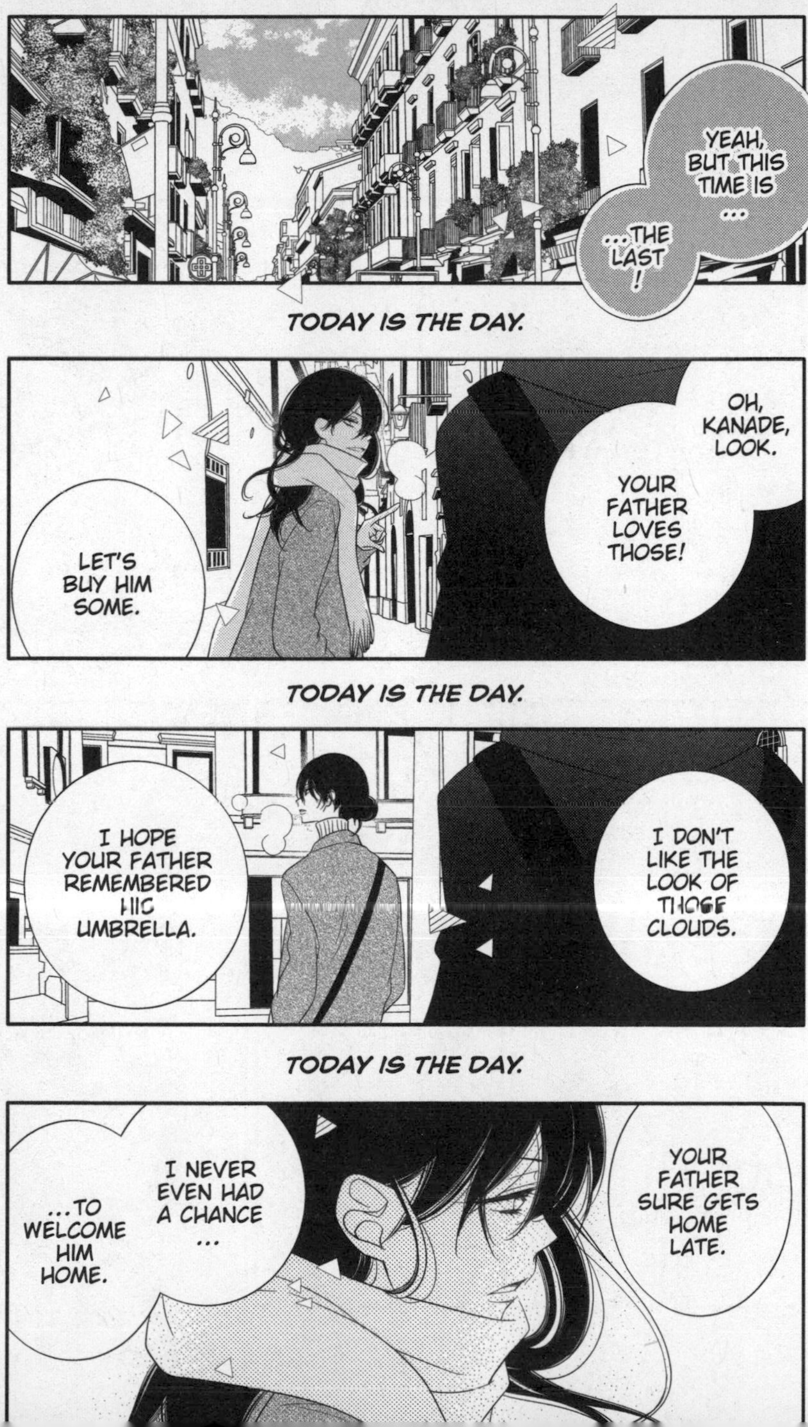
YEAH, BUT THIS TIME IS ...
...THE LAST!
TODAY IS THE DAY.
OH, KANADE, LOOK.
YOUR FATHER LOVES THOSE!
LET'S BUY HIM SOME.
TODAY IS THE DAY.
I DON'T LIKE THE LOOK OF THOSE CLOUDS.
I HOPE YOUR FATHER REMEMBERED HIS UMBRELLA.
TODAY IS THE DAY.
YOUR FATHER SURE GETS HOME LATE.
I NEVER EVEN HAD A CHANCE ...
...TO WELCOME HIM HOME.

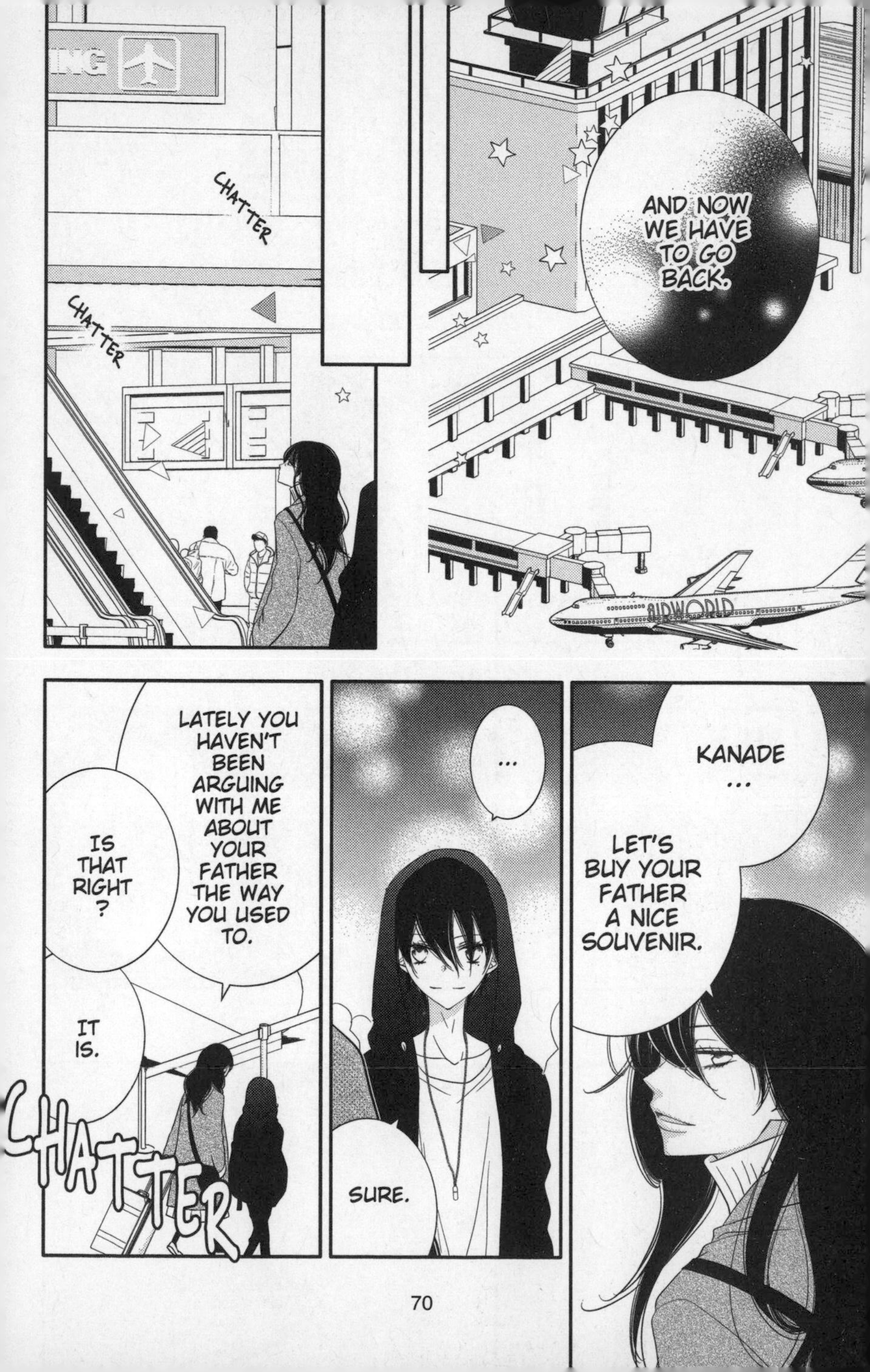
AND NOW WE HAVE TO GO BACK.
CHATTER
CHATTER
AIRWORLD
KANADE...
LET'S BUY YOUR FATHER A NICE SOUVENIR.
...
SURE.
LATELY YOU HAVEN'T BEEN ARGUING WITH ME ABOUT YOUR FATHER THE WAY YOU USED TO.
IS THAT RIGHT?
IT IS.
CHATTER

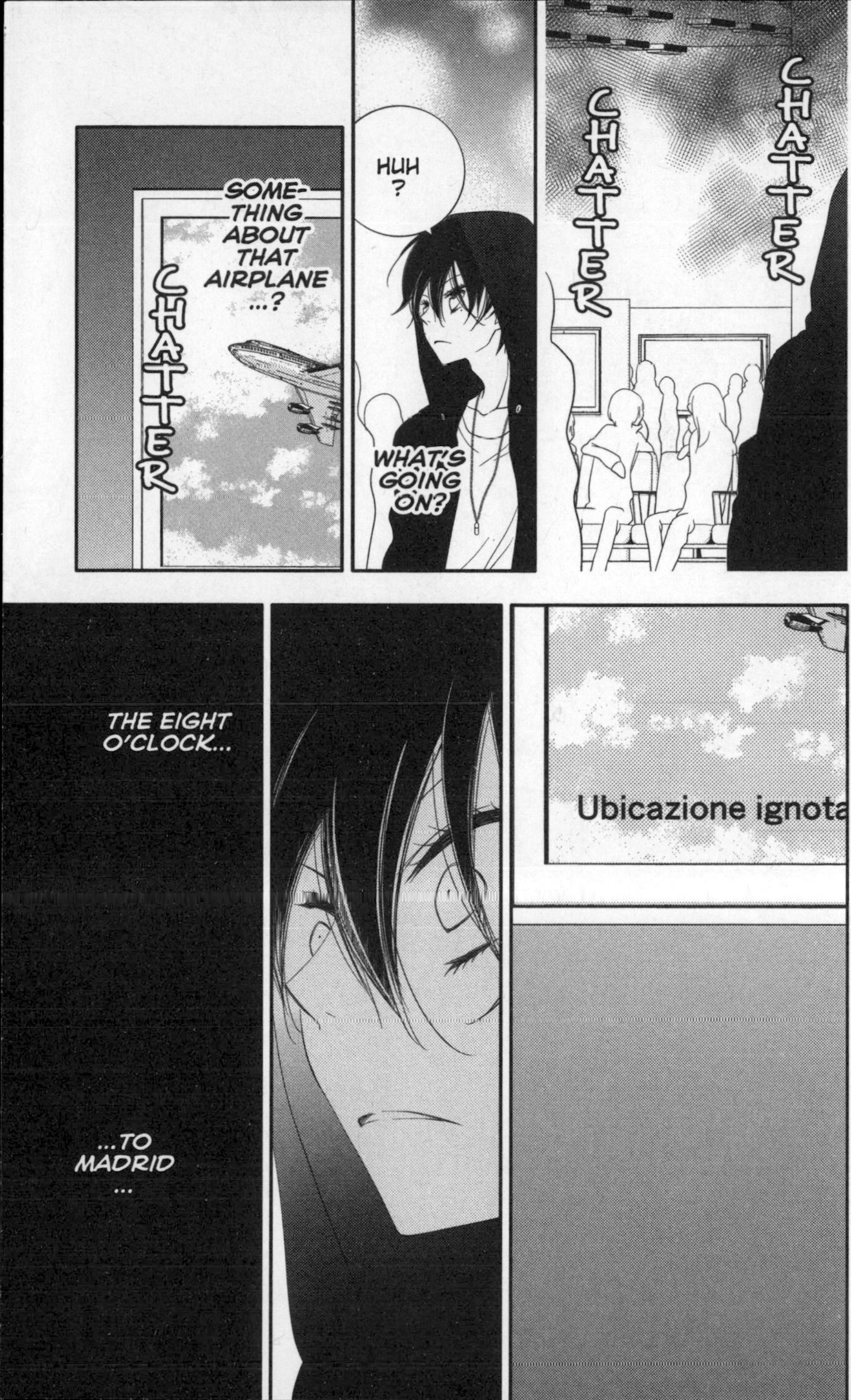
CHATTER
CHATTER
HUH?
WHAT'S GOING ON?
SOME-THING ABOUT THAT AIRPLANE ...?
CHATTER
Ubicazione ignota
THE EIGHT O'CLOCK...
...TO MADRID ...

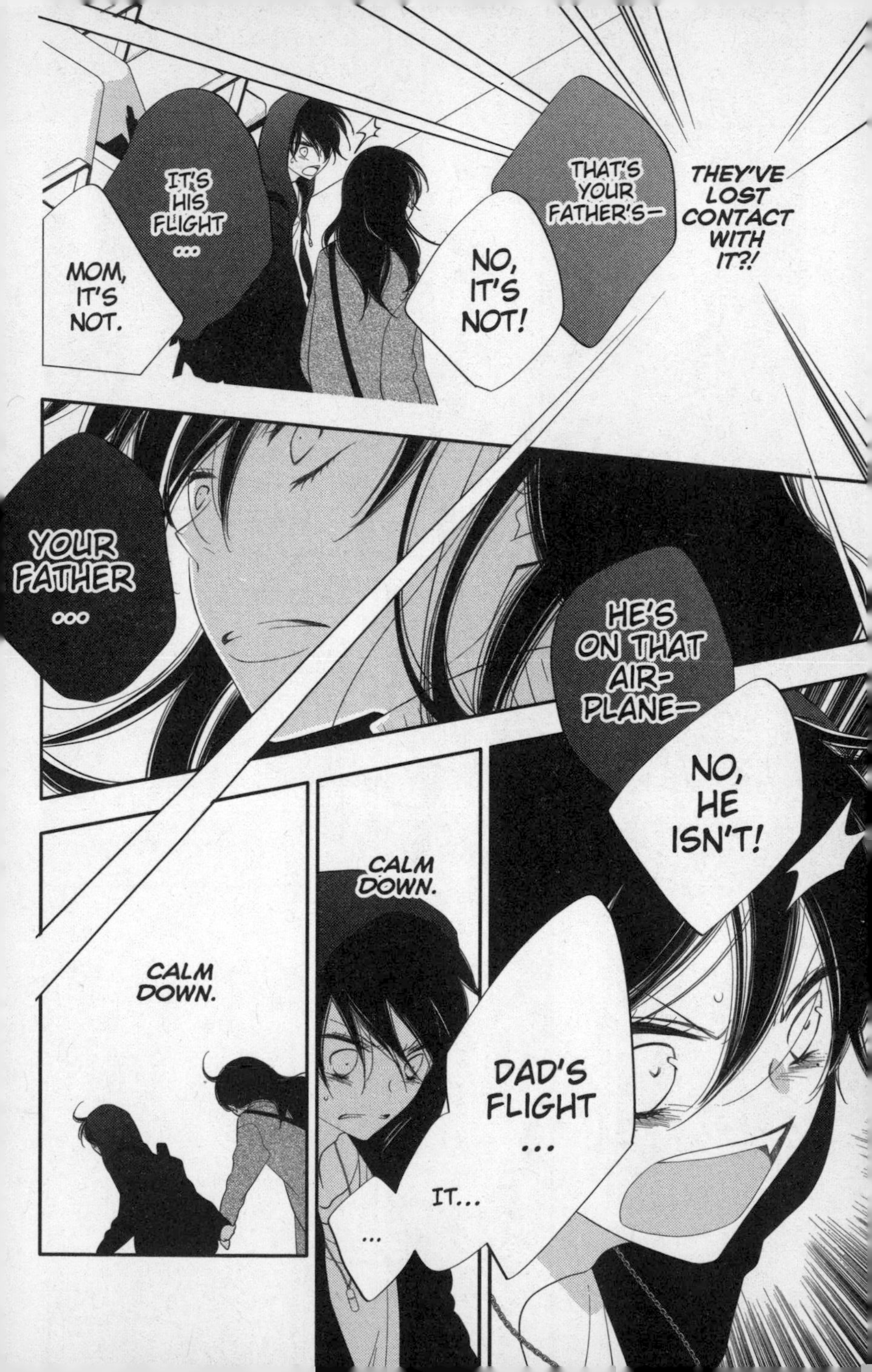
THEY'VE LOST CONTACT WITH IT?!
THAT'S YOUR FATHER'S—
NO, IT'S NOT!
IT'S HIS FLIGHT ...
MOM, IT'S NOT.
YOUR FATHER ...
HE'S ON THAT AIR-PLANE—
NO, HE ISN'T!
DAD'S FLIGHT ...
CALM DOWN.
IT...
...
CALM DOWN.

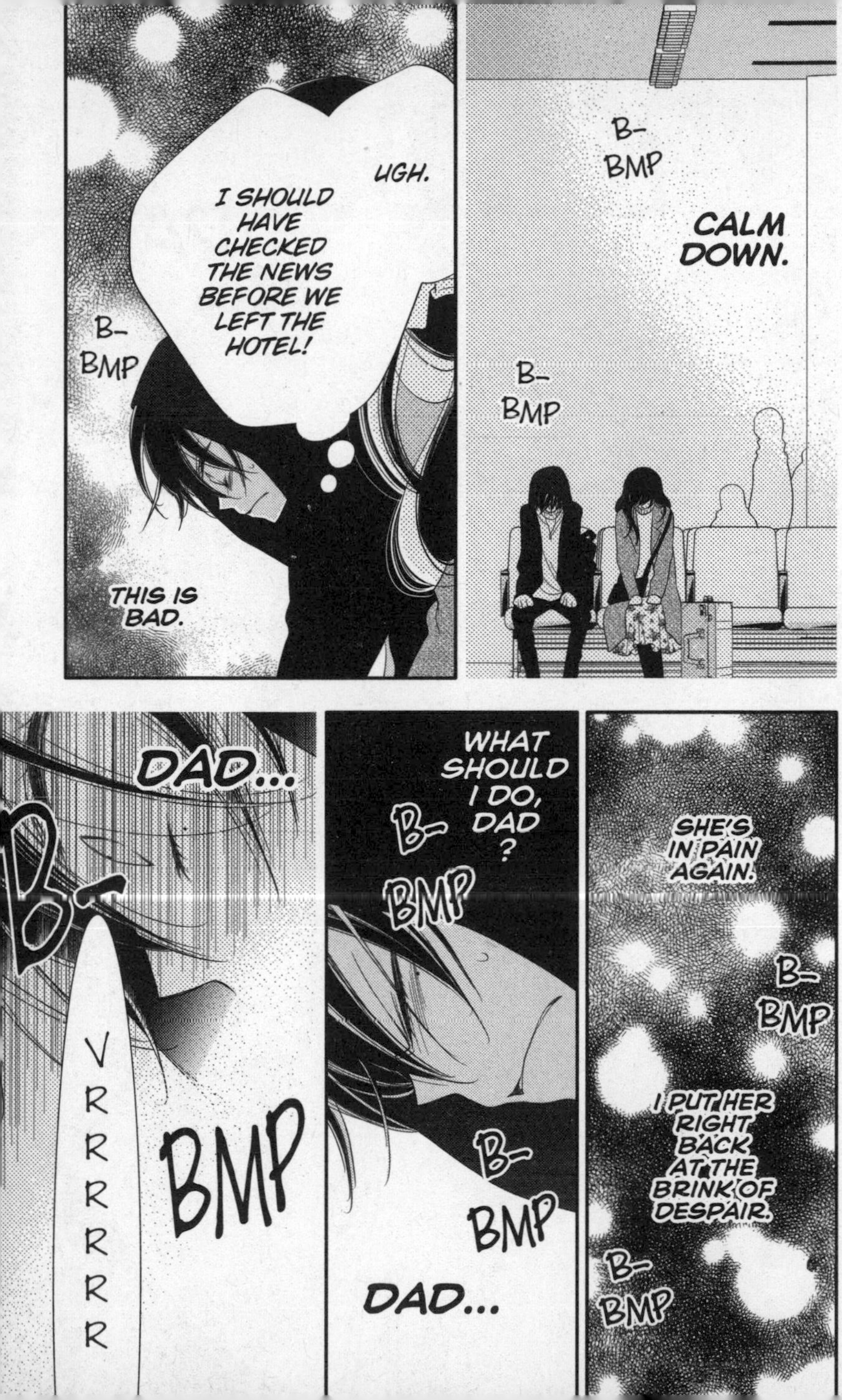
B-BMP
CALM DOWN.
B-BMP
UGH.
I SHOULD HAVE CHECKED THE NEWS BEFORE WE LEFT THE HOTEL!
B-BMP
THIS IS BAD.
SHE'S IN PAIN AGAIN.
B-BMP
I PUT HER RIGHT BACK AT THE BRINK OF DESPAIR.
B-BMP
WHAT SHOULD I DO, DAD?
B-BMP
B-BMP
DAD...
DAD...
B-BMP
VRRRRRR

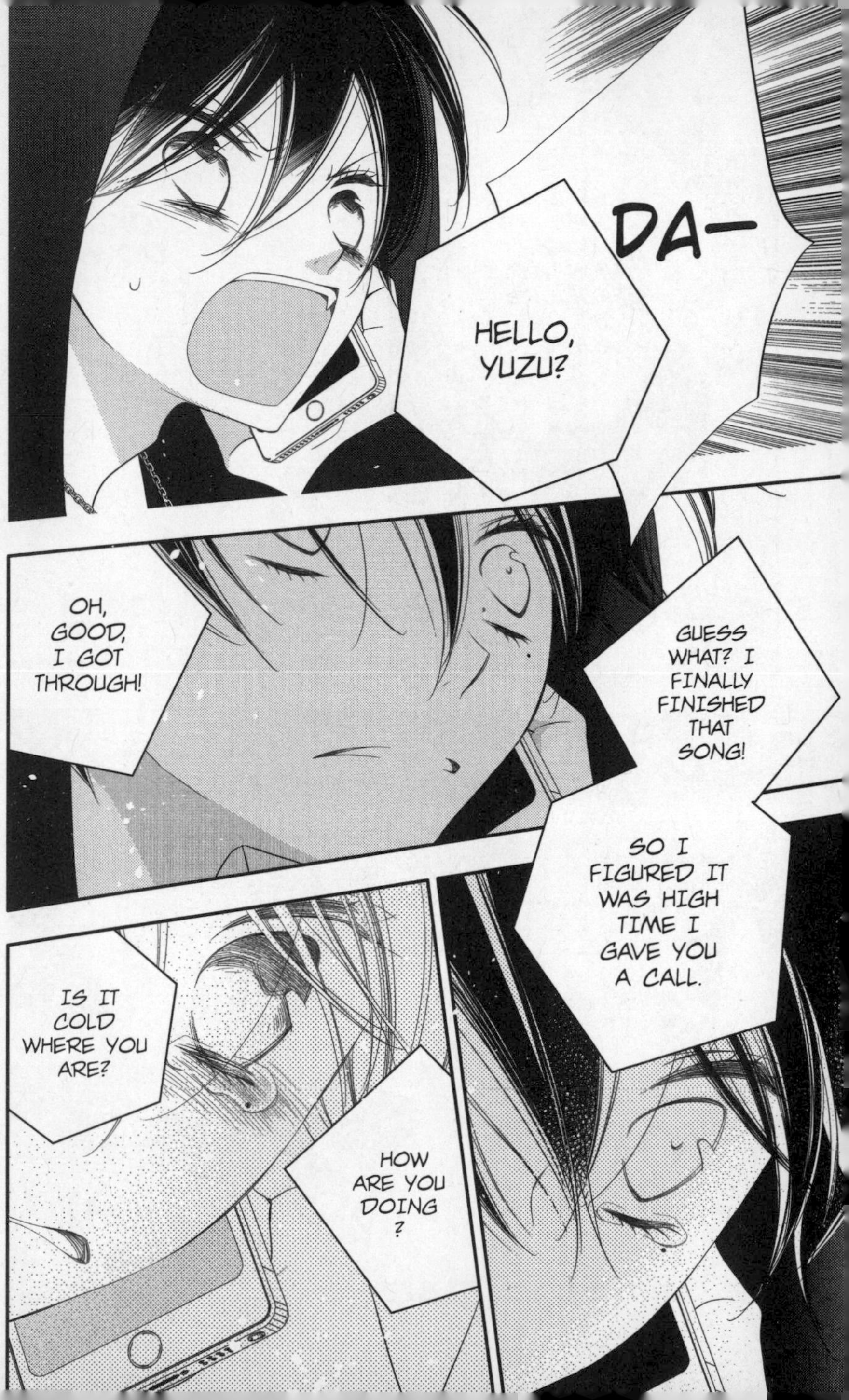
DA—
HELLO, YUZU?
OH, GOOD, I GOT THROUGH!
GUESS WHAT? I FINALLY FINISHED THAT SONG!
SO I FIGURED IT WAS HIGH TIME I GAVE YOU A CALL.
IS IT COLD WHERE YOU ARE?
HOW ARE YOU DOING?

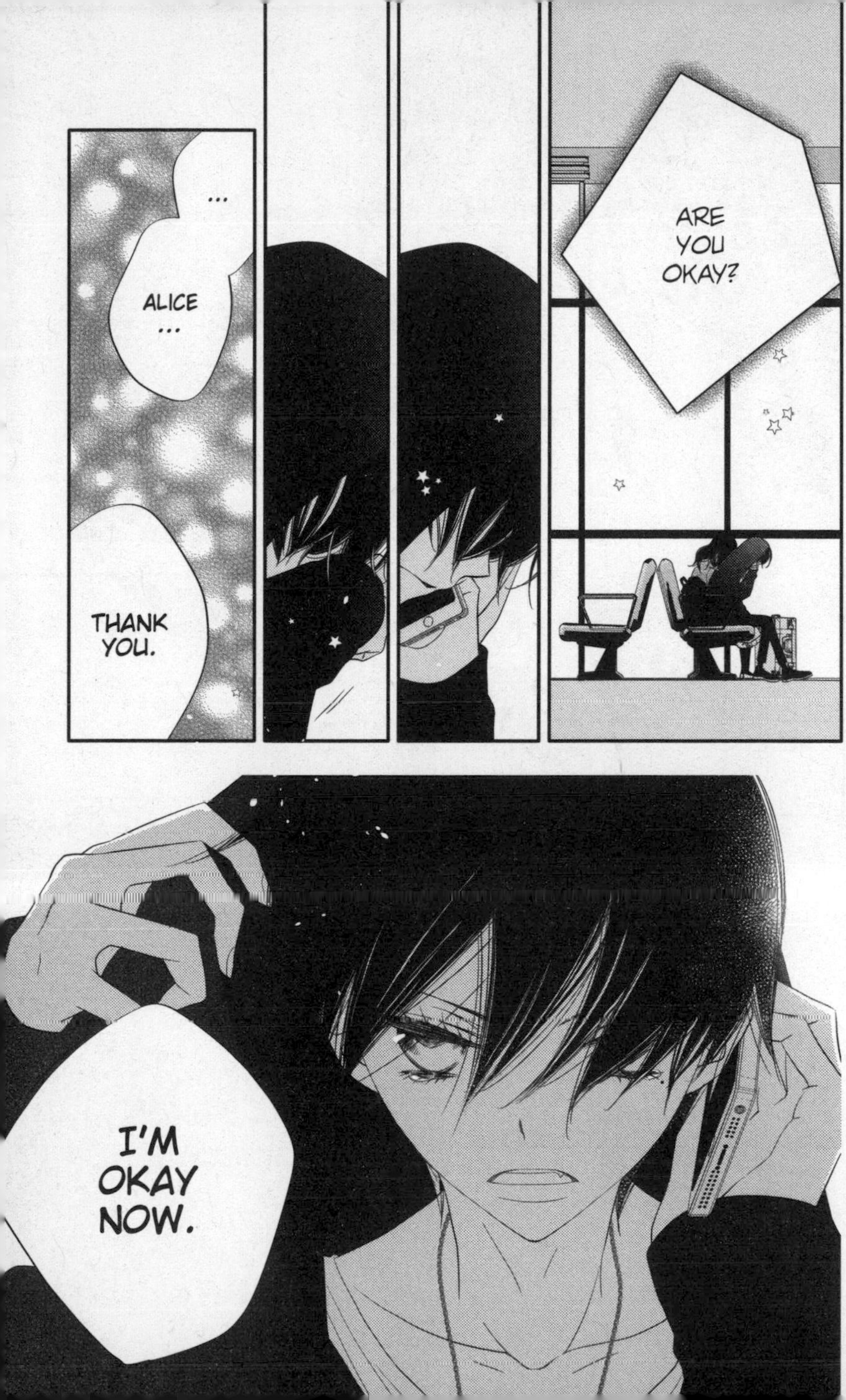
ARE YOU OKAY?
...
ALICE ...
THANK YOU.
I'M OKAY NOW.

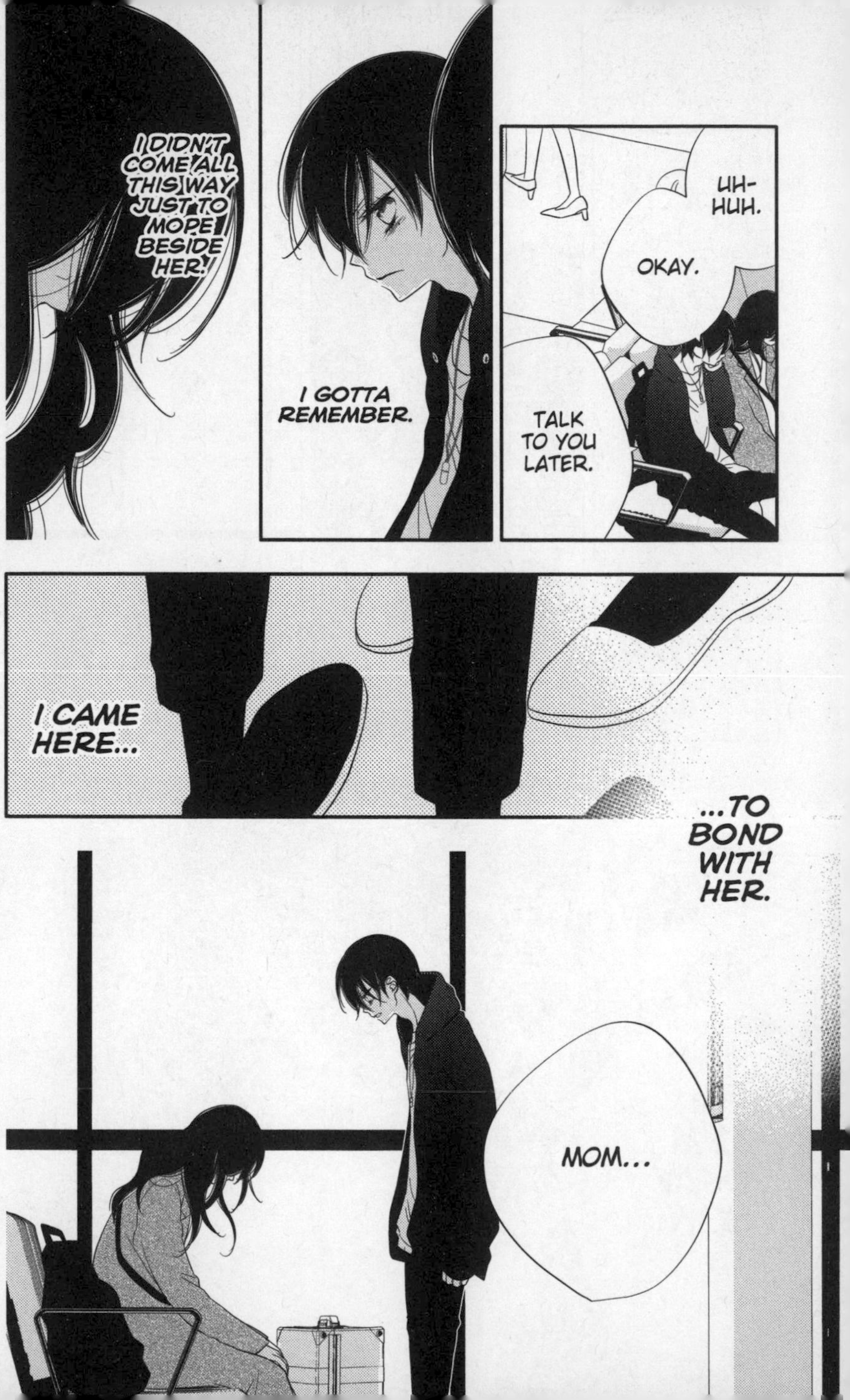
UH-HUH.
OKAY.
TALK TO YOU LATER.
I GOTTA REMEMBER.
I DIDN'T COME ALL THIS WAY JUST TO MOPE BESIDE HER!
I CAME HERE...
...TO BOND WITH HER.
MOM...

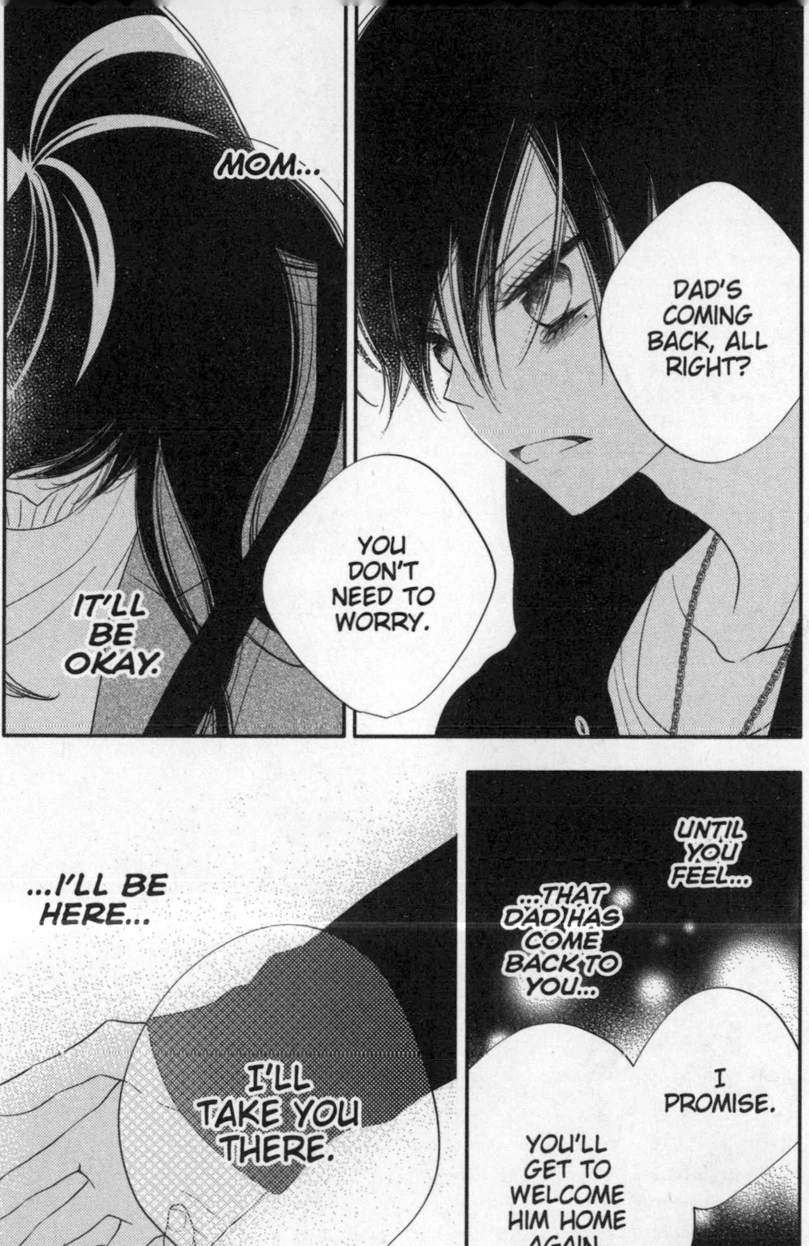
DAD'S COMING BACK, ALL RIGHT?
YOU DON'T NEED TO WORRY.
MOM...
IT'LL BE OKAY.
UNTIL YOU FEEL...
...THAT DAD HAS COME BACK TO YOU...
I PROMISE.
YOU'LL GET TO WELCOME HIM HOME AGAIN.
...I'LL BE HERE...
I'LL TAKE YOU THERE.

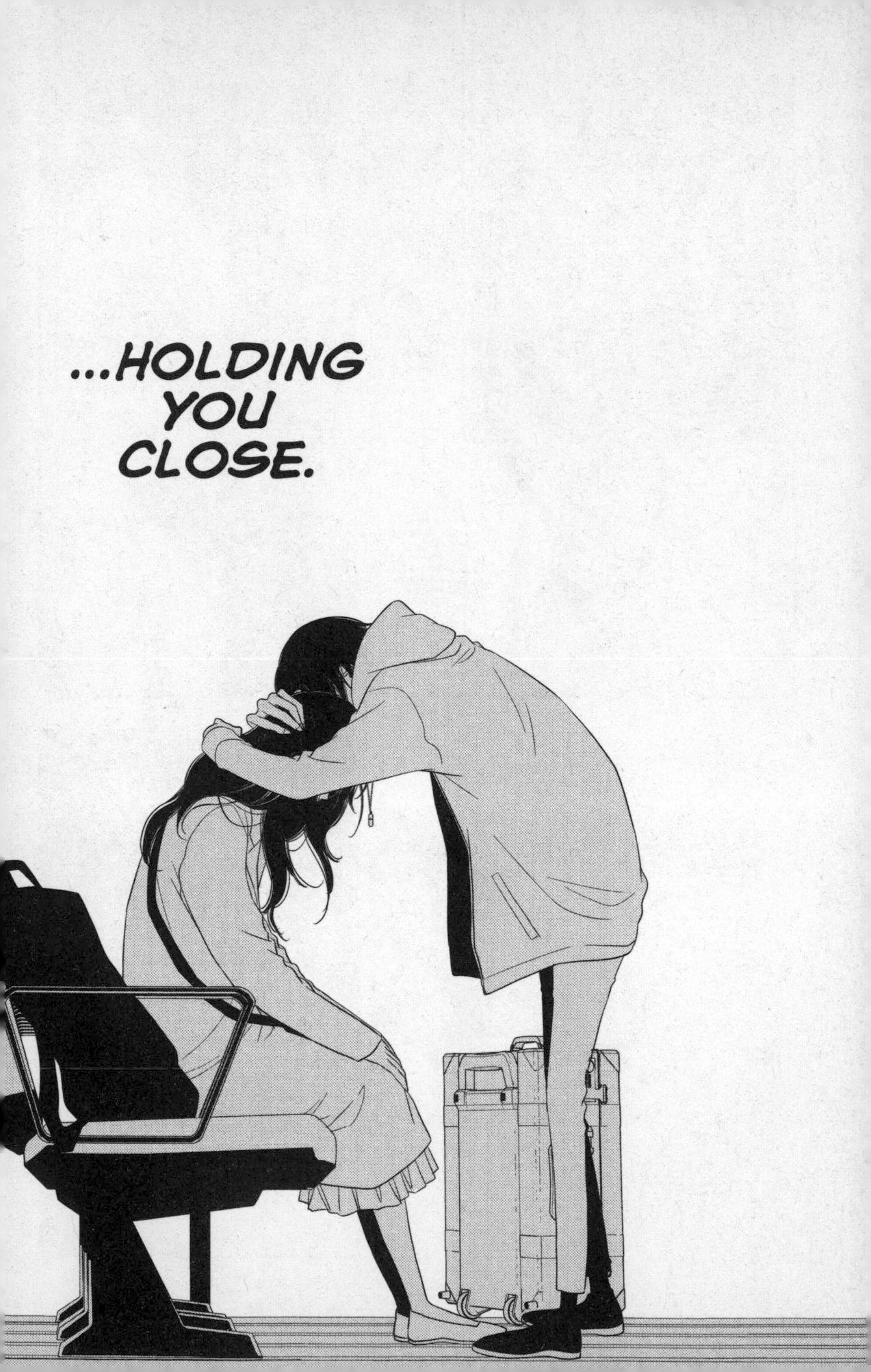
...HOLDING YOU CLOSE.

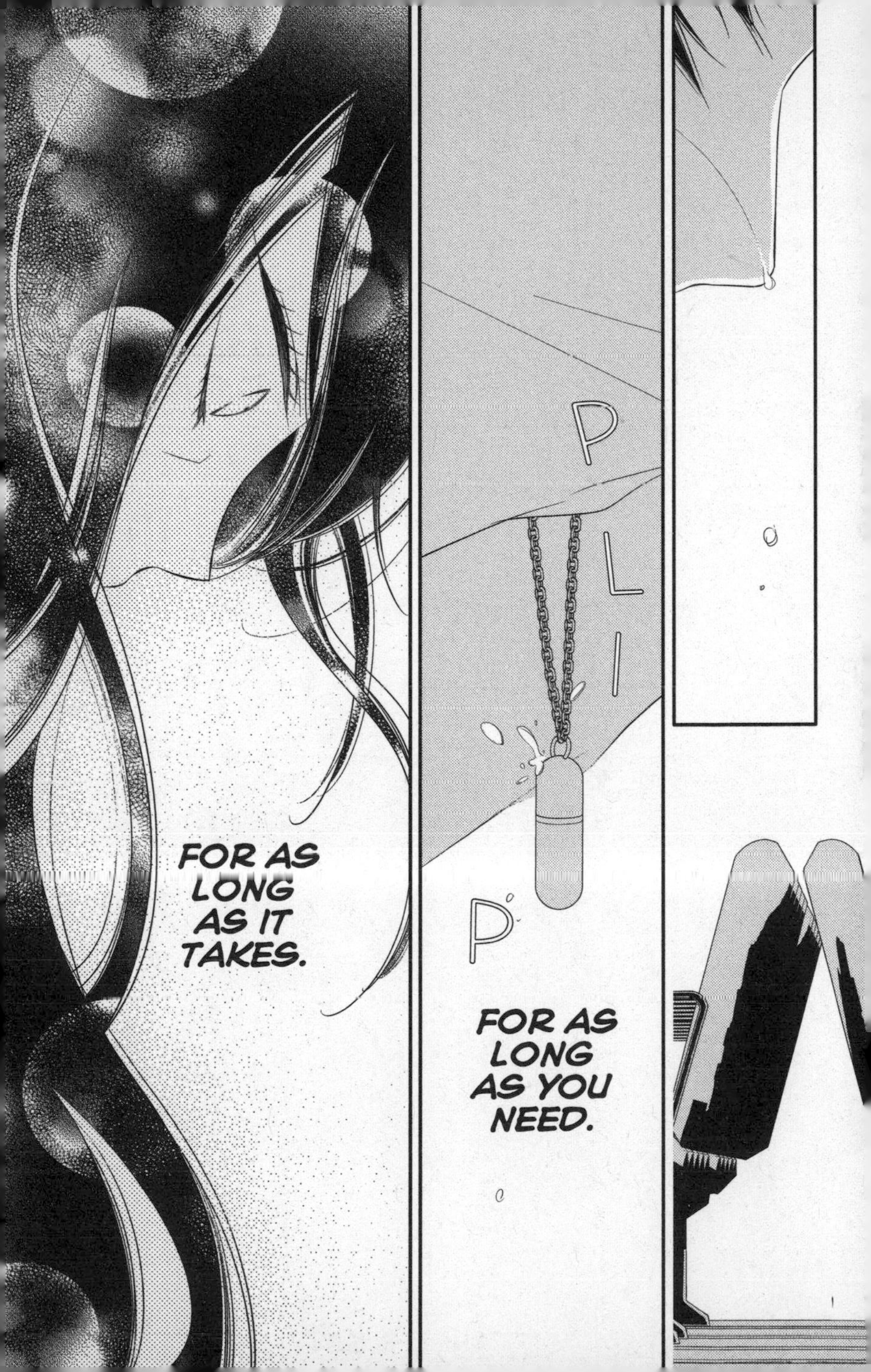
PLIP
FOR AS LONG AS YOU NEED.
FOR AS LONG AS IT TAKES.

I'LL
BE
HERE.

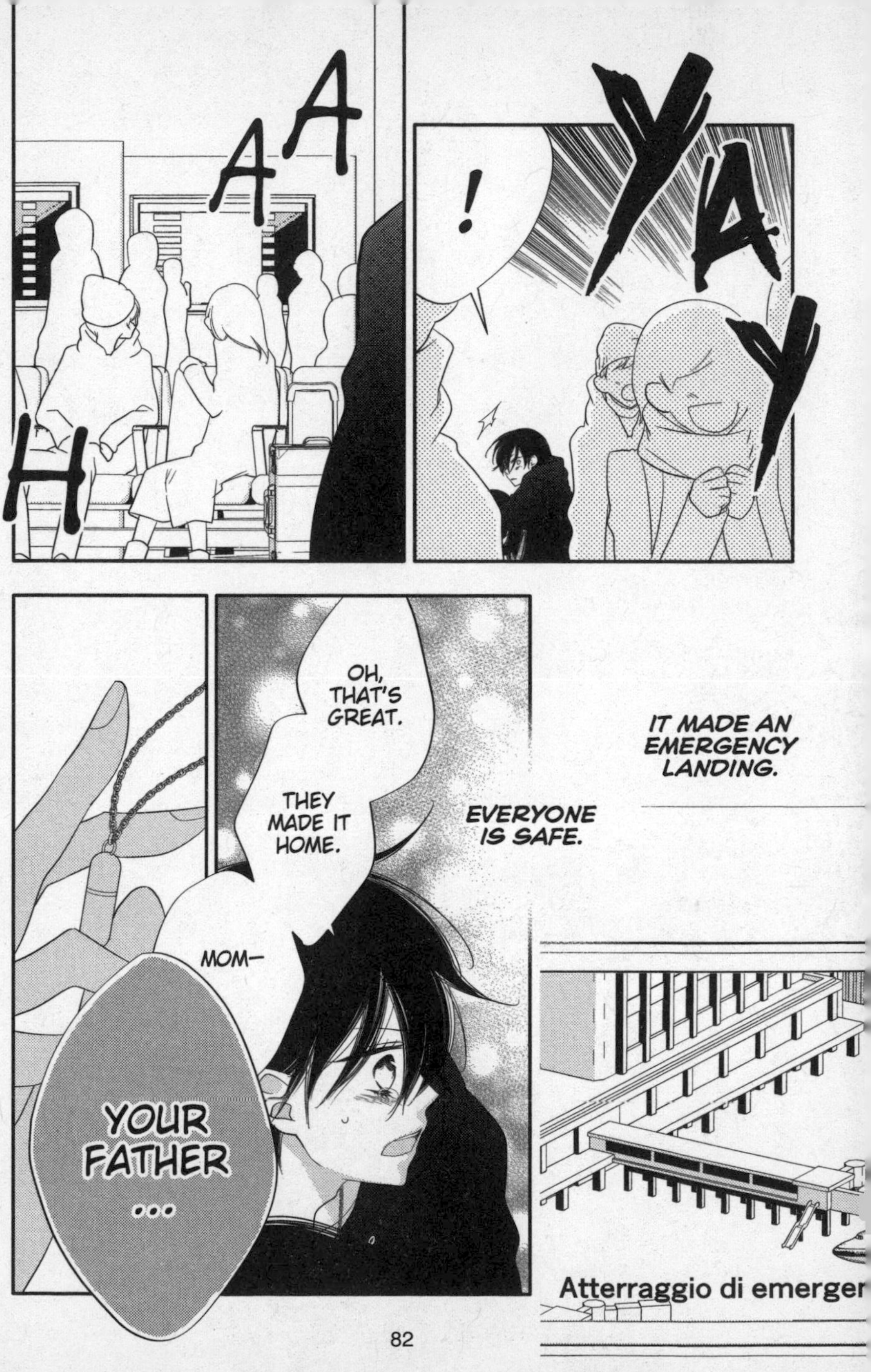
!
YAY!
AAH
IT MADE AN EMERGENCY LANDING.
Atterraggio di emerger
EVERYONE IS SAFE.
OH, THAT'S GREAT.
THEY MADE IT HOME.
MOM—
YOUR FATHER...

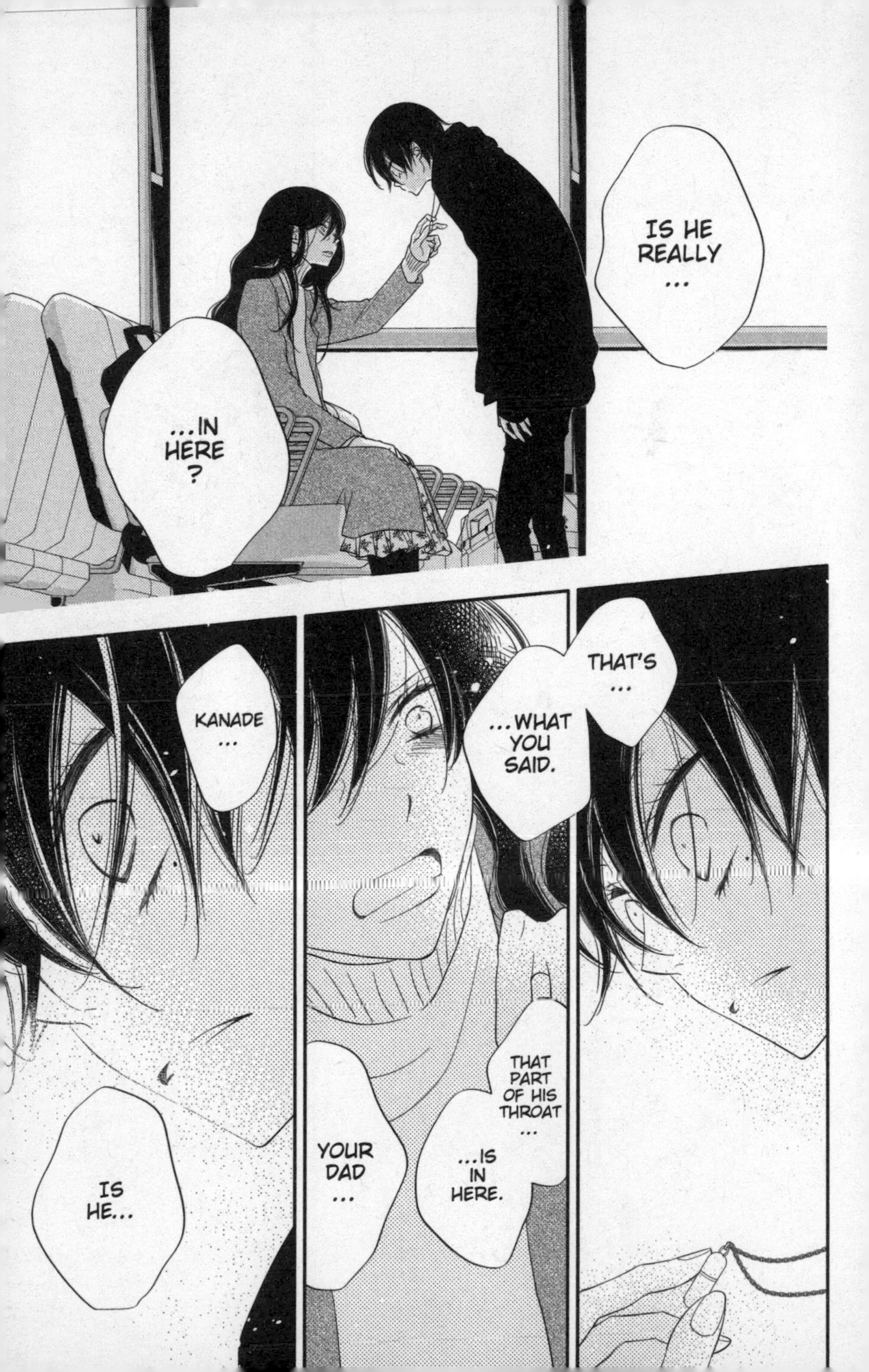
IS HE REALLY ...
...IN HERE?
THAT'S ...
...WHAT YOU SAID.
THAT PART OF HIS THROAT ...
...IS IN HERE.
YOUR DAD ...
KANADE ...
IS HE...

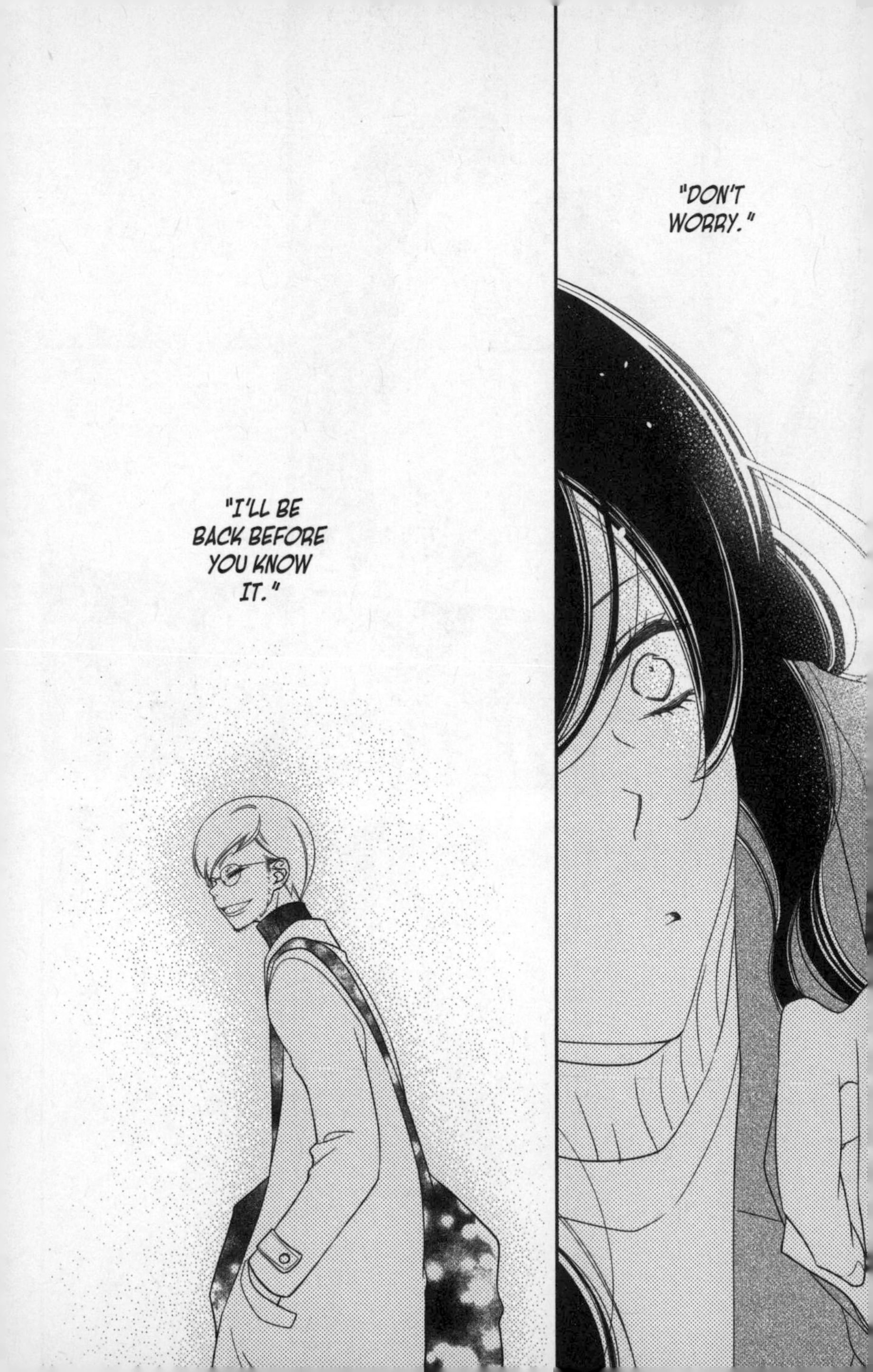
"DON'T WORRY."
"I'LL BE BACK BEFORE YOU KNOW IT."

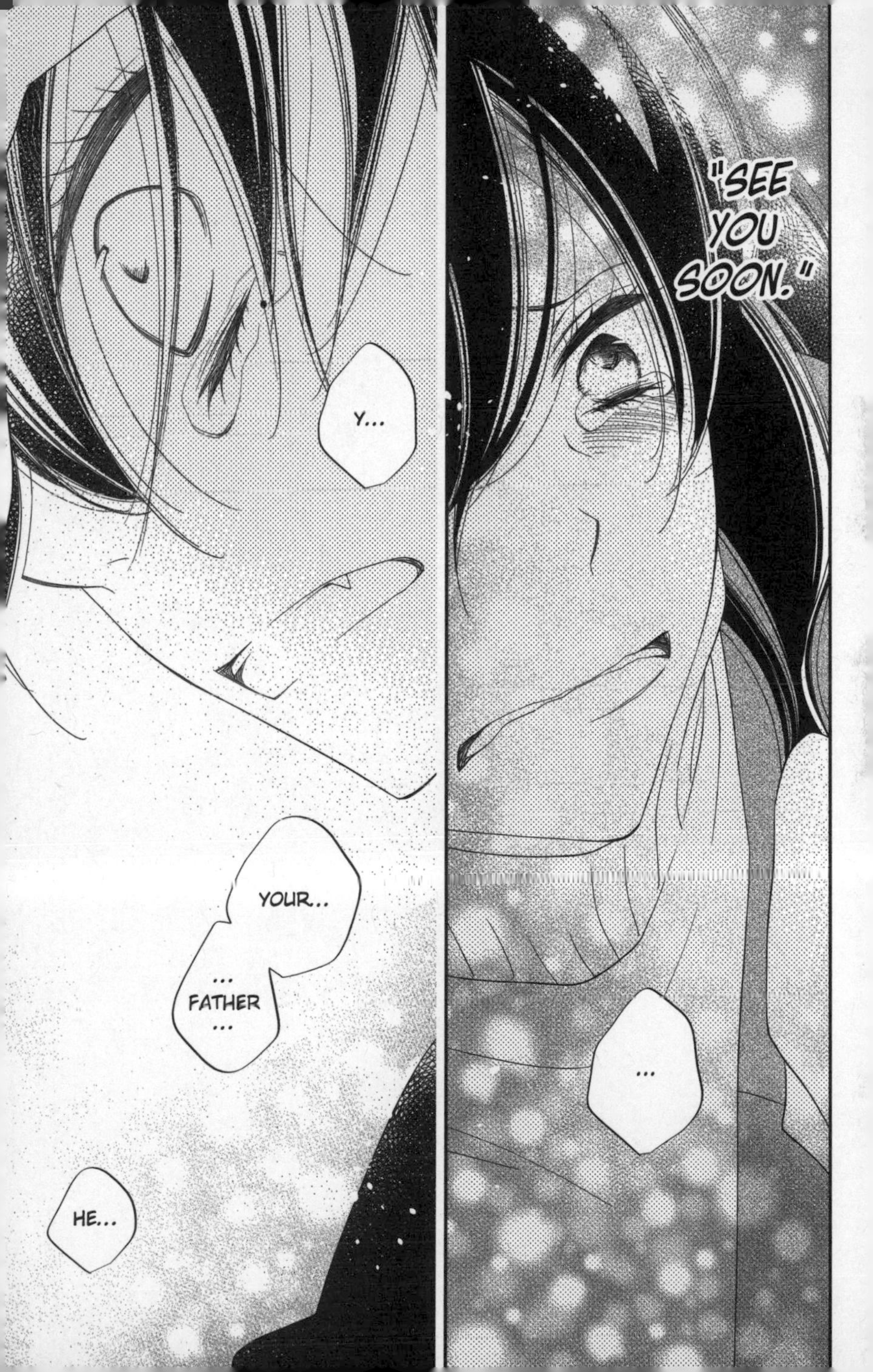
"SEE YOU SOON."
...
Y...
YOUR...
... FATHER ...
HE...

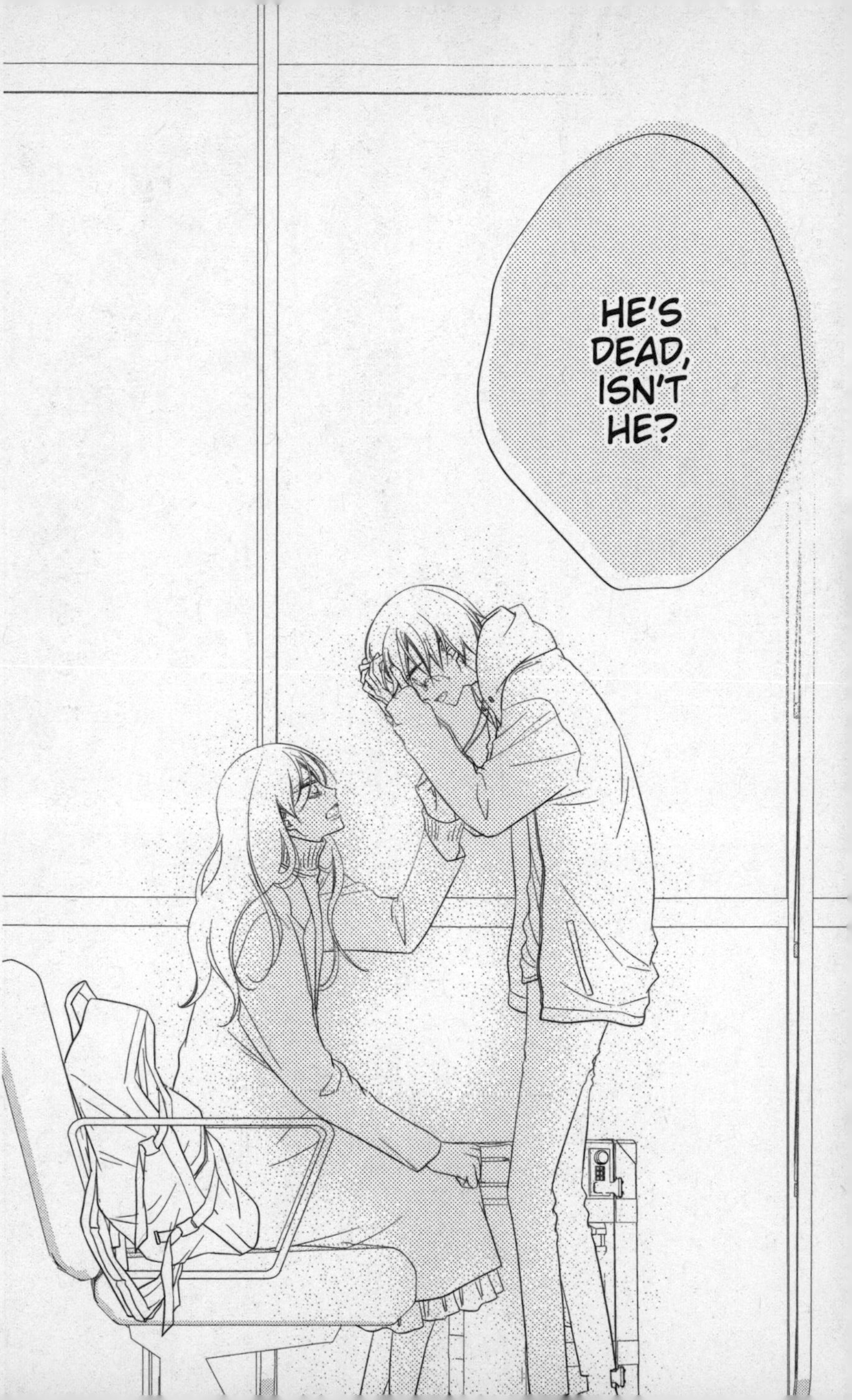
HE'S DEAD, ISN'T HE?

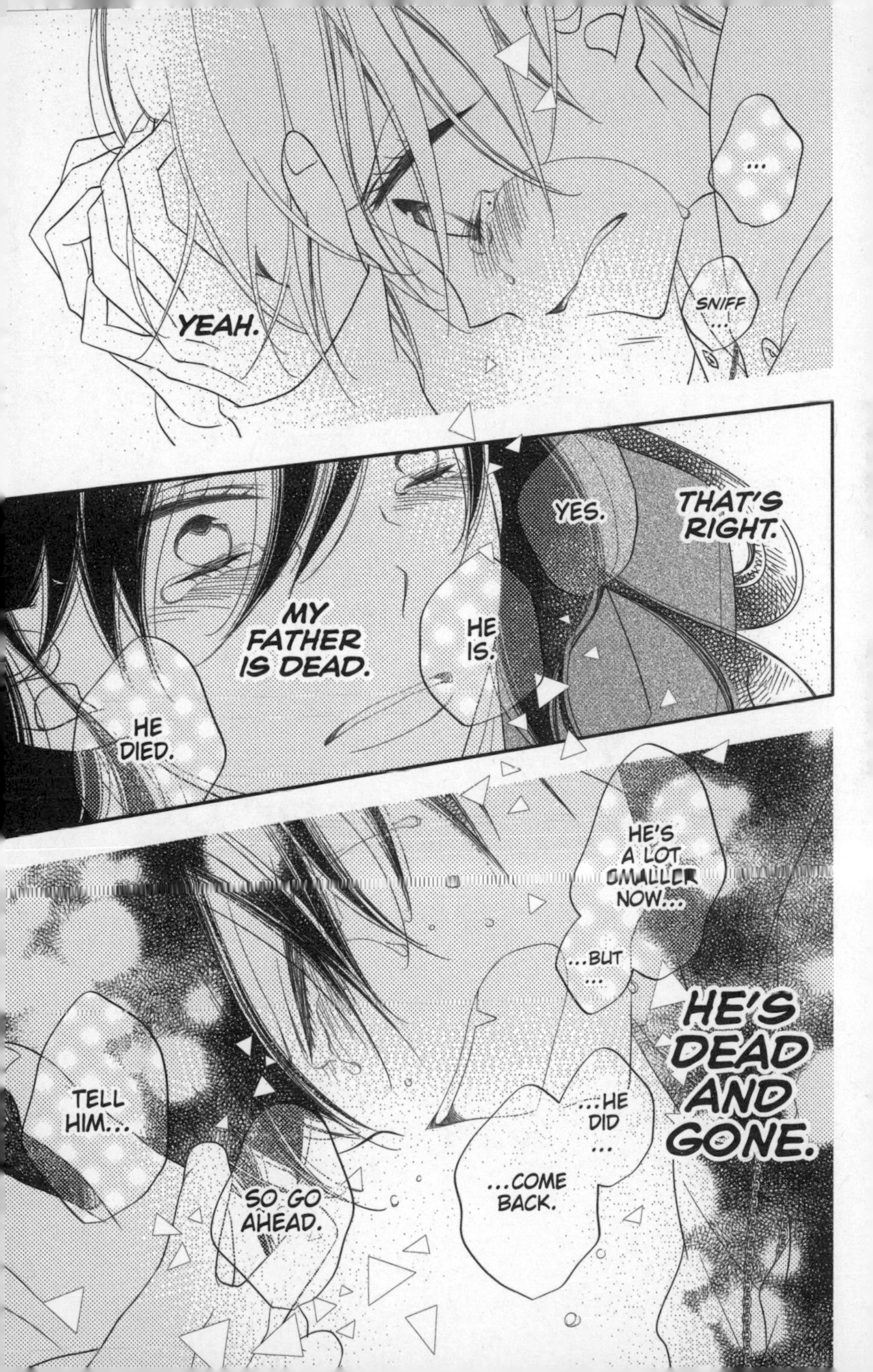
...
SNIFF ...
YEAH.
THAT'S RIGHT.
YES.
HE IS.
MY FATHER IS DEAD.
HE DIED.
HE'S A LOT SMALLER NOW...
...BUT ...
...HE DID ...
...COME BACK.
HE'S DEAD AND GONE.
TELL HIM...
SO GO AHEAD.

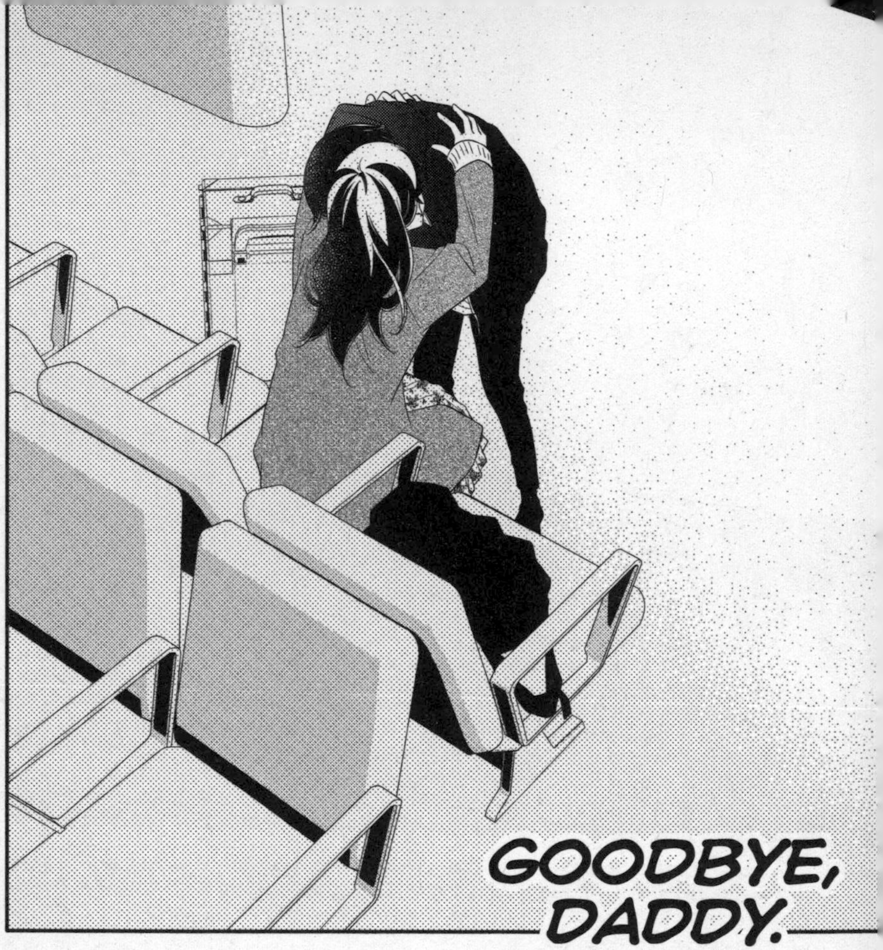
GOODBYE, DADDY.

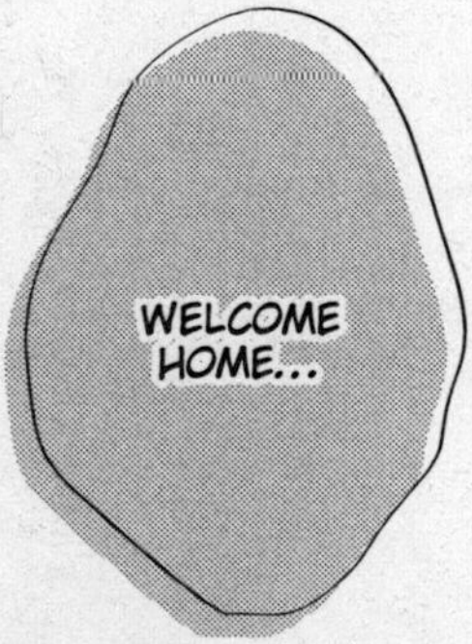
WELCOME HOME...

in NO
hurry
to shout;

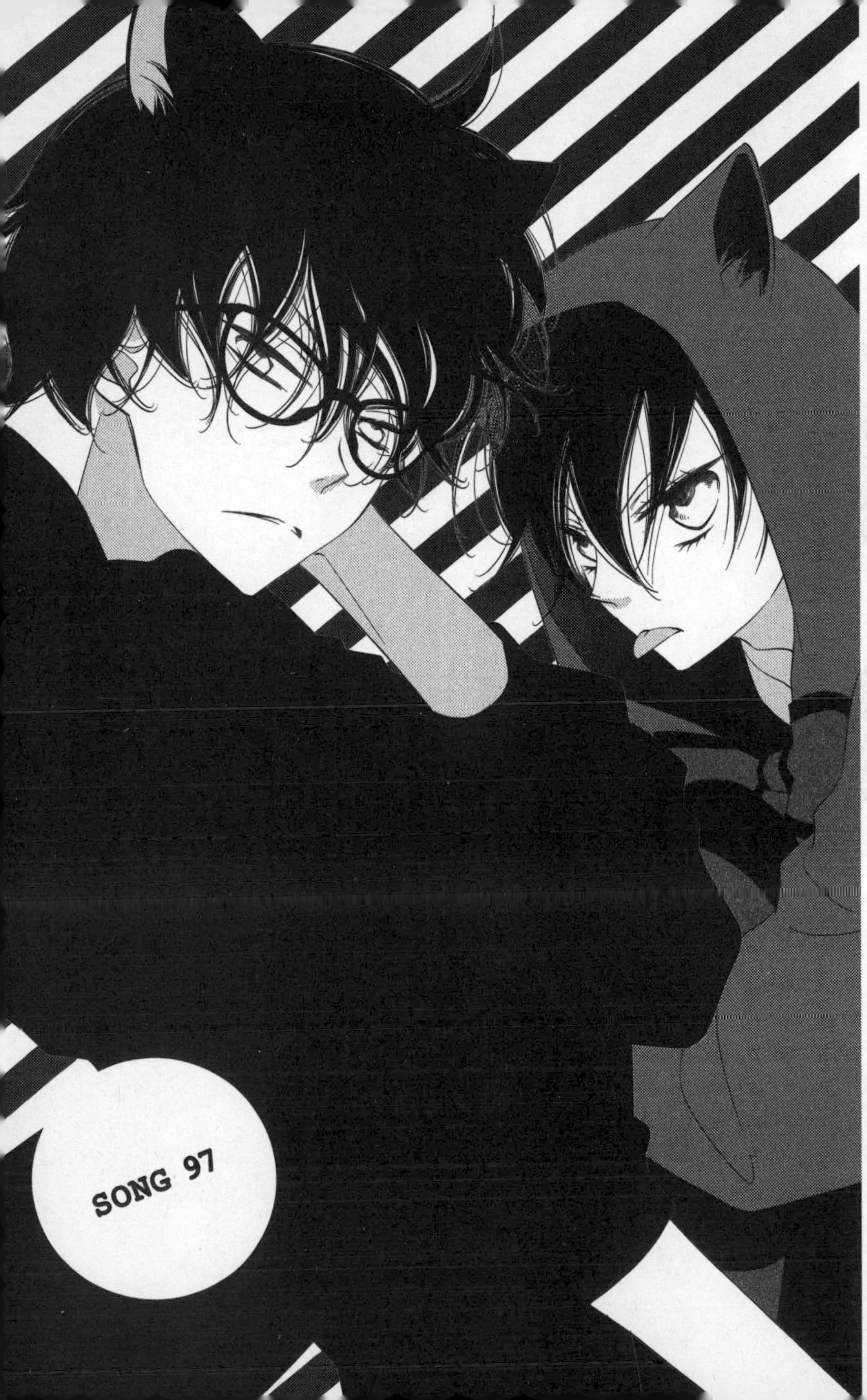
SONG 97

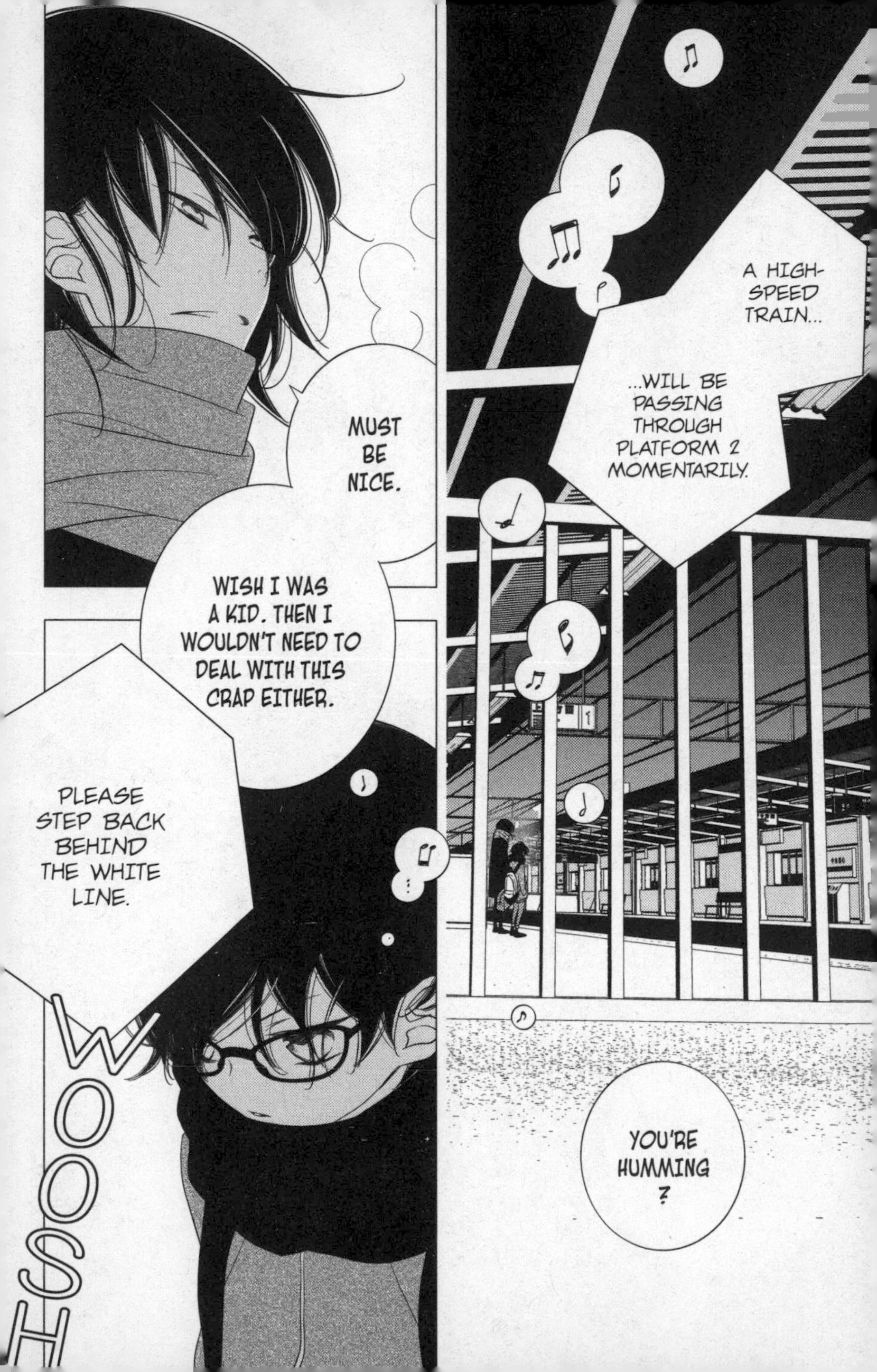
A HIGH-SPEED TRAIN...
...WILL BE PASSING THROUGH PLATFORM 2 MOMENTARILY.
YOU'RE HUMMING?
MUST BE NICE.
WISH I WAS A KID. THEN I WOULDN'T NEED TO DEAL WITH THIS CRAP EITHER.
PLEASE STEP BACK BEHIND THE WHITE LINE.
WHOOSH

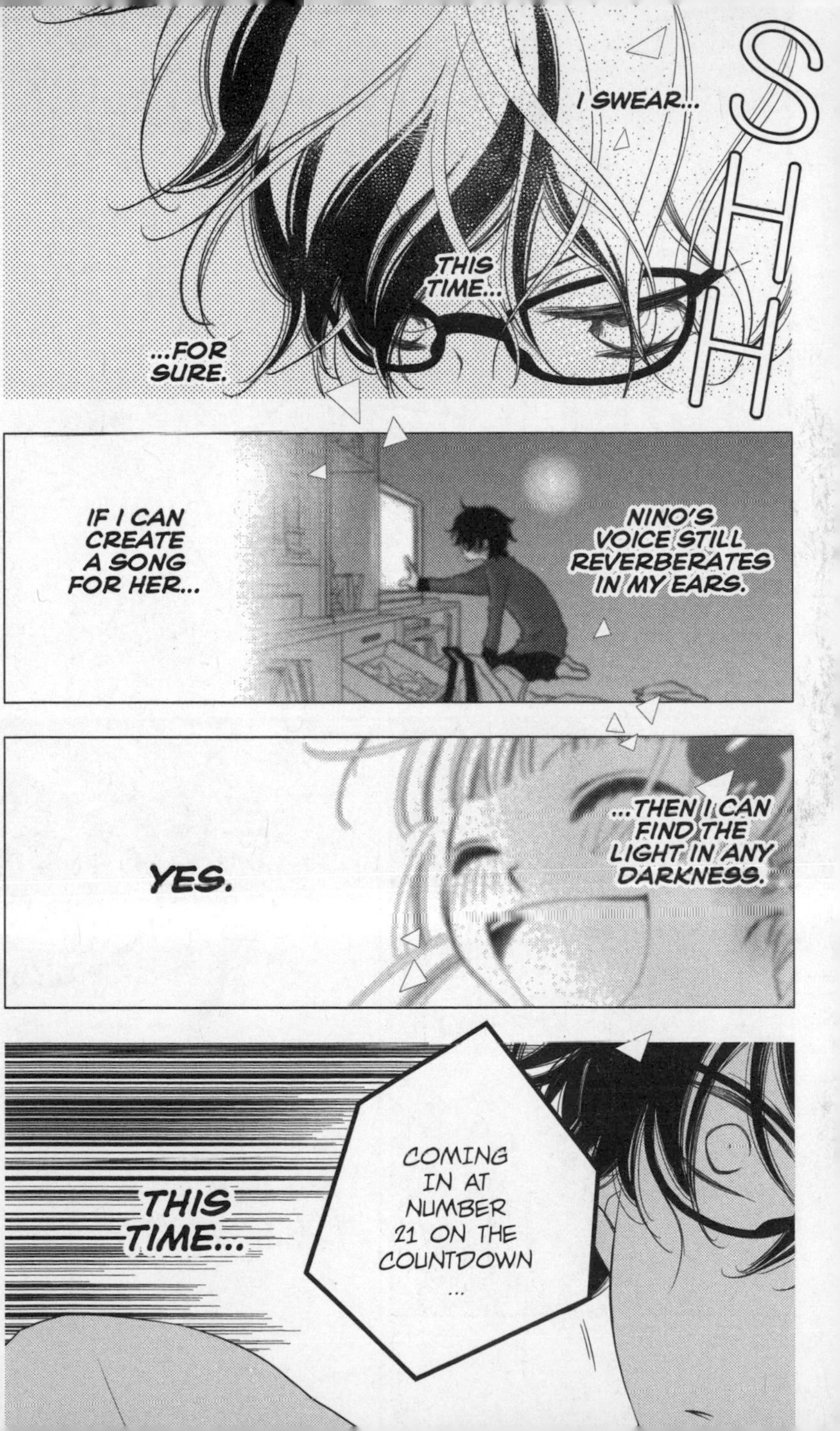
SHH
I SWEAR...
THIS TIME...
...FOR SURE.
NINO'S VOICE STILL REVERBERATES IN MY EARS.
IF I CAN CREATE A SONG FOR HER...
...THEN I CAN FIND THE LIGHT IN ANY DARKNESS.
YES.
COMING IN AT NUMBER 21 ON THE COUNTDOWN...
THIS TIME...

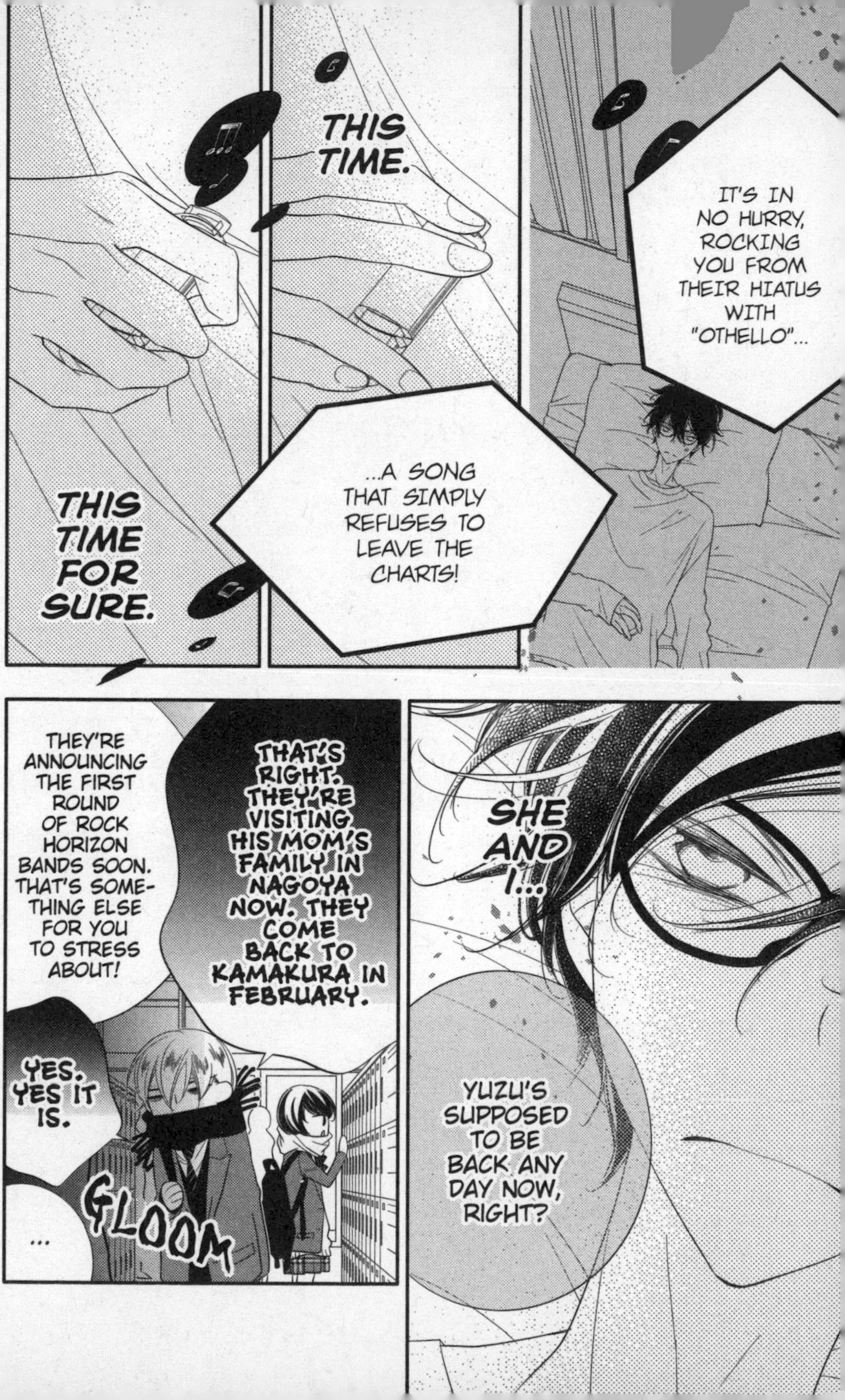
IT'S IN NO HURRY, ROCKING YOU FROM THEIR HIATUS WITH "OTHELLO"...
...A SONG THAT SIMPLY REFUSES TO LEAVE THE CHARTS!
THIS TIME.
THIS TIME FOR SURE.
SHE AND I...
YUZU'S SUPPOSED TO BE BACK ANY DAY NOW, RIGHT?
THAT'S RIGHT. THEY'RE VISITING HIS MOM'S FAMILY IN NAGOYA NOW. THEY COME BACK TO KAMAKURA IN FEBRUARY.
THEY'RE ANNOUNCING THE FIRST ROUND OF ROCK HORIZON BANDS SOON. THAT'S SOMETHING ELSE FOR YOU TO STRESS ABOUT!
YES. YES IT IS.
GLOOM
...

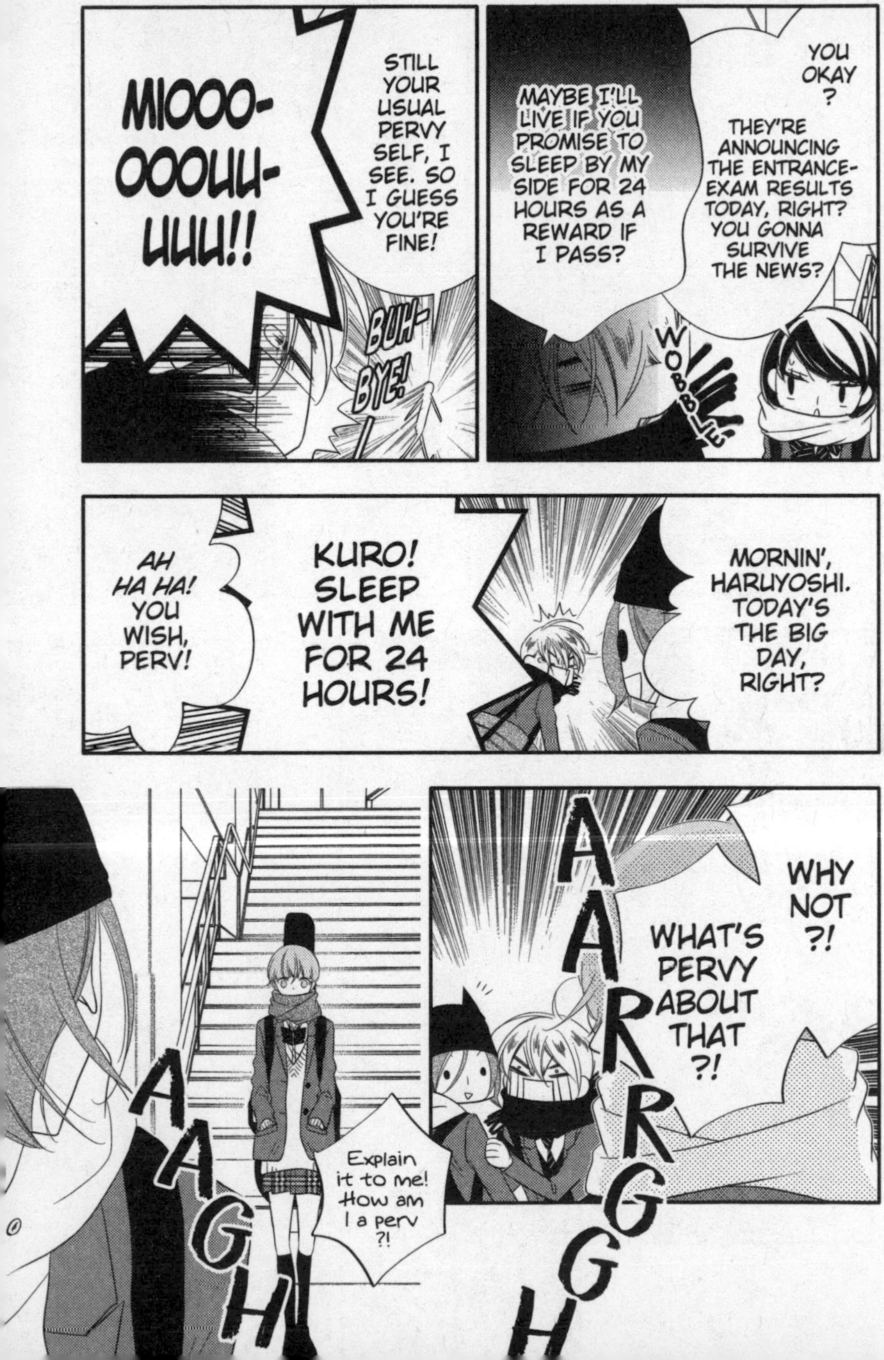
YOU OKAY?
THEY'RE ANNOUNCING THE ENTRANCE-EXAM RESULTS TODAY, RIGHT? YOU GONNA SURVIVE THE NEWS?
WOBBLE
MAYBE I'LL LIVE IF YOU PROMISE TO SLEEP BY MY SIDE FOR 24 HOURS AS A REWARD IF I PASS?
STILL YOUR USUAL PERVY SELF, I SEE. SO I GUESS YOU'RE FINE!
BUH-BYE!
MIOOO-OOOUU-UUU!!
MORNIN', HARUYOSHI. TODAY'S THE BIG DAY, RIGHT?
KURO! SLEEP WITH ME FOR 24 HOURS!
AH HA HA! YOU WISH, PERV!
WHY NOT?!
WHAT'S PERVY ABOUT THAT?!
AARRGGH
Explain it to me! How am I a perv?!
AAGH

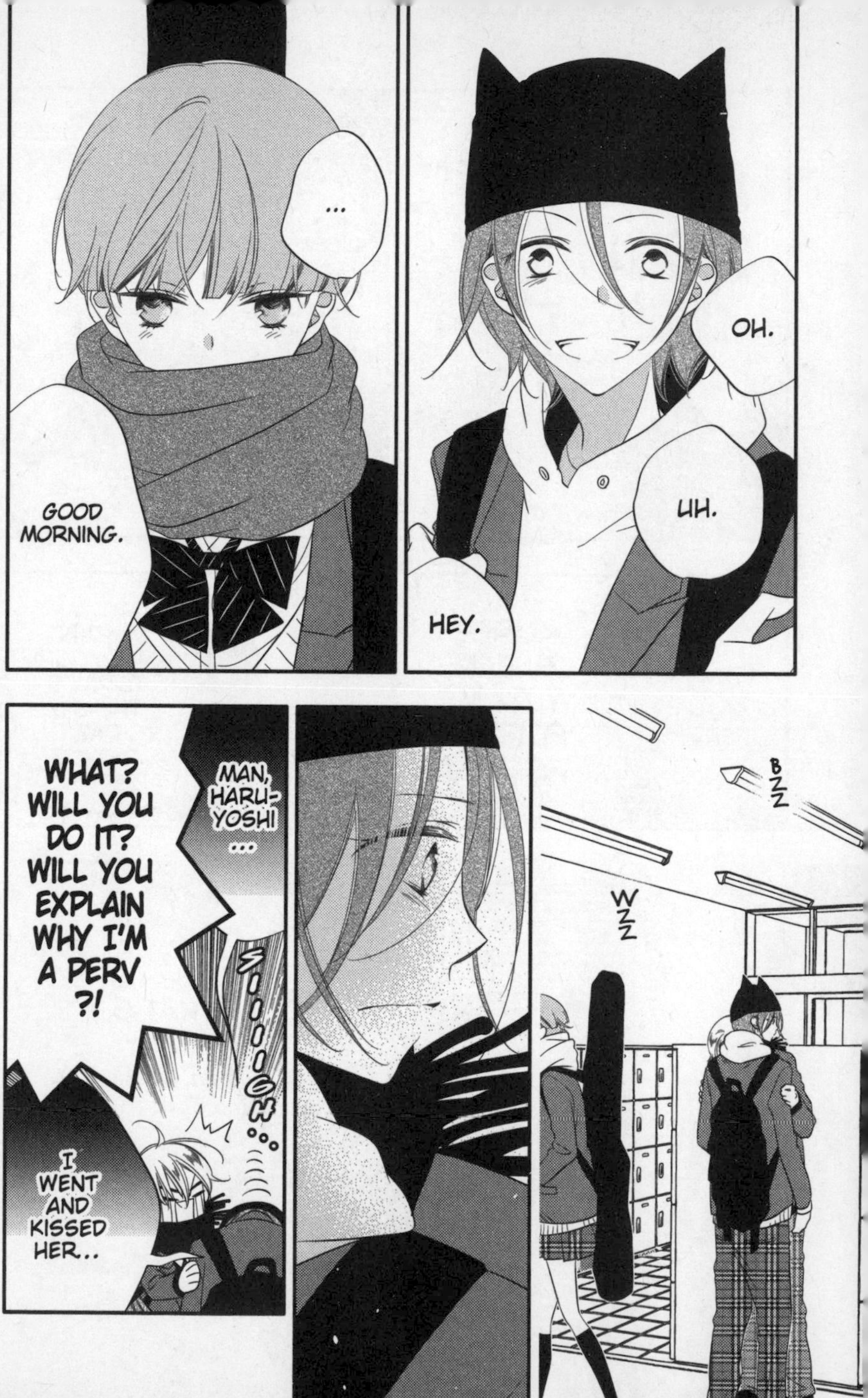
OH.
UH.
HEY.
...
GOOD MORNING.
BZZ
WZZ
SIIIIIGH...
MAN, HARUYOSHI...
WHAT? WILL YOU DO IT? WILL YOU EXPLAIN WHY I'M A PERV?!
I WENT AND KISSED HER..

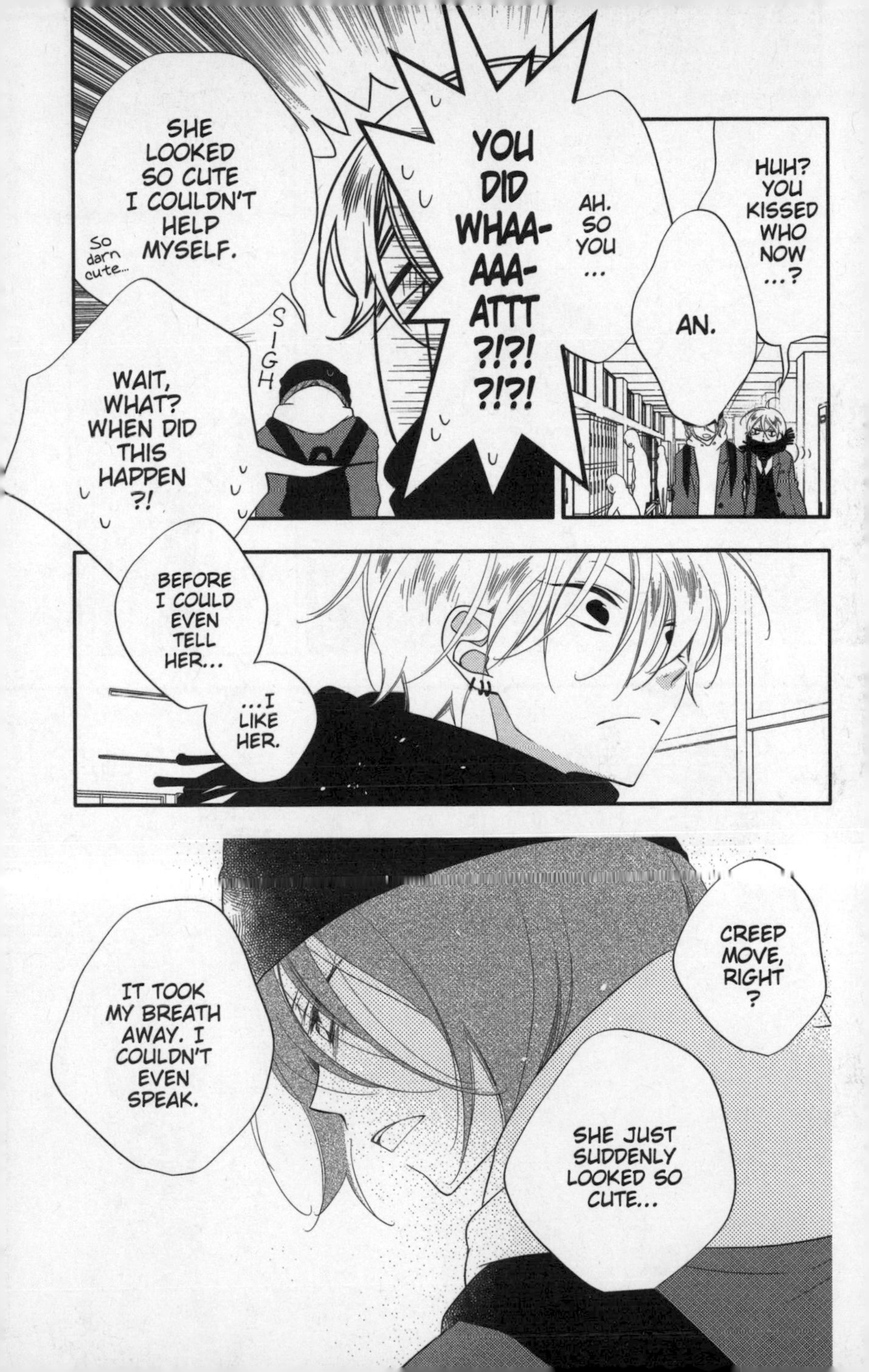
HUH? YOU KISSED WHO NOW...?
AN.
AH. SO YOU...
YOU DID WHAAAAA-ATTT?!?!?!?!
SHE LOOKED SO CUTE I COULDN'T HELP MYSELF.
So darn cute...
SIGH
WAIT, WHAT? WHEN DID THIS HAPPEN?!
BEFORE I COULD EVEN TELL HER...
...I LIKE HER.
CREEP MOVE, RIGHT?
SHE JUST SUDDENLY LOOKED SO CUTE...
IT TOOK MY BREATH AWAY. I COULDN'T EVEN SPEAK.

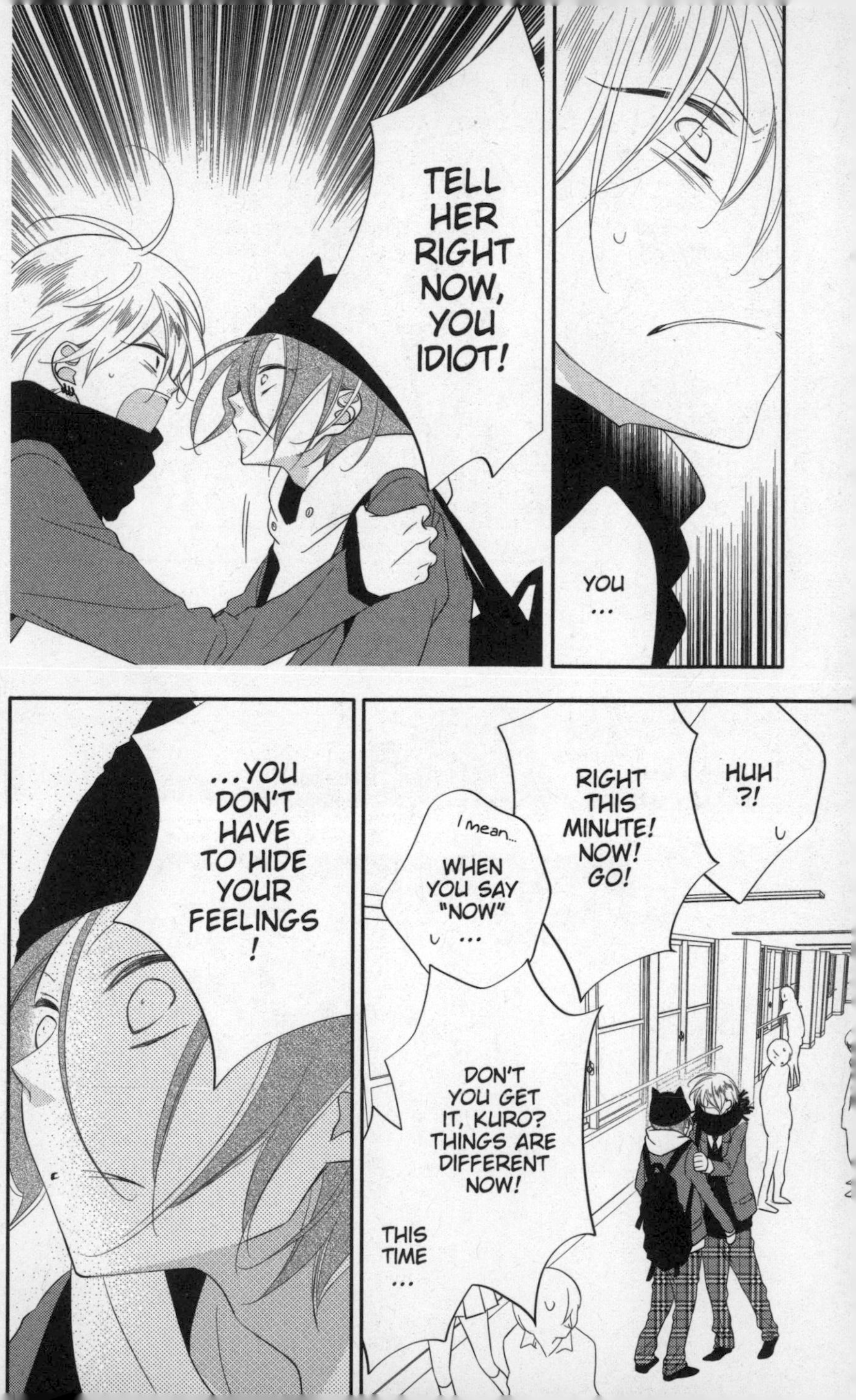
YOU ...
TELL HER RIGHT NOW, YOU IDIOT!
HUH?!
RIGHT THIS MINUTE! NOW! GO!
I mean... WHEN YOU SAY "NOW" ...
DON'T YOU GET IT, KURO? THINGS ARE DIFFERENT NOW!
THIS TIME ...
...YOU DON'T HAVE TO HIDE YOUR FEELINGS!

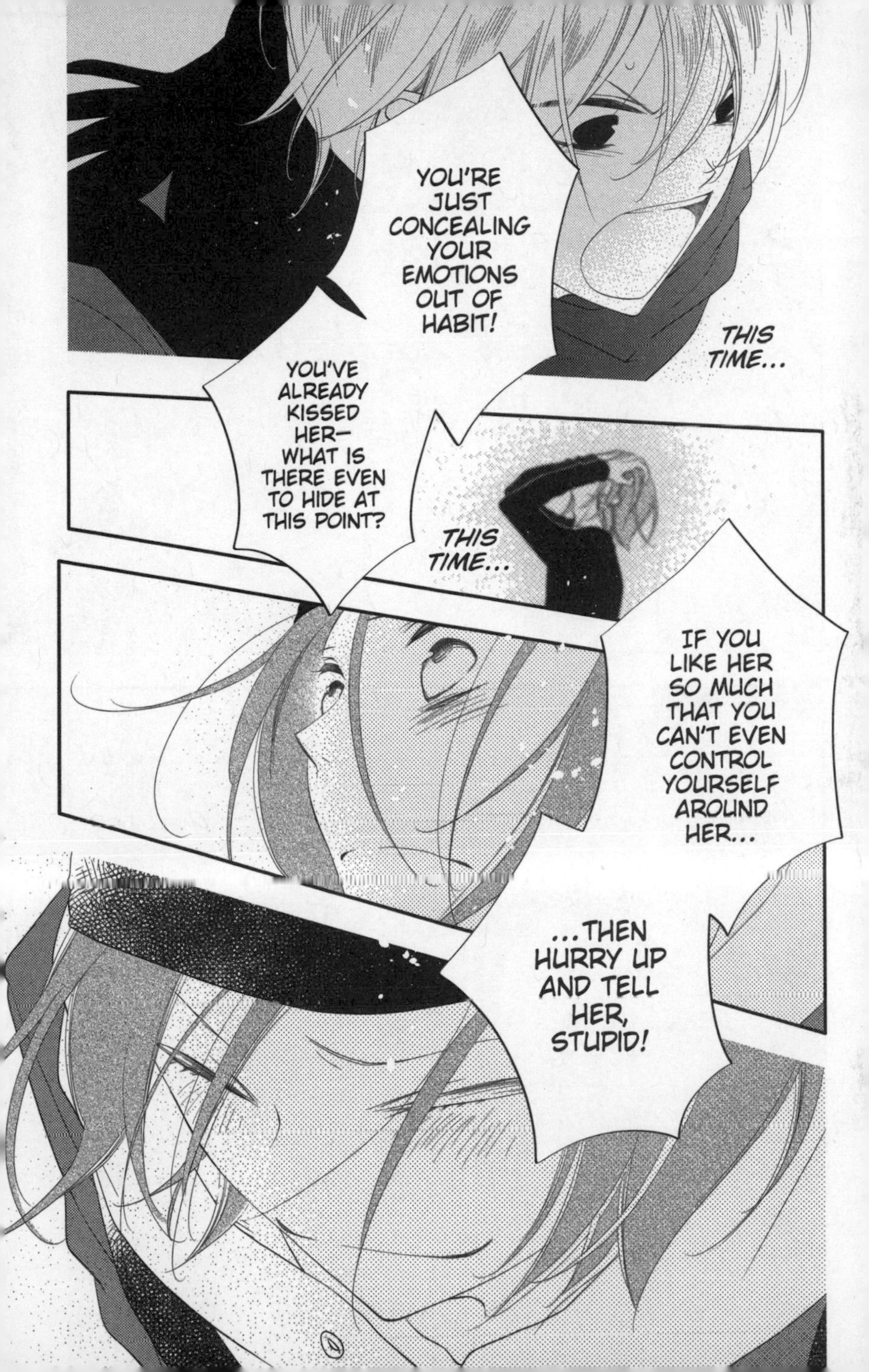
YOU'RE JUST CONCEALING YOUR EMOTIONS OUT OF HABIT!
THIS TIME...
YOU'VE ALREADY KISSED HER— WHAT IS THERE EVEN TO HIDE AT THIS POINT?
THIS TIME...
IF YOU LIKE HER SO MUCH THAT YOU CAN'T EVEN CONTROL YOURSELF AROUND HER...
...THEN HURRY UP AND TELL HER, STUPID!

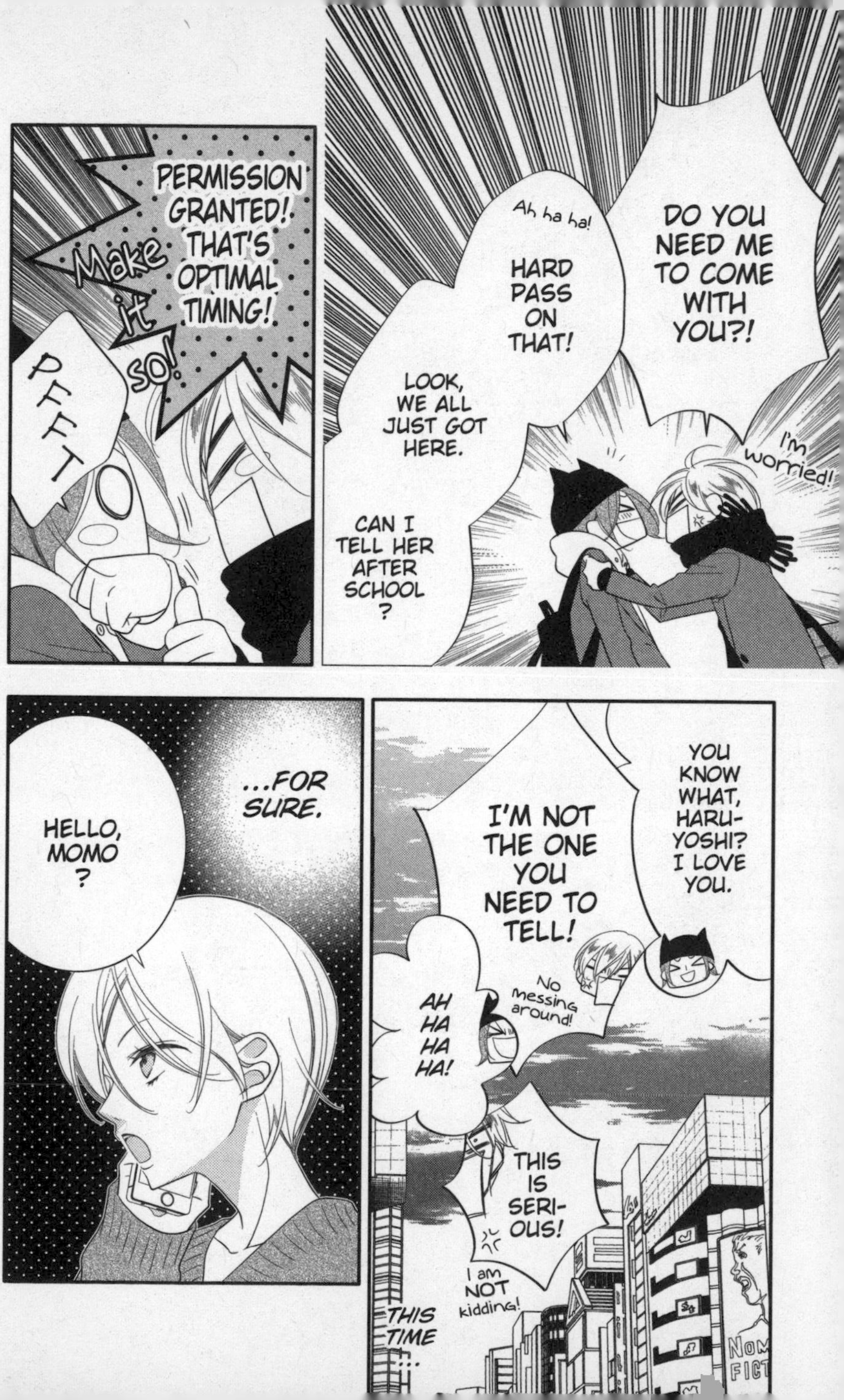
DO YOU NEED ME TO COME WITH YOU?!
Ah ha ha!
HARD PASS ON THAT!
I'm worried!
LOOK, WE ALL JUST GOT HERE.
CAN I TELL HER AFTER SCHOOL?
PERMISSION GRANTED! THAT'S OPTIMAL TIMING!
Make it so!
PFFT
YOU KNOW WHAT, HARU-YOSHI? I LOVE YOU.
I'M NOT THE ONE YOU NEED TO TELL!
No messing around!
AH HA HA HA!
THIS IS SERI-OUS!
I am NOT kidding!
THIS TIME...
...FOR SURE.
HELLO, MOMO?

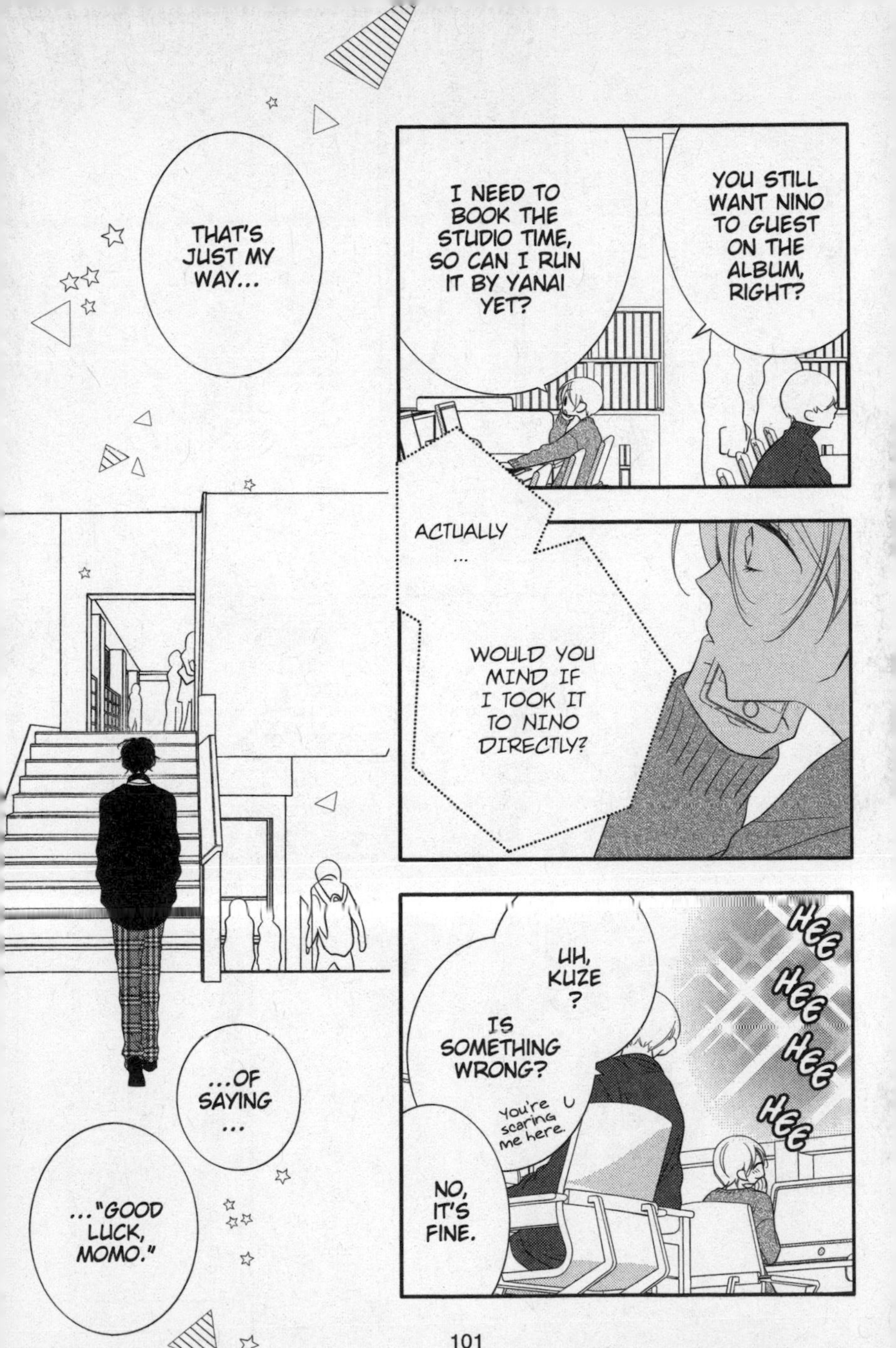
YOU STILL WANT NINO TO GUEST ON THE ALBUM, RIGHT?
I NEED TO BOOK THE STUDIO TIME, SO CAN I RUN IT BY YANAI YET?
ACTUALLY ...
WOULD YOU MIND IF I TOOK IT TO NINO DIRECTLY?
HEE HEE HEE HEE
UH, KUZE? IS SOMETHING WRONG?
You're scaring me here.
NO, IT'S FINE.
THAT'S JUST MY WAY...
...OF SAYING ...
..."GOOD LUCK, MOMO."

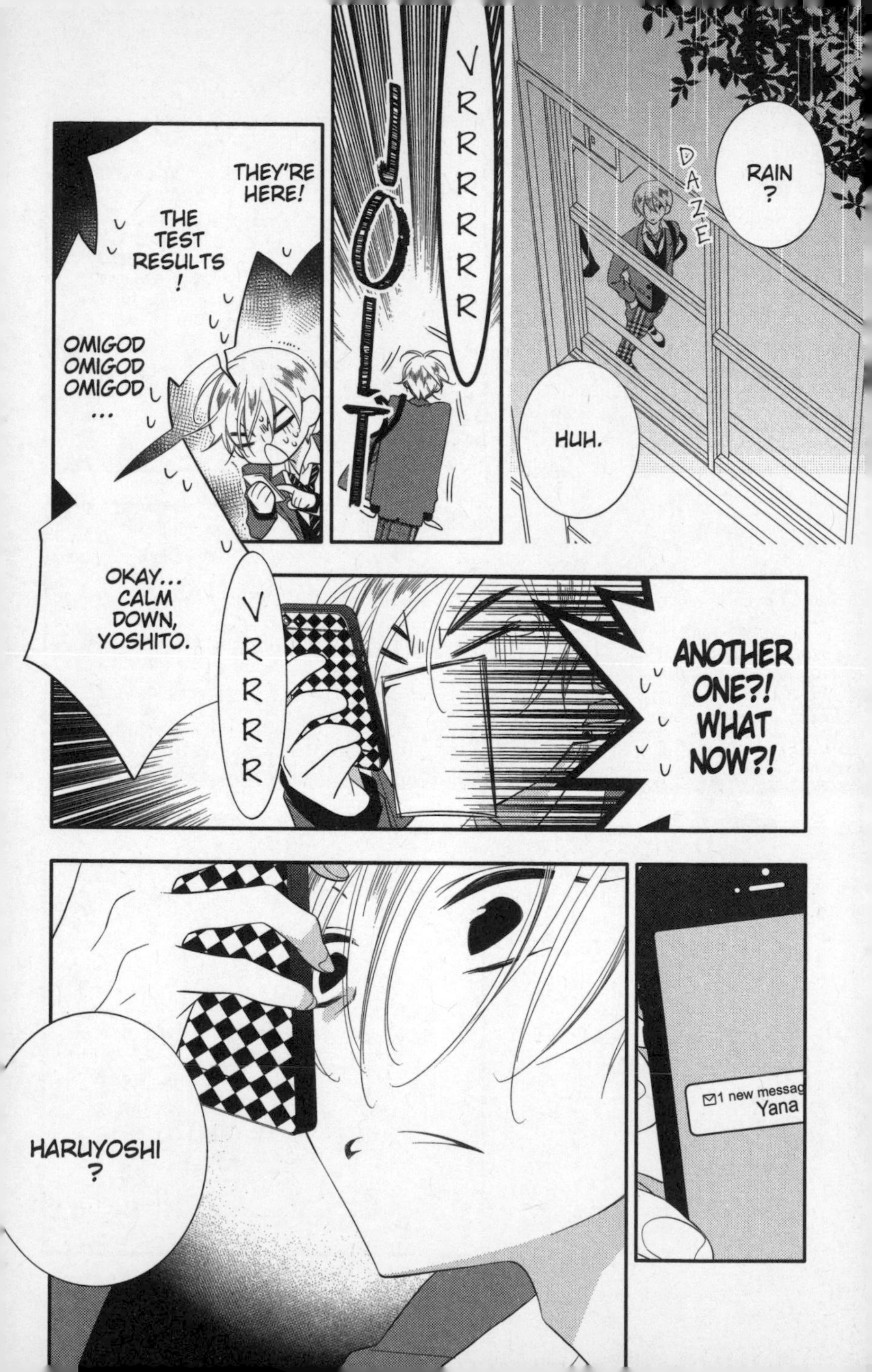
RAIN?
DAZE
HUH.
VRRRRRR
JOLT
THEY'RE HERE!
THE TEST RESULTS!
OMIGOD OMIGOD OMIGOD...
OKAY... CALM DOWN, YOSHITO.
VRRRR
ANOTHER ONE?! WHAT NOW?!
1 new messag
Yana
HARUYOSHI?

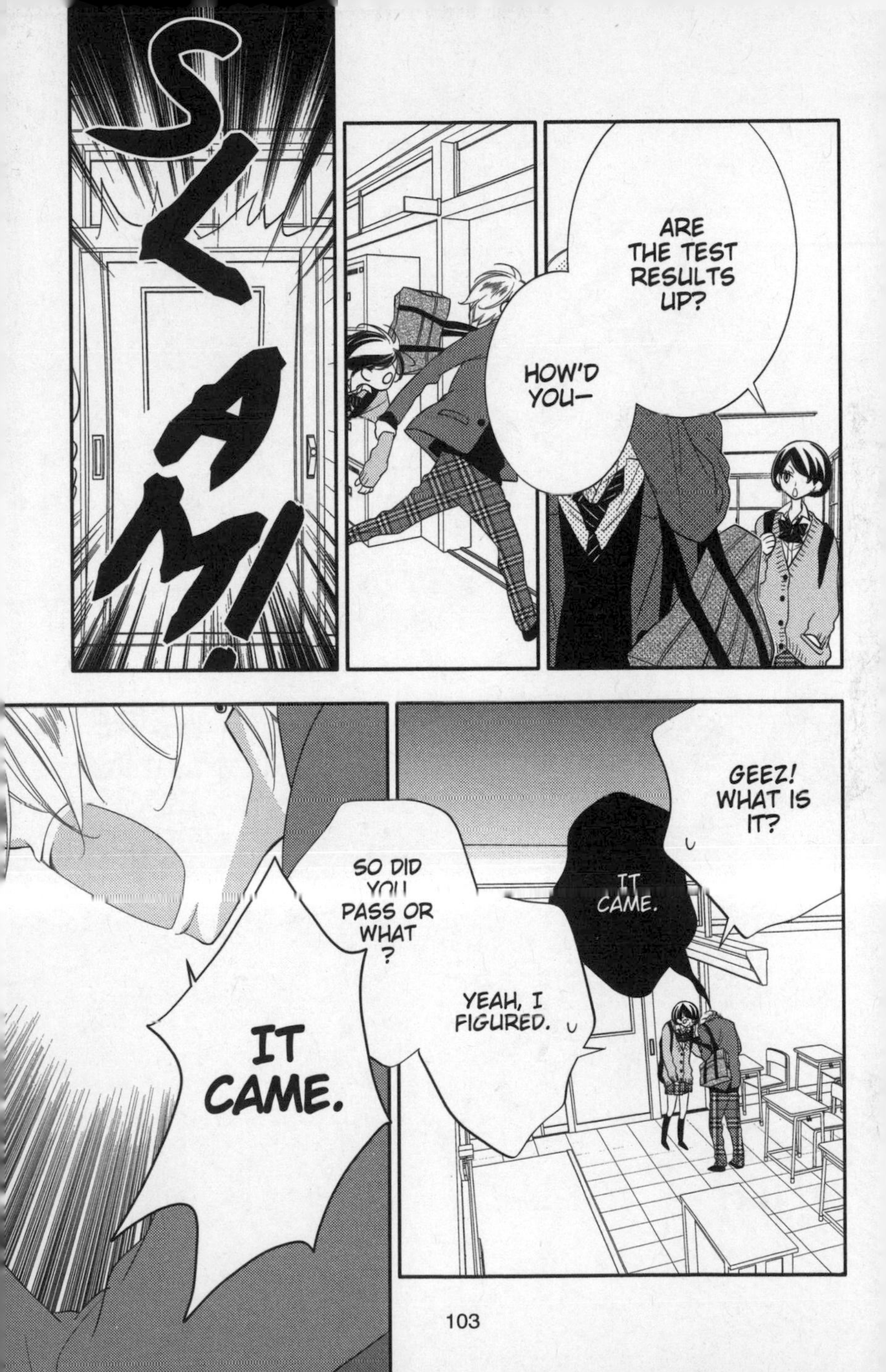
ARE THE TEST RESULTS UP?
HOW'D YOU—
SLAM!
GEEZ! WHAT IS IT?
IT CAME.
SO DID YOU PASS OR WHAT?
YEAH, I FIGURED.
IT CAME.

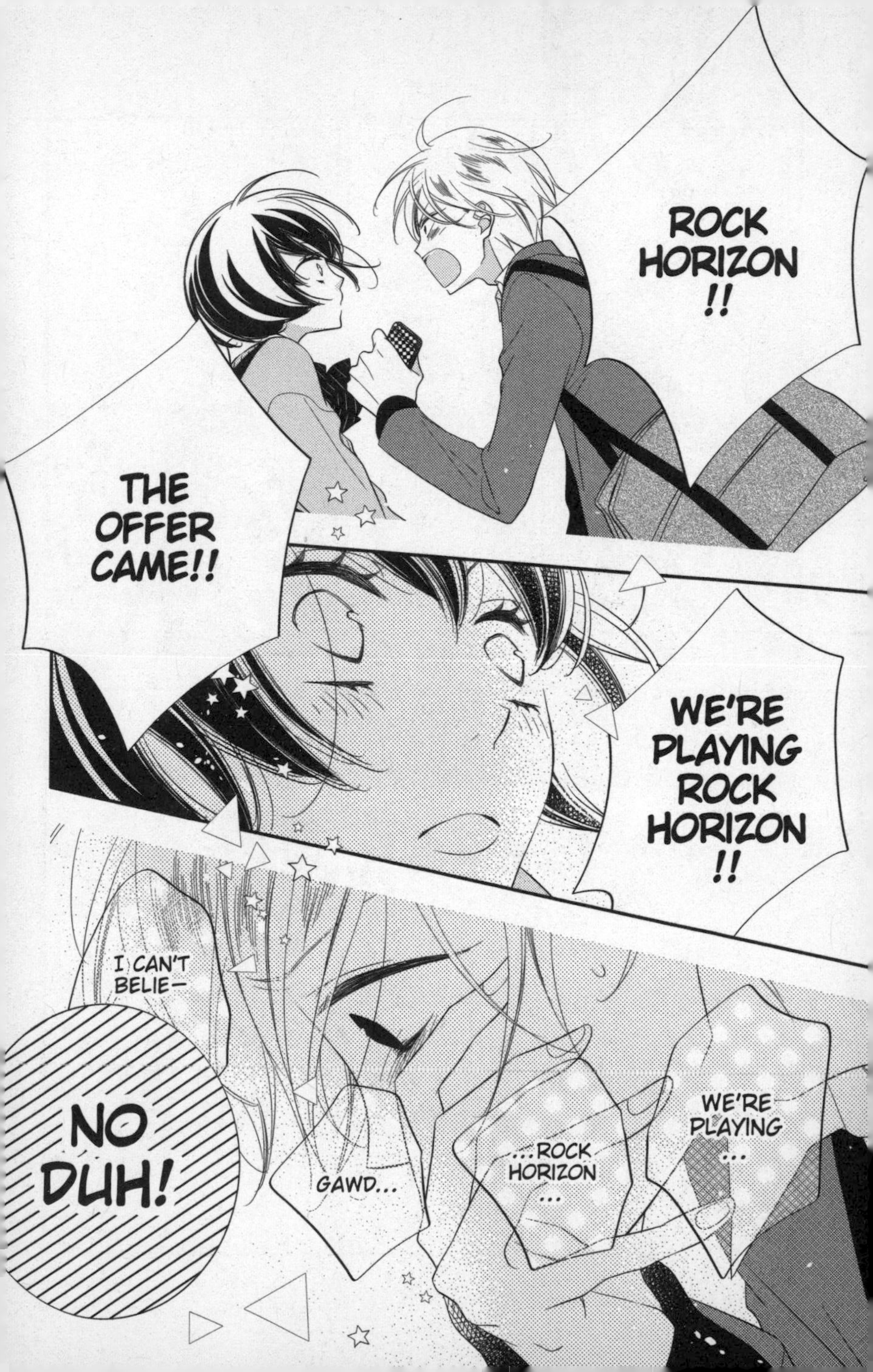
ROCK HORIZON!!
THE OFFER CAME!!
WE'RE PLAYING ROCK HORIZON!!
WE'RE PLAYING...
...ROCK HORIZON...
GAWD...
I CAN'T BELIE—
NO DUH!

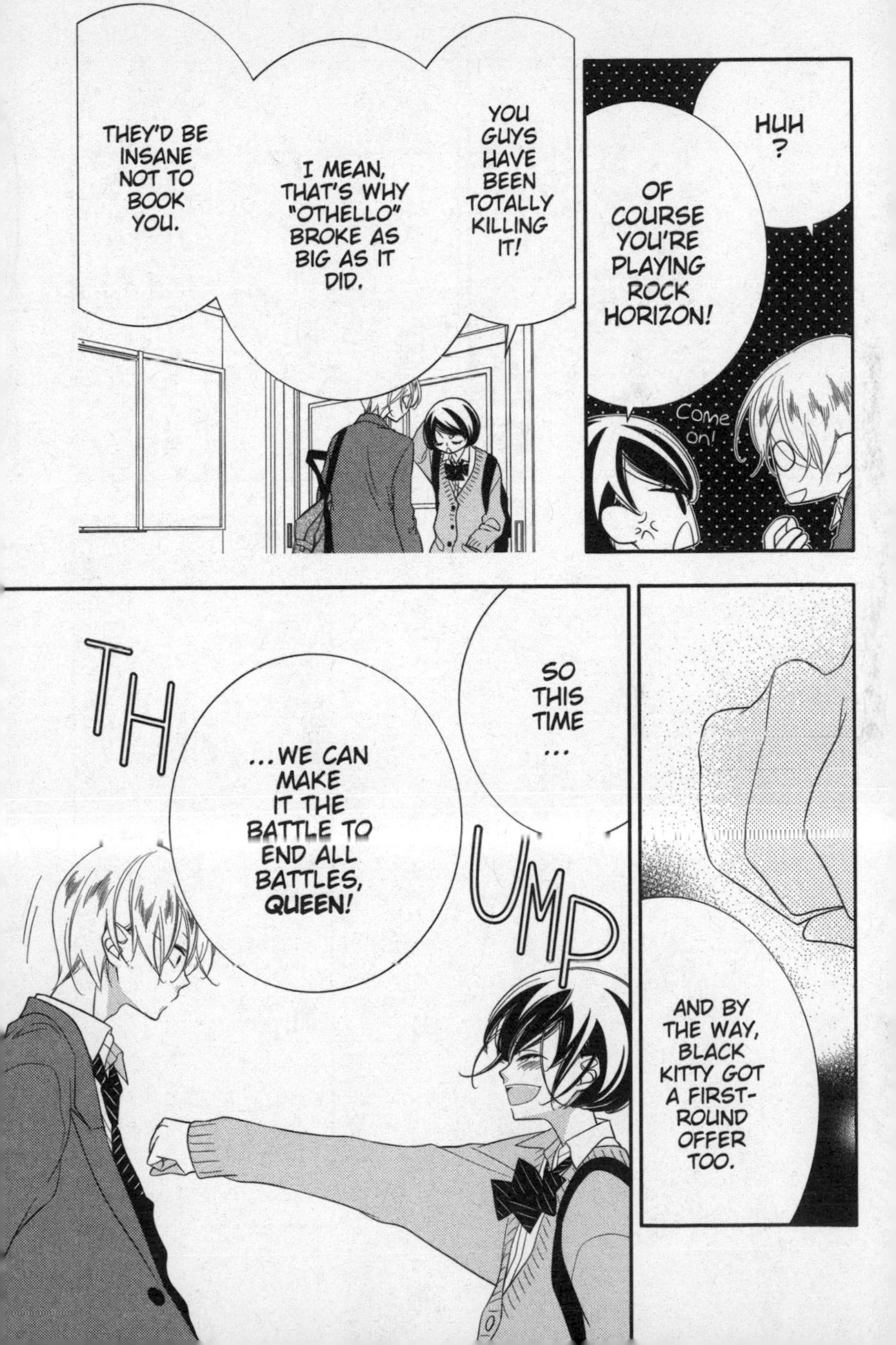
HUH?
OF COURSE YOU'RE PLAYING ROCK HORIZON!
Come on!
YOU GUYS HAVE BEEN TOTALLY KILLING IT!
I MEAN, THAT'S WHY "OTHELLO" BROKE AS BIG AS IT DID.
THEY'D BE INSANE NOT TO BOOK YOU.
AND BY THE WAY, BLACK KITTY GOT A FIRST-ROUND OFFER TOO.
SO THIS TIME...
...WE CAN MAKE IT THE BATTLE TO END ALL BATTLES, QUEEN!
THUMP

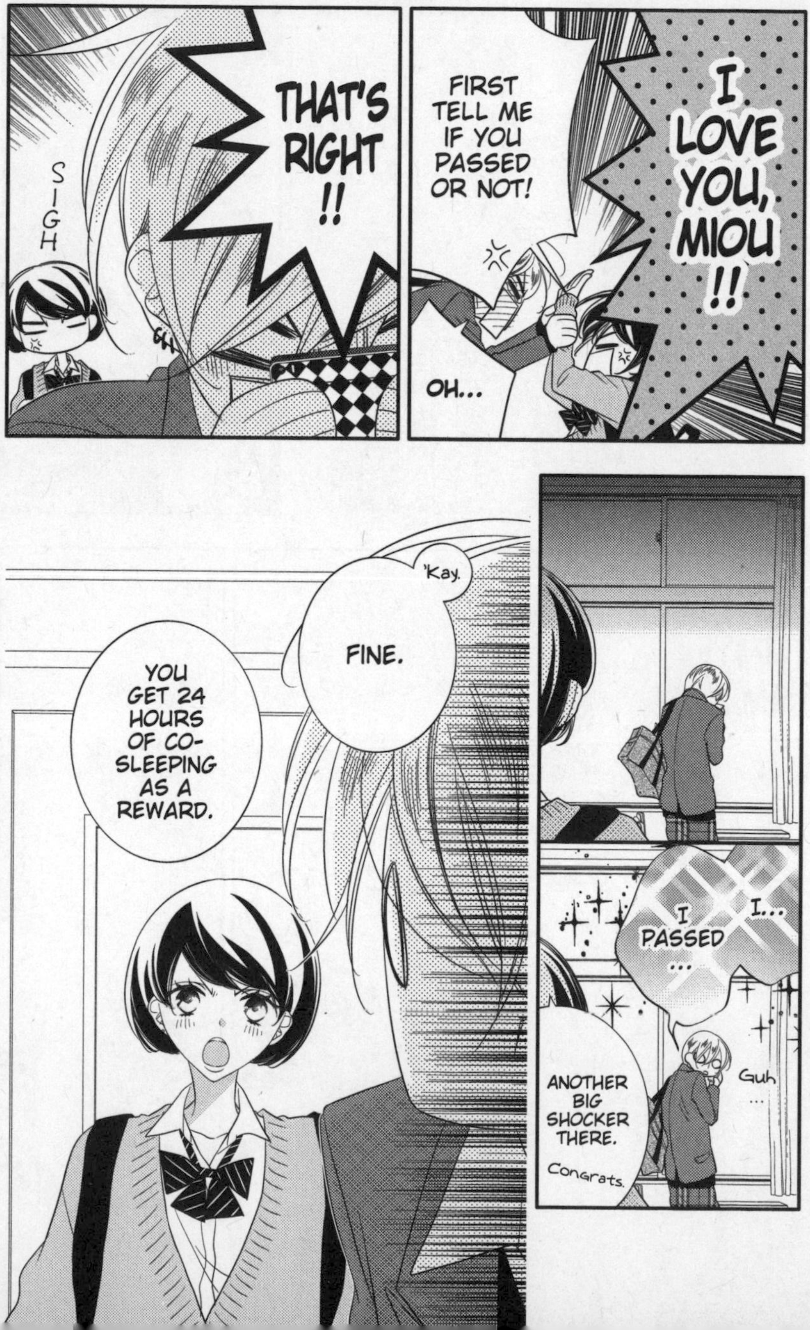
I LOVE YOU, MIOU!!
FIRST TELL ME IF YOU PASSED OR NOT!
OH...
THAT'S RIGHT!!
SIGH
I...
I PASSED...
ANOTHER BIG SHOCKER THERE.
Congrats.
Guh...
'Kay.
FINE.
YOU GET 24 HOURS OF CO-SLEEPING AS A REWARD.

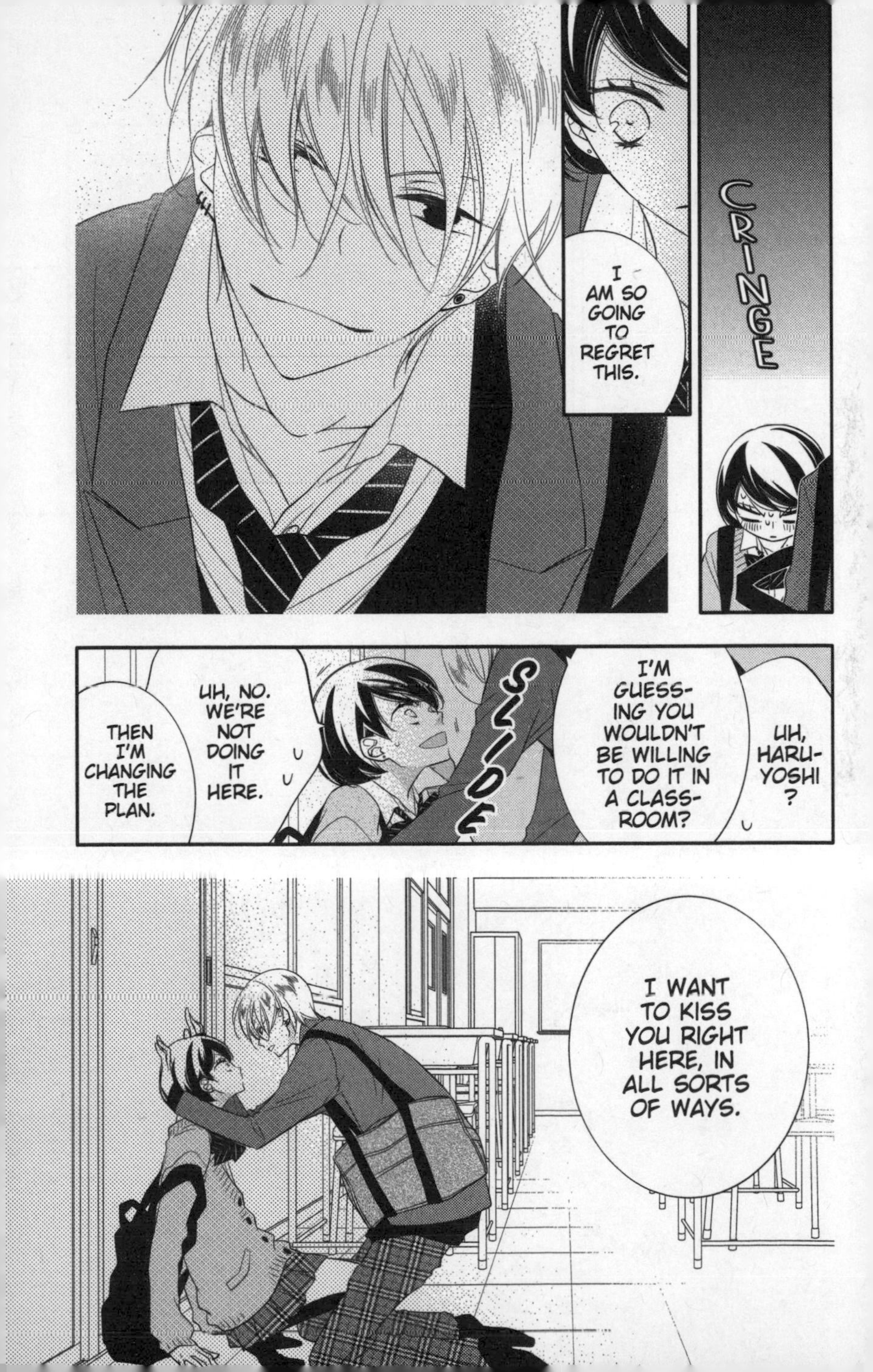
CRINGE
I AM SO GOING TO REGRET THIS.
UH, HARU-YOSHI?
I'M GUESSING YOU WOULDN'T BE WILLING TO DO IT IN A CLASSROOM?
SLIDE
UH, NO. WE'RE NOT DOING IT HERE.
THEN I'M CHANGING THE PLAN.
I WANT TO KISS YOU RIGHT HERE, IN ALL SORTS OF WAYS.

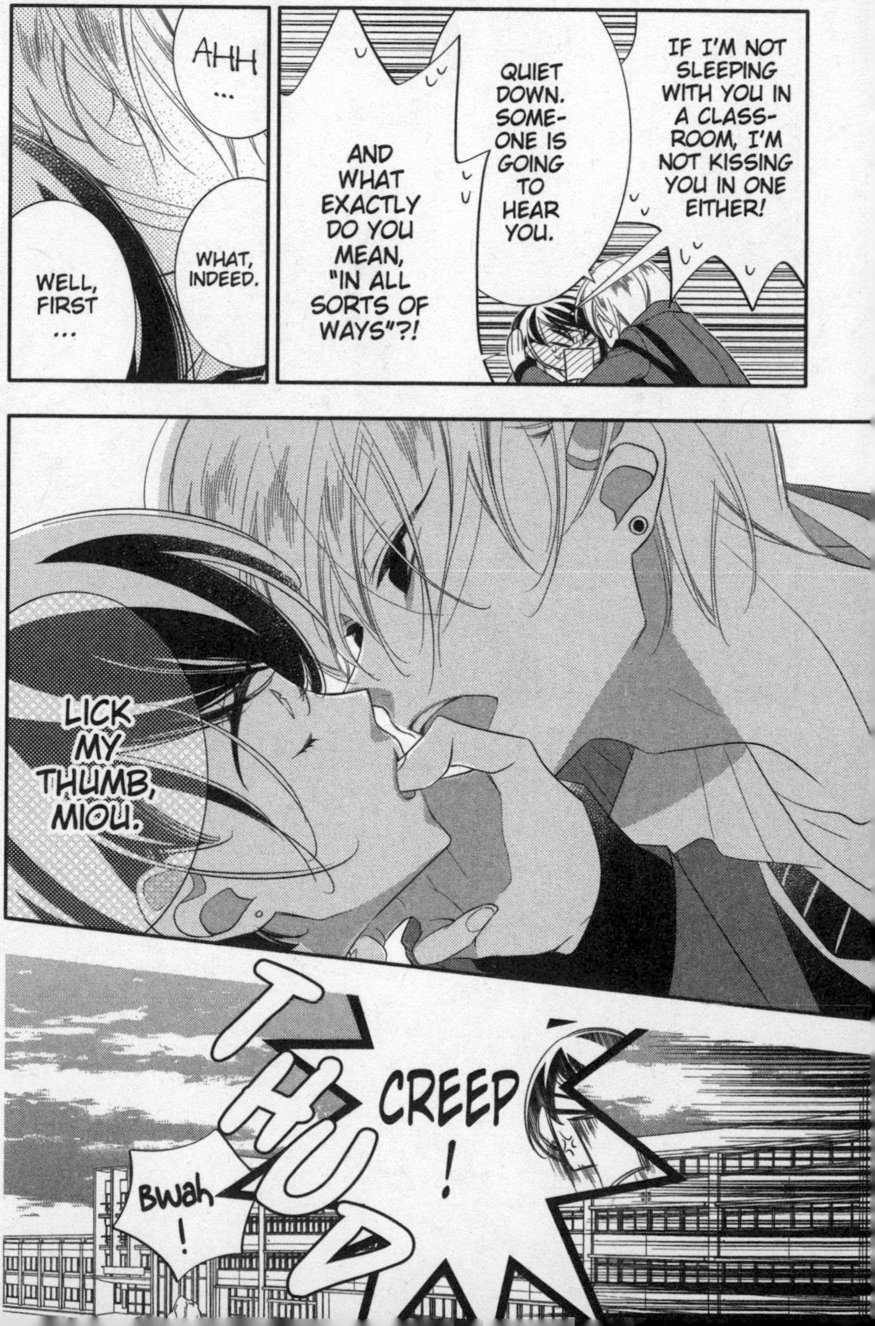
IF I'M NOT SLEEPING WITH YOU IN A CLASSROOM, I'M NOT KISSING YOU IN ONE EITHER!
QUIET DOWN. SOMEONE IS GOING TO HEAR YOU.
AND WHAT EXACTLY DO YOU MEAN, "IN ALL SORTS OF WAYS"?!
AHH ...
WHAT, INDEED.
WELL, FIRST ...
LICK MY THUMB, MIOU.
CREEP!
THUD
Bwah!

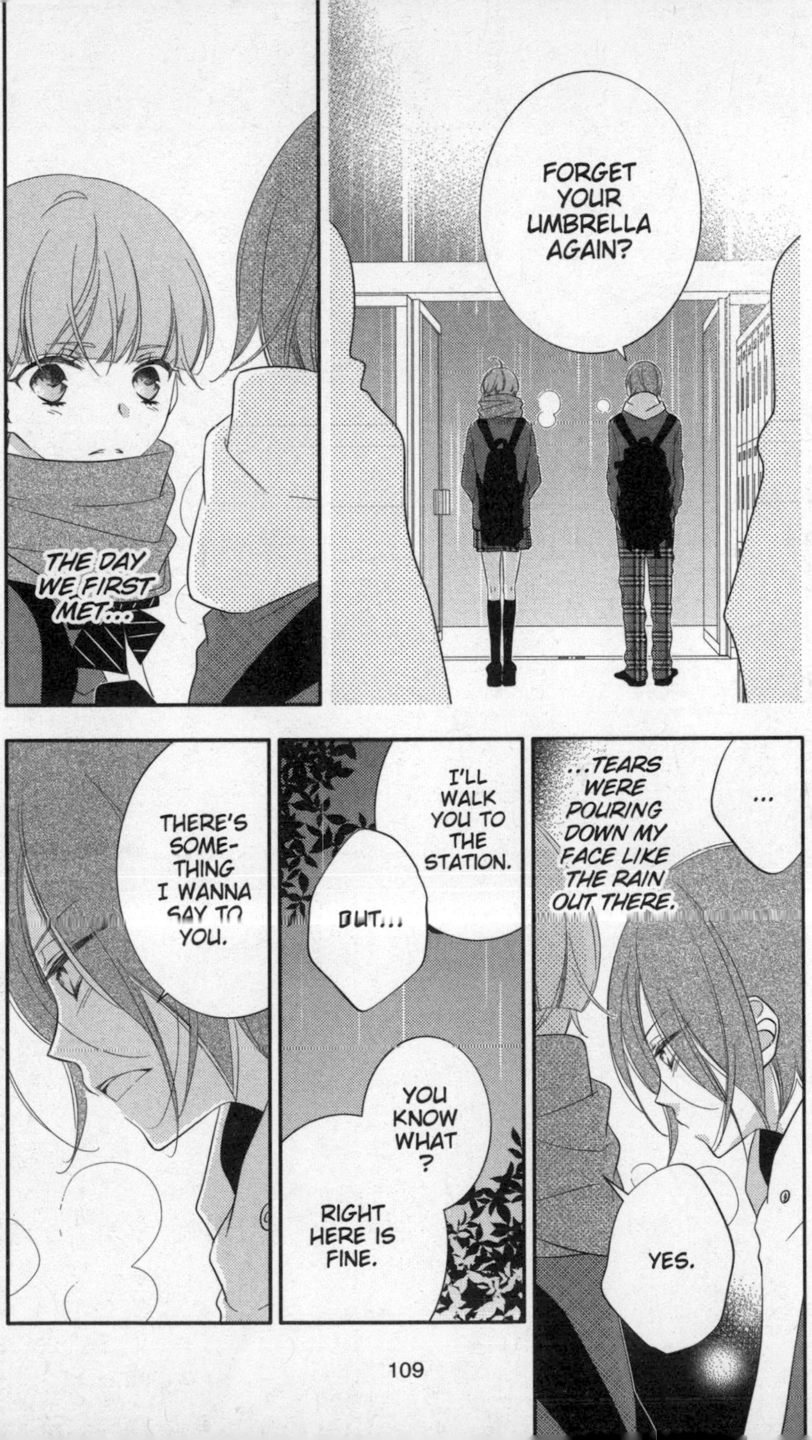
FORGET YOUR UMBRELLA AGAIN?
THE DAY WE FIRST MET...
...
...TEARS WERE POURING DOWN MY FACE LIKE THE RAIN OUT THERE.
YES.
I'LL WALK YOU TO THE STATION.
BUT...
YOU KNOW WHAT?
RIGHT HERE IS FINE.
THERE'S SOME-THING I WANNA SAY TO YOU.

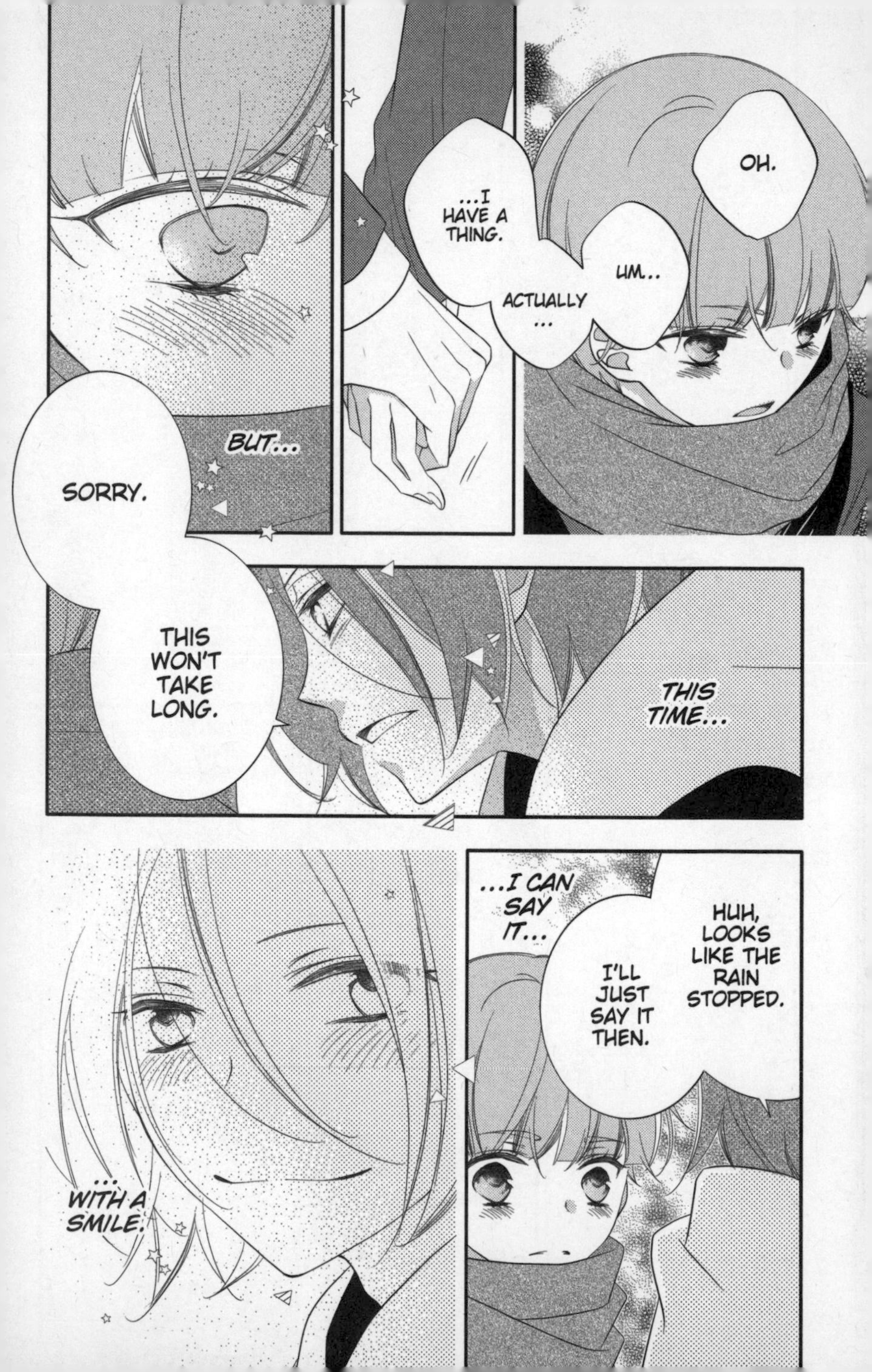
OH.
UM...
ACTUALLY ...
...I HAVE A THING.
BUT...
SORRY.
THIS WON'T TAKE LONG.
THIS TIME...
HUH, LOOKS LIKE THE RAIN STOPPED.
I'LL JUST SAY IT THEN.
...I CAN SAY IT...
...WITH A SMILE.

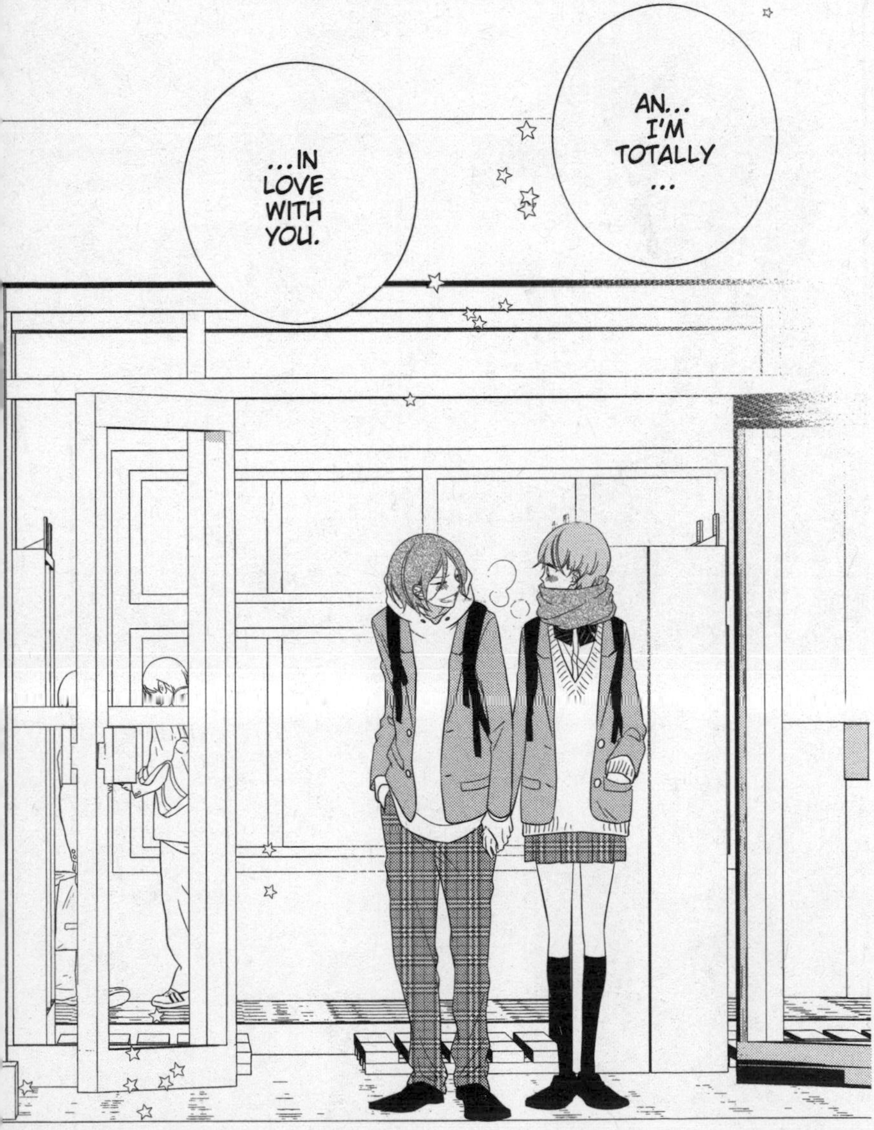
AN... I'M TOTALLY ...
...IN LOVE WITH YOU.

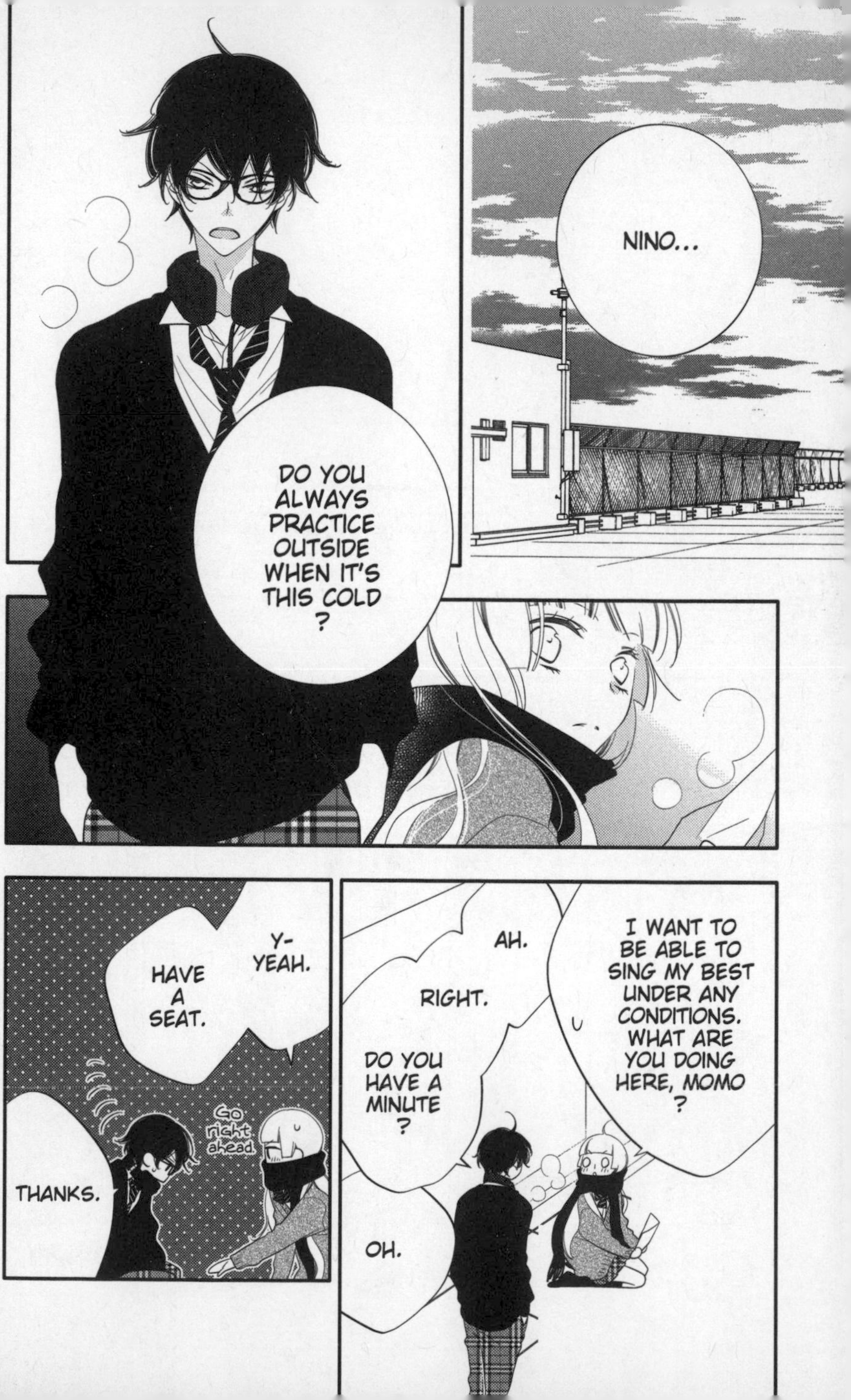
NINO...
DO YOU ALWAYS PRACTICE OUTSIDE WHEN IT'S THIS COLD?
I WANT TO BE ABLE TO SING MY BEST UNDER ANY CONDITIONS. WHAT ARE YOU DOING HERE, MOMO?
AH.
RIGHT.
DO YOU HAVE A MINUTE?
OH.
Y-YEAH.
HAVE A SEAT.
Go right ahead.
THANKS.

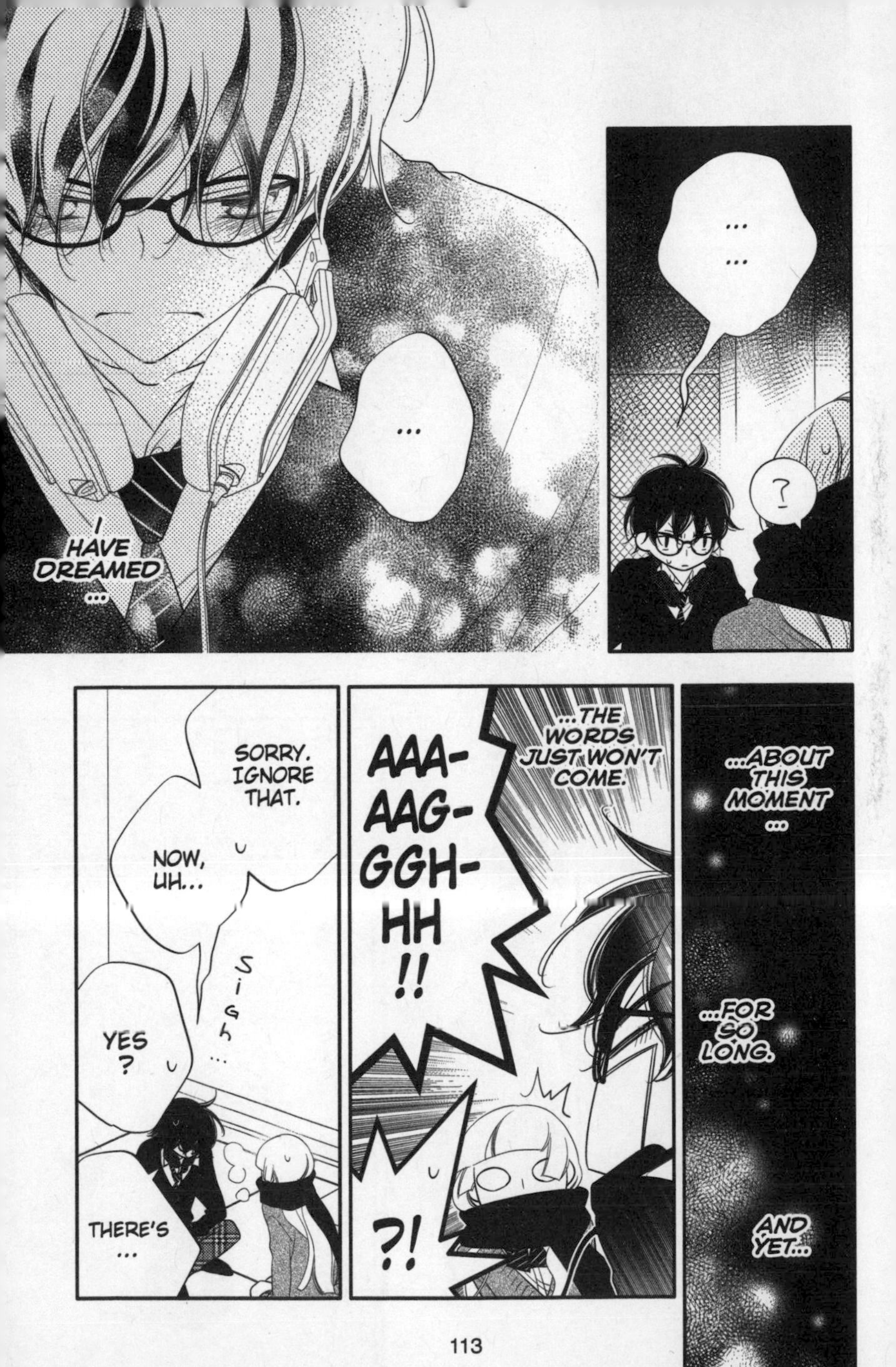

... ...
?
...
I HAVE DREAMED ...
...ABOUT THIS MOMENT ...
...FOR SO LONG.
AND YET...
...THE WORDS JUST WON'T COME.
AAAAAGGGHHH!!
?!
SORRY. IGNORE THAT.
NOW, UH...
Sigh...
YES?
THERE'S ...

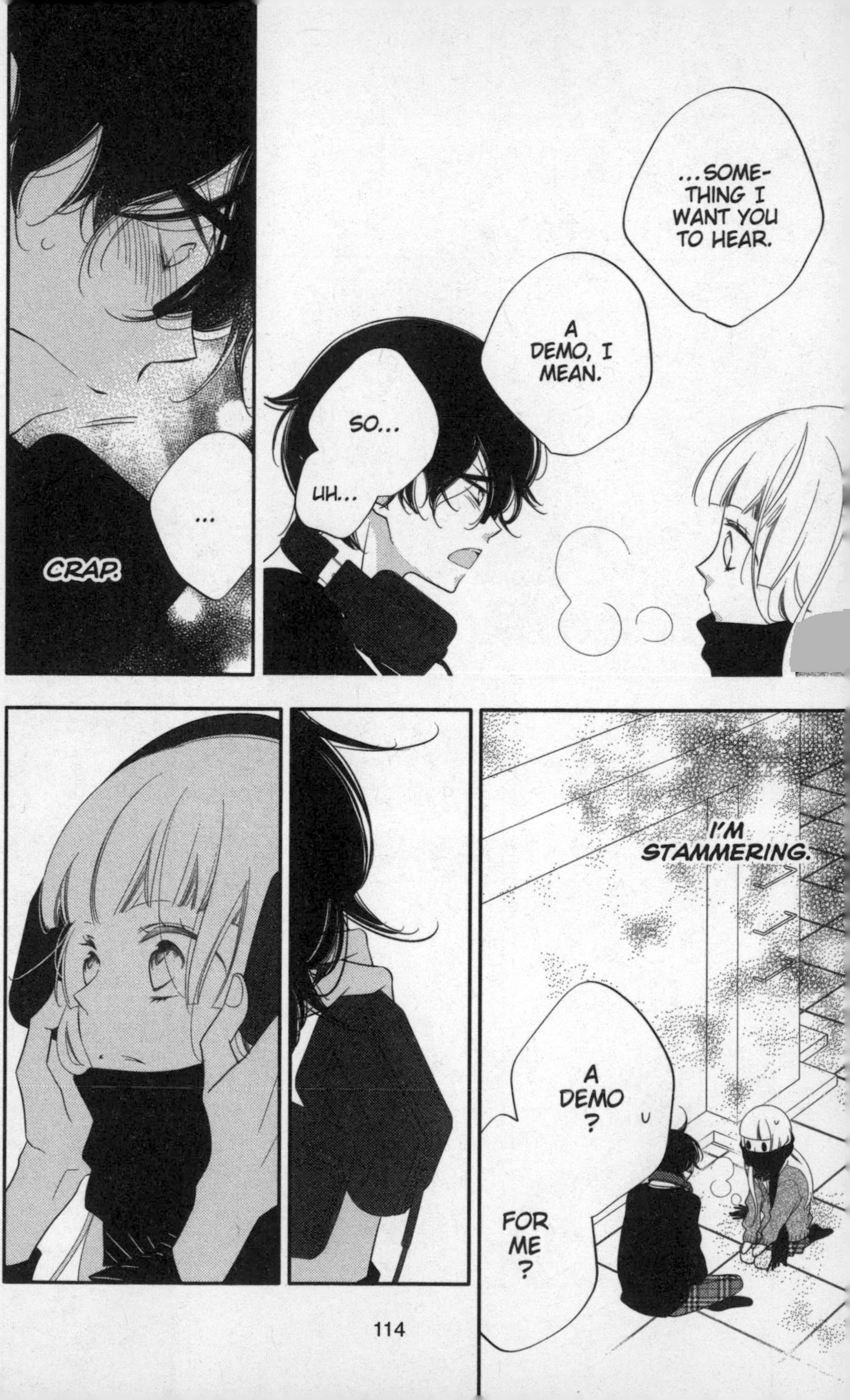
...SOME-THING I WANT YOU TO HEAR.
A DEMO, I MEAN.
SO...
UH...
...
CRAP.
I'M STAMMERING.
A DEMO?
FOR ME?

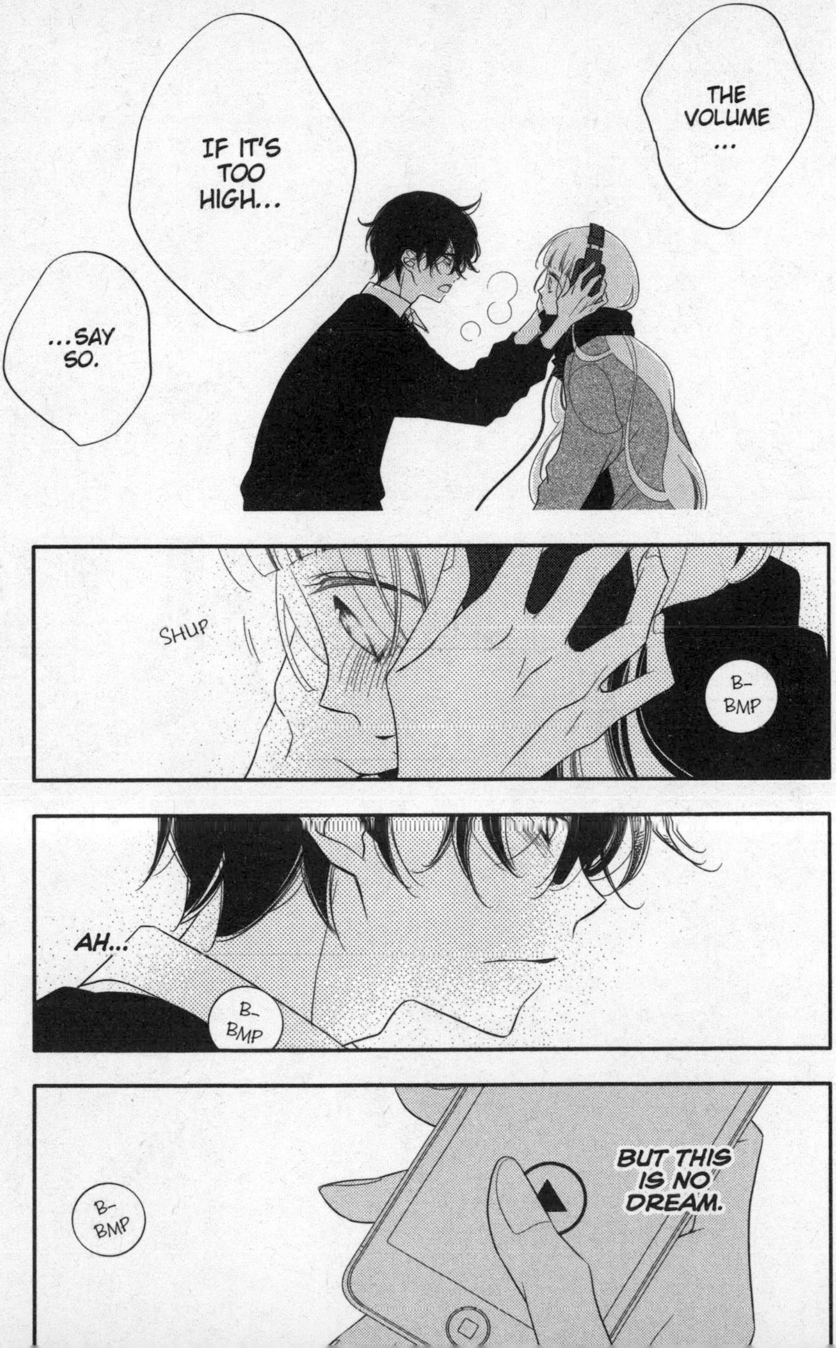
THE VOLUME ...
IF IT'S TOO HIGH...
...SAY SO.
B-BMP
SHUP
AH...
B-BMP
BUT THIS IS NO DREAM.
B-BMP

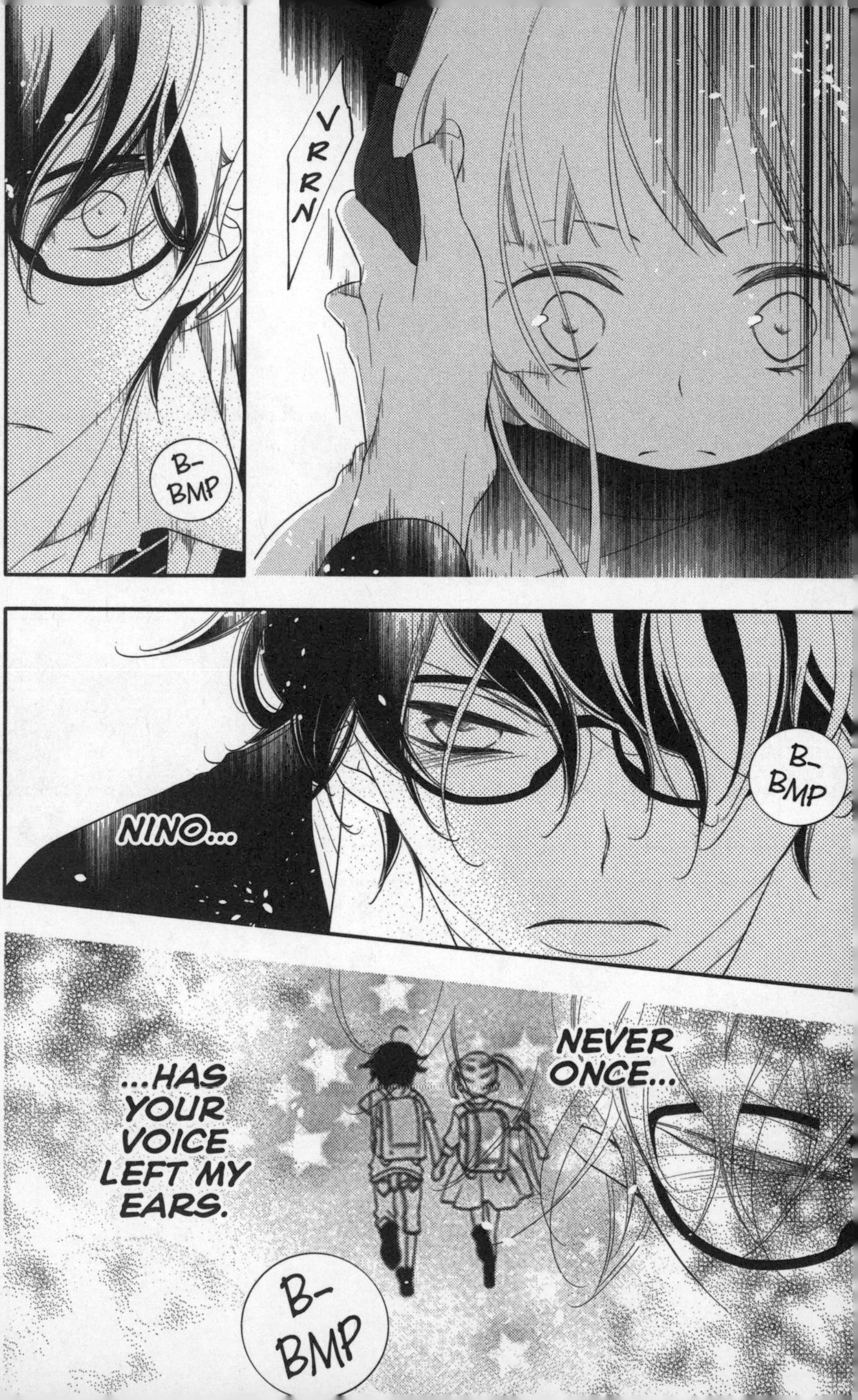
VRRN
B-BMP
B-BMP
NINO...
NEVER ONCE...
...HAS YOUR VOICE LEFT MY EARS.
B-BMP

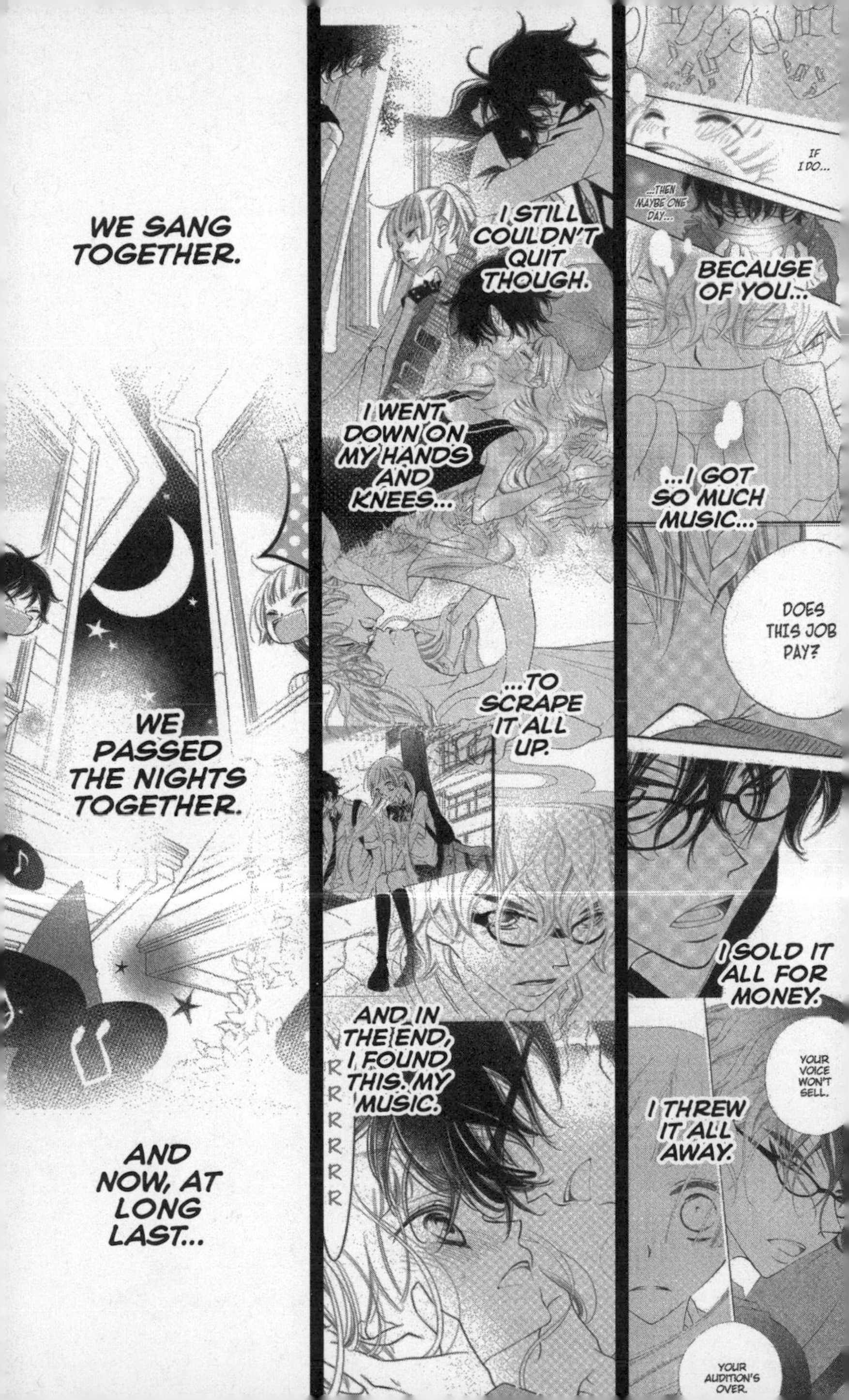
IF I DO...
...THEN MAYBE ONE DAY...
BECAUSE OF YOU...
...I GOT SO MUCH MUSIC...
DOES THIS JOB PAY?
I SOLD IT ALL FOR MONEY.
YOUR VOICE WON'T SELL.
I THREW IT ALL AWAY.
YOUR AUDITION'S OVER.
I STILL COULDN'T QUIT THOUGH.
I WENT DOWN ON MY HANDS AND KNEES...
...TO SCRAPE IT ALL UP.
AND IN THE END, I FOUND THIS. MY MUSIC.
VRRRRRRR
WE SANG TOGETHER.
WE PASSED THE NIGHTS TOGETHER.
AND NOW, AT LONG LAST...

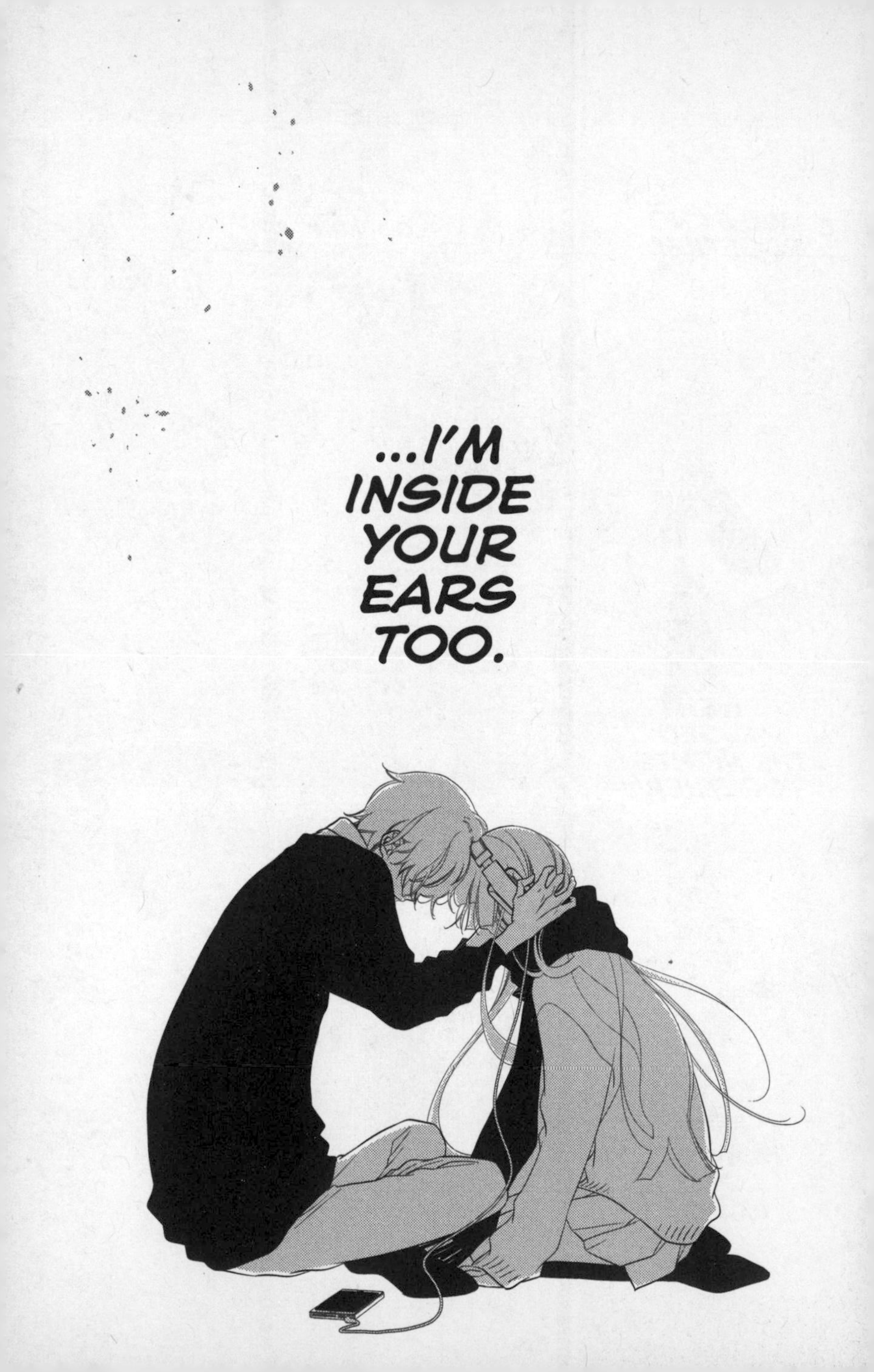
...I'M INSIDE YOUR EARS TOO.

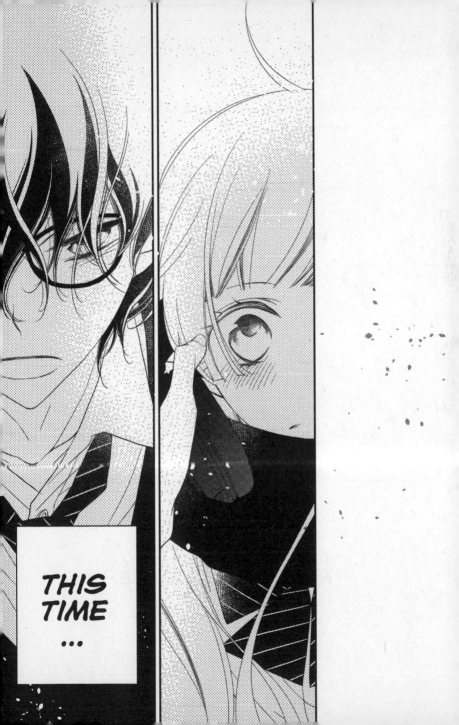

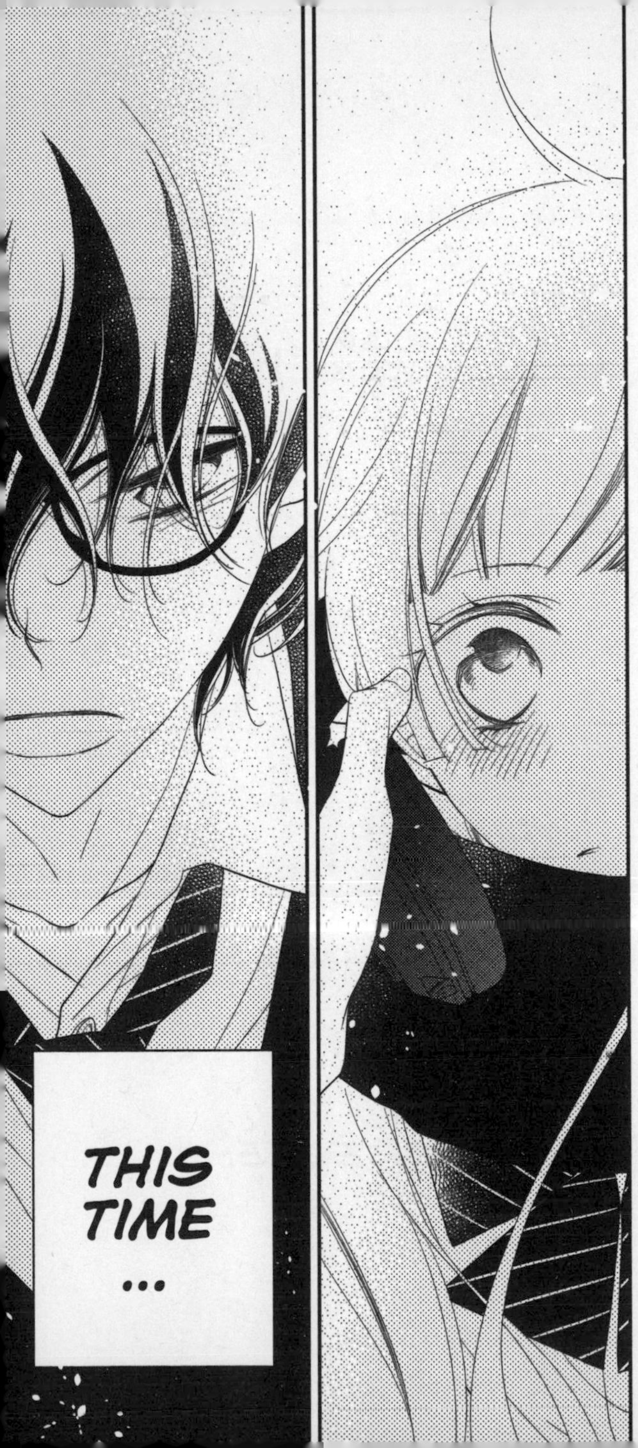
THIS TIME ...

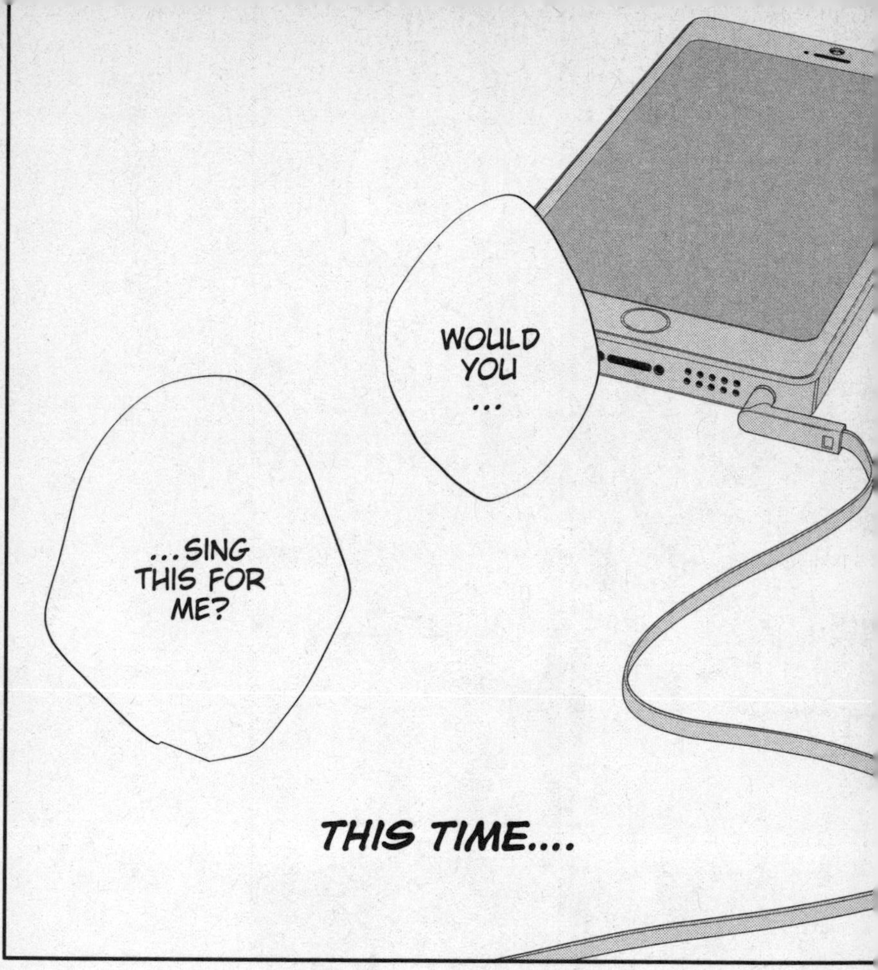
WOULD YOU ...
...SING THIS FOR ME?
THIS TIME....

THIS TIME FOR SURE.

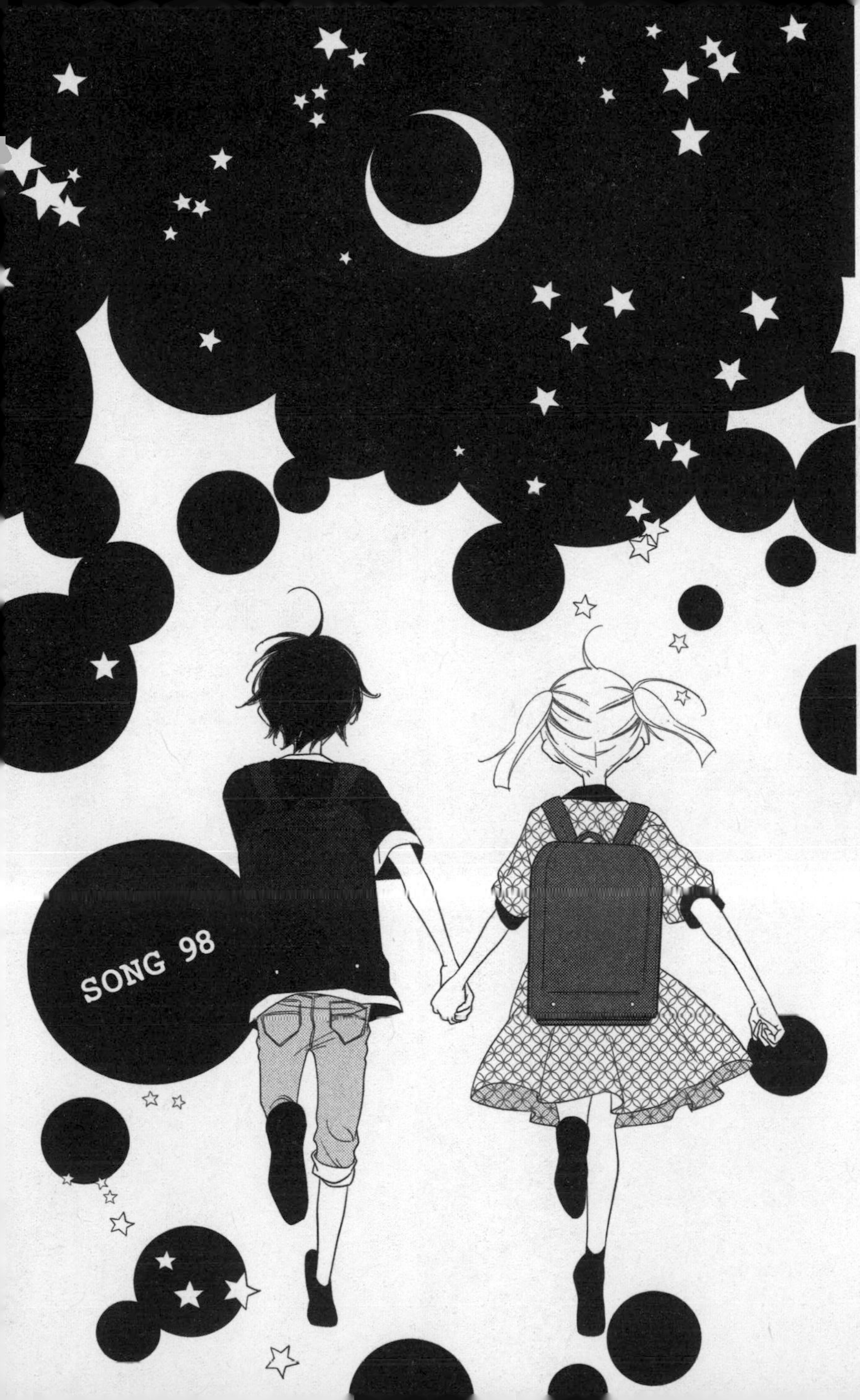
SONG 98

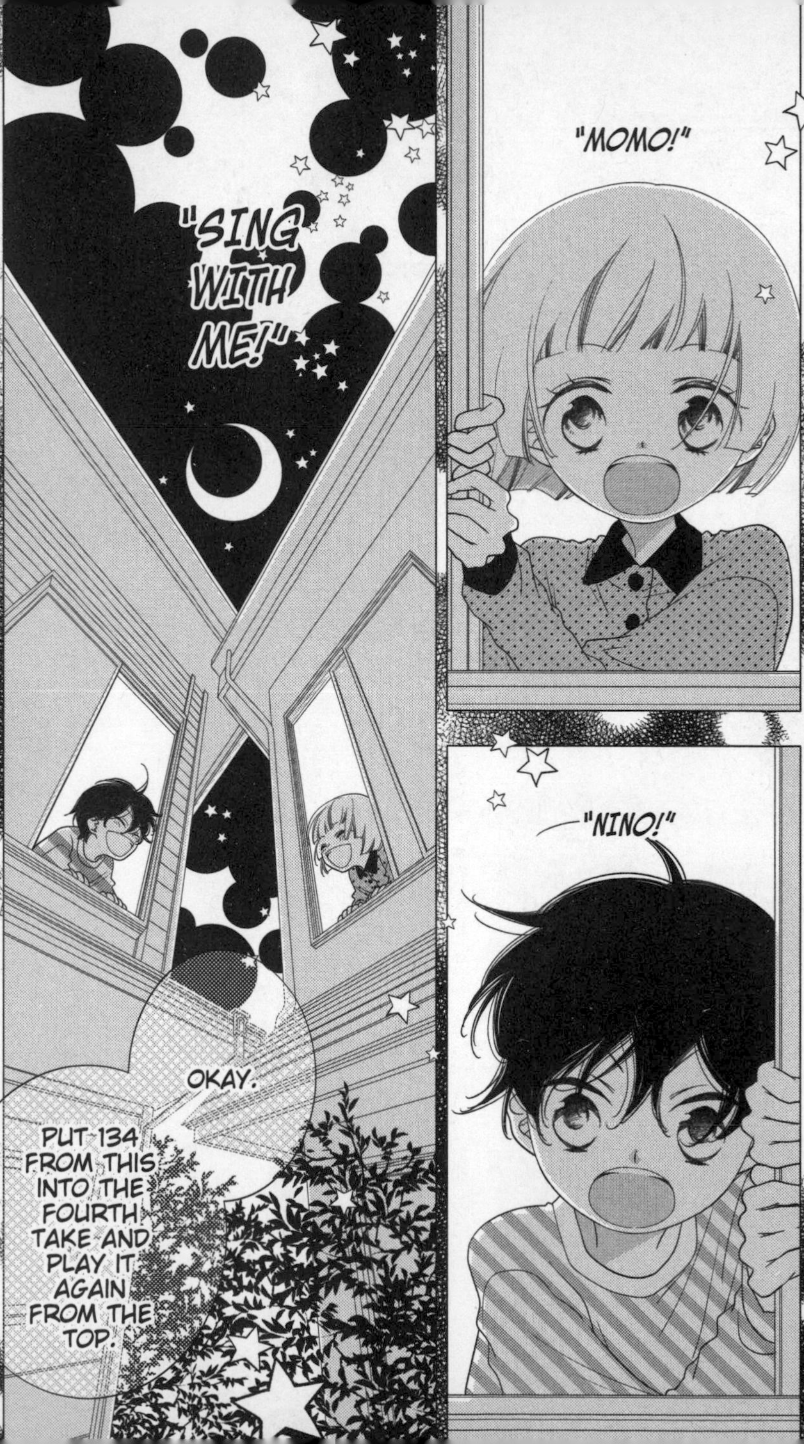
"MOMO!"
"NINO!"
"SING WITH ME!"
OKAY.
PUT 134 FROM THIS INTO THE FOURTH TAKE AND PLAY IT AGAIN FROM THE TOP.

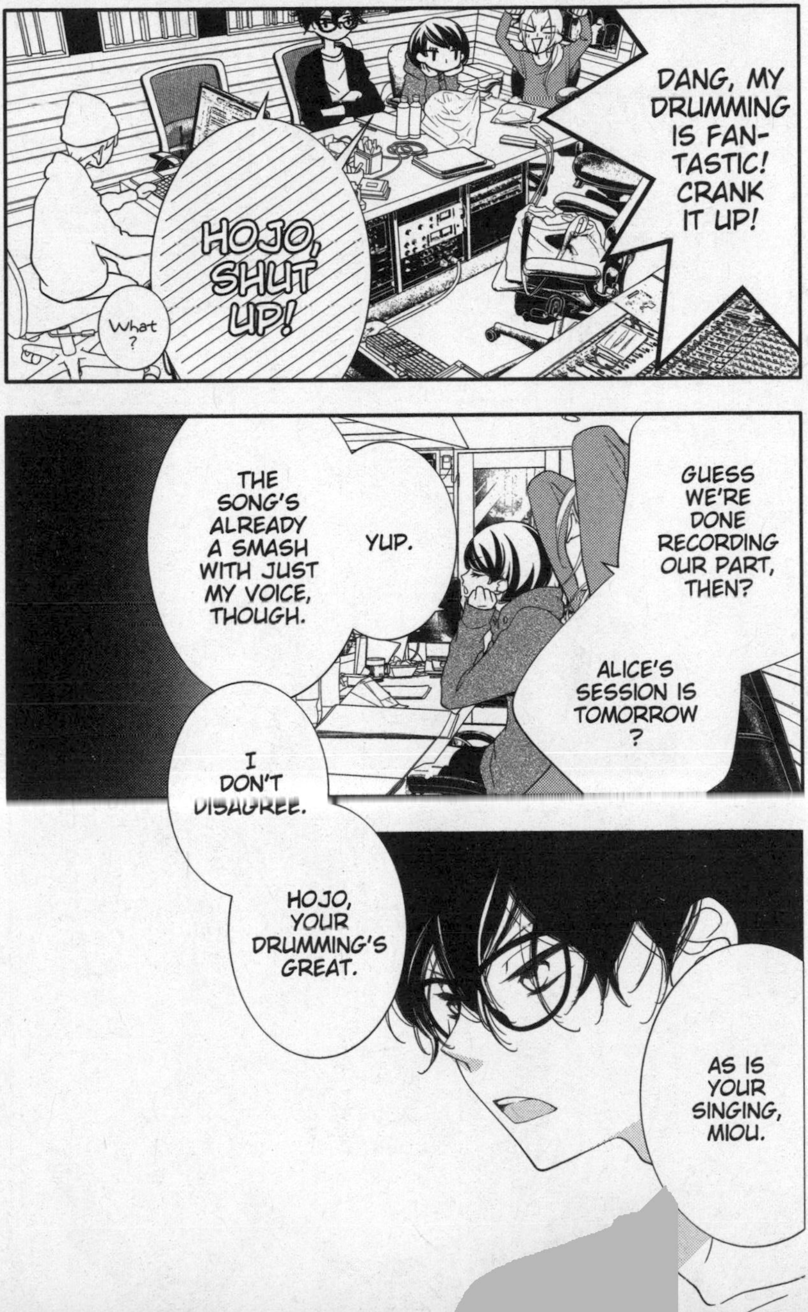
DANG, MY DRUMMING IS FAN-TASTIC! CRANK IT UP!
HOJO, SHUT UP!
What?
GUESS WE'RE DONE RECORDING OUR PART, THEN?
ALICE'S SESSION IS TOMORROW?
YUP.
THE SONG'S ALREADY A SMASH WITH JUST MY VOICE, THOUGH.
I DON'T DISAGREE.
HOJO, YOUR DRUMMING'S GREAT.
AS IS YOUR SINGING, MIOU.

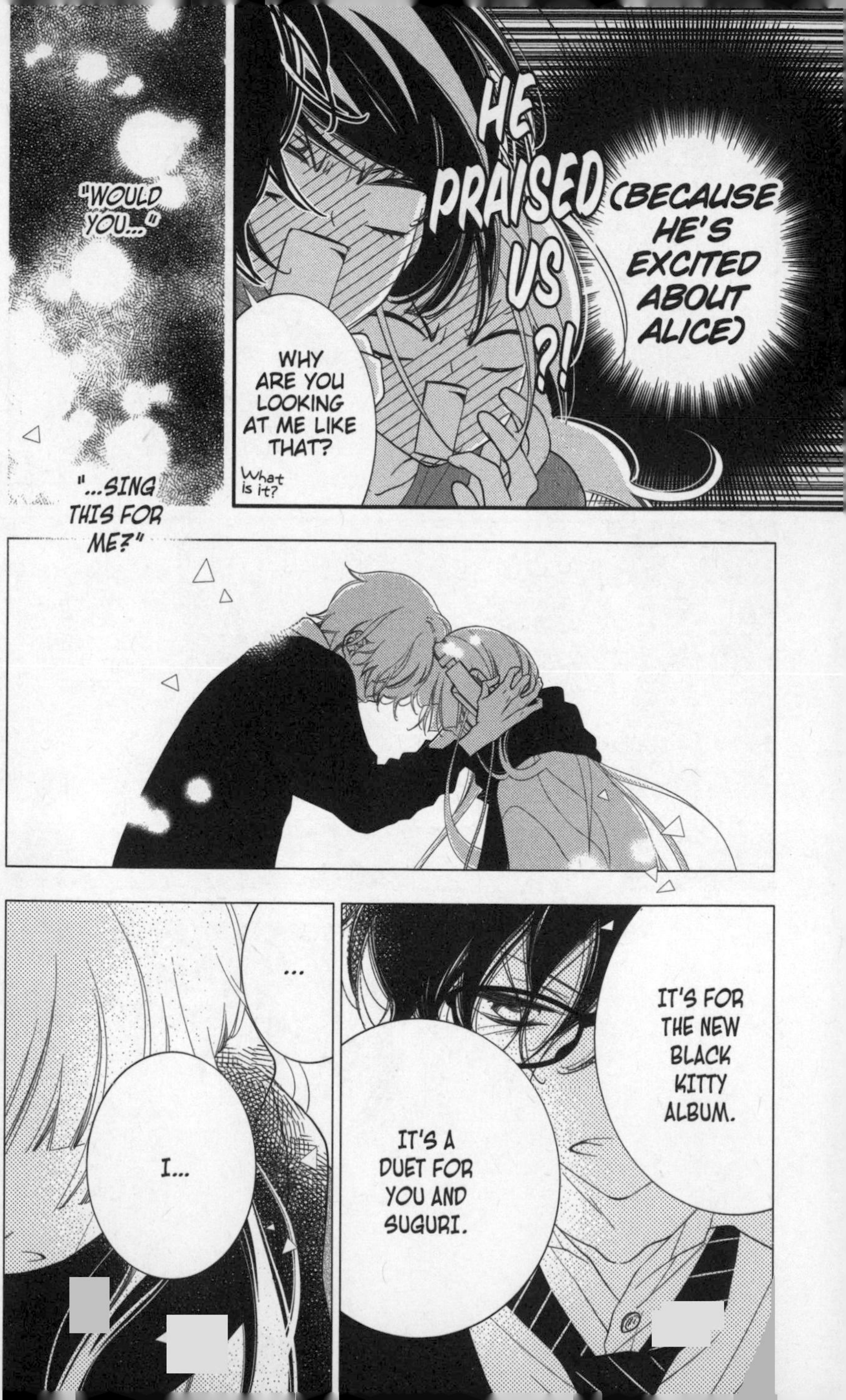
HE PRAISED US?!
(BECAUSE HE'S EXCITED ABOUT ALICE)
WHY ARE YOU LOOKING AT ME LIKE THAT?
What is it?
"WOULD YOU..."
"...SING THIS FOR ME?"
IT'S FOR THE NEW BLACK KITTY ALBUM.
IT'S A DUET FOR YOU AND SUGURI.
...
I...

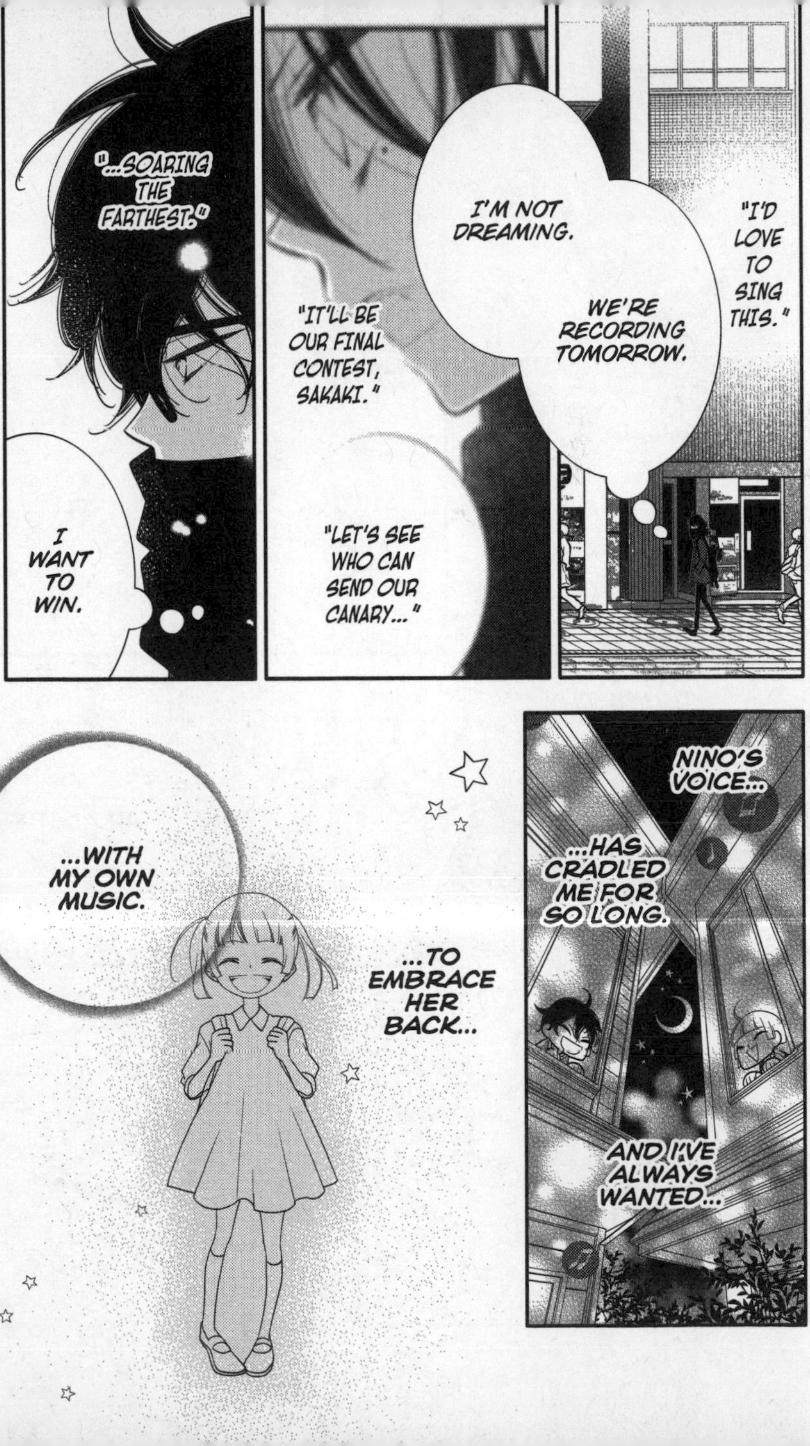
"I'D LOVE TO SING THIS."
I'M NOT DREAMING.
WE'RE RECORDING TOMORROW.
"IT'LL BE OUR FINAL CONTEST, SAKAKI."
"LET'S SEE WHO CAN SEND OUR CANARY..."
"...SOARING THE FARTHEST."
I WANT TO WIN.
NINO'S VOICE...
...HAS CRADLED ME FOR SO LONG.
AND I'VE ALWAYS WANTED...
...TO EMBRACE HER BACK...
...WITH MY OWN MUSIC.

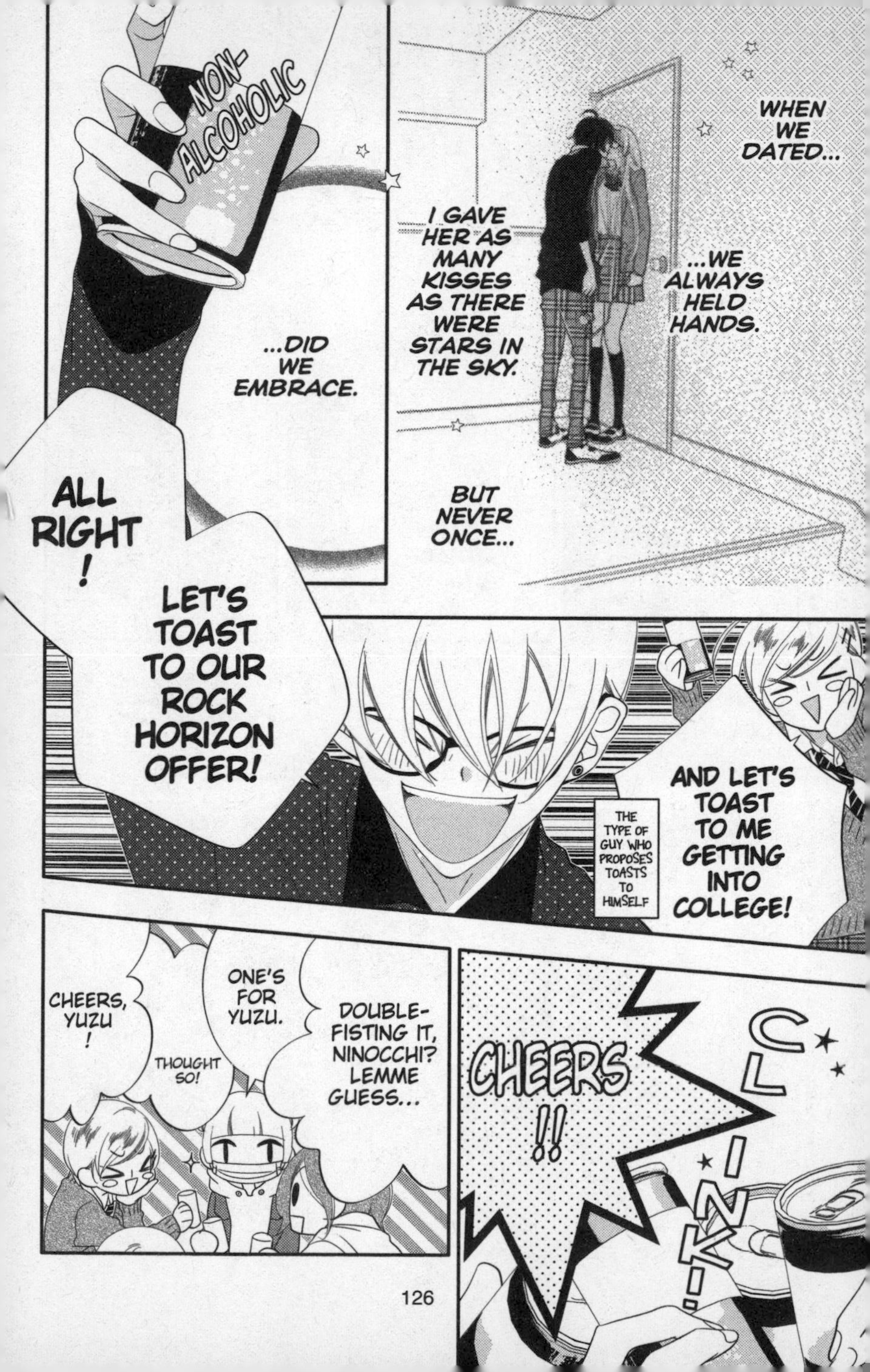
WHEN WE DATED...
...WE ALWAYS HELD HANDS.
I GAVE HER AS MANY KISSES AS THERE WERE STARS IN THE SKY.
BUT NEVER ONCE...
...DID WE EMBRACE.
NON-ALCOHOLIC
ALL RIGHT!
LET'S TOAST TO OUR ROCK HORIZON OFFER!
AND LET'S TOAST TO ME GETTING INTO COLLEGE!
THE TYPE OF GUY WHO PROPOSES TOASTS TO HIMSELF
CHEERS!!
CLINK!
DOUBLE-FISTING IT, NINOCCHI? LEMME GUESS...
ONE'S FOR YUZU.
THOUGHT SO!
CHEERS, YUZU!

4

Well, how did you all enjoy volume 17? Remember, the next one is the long-awaited final volume!

Whoa. I'm so nervous! I really hope I'll see you again in the pages of our finale!
Until then...! ✧

XXX
Ryoko Fukuyama
12/9/2018

THANK YOU!

[SPECIAL THANKS]
MOSAGE
TAKAYUKI NAGASHIMA
IKUMI ISHIGAKI
AYAKA TOKUSHIGE
KENJU NORO
MY FAMILY
MY FRIENDS
AND YOU!!

Ryoko Fukuyama
c/o Anonymous
Noise Editor
VIZ Media
P.O. Box 77010
San Francisco, CA
94107

HP http://ryoconet/
@ryocoryocoryoco
https://www.instagram.com/ryocofukuyama/

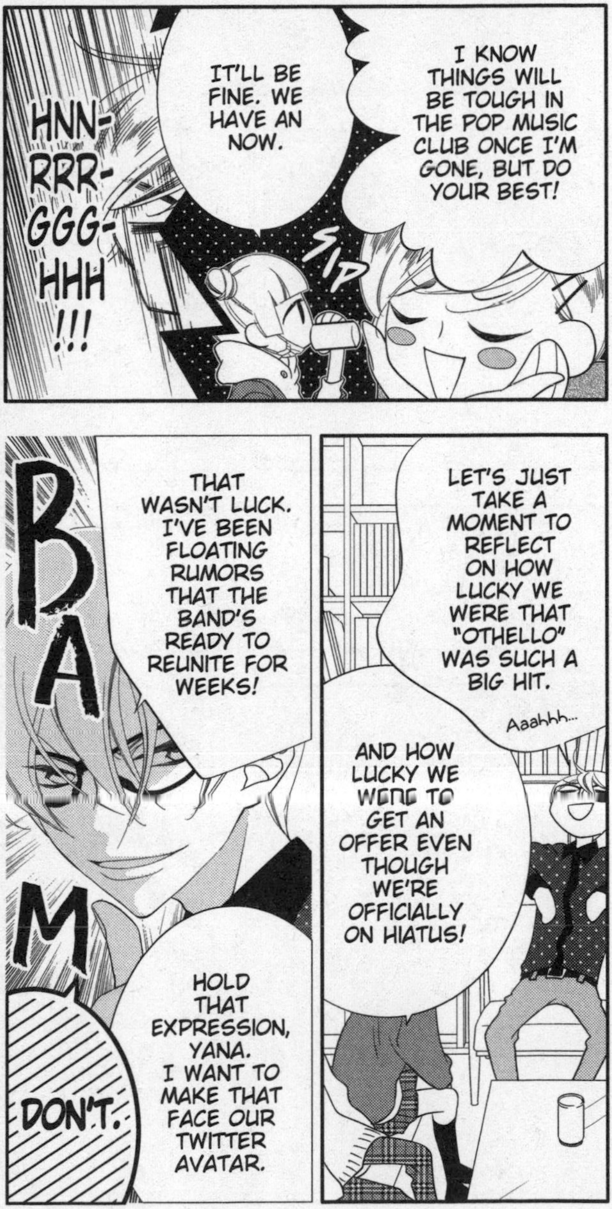
I KNOW THINGS WILL BE TOUGH IN THE POP MUSIC CLUB ONCE I'M GONE, BUT DO YOUR BEST!
IT'LL BE FINE. WE HAVE AN NOW.
SIP
HNN-RRR-GGG-HHH!!!
LET'S JUST TAKE A MOMENT TO REFLECT ON HOW LUCKY WE WERE THAT "OTHELLO" WAS SUCH A BIG HIT.
Aaahhh...
AND HOW LUCKY WE WERE TO GET AN OFFER EVEN THOUGH WE'RE OFFICIALLY ON HIATUS!
THAT WASN'T LUCK. I'VE BEEN FLOATING RUMORS THAT THE BAND'S READY TO REUNITE FOR WEEKS!
BAM
HOLD THAT EXPRESSION, YANA. I WANT TO MAKE THAT FACE OUR TWITTER AVATAR.
DON'T.

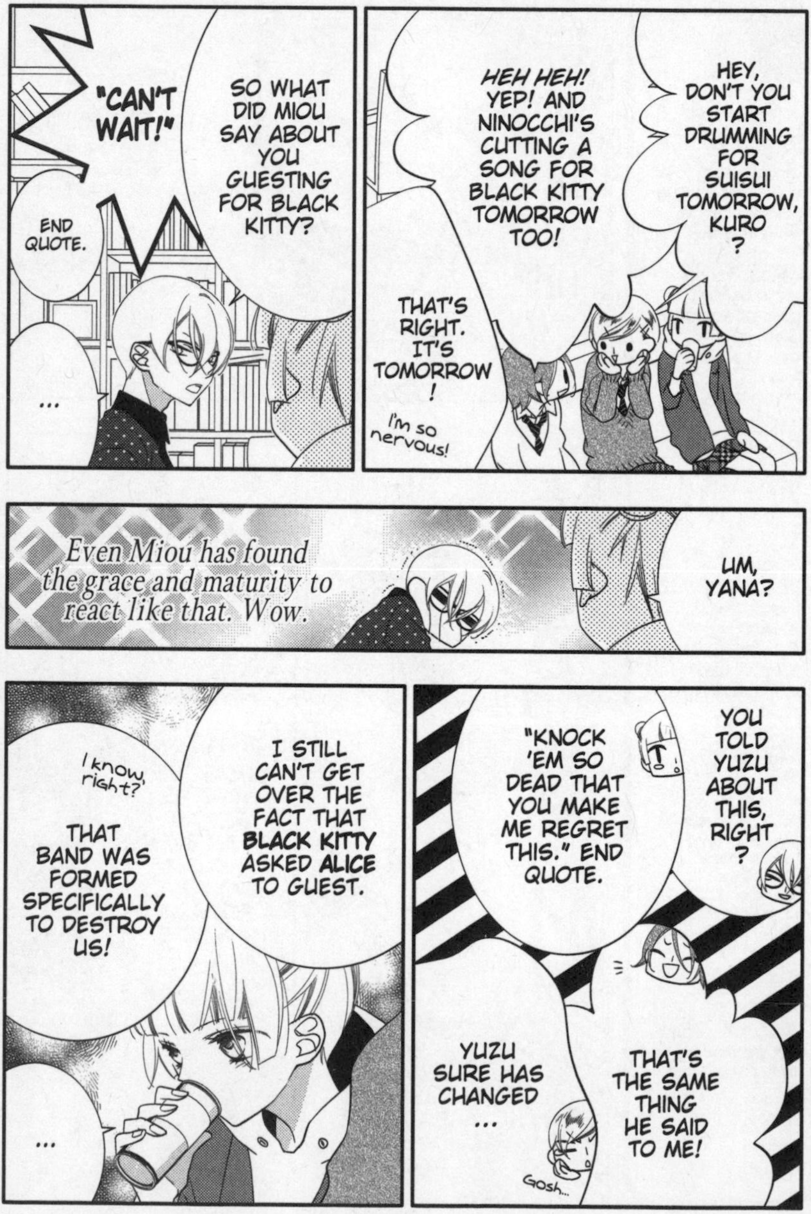
HEY, DON'T YOU START DRUMMING FOR SUISUI TOMORROW, KURO?
HEH HEH! YEP! AND NINOCCHI'S CUTTING A SONG FOR BLACK KITTY TOMORROW TOO!
THAT'S RIGHT. IT'S TOMORROW!
I'm so nervous!
SO WHAT DID MIOU SAY ABOUT YOU GUESTING FOR BLACK KITTY?
"CAN'T WAIT!"
END QUOTE.
...
UM, YANA?
Even Miou has found the grace and maturity to react like that. Wow.
YOU TOLD YUZU ABOUT THIS, RIGHT?
"KNOCK 'EM SO DEAD THAT YOU MAKE ME REGRET THIS." END QUOTE.
THAT'S THE SAME THING HE SAID TO ME!
YUZU SURE HAS CHANGED...
Gosh...
I STILL CAN'T GET OVER THE FACT THAT BLACK KITTY ASKED ALICE TO GUEST.
I know, right?
THAT BAND WAS FORMED SPECIFICALLY TO DESTROY US!
...

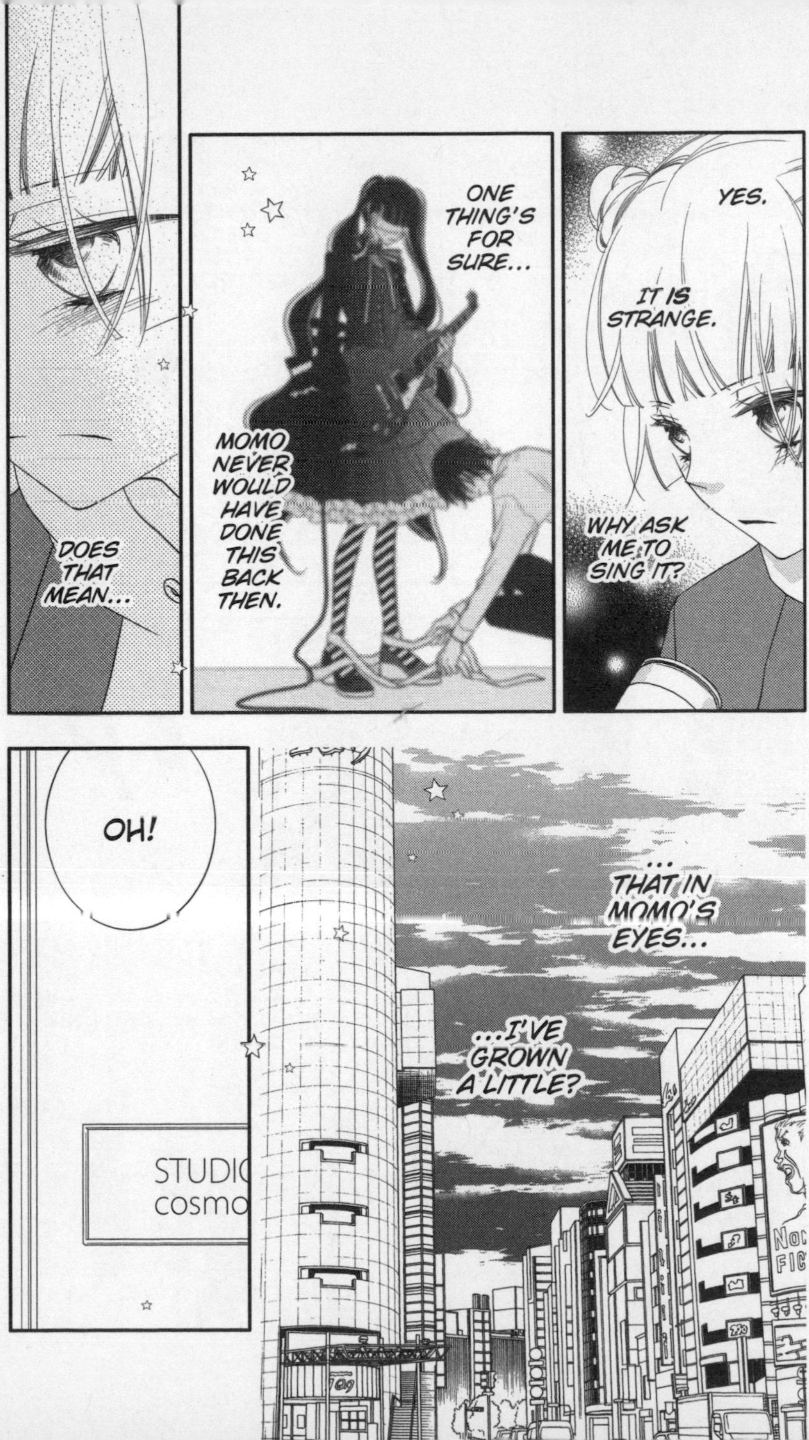
YES.
IT IS STRANGE.
WHY ASK ME TO SING IT?
ONE THING'S FOR SURE...
MOMO NEVER WOULD HAVE DONE THIS BACK THEN.
DOES THAT MEAN...
...THAT IN MOMO'S EYES...
...I'VE GROWN A LITTLE?
OH!

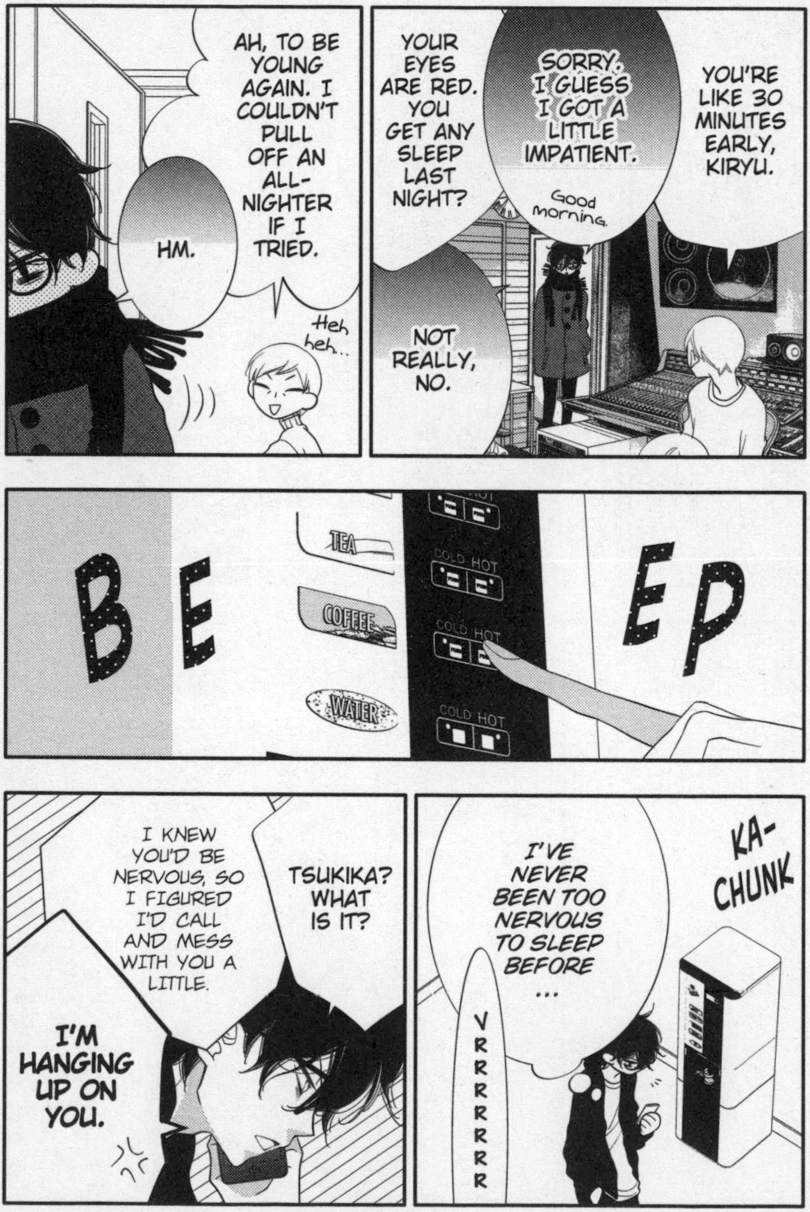
YOU'RE LIKE 30 MINUTES EARLY, KIRYU.
SORRY. I GUESS I GOT A LITTLE IMPATIENT.
Good morning.
YOUR EYES ARE RED. YOU GET ANY SLEEP LAST NIGHT?
NOT REALLY, NO.
AH, TO BE YOUNG AGAIN. I COULDN'T PULL OFF AN ALL-NIGHTER IF I TRIED.
Heh heh...
HM.
BEEP
TEA
COFFEE
WATER
COLD HOT
COLD HOT
COLD HOT
KA-CHUNK
I'VE NEVER BEEN TOO NERVOUS TO SLEEP BEFORE ...
VRRRRRRR
TSUKIKA? WHAT IS IT?
I KNEW YOU'D BE NERVOUS, SO I FIGURED I'D CALL AND MESS WITH YOU A LITTLE.
I'M HANGING UP ON YOU.

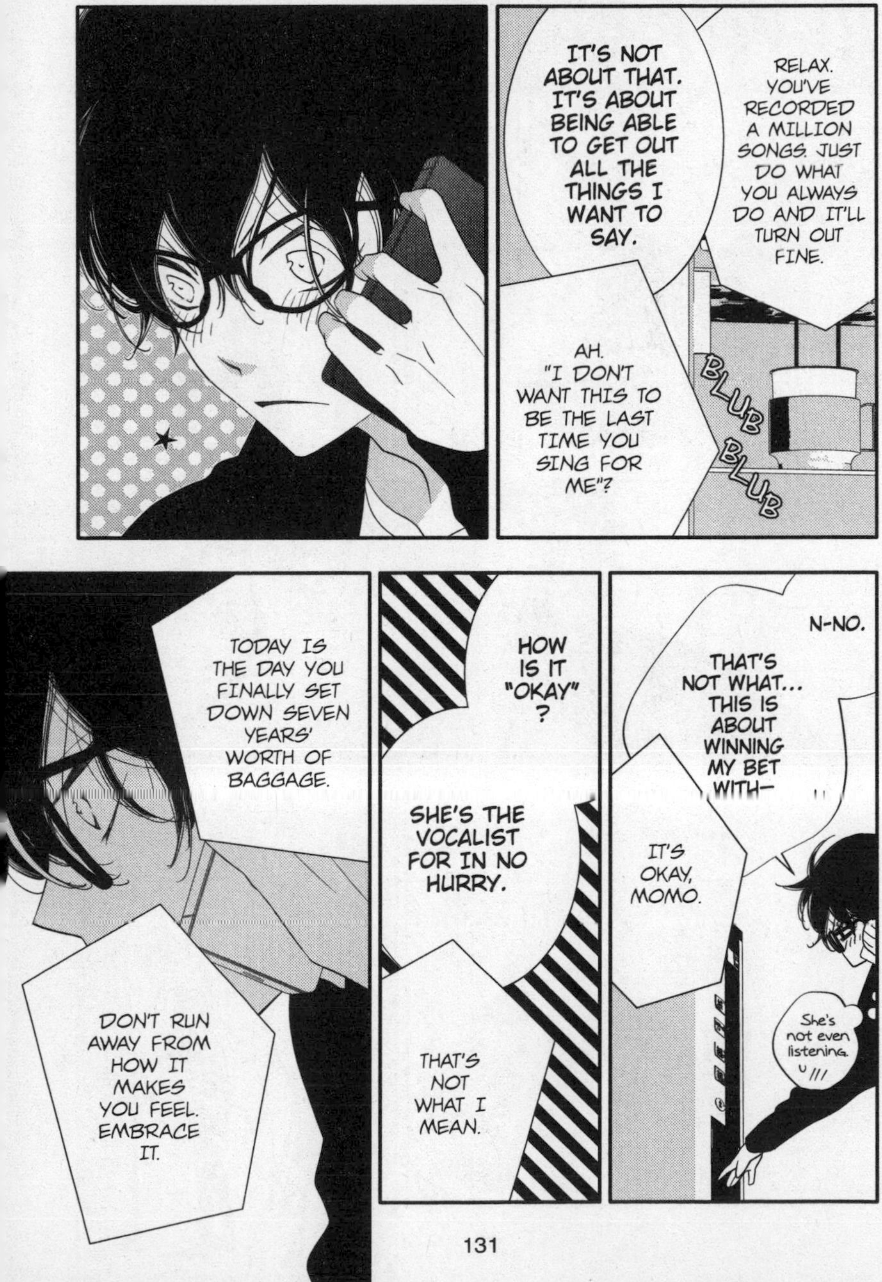
RELAX. YOU'VE RECORDED A MILLION SONGS. JUST DO WHAT YOU ALWAYS DO AND IT'LL TURN OUT FINE.
IT'S NOT ABOUT THAT. IT'S ABOUT BEING ABLE TO GET OUT ALL THE THINGS I WANT TO SAY.
AH. "I DON'T WANT THIS TO BE THE LAST TIME YOU SING FOR ME"?
BLUB BLUB
N-NO.
THAT'S NOT WHAT... THIS IS ABOUT WINNING MY BET WITH—
IT'S OKAY, MOMO.
She's not even listening.
HOW IS IT "OKAY"?
SHE'S THE VOCALIST FOR IN NO HURRY.
THAT'S NOT WHAT I MEAN.
TODAY IS THE DAY YOU FINALLY SET DOWN SEVEN YEARS' WORTH OF BAGGAGE.
DON'T RUN AWAY FROM HOW IT MAKES YOU FEEL. EMBRACE IT.

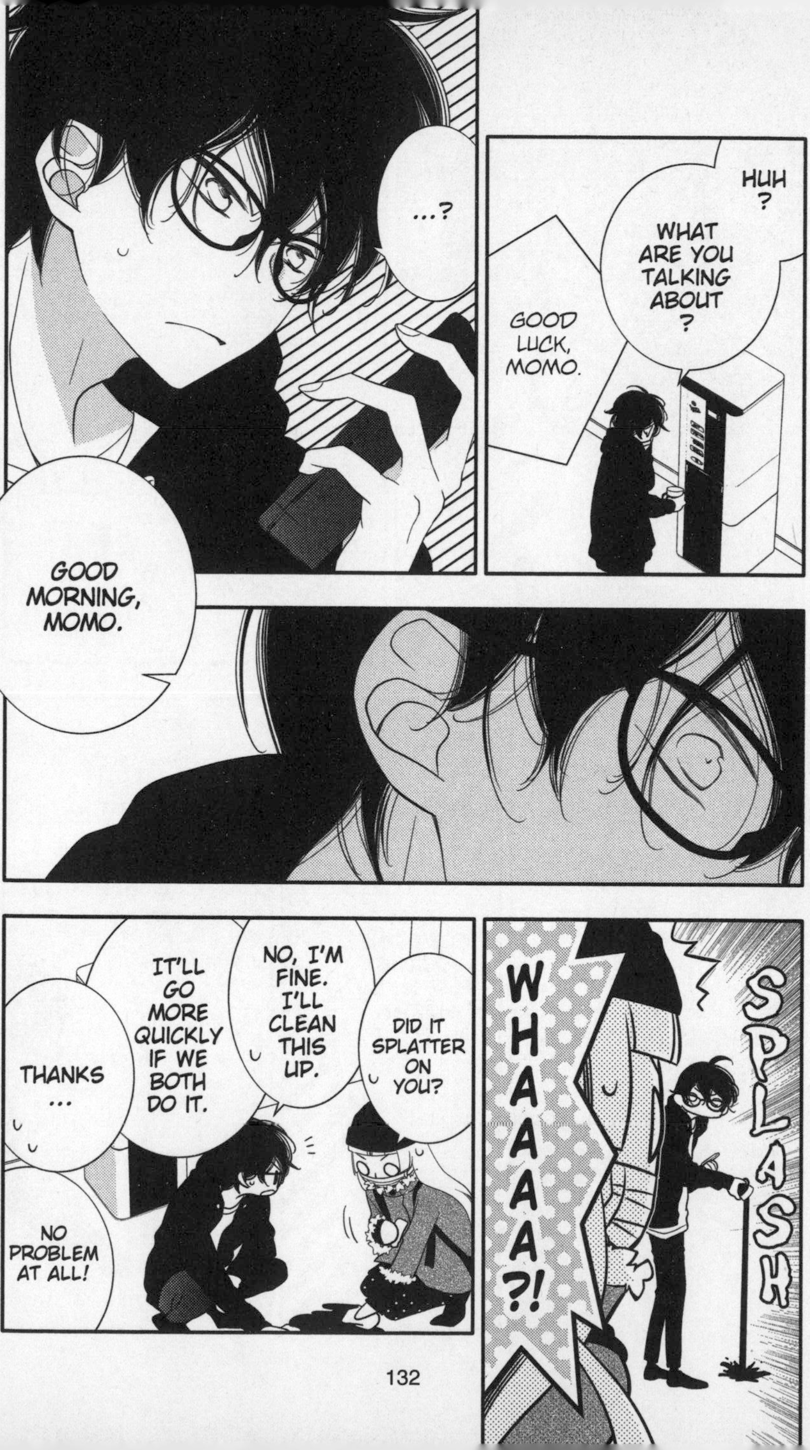

HUH?
WHAT ARE YOU TALKING ABOUT?
GOOD LUCK, MOMO.
...?
GOOD MORNING, MOMO.
SPLASH
WHAAAAA?!
DID IT SPLATTER ON YOU?
NO, I'M FINE. I'LL CLEAN THIS UP.
IT'LL GO MORE QUICKLY IF WE BOTH DO IT.
THANKS...
NO PROBLEM AT ALL!

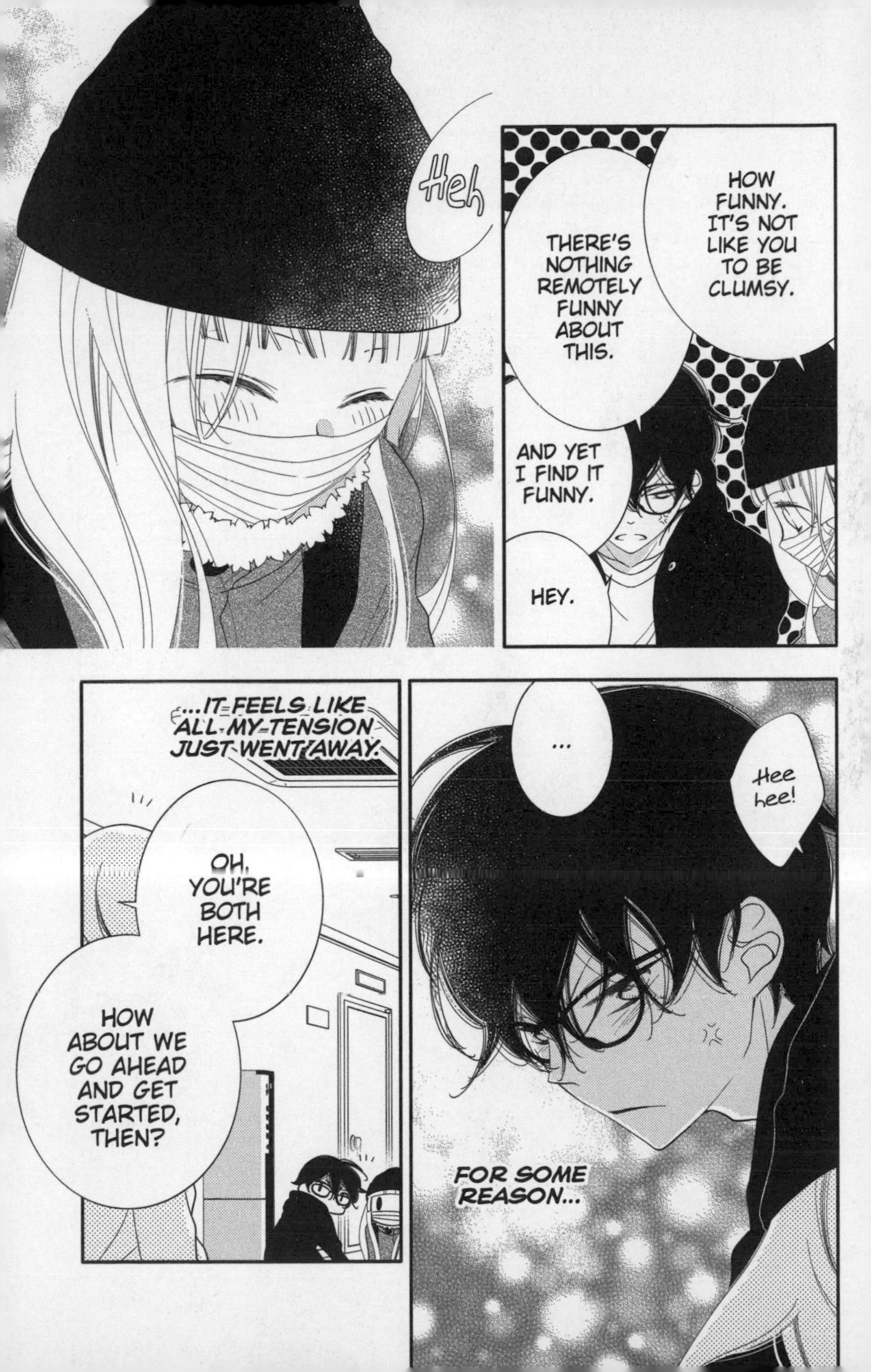
HOW FUNNY. IT'S NOT LIKE YOU TO BE CLUMSY.
THERE'S NOTHING REMOTELY FUNNY ABOUT THIS.
AND YET I FIND IT FUNNY.
HEY.
Heh
Hee hee!
...
FOR SOME REASON...
...IT FEELS LIKE ALL MY TENSION JUST WENT AWAY.
OH, YOU'RE BOTH HERE.
HOW ABOUT WE GO AHEAD AND GET STARTED, THEN?

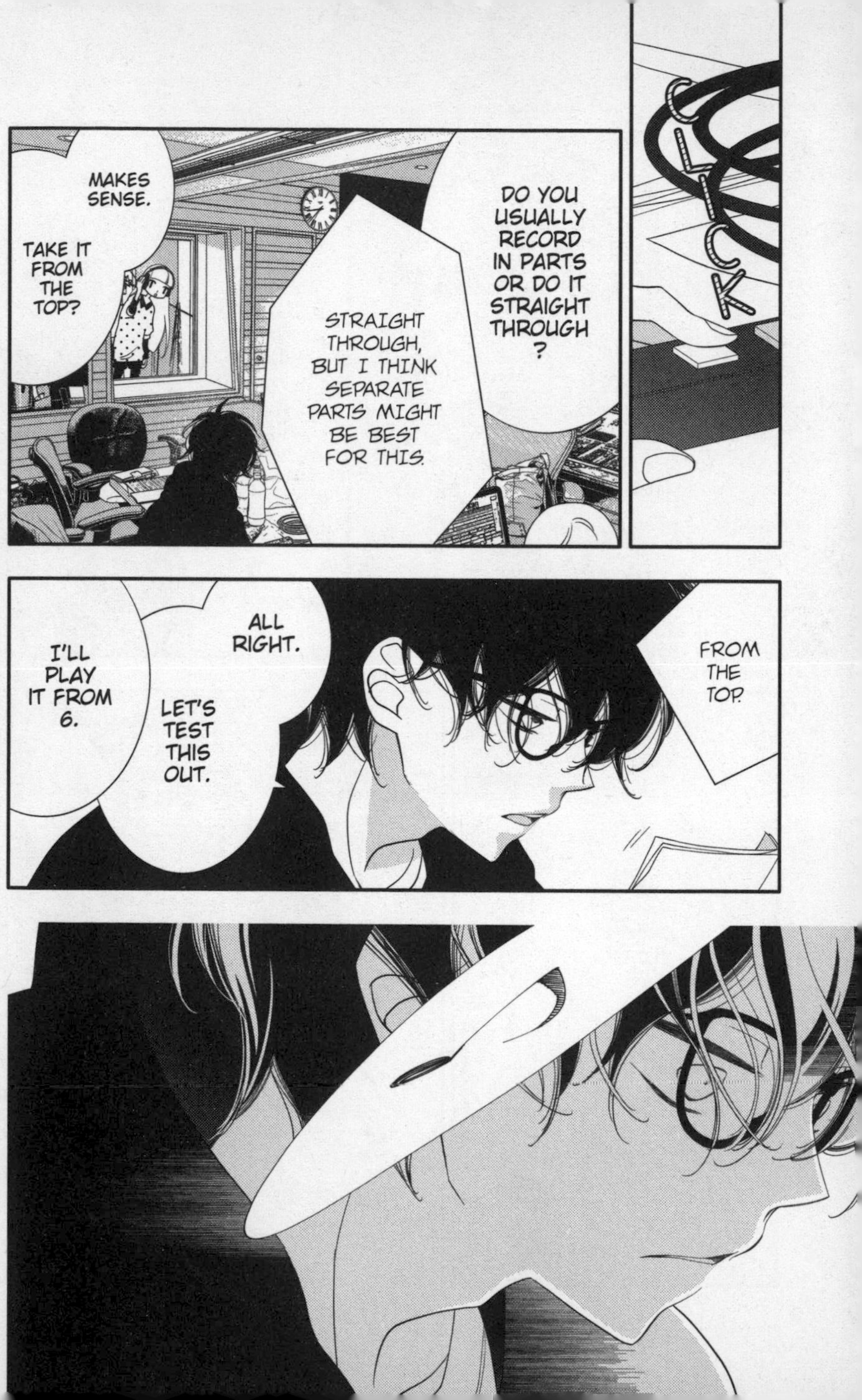
CLICK
DO YOU USUALLY RECORD IN PARTS OR DO IT STRAIGHT THROUGH?
STRAIGHT THROUGH, BUT I THINK SEPARATE PARTS MIGHT BE BEST FOR THIS.
MAKES SENSE.
TAKE IT FROM THE TOP?
FROM THE TOP.
ALL RIGHT.
LET'S TEST THIS OUT.
I'LL PLAY IT FROM 6.

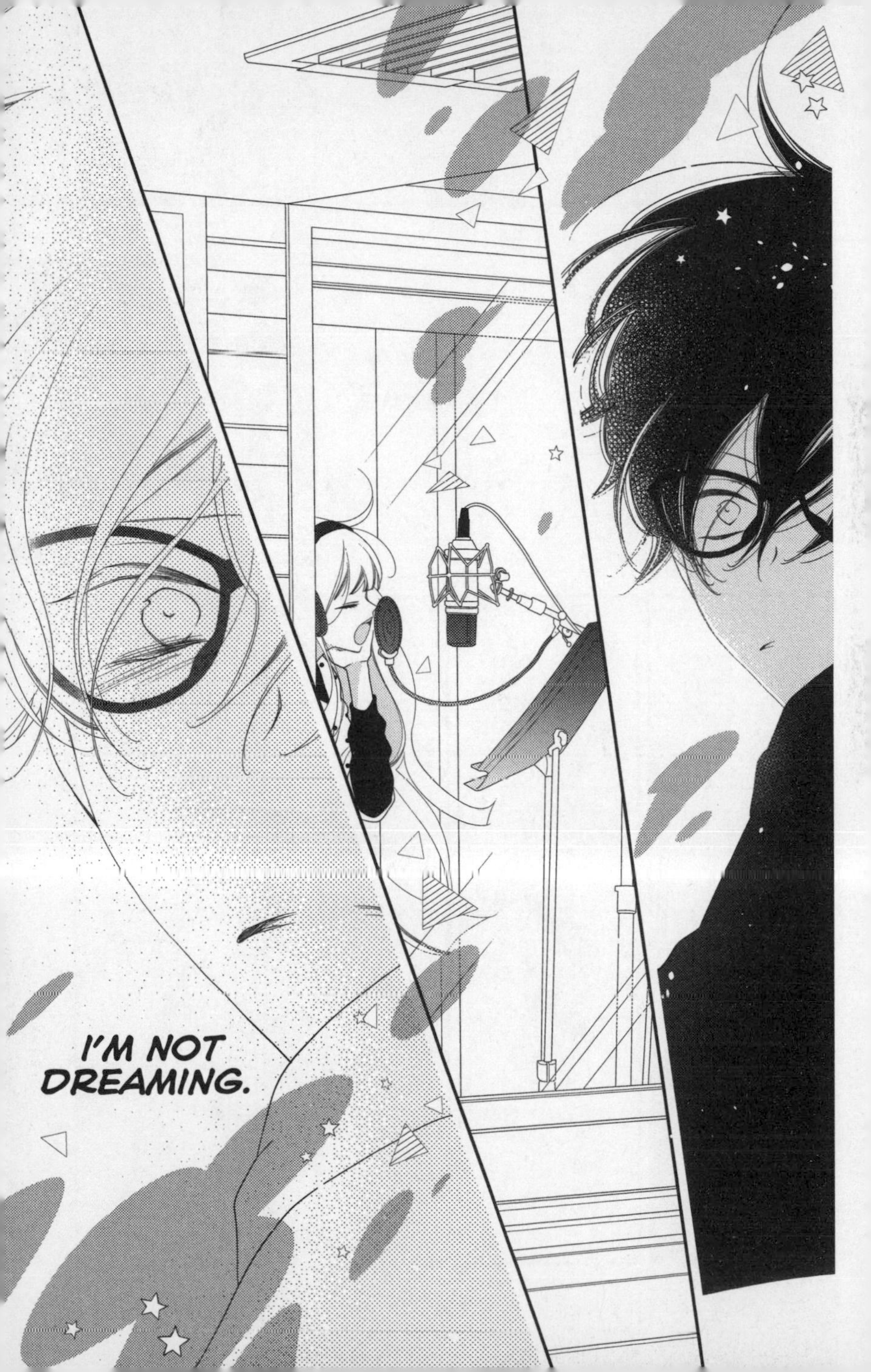
I'M NOT DREAMING.

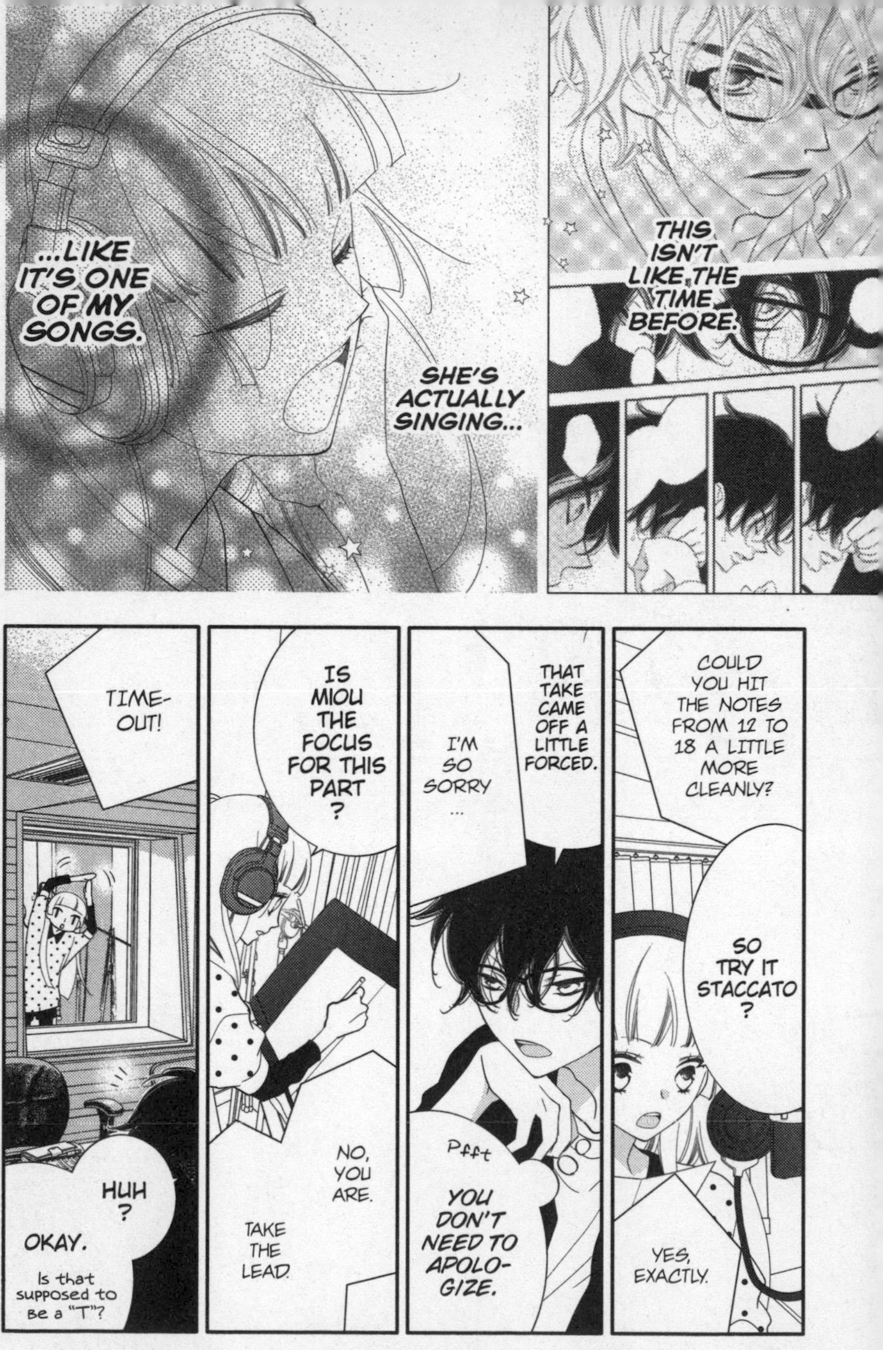
THIS ISN'T LIKE THE TIME BEFORE.
SHE'S ACTUALLY SINGING...
...LIKE IT'S ONE OF MY SONGS.
COULD YOU HIT THE NOTES FROM 12 TO 18 A LITTLE MORE CLEANLY?
SO TRY IT STACCATO?
YES, EXACTLY.
THAT TAKE CAME OFF A LITTLE FORCED.
I'M SO SORRY...
Pfft
YOU DON'T NEED TO APOLO-GIZE.
IS MIOU THE FOCUS FOR THIS PART?
NO, YOU ARE.
TAKE THE LEAD.
TIME-OUT!
HUH?
OKAY.
Is that supposed to be a "T"?

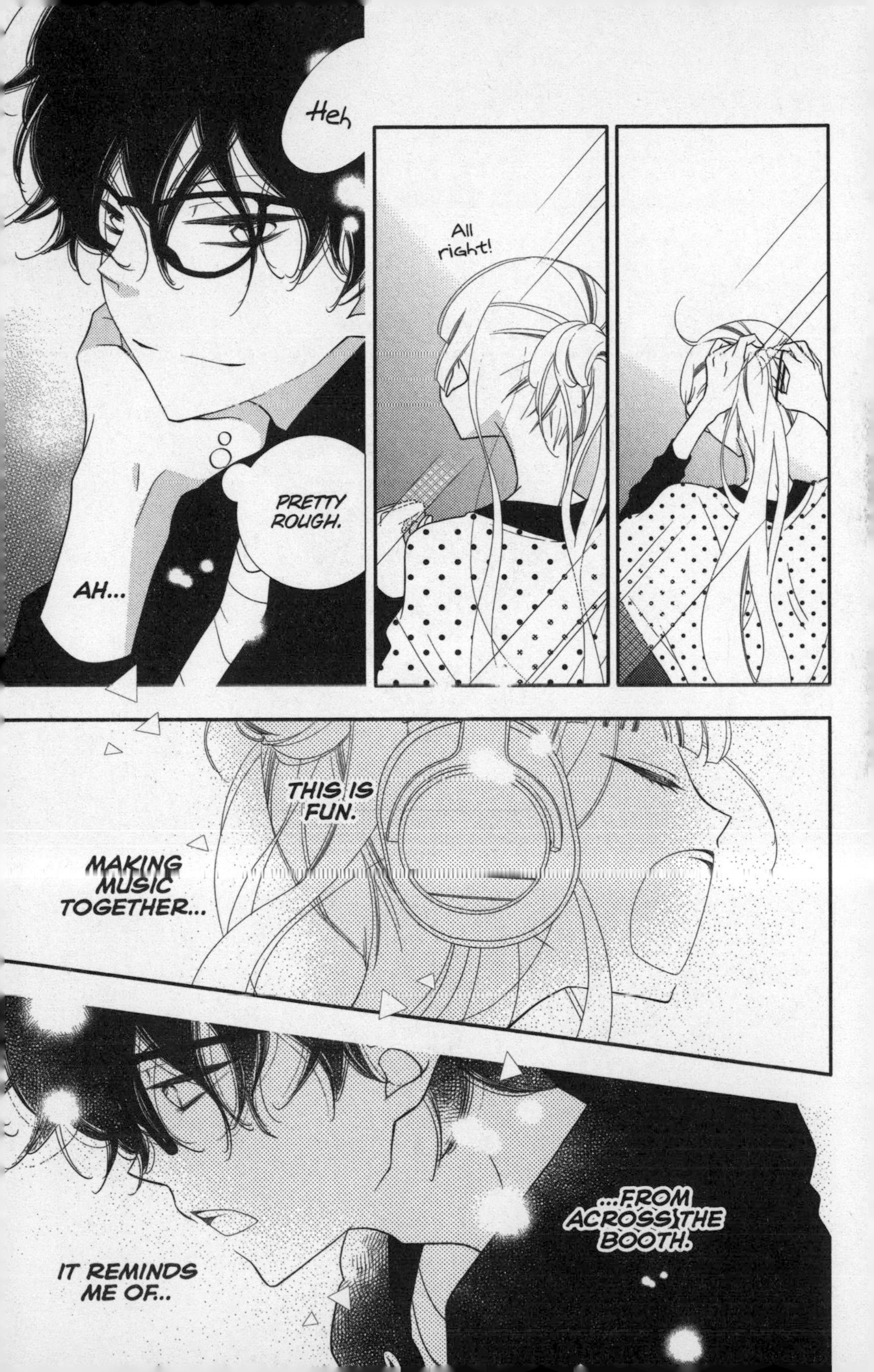
All right!
Heh
PRETTY ROUGH.
AH...
THIS IS FUN.
MAKING MUSIC TOGETHER...
...FROM ACROSS THE BOOTH.
IT REMINDS ME OF...

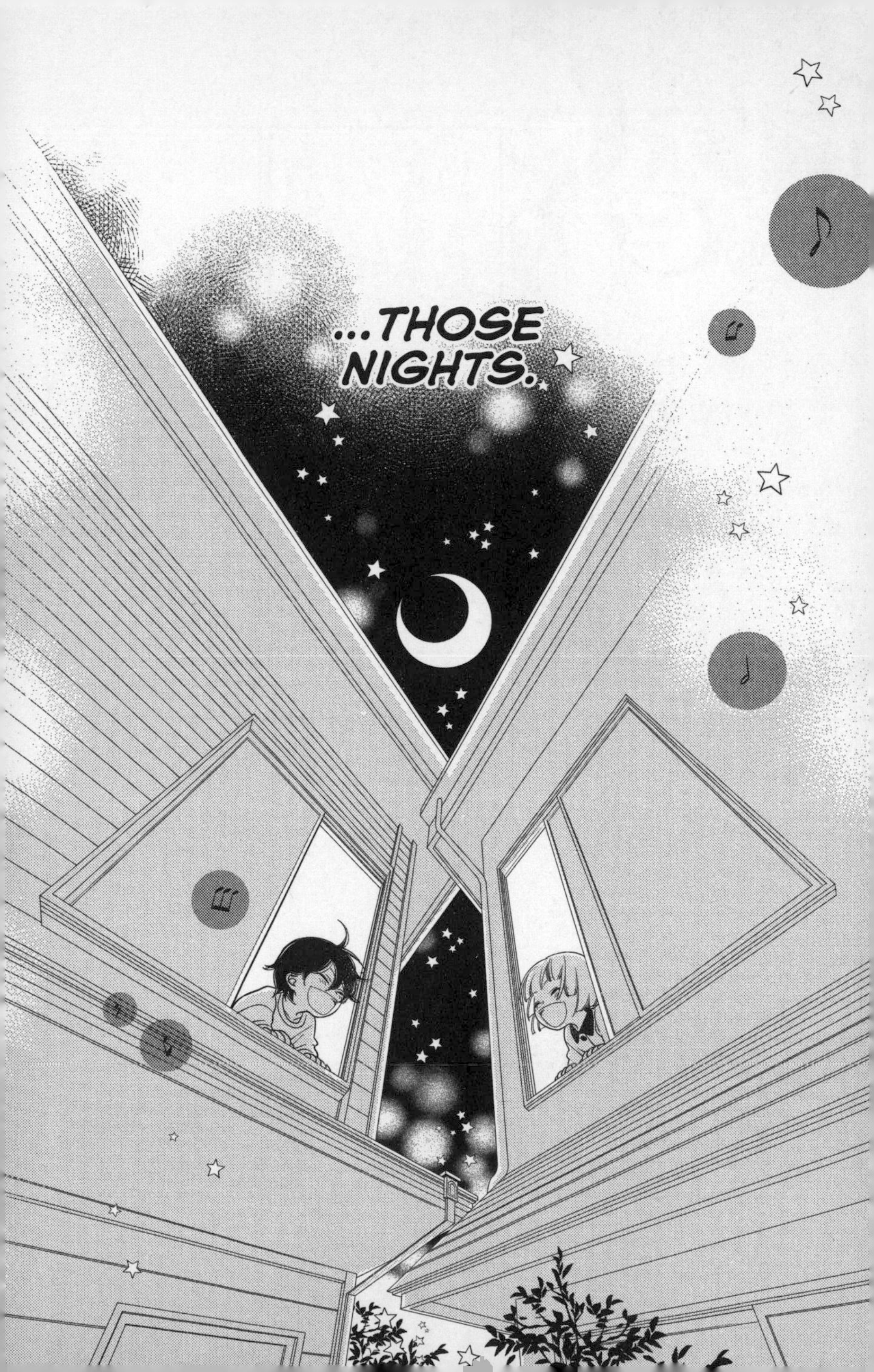
...THOSE NIGHTS.

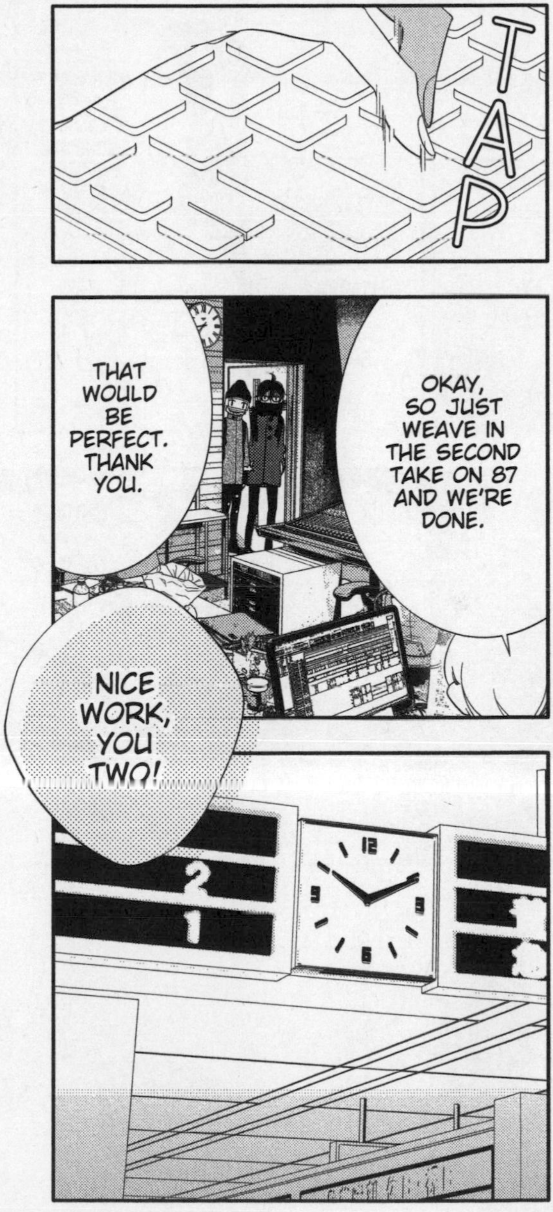
TAP
OKAY, SO JUST WEAVE IN THE SECOND TAKE ON 87 AND WE'RE DONE.
THAT WOULD BE PERFECT. THANK YOU.
NICE WORK, YOU TWO!
2
1

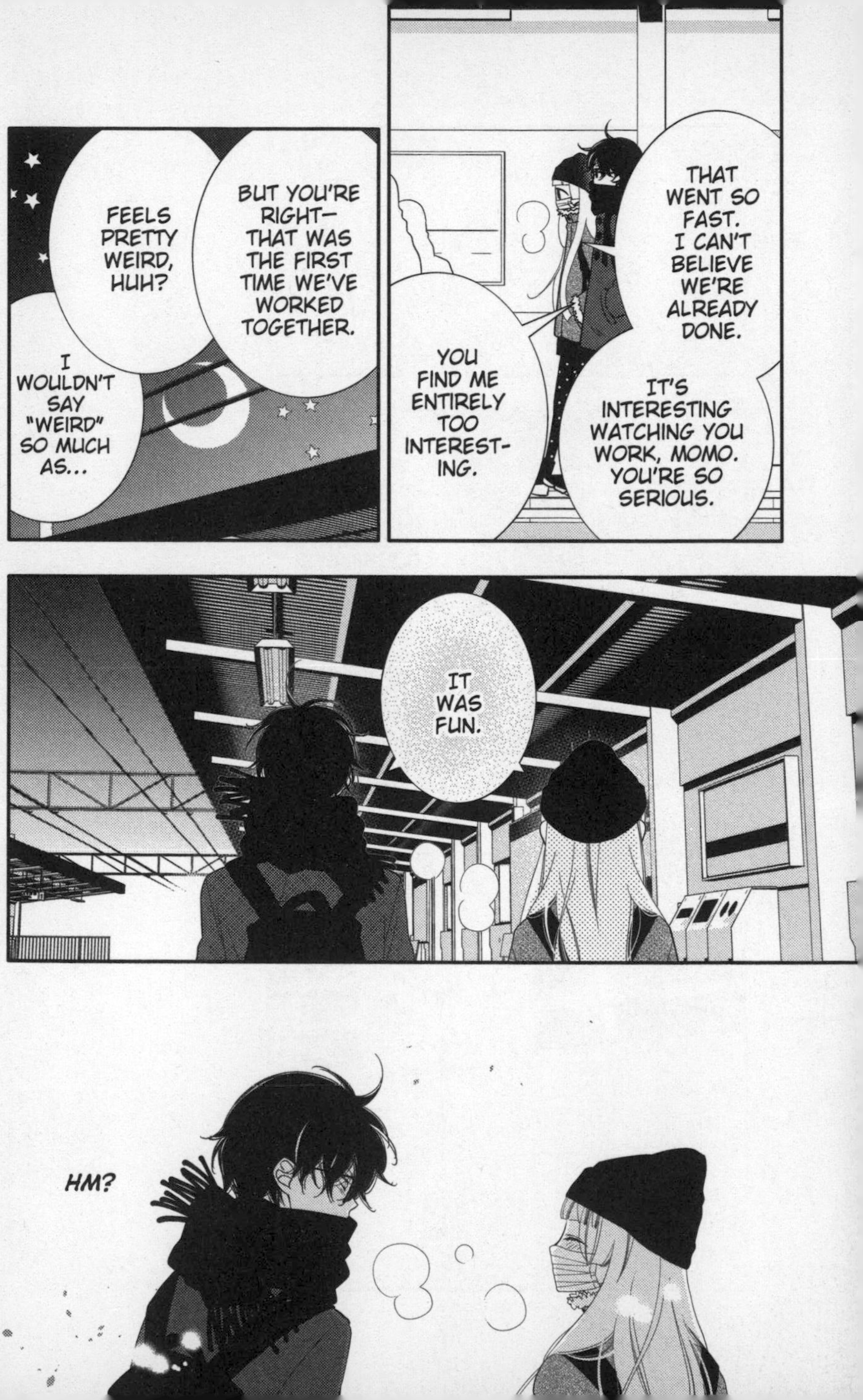
THAT WENT SO FAST. I CAN'T BELIEVE WE'RE ALREADY DONE.
IT'S INTERESTING WATCHING YOU WORK, MOMO. YOU'RE SO SERIOUS.
YOU FIND ME ENTIRELY TOO INTEREST-ING.
FEELS PRETTY WEIRD, HUH?
I WOULDN'T SAY "WEIRD" SO MUCH AS...
BUT YOU'RE RIGHT—THAT WAS THE FIRST TIME WE'VE WORKED TOGETHER.
IT WAS FUN.
HM?

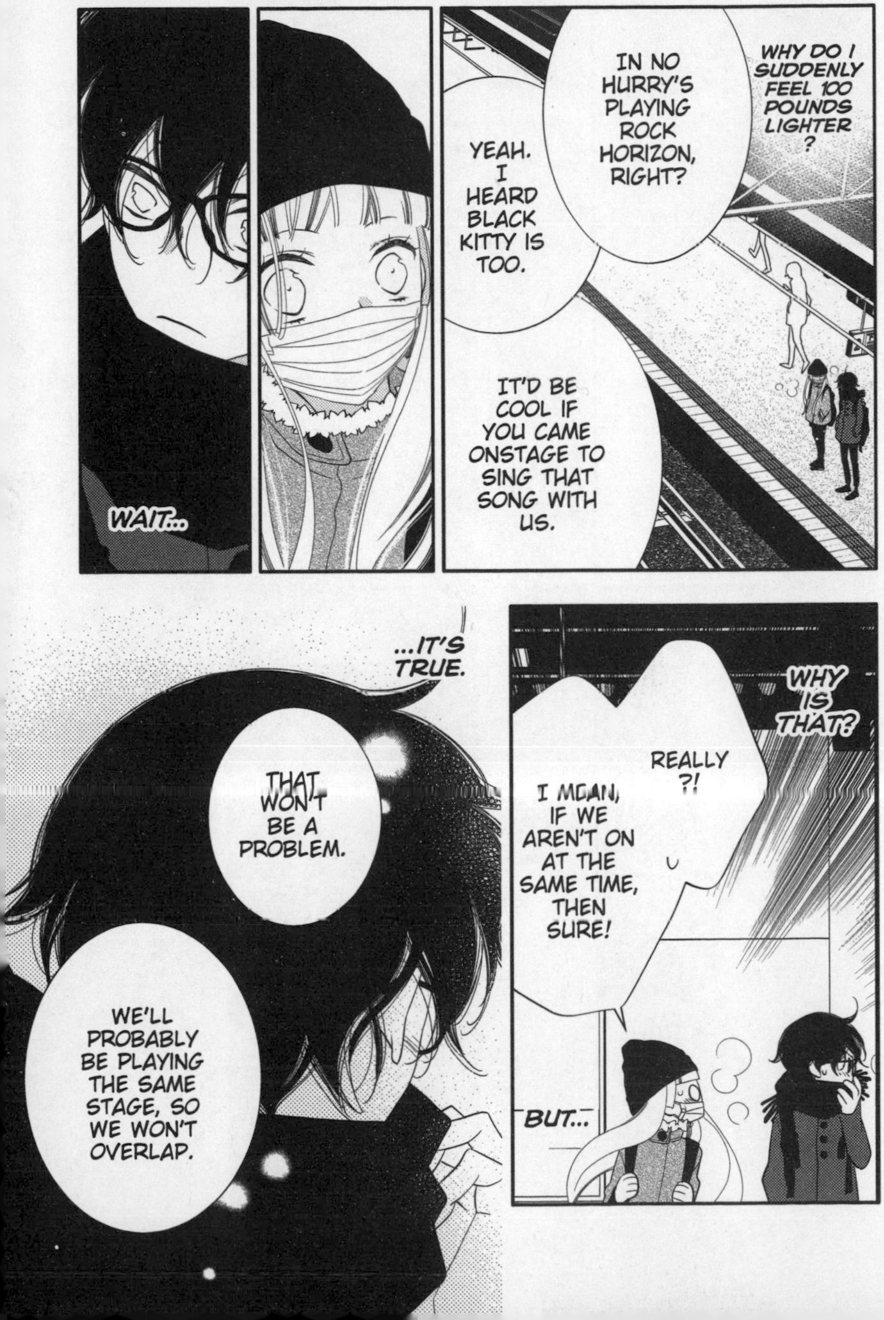
WHY DO I SUDDENLY FEEL 100 POUNDS LIGHTER?
IN NO HURRY'S PLAYING ROCK HORIZON, RIGHT?
YEAH. I HEARD BLACK KITTY IS TOO.
IT'D BE COOL IF YOU CAME ONSTAGE TO SING THAT SONG WITH US.
WAIT...
WHY IS THAT?
REALLY?!
I MEAN, IF WE AREN'T ON AT THE SAME TIME, THEN SURE!
BUT...
...IT'S TRUE.
THAT WON'T BE A PROBLEM.
WE'LL PROBABLY BE PLAYING THE SAME STAGE, SO WE WON'T OVERLAP.

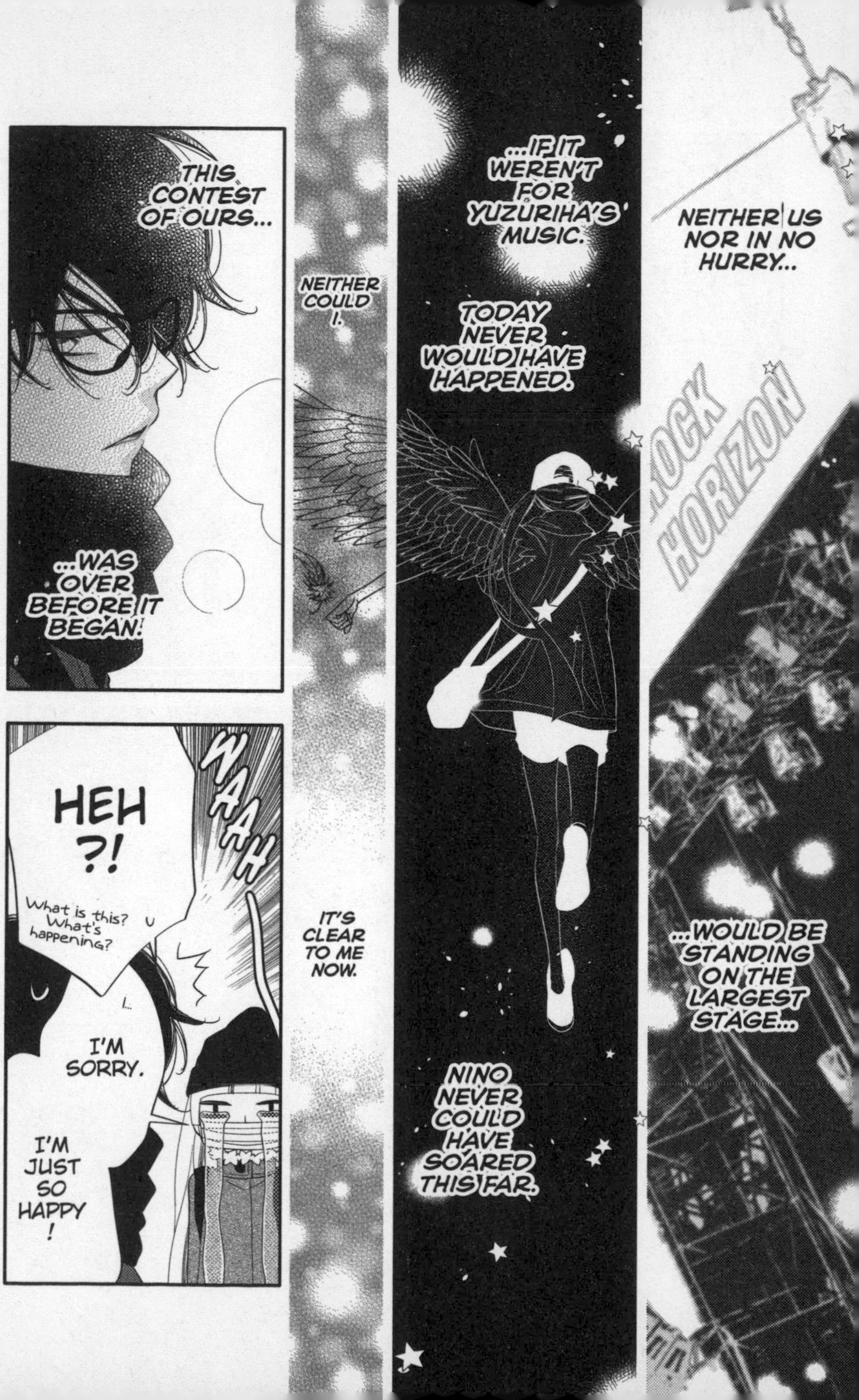
NEITHER US NOR IN NO HURRY...
ROCK HORIZON
...WOULD BE STANDING ON THE LARGEST STAGE...
...IF IT WEREN'T FOR YUZURIHA'S MUSIC.
TODAY NEVER WOULD HAVE HAPPENED.
NINO NEVER COULD HAVE SOARED THIS FAR.
NEITHER COULD I.
IT'S CLEAR TO ME NOW.
THIS CONTEST OF OURS...
...WAS OVER BEFORE IT BEGAN.
WAAAH
HEH ?!
What is this? What's happening?
I...
I'M SORRY.
I'M JUST SO HAPPY!

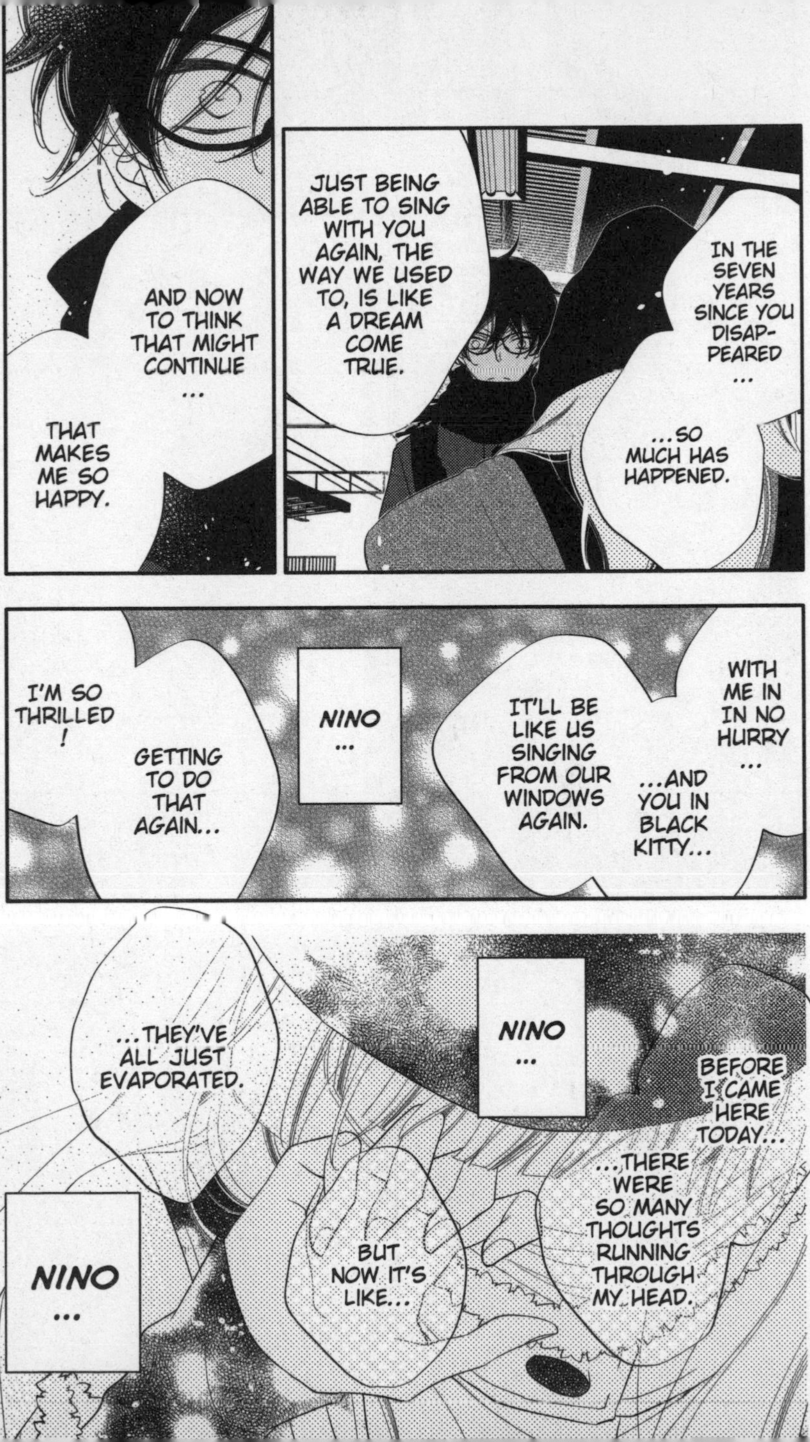
IN THE SEVEN YEARS SINCE YOU DISAPPEARED...
...SO MUCH HAS HAPPENED.
JUST BEING ABLE TO SING WITH YOU AGAIN, THE WAY WE USED TO, IS LIKE A DREAM COME TRUE.
AND NOW TO THINK THAT MIGHT CONTINUE...
THAT MAKES ME SO HAPPY.
WITH ME IN IN NO HURRY...
...AND YOU IN BLACK KITTY...
IT'LL BE LIKE US SINGING FROM OUR WINDOWS AGAIN.
NINO...
GETTING TO DO THAT AGAIN...
I'M SO THRILLED!
NINO...
BEFORE I CAME HERE TODAY...
...THERE WERE SO MANY THOUGHTS RUNNING THROUGH MY HEAD.
BUT NOW IT'S LIKE...
...THEY'VE ALL JUST EVAPORATED.
NINO...

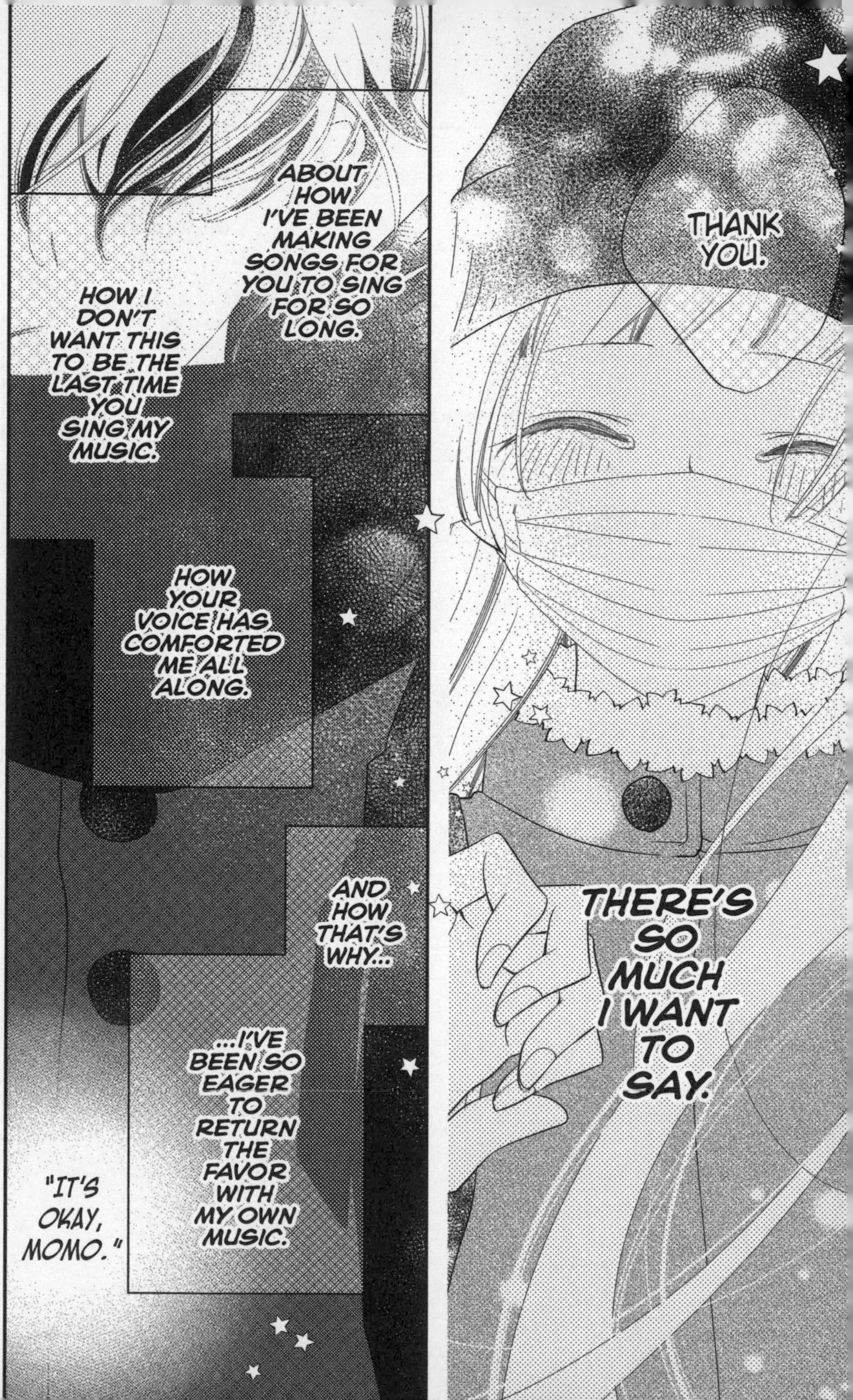
THANK YOU.
THERE'S SO MUCH I WANT TO SAY.
ABOUT HOW I'VE BEEN MAKING SONGS FOR YOU TO SING FOR SO LONG.
HOW I DON'T WANT THIS TO BE THE LAST TIME YOU SING MY MUSIC.
HOW YOUR VOICE HAS COMFORTED ME ALL ALONG.
AND HOW THAT'S WHY...
...I'VE BEEN SO EAGER TO RETURN THE FAVOR WITH MY OWN MUSIC.
"IT'S OKAY, MOMO."

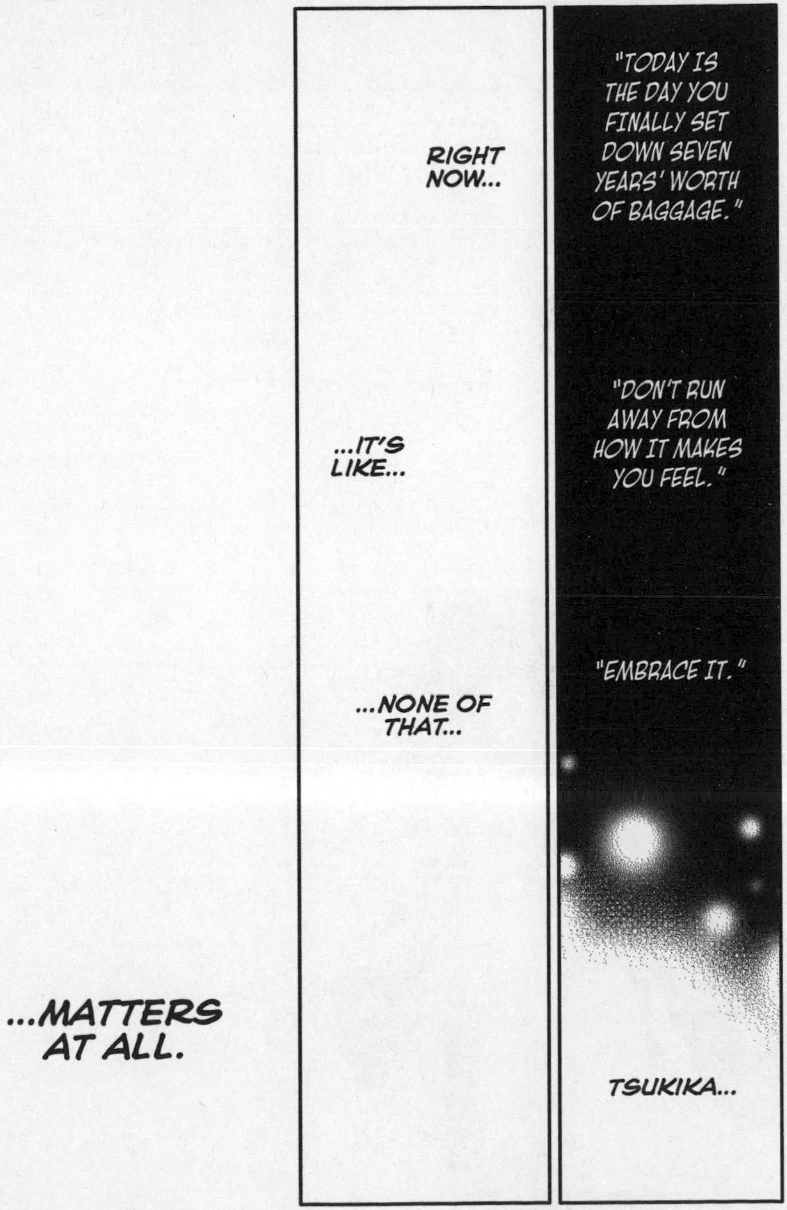
"TODAY IS THE DAY YOU FINALLY SET DOWN SEVEN YEARS' WORTH OF BAGGAGE."
"DON'T RUN AWAY FROM HOW IT MAKES YOU FEEL."
"EMBRACE IT."
TSUKIKA...
RIGHT NOW...
...IT'S LIKE...
...NONE OF THAT...
...MATTERS AT ALL.

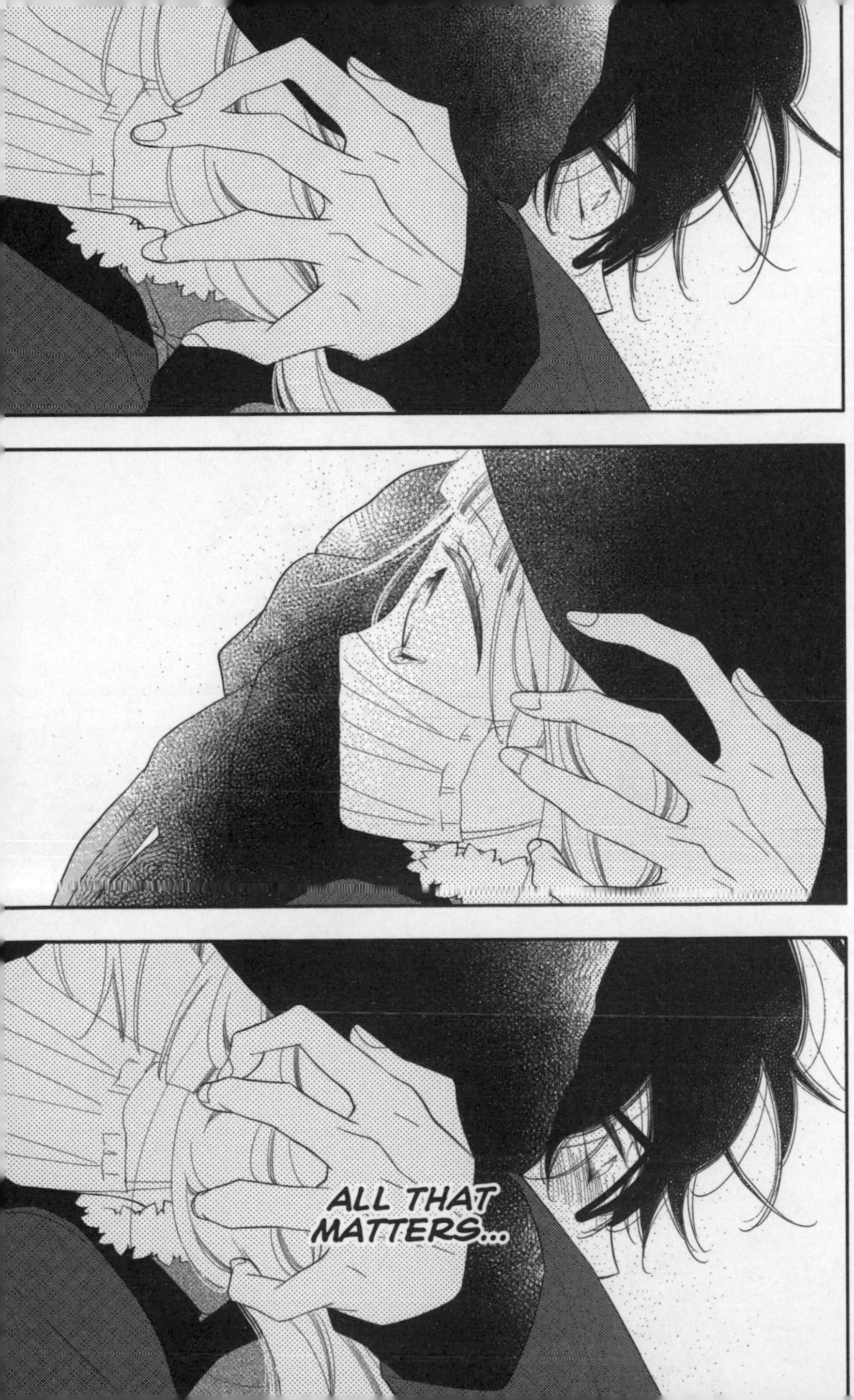
ALL THAT
MATTERS...

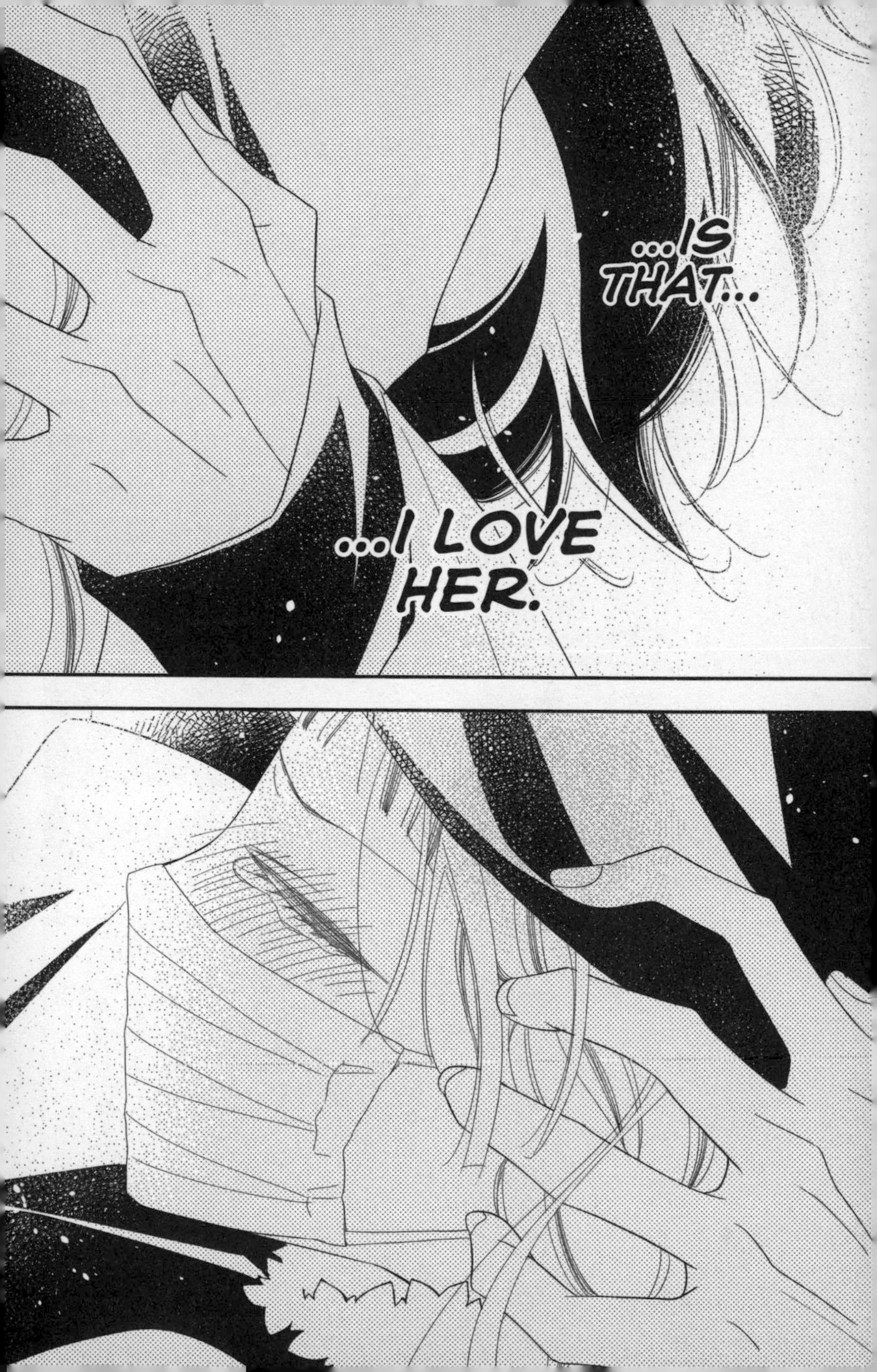
...IS THAT...
...I LOVE HER.

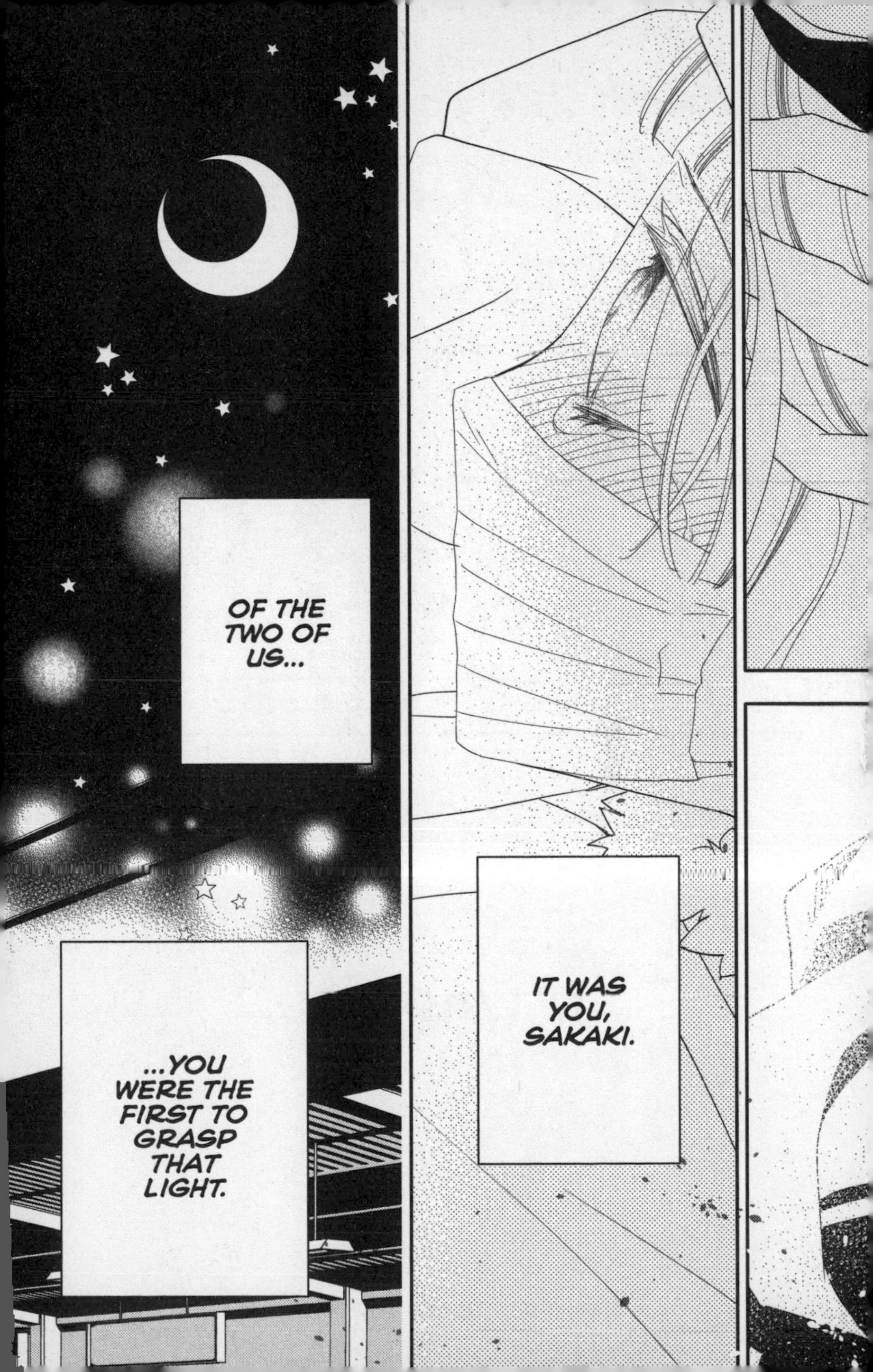
IT WAS YOU, SAKAKI.
OF THE TWO OF US...
...YOU WERE THE FIRST TO GRASP THAT LIGHT.

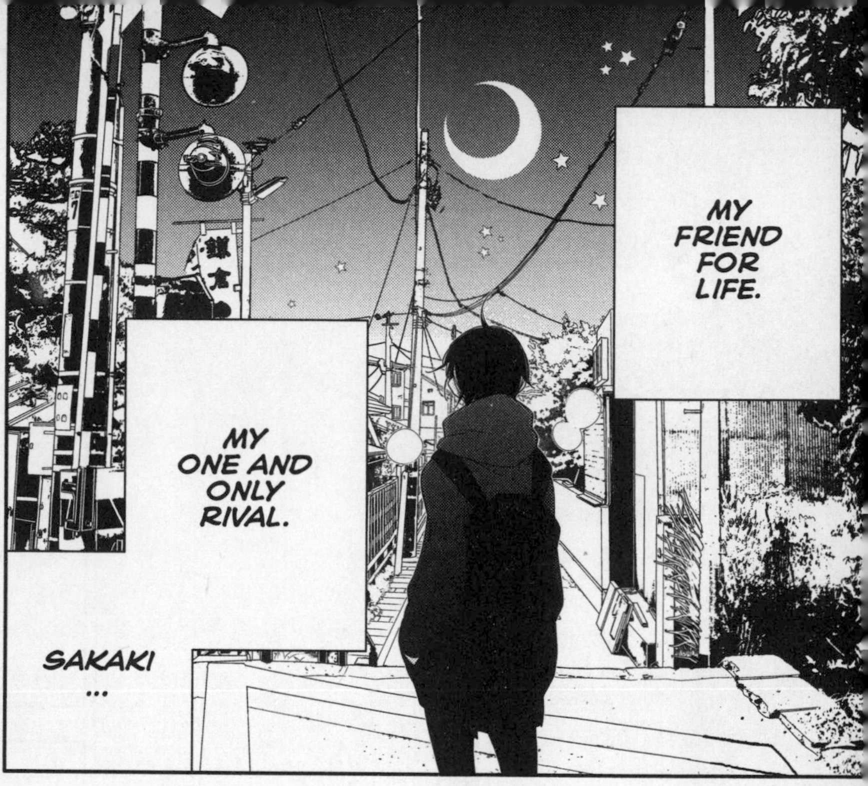
MY FRIEND FOR LIFE.
MY ONE AND ONLY RIVAL.
SAKAKI ...

IT WAS YOU.

ANONYMOUS NOISE ⑰ / THE END

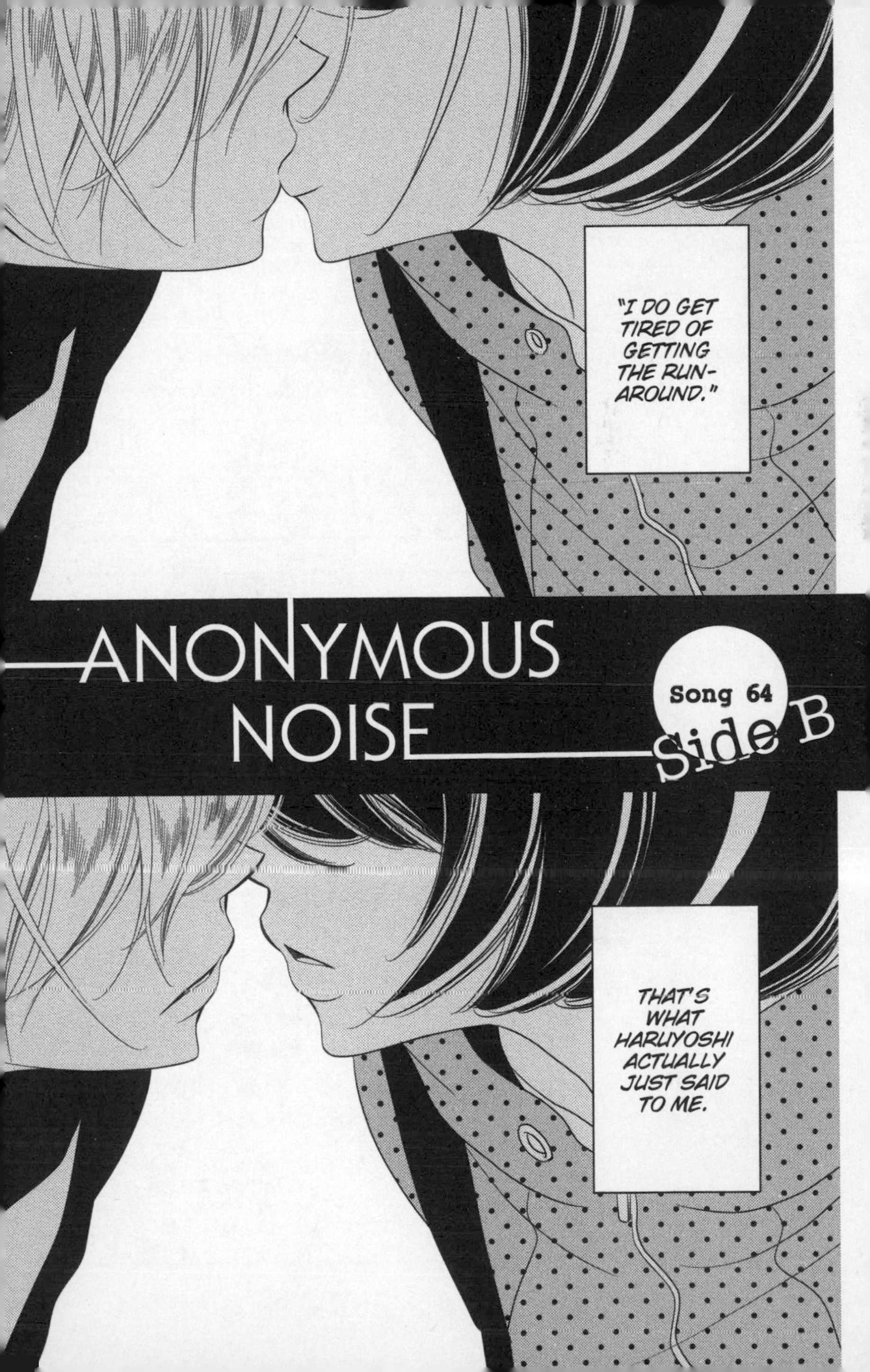
"I DO GET TIRED OF GETTING THE RUN-AROUND."
ANONYMOUS NOISE
Song 64
Side B
THAT'S WHAT HARUYOSHI ACTUALLY JUST SAID TO ME.

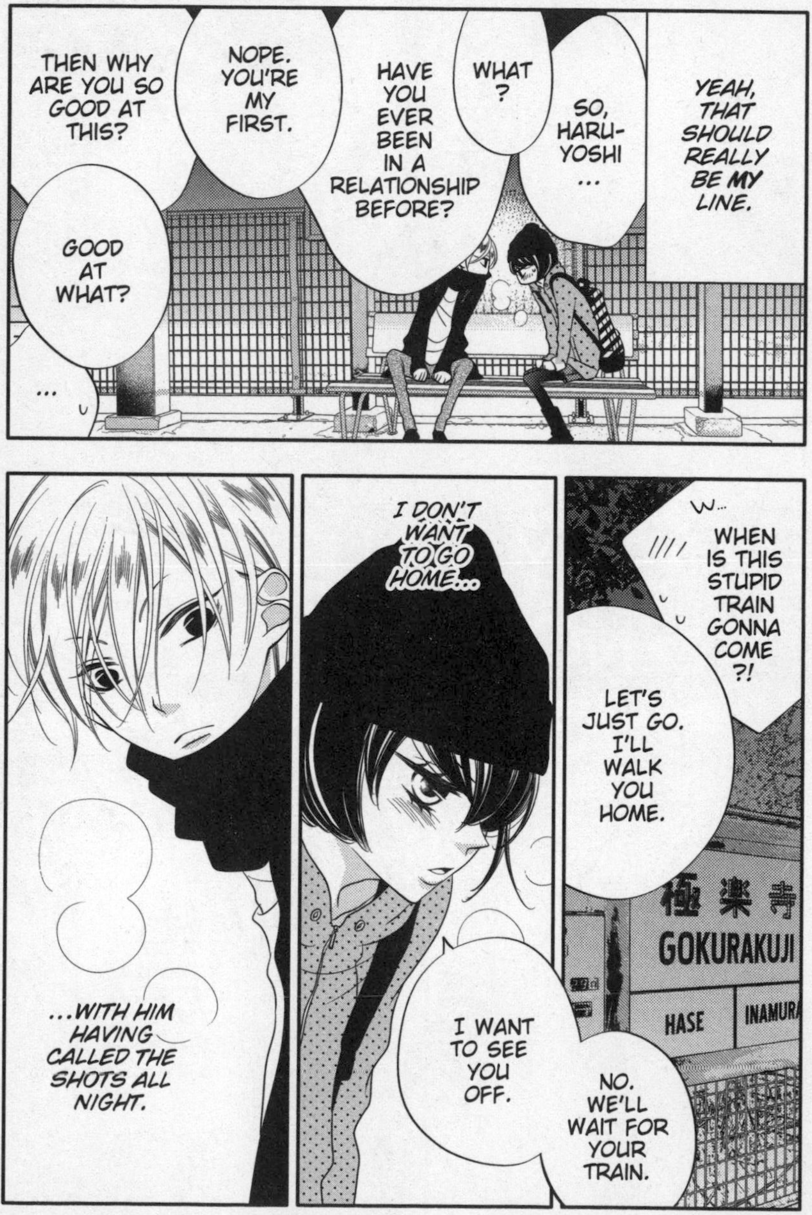
YEAH, THAT SHOULD REALLY BE MY LINE.
SO, HARU-YOSHI…
WHAT?
HAVE YOU EVER BEEN IN A RELATIONSHIP BEFORE?
NOPE. YOU'RE MY FIRST.
THEN WHY ARE YOU SO GOOD AT THIS?
GOOD AT WHAT?
…
W…
WHEN IS THIS STUPID TRAIN GONNA COME?!
LET'S JUST GO. I'LL WALK YOU HOME.
極楽寺
GOKURAKUJI
HASE
INAMURA
NO. WE'LL WAIT FOR YOUR TRAIN.
I DON'T WANT TO GO HOME…
I WANT TO SEE YOU OFF.
…WITH HIM HAVING CALLED THE SHOTS ALL NIGHT.

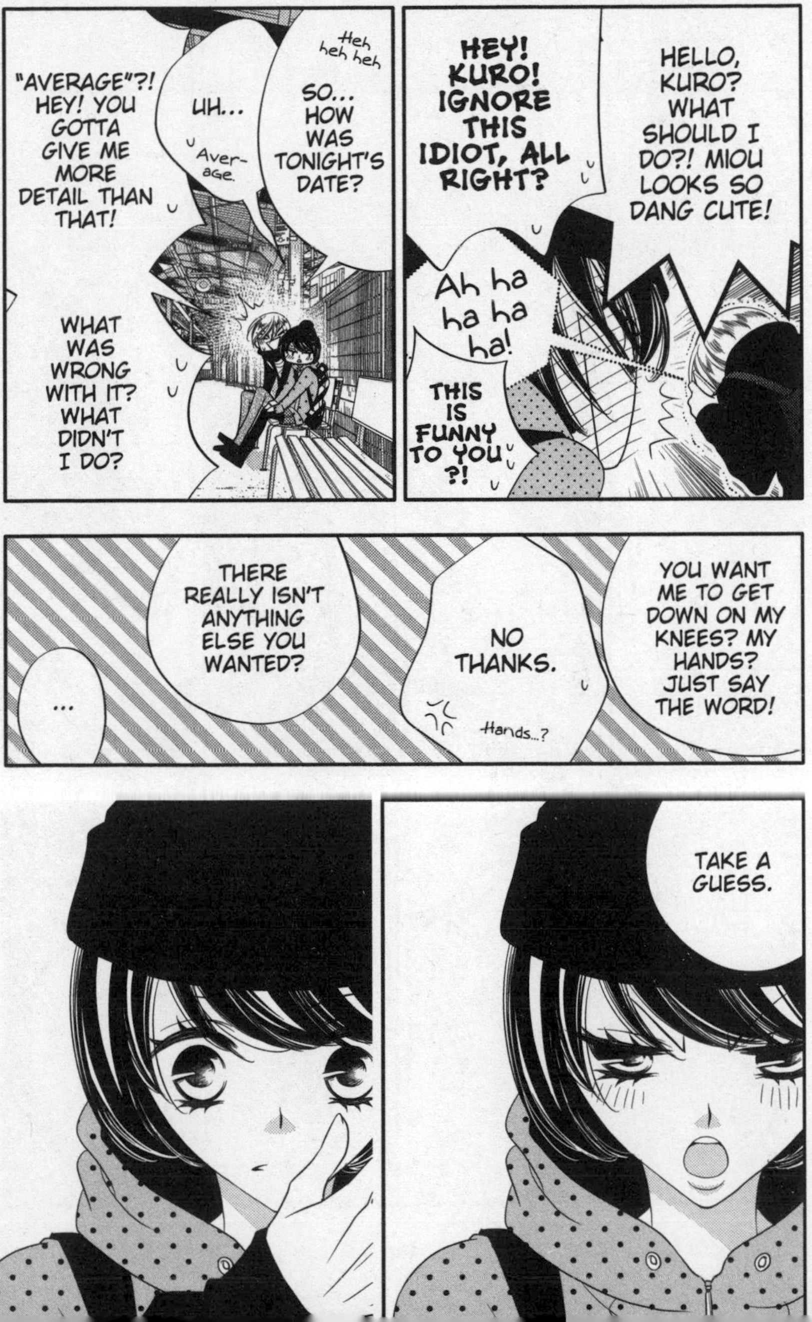
HELLO, KURO? WHAT SHOULD I DO?! MIOU LOOKS SO DANG CUTE!
HEY! KURO! IGNORE THIS IDIOT, ALL RIGHT?
Ah ha ha ha ha!
THIS IS FUNNY TO YOU?!
Heh heh heh
SO... HOW WAS TONIGHT'S DATE?
UH...
Aver-age.
"AVERAGE"?! HEY! YOU GOTTA GIVE ME MORE DETAIL THAN THAT!
WHAT WAS WRONG WITH IT? WHAT DIDN'T I DO?
YOU WANT ME TO GET DOWN ON MY KNEES? MY HANDS? JUST SAY THE WORD!
NO THANKS.
Hands...?
THERE REALLY ISN'T ANYTHING ELSE YOU WANTED?
...
TAKE A GUESS.

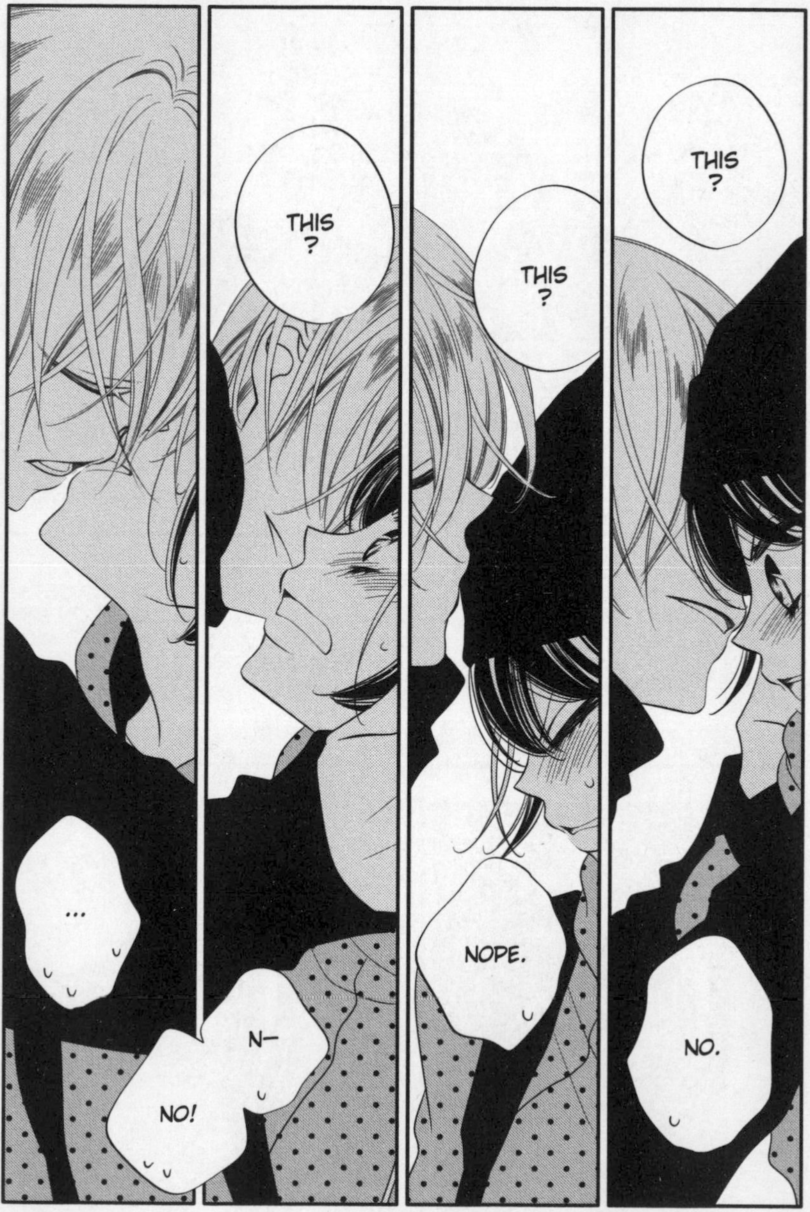
THIS ?
NO.
THIS ?
NOPE.
THIS ?
N—
NO!
...

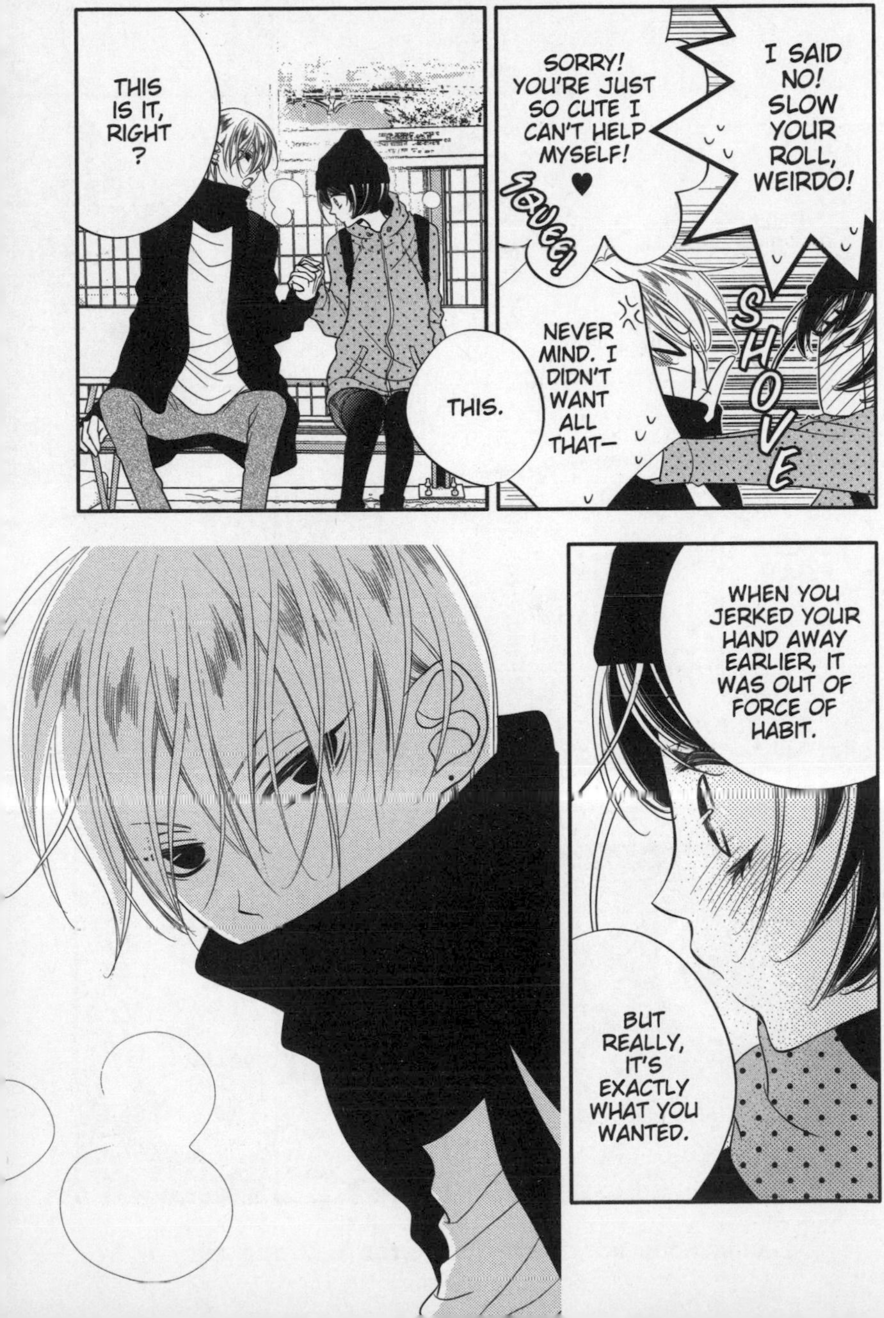
I SAID NO! SLOW YOUR ROLL, WEIRDO!
SORRY! YOU'RE JUST SO CUTE I CAN'T HELP MYSELF! ♥
SQUEE!
SHOVE
NEVER MIND. I DIDN'T WANT ALL THAT—
THIS.
THIS IS IT, RIGHT?
WHEN YOU JERKED YOUR HAND AWAY EARLIER, IT WAS OUT OF FORCE OF HABIT.
BUT REALLY, IT'S EXACTLY WHAT YOU WANTED.

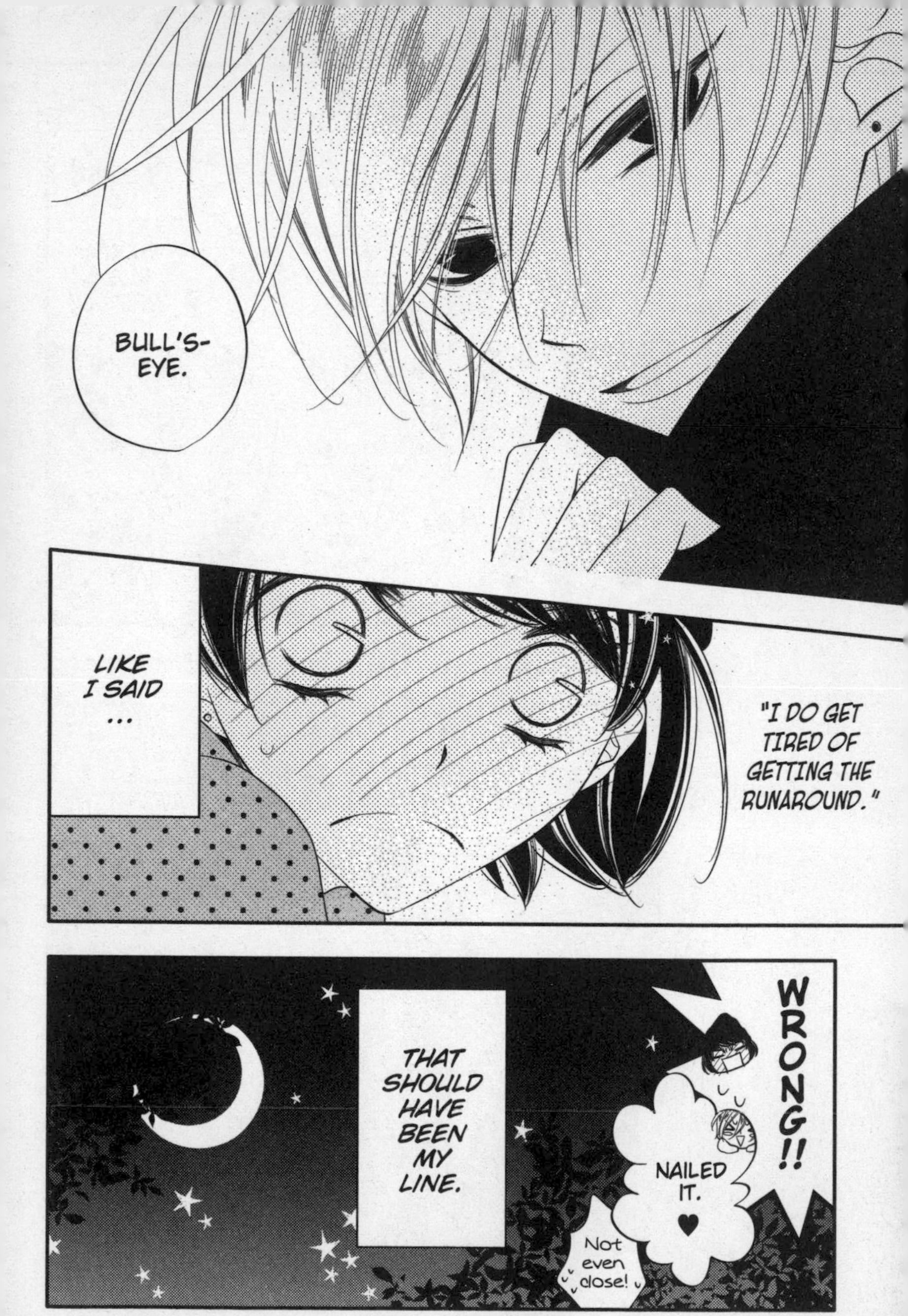
BULL'S-EYE.
LIKE I SAID ...
"I DO GET TIRED OF GETTING THE RUNAROUND."
WRONG!!
NAILED IT. ♥
Not even close!
THAT SHOULD HAVE BEEN MY LINE.

ANONYMOUS NOISE SONG 64 SIDE B / THE END

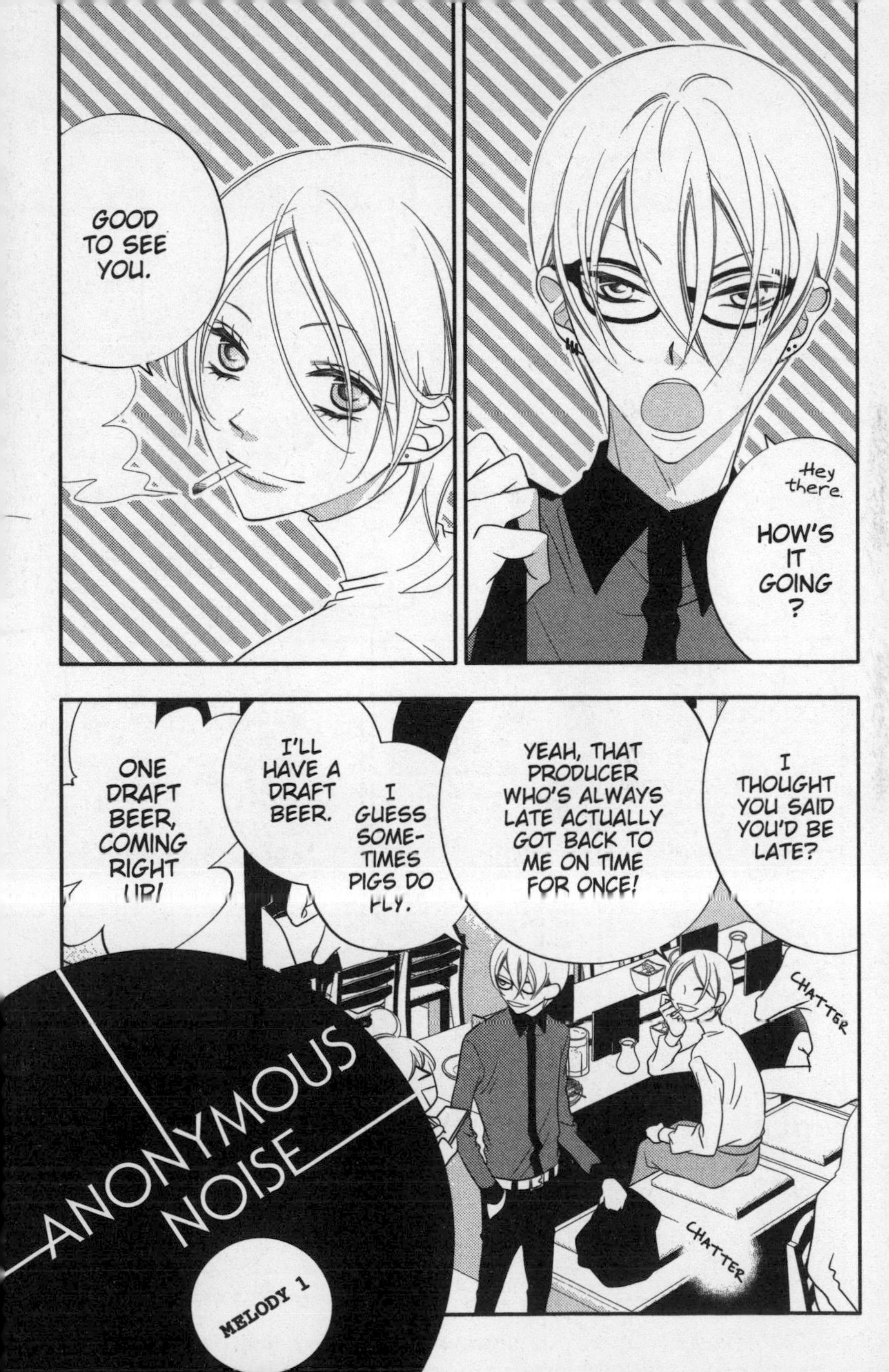
Hey there.
HOW'S IT GOING?
GOOD TO SEE YOU.
I THOUGHT YOU SAID YOU'D BE LATE?
YEAH, THAT PRODUCER WHO'S ALWAYS LATE ACTUALLY GOT BACK TO ME ON TIME FOR ONCE!
I GUESS SOME-TIMES PIGS DO FLY.
I'LL HAVE A DRAFT BEER.
ONE DRAFT BEER, COMING RIGHT UP!
CHATTER
CHATTER
ANONYMOUS NOISE
MELODY 1

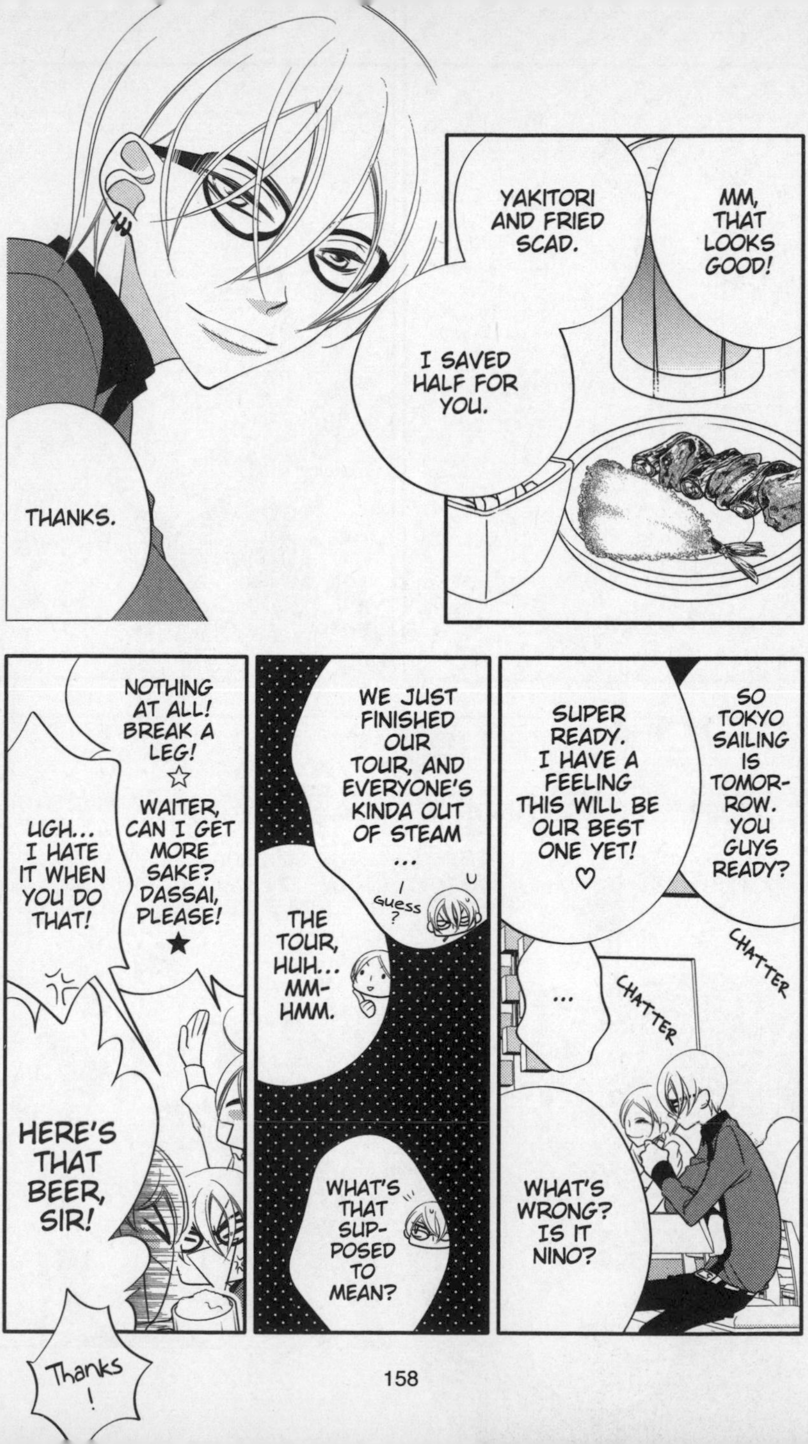
MM, THAT LOOKS GOOD!
YAKITORI AND FRIED SCAD.
I SAVED HALF FOR YOU.
THANKS.
SO TOKYO SAILING IS TOMORROW. YOU GUYS READY?
SUPER READY. I HAVE A FEELING THIS WILL BE OUR BEST ONE YET! ♡
CHATTER
CHATTER
...
WHAT'S WRONG? IS IT NINO?
WE JUST FINISHED OUR TOUR, AND EVERYONE'S KINDA OUT OF STEAM...
I guess?
THE TOUR, HUH... MM-HMM.
WHAT'S THAT SUPPOSED TO MEAN?
NOTHING AT ALL! BREAK A LEG! ☆
WAITER, CAN I GET MORE SAKE? DASSAI, PLEASE! ★
UGH... I HATE IT WHEN YOU DO THAT!
HERE'S THAT BEER, SIR!
Thanks!

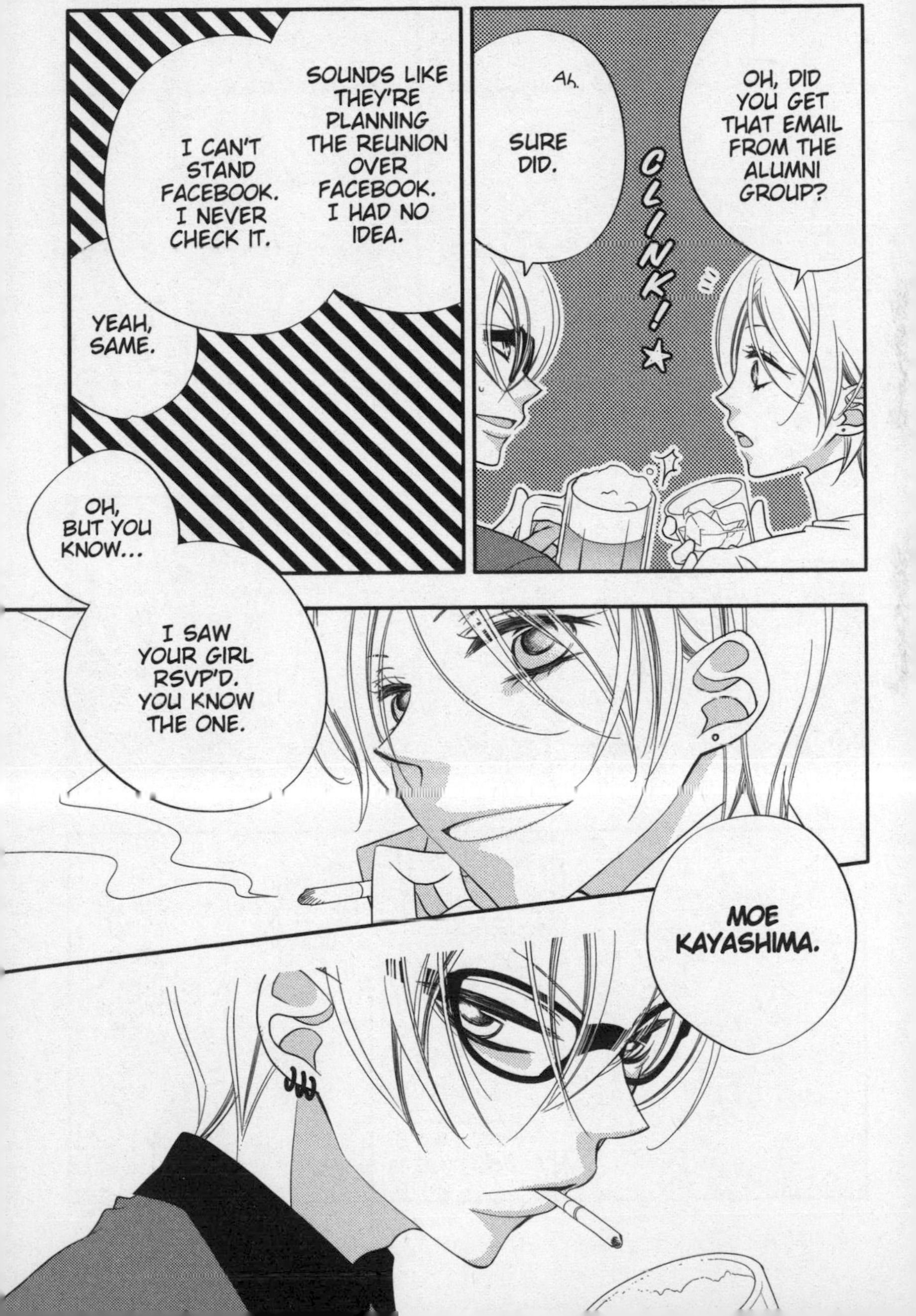
OH, DID YOU GET THAT EMAIL FROM THE ALUMNI GROUP?
CLINK!★
Ah.
SURE DID.
SOUNDS LIKE THEY'RE PLANNING THE REUNION OVER FACEBOOK. I HAD NO IDEA.
I CAN'T STAND FACEBOOK. I NEVER CHECK IT.
YEAH, SAME.
OH, BUT YOU KNOW...
I SAW YOUR GIRL RSVP'D. YOU KNOW THE ONE.
MOE KAYASHIMA.

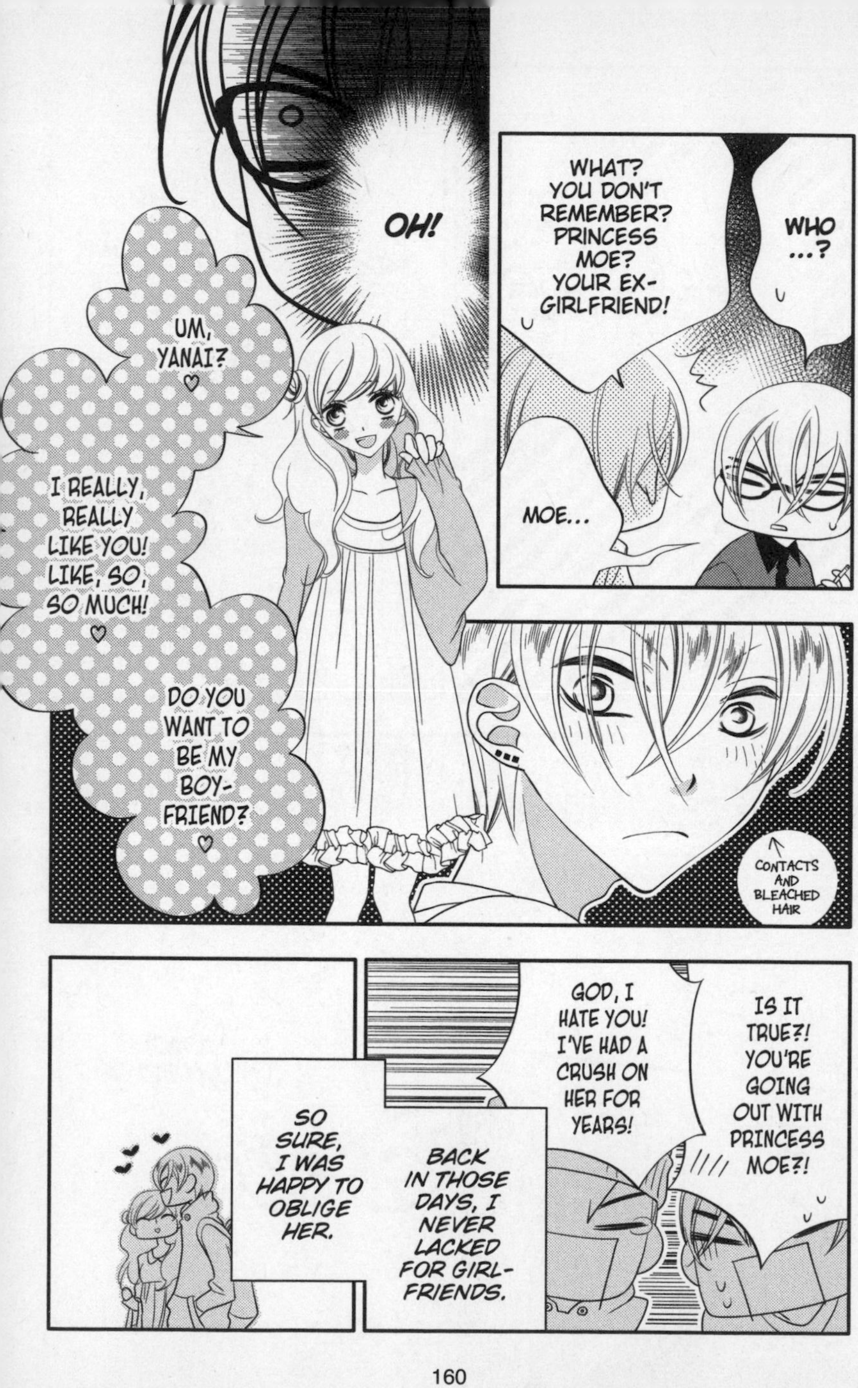
WHO ...?
WHAT? YOU DON'T REMEMBER? PRINCESS MOE? YOUR EX-GIRLFRIEND!
MOE...
CONTACTS AND BLEACHED HAIR
OH!
UM, YANAI? ♡
I REALLY, REALLY LIKE YOU! LIKE, SO, SO MUCH! ♡
DO YOU WANT TO BE MY BOY-FRIEND? ♡
IS IT TRUE?! YOU'RE GOING OUT WITH PRINCESS MOE?!
GOD, I HATE YOU! I'VE HAD A CRUSH ON HER FOR YEARS!
BACK IN THOSE DAYS, I NEVER LACKED FOR GIRL-FRIENDS.
SO SURE, I WAS HAPPY TO OBLIGE HER.

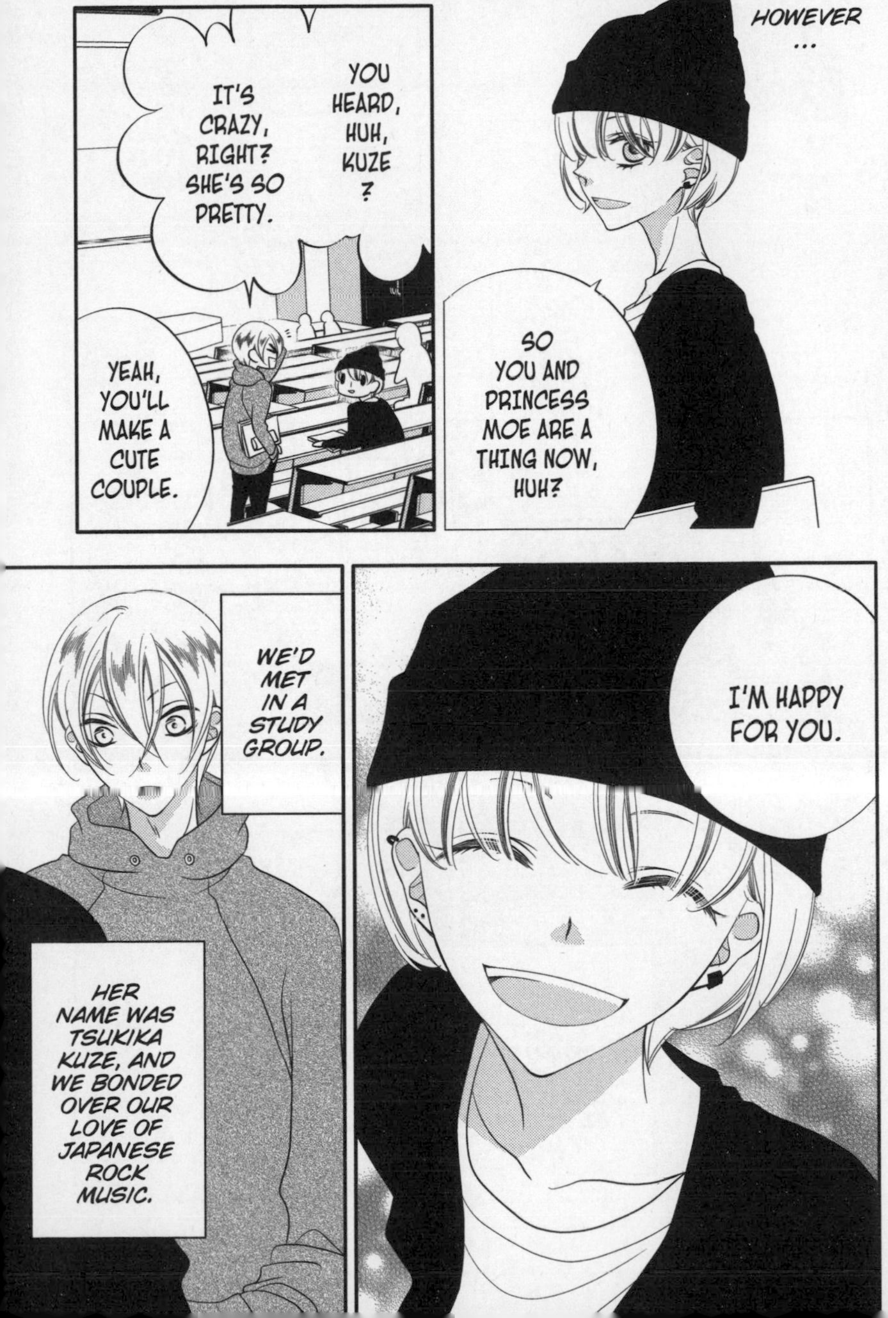
HOWEVER ...
SO YOU AND PRINCESS MOE ARE A THING NOW, HUH?
YOU HEARD, HUH, KUZE?
IT'S CRAZY, RIGHT? SHE'S SO PRETTY.
YEAH, YOU'LL MAKE A CUTE COUPLE.
I'M HAPPY FOR YOU.
WE'D MET IN A STUDY GROUP.
HER NAME WAS TSUKIKA KUZE, AND WE BONDED OVER OUR LOVE OF JAPANESE ROCK MUSIC.

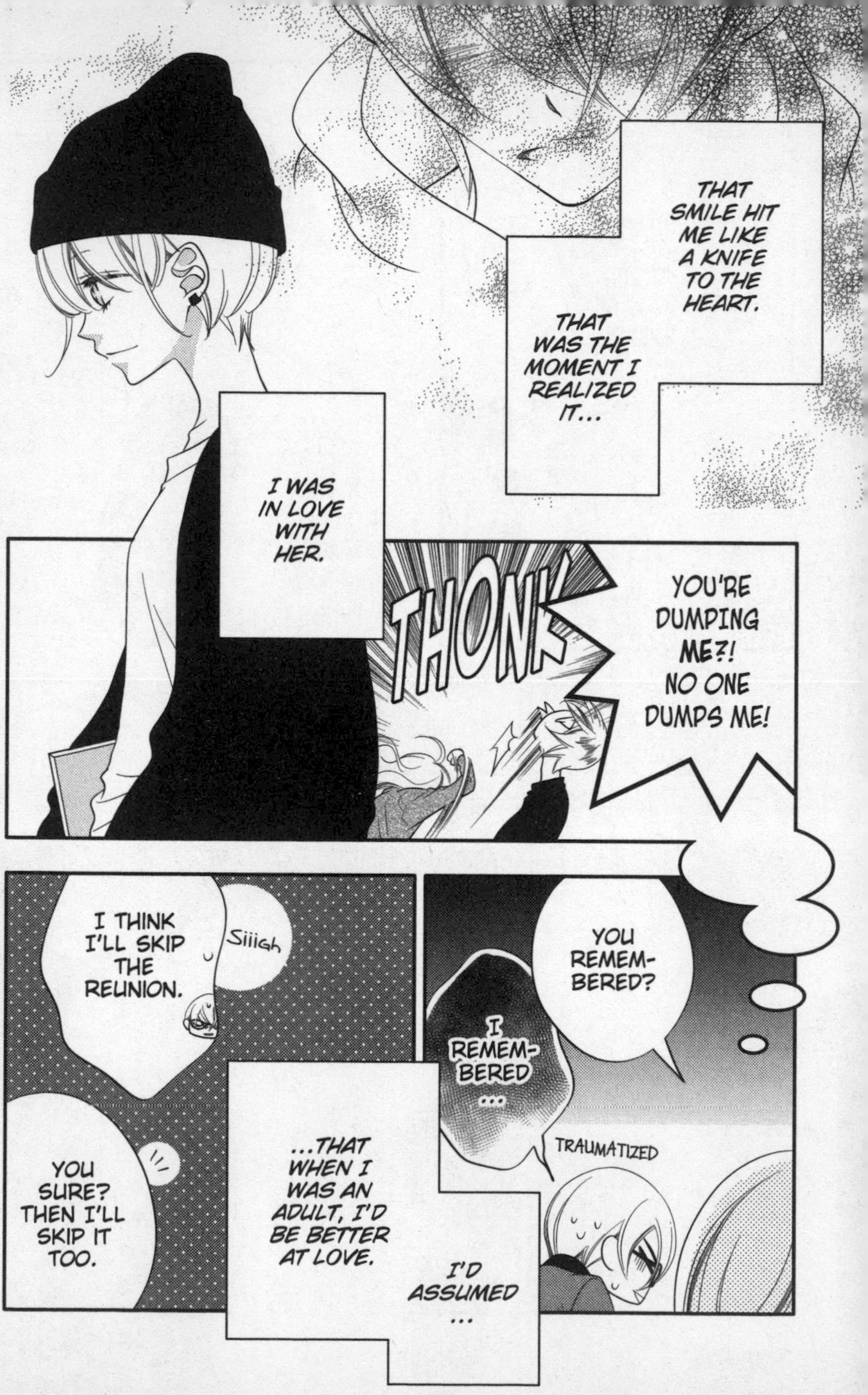
THAT SMILE HIT ME LIKE A KNIFE TO THE HEART.
THAT WAS THE MOMENT I REALIZED IT...
I WAS IN LOVE WITH HER.
YOU'RE DUMPING ME?! NO ONE DUMPS ME!
THONK
YOU REMEMBERED?
I REMEMBERED...
TRAUMATIZED
I'D ASSUMED...
...THAT WHEN I WAS AN ADULT, I'D BE BETTER AT LOVE.
I THINK I'LL SKIP THE REUNION.
Siiigh
YOU SURE? THEN I'LL SKIP IT TOO.

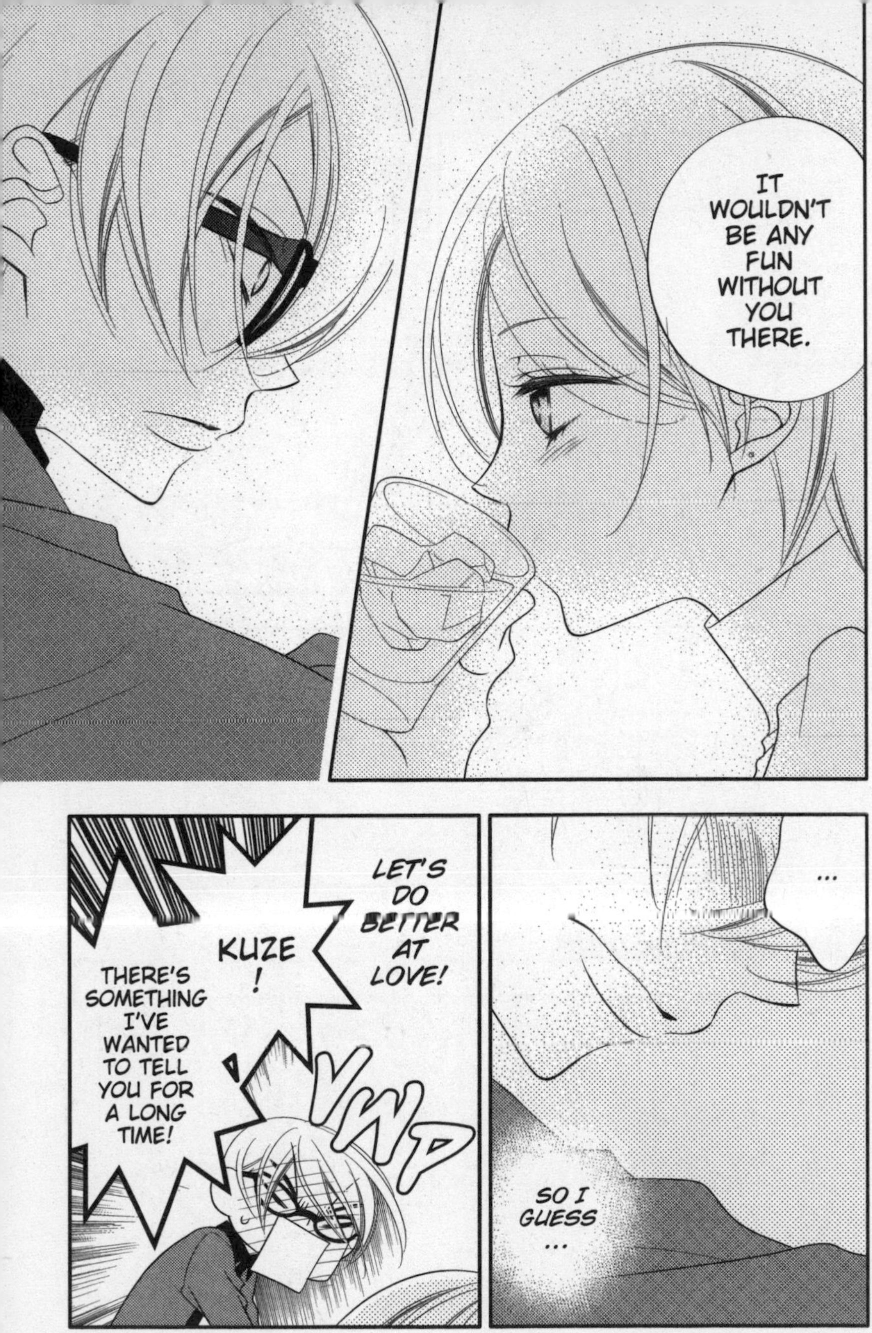
IT WOULDN'T BE ANY FUN WITHOUT YOU THERE.
...
SO I GUESS ...
LET'S DO BETTER AT LOVE!
KUZE!
THERE'S SOMETHING I'VE WANTED TO TELL YOU FOR A LONG TIME!

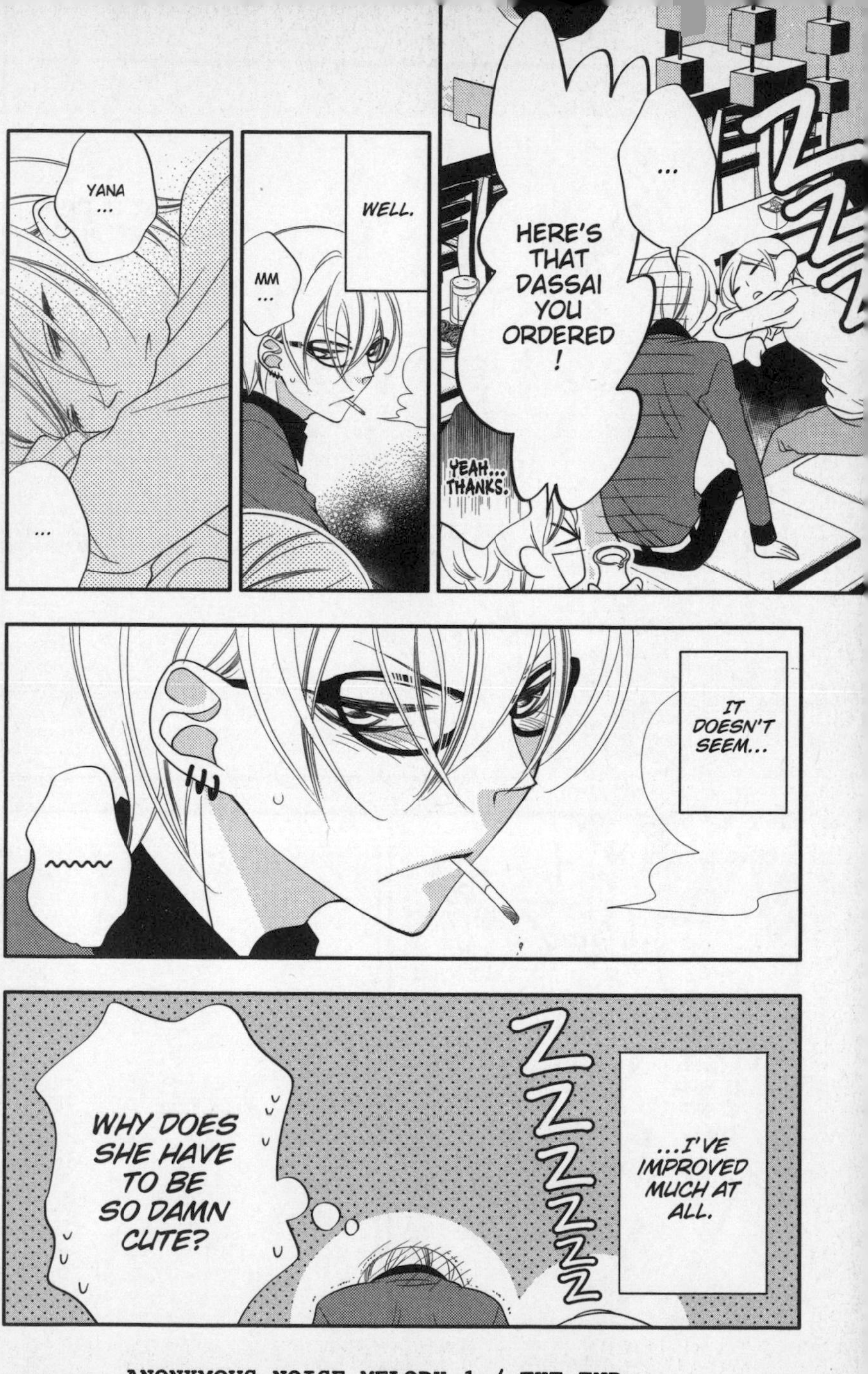
ZZZ
...
HERE'S THAT DASSAI YOU ORDERED!
YEAH... THANKS.
WELL.
MM ...
YANA ...
...
IT DOESN'T SEEM...
...I'VE IMPROVED MUCH AT ALL.
ZZZZZZ
WHY DOES SHE HAVE TO BE SO DAMN CUTE?

ANONYMOUS NOISE MELODY 1 / THE END

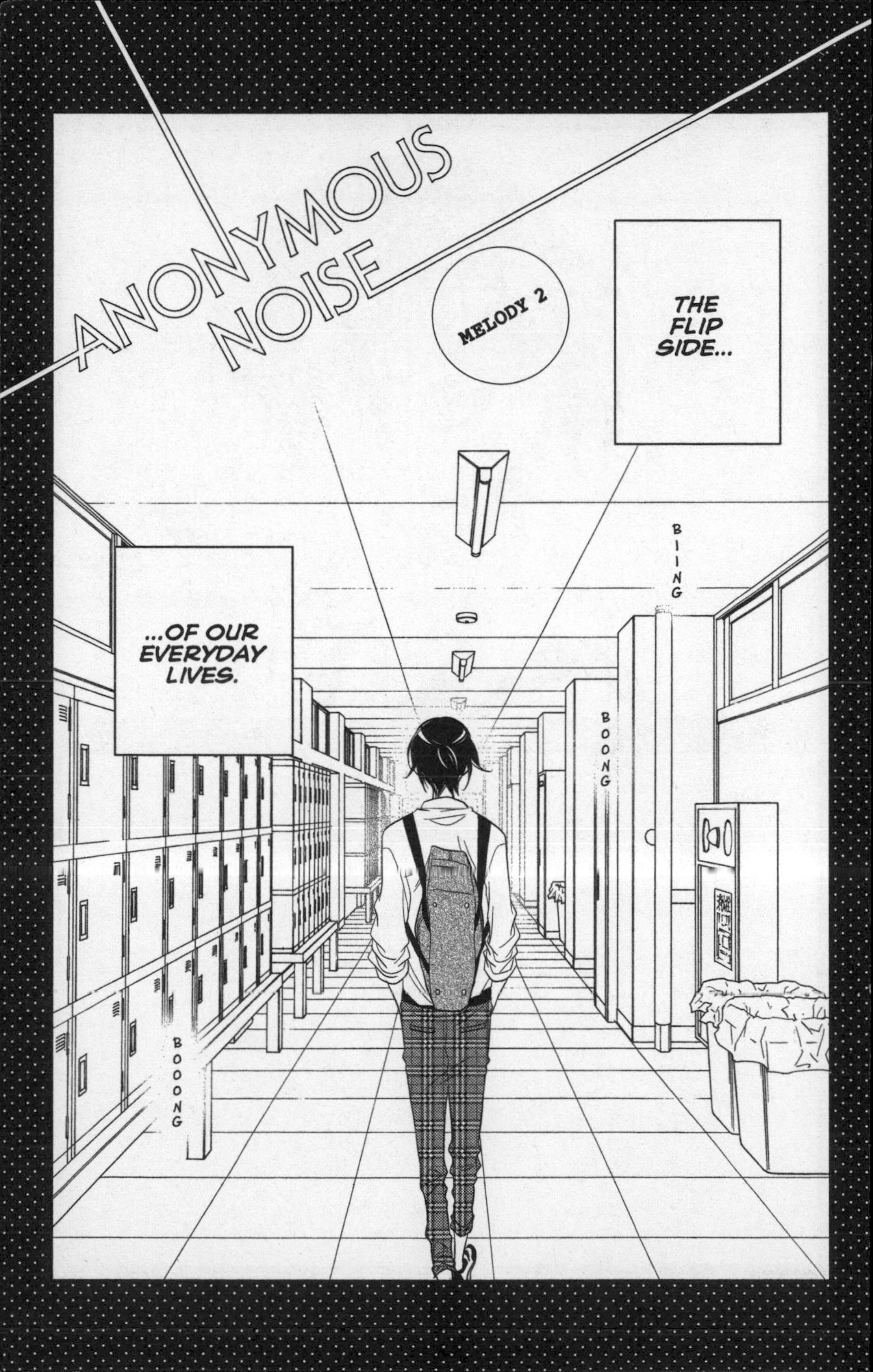
ANONYMOUS NOISE
MELODY 2
THE FLIP SIDE...
BIING
...OF OUR EVERYDAY LIVES.
BOONG
BOOONG

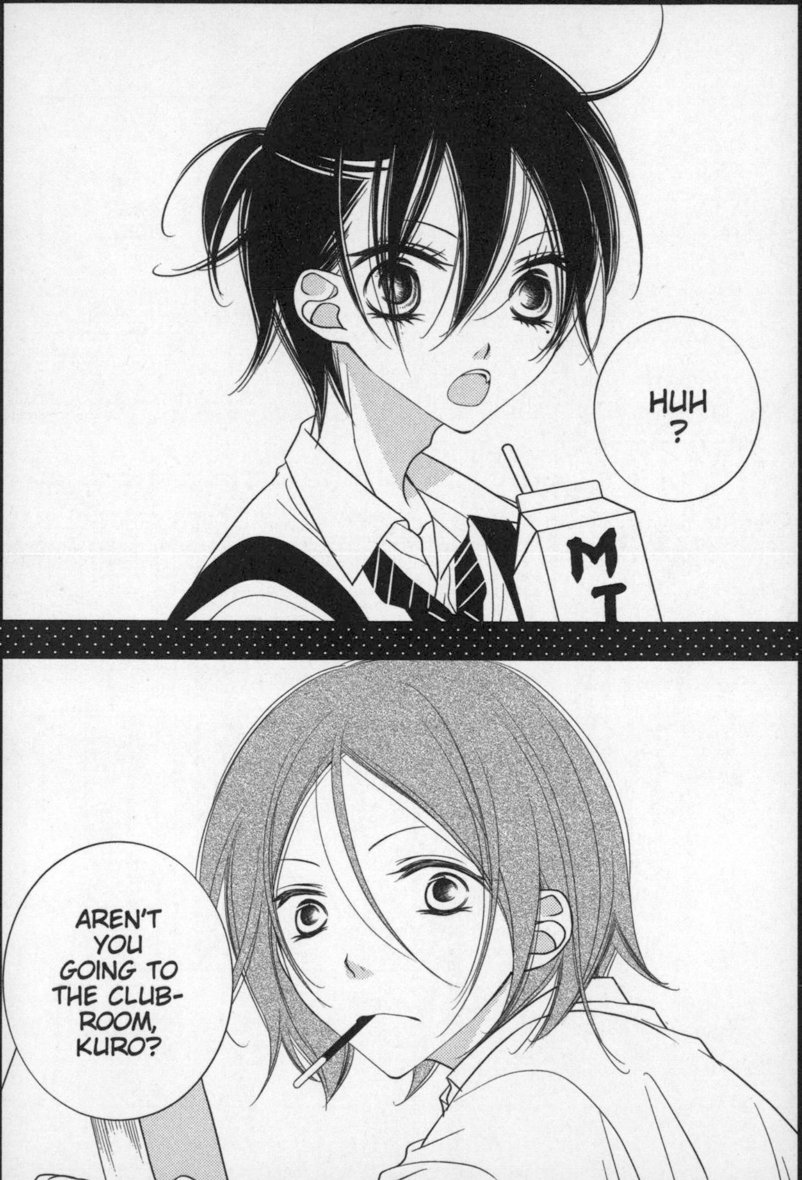
HUH ?
AREN'T YOU GOING TO THE CLUB-ROOM, KURO?

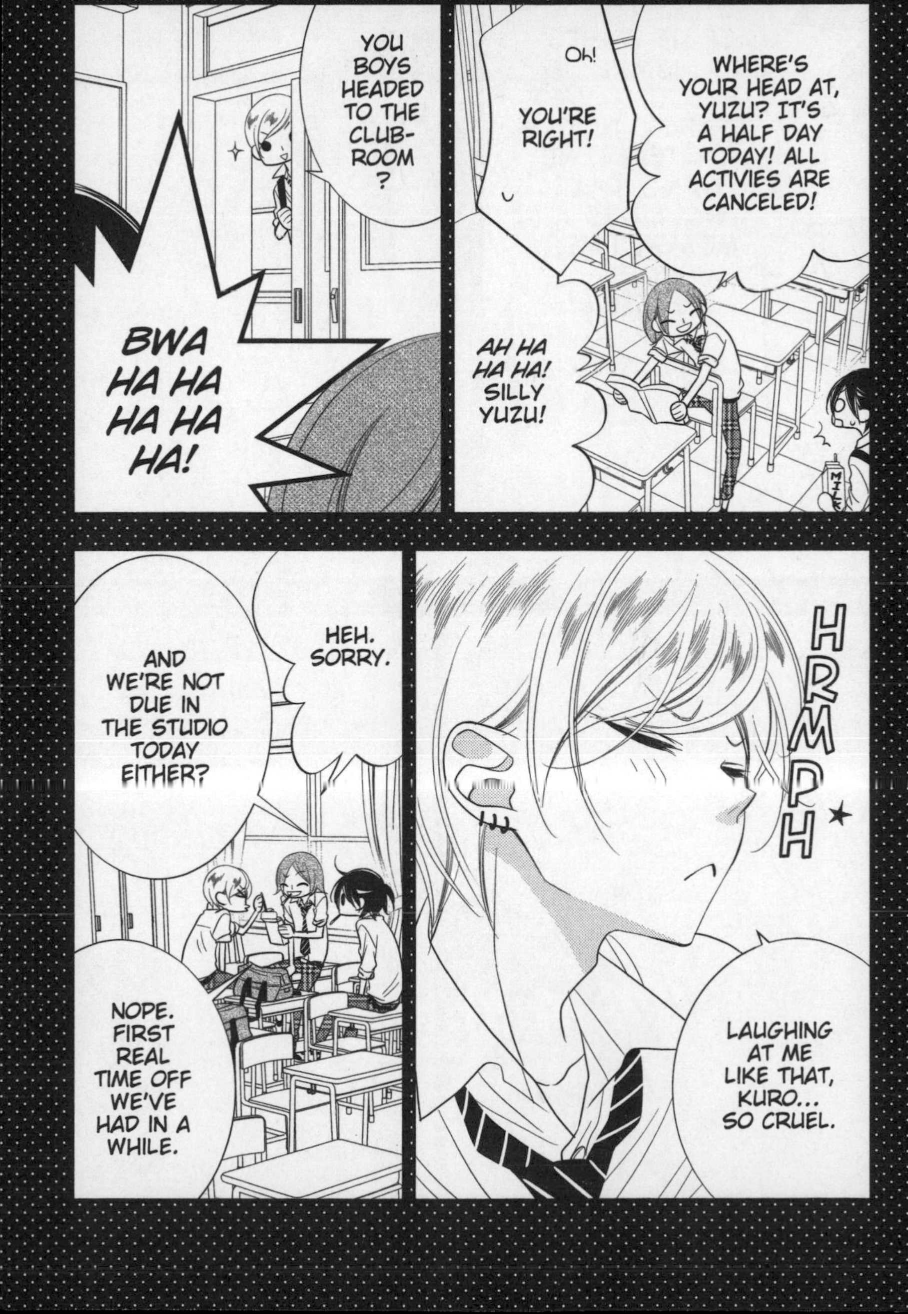
WHERE'S YOUR HEAD AT, YUZU? IT'S A HALF DAY TODAY! ALL ACTIVIES ARE CANCELED!
Oh! YOU'RE RIGHT!
AH HA HA HA! SILLY YUZU!
MILK
YOU BOYS HEADED TO THE CLUB-ROOM?
BWA HA HA HA HA HA!
HRMPH
LAUGHING AT ME LIKE THAT, KURO... SO CRUEL.
HEH. SORRY.
AND WE'RE NOT DUE IN THE STUDIO TODAY EITHER?
NOPE. FIRST REAL TIME OFF WE'VE HAD IN A WHILE.

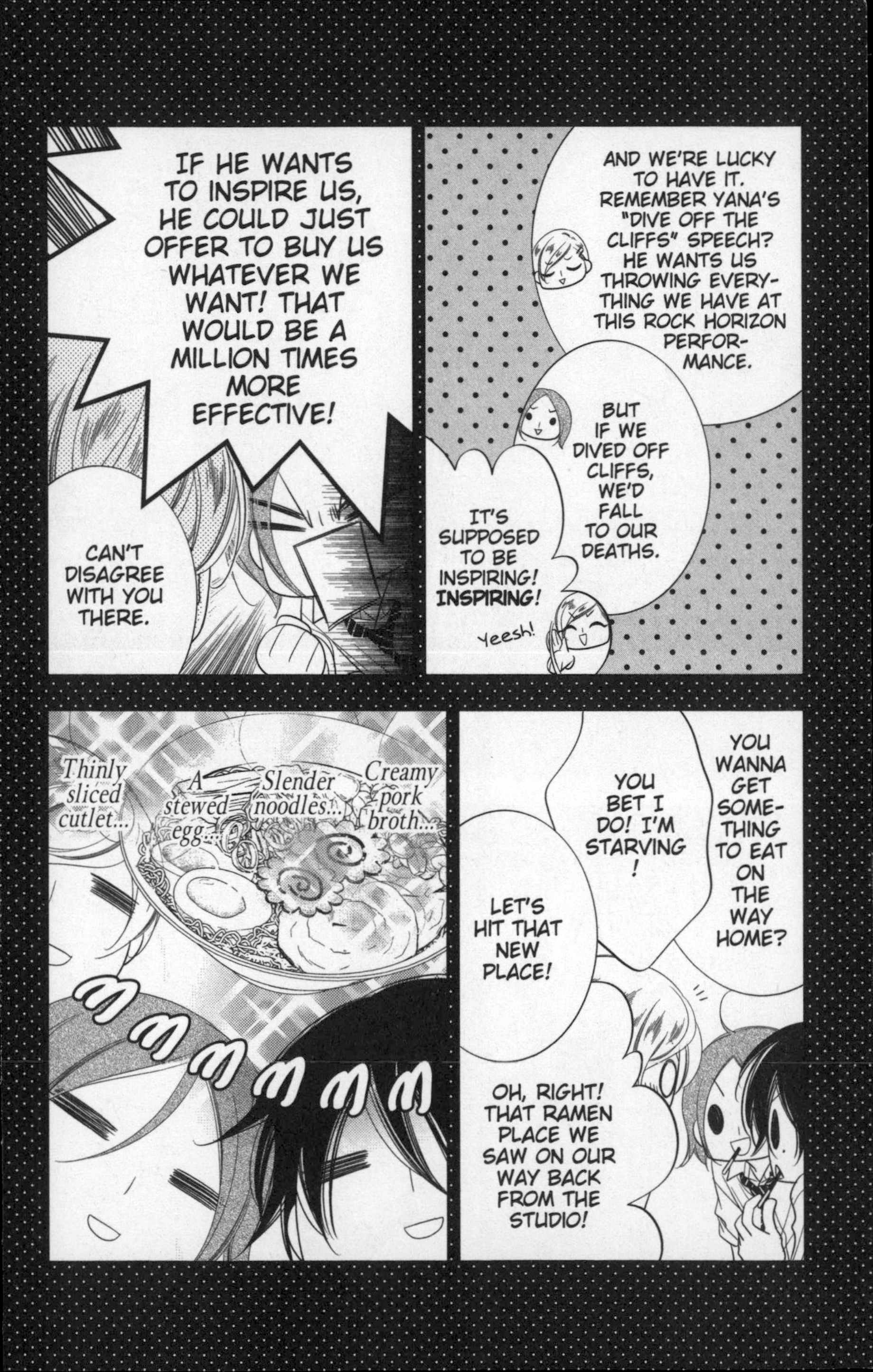
AND WE'RE LUCKY TO HAVE IT. REMEMBER YANA'S "DIVE OFF THE CLIFFS" SPEECH? HE WANTS US THROWING EVERY-THING WE HAVE AT THIS ROCK HORIZON PERFOR-MANCE.
BUT IF WE DIVED OFF CLIFFS, WE'D FALL TO OUR DEATHS.
IT'S SUPPOSED TO BE INSPIRING! **INSPIRING!**
Yeesh!
IF HE WANTS TO INSPIRE US, HE COULD JUST OFFER TO BUY US WHATEVER WE WANT! THAT WOULD BE A MILLION TIMES MORE EFFECTIVE!
CAN'T DISAGREE WITH YOU THERE.
YOU WANNA GET SOME-THING TO EAT ON THE WAY HOME?
YOU BET I DO! I'M STARVING!
LET'S HIT THAT NEW PLACE!
OH, RIGHT! THAT RAMEN PLACE WE SAW ON OUR WAY BACK FROM THE STUDIO!
Creamy pork broth...
Slender noodles...
A stewed egg...
Thinly sliced cutlet...

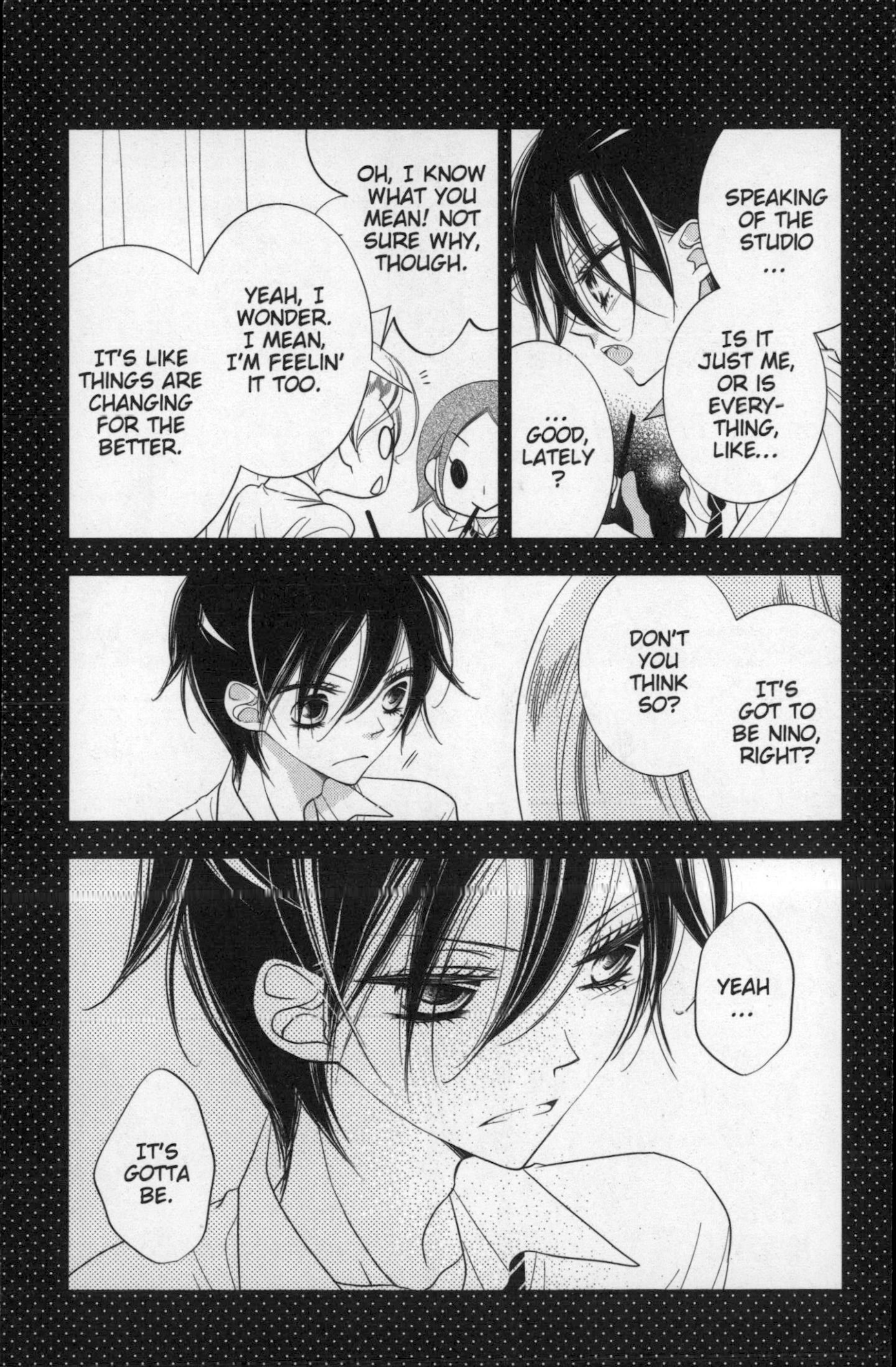
SPEAKING OF THE STUDIO ...
IS IT JUST ME, OR IS EVERY-THING, LIKE...
... GOOD, LATELY ?
OH, I KNOW WHAT YOU MEAN! NOT SURE WHY, THOUGH.
YEAH, I WONDER. I MEAN, I'M FEELIN' IT TOO.
IT'S LIKE THINGS ARE CHANGING FOR THE BETTER.
IT'S GOT TO BE NINO, RIGHT?
DON'T YOU THINK SO?
YEAH ...
IT'S GOTTA BE.

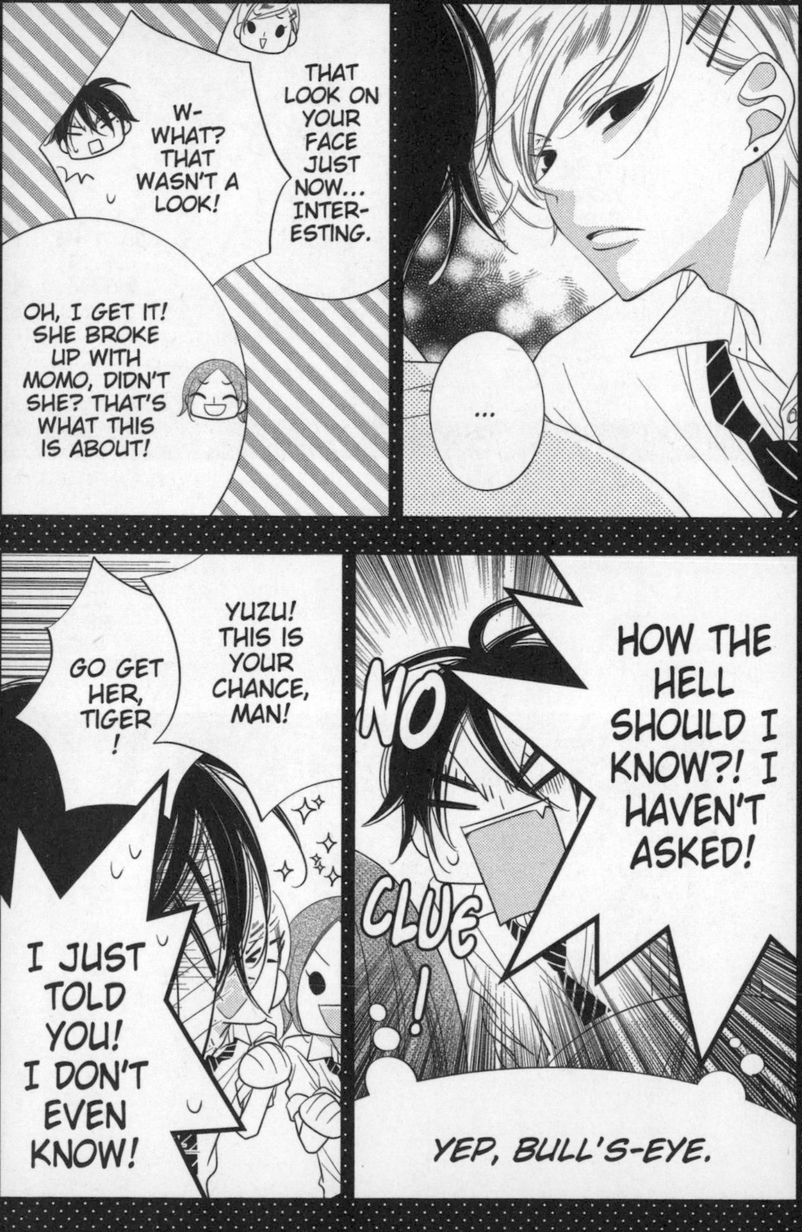
...
THAT LOOK ON YOUR FACE JUST NOW... INTER-ESTING.
W-WHAT? THAT WASN'T A LOOK!
OH, I GET IT! SHE BROKE UP WITH MOMO, DIDN'T SHE? THAT'S WHAT THIS IS ABOUT!
HOW THE HELL SHOULD I KNOW?! I HAVEN'T ASKED!
NO CLUE!
YEP, BULL'S-EYE.
YUZU! THIS IS YOUR CHANCE, MAN!
GO GET HER, TIGER!
I JUST TOLD YOU! I DON'T EVEN KNOW!

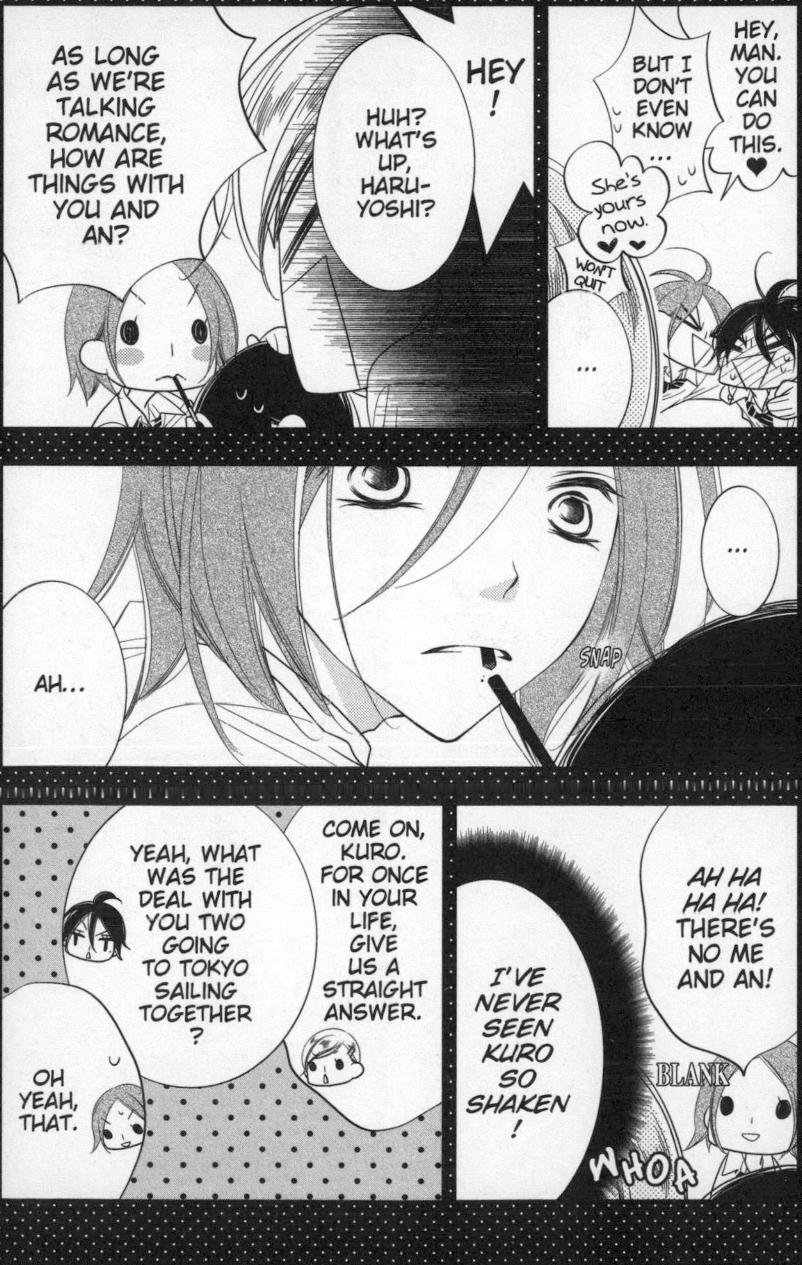
HEY, MAN. YOU CAN DO THIS. ❤
BUT I DON'T EVEN KNOW...
She's yours now. ❤❤
WON'T QUIT
...
HEY!
HUH? WHAT'S UP, HARU-YOSHI?
AS LONG AS WE'RE TALKING ROMANCE, HOW ARE THINGS WITH YOU AND AN?
...
SNAP
AH...
AH HA HA HA! THERE'S NO ME AND AN!
BLANK
I'VE NEVER SEEN KURO SO SHAKEN!
WHOA
COME ON, KURO. FOR ONCE IN YOUR LIFE, GIVE US A STRAIGHT ANSWER.
YEAH, WHAT WAS THE DEAL WITH YOU TWO GOING TO TOKYO SAILING TOGETHER?
OH YEAH, THAT.

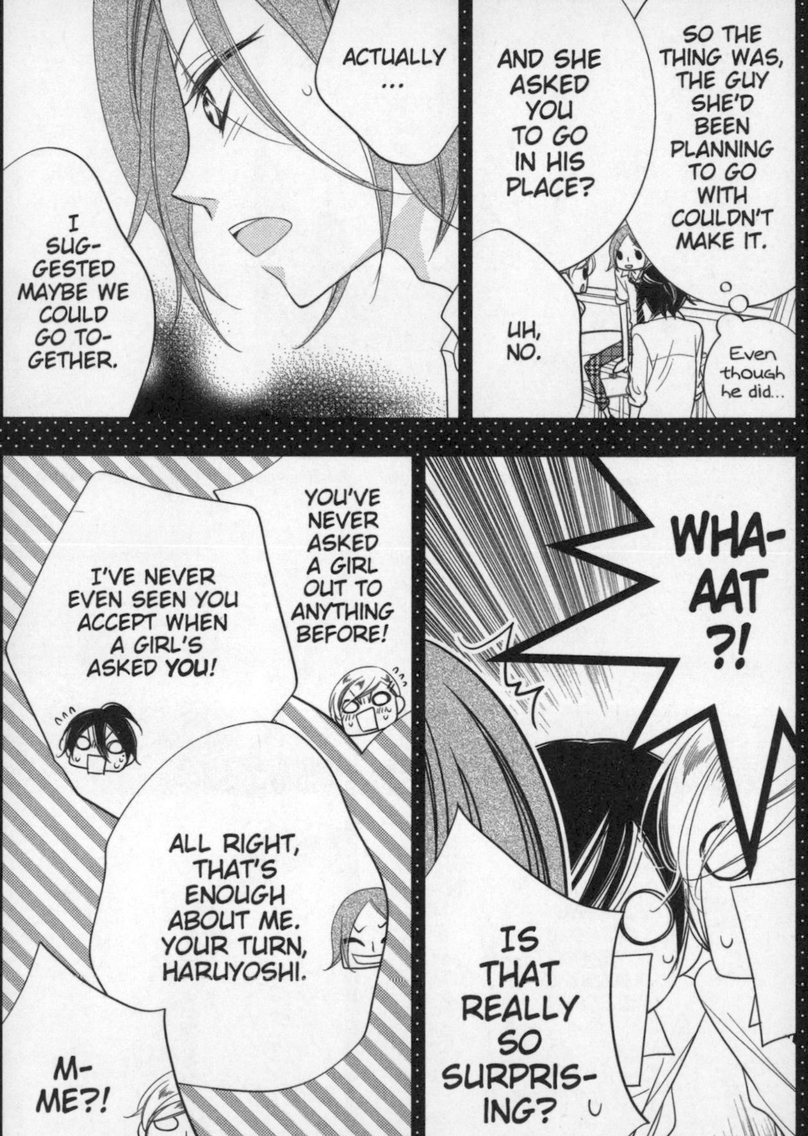
SO THE THING WAS, THE GUY SHE'D BEEN PLANNING TO GO WITH COULDN'T MAKE IT.
AND SHE ASKED YOU TO GO IN HIS PLACE?
UH, NO.
Even though he did...
ACTUALLY...
I SUG-GESTED MAYBE WE COULD GO TO-GETHER.
WHA-AAT?!
IS THAT REALLY SO SURPRIS-ING?
YOU'VE NEVER ASKED A GIRL OUT TO ANYTHING BEFORE!
I'VE NEVER EVEN SEEN YOU ACCEPT WHEN A GIRL'S ASKED YOU!
ALL RIGHT, THAT'S ENOUGH ABOUT ME. YOUR TURN, HARUYOSHI.
M-ME?!

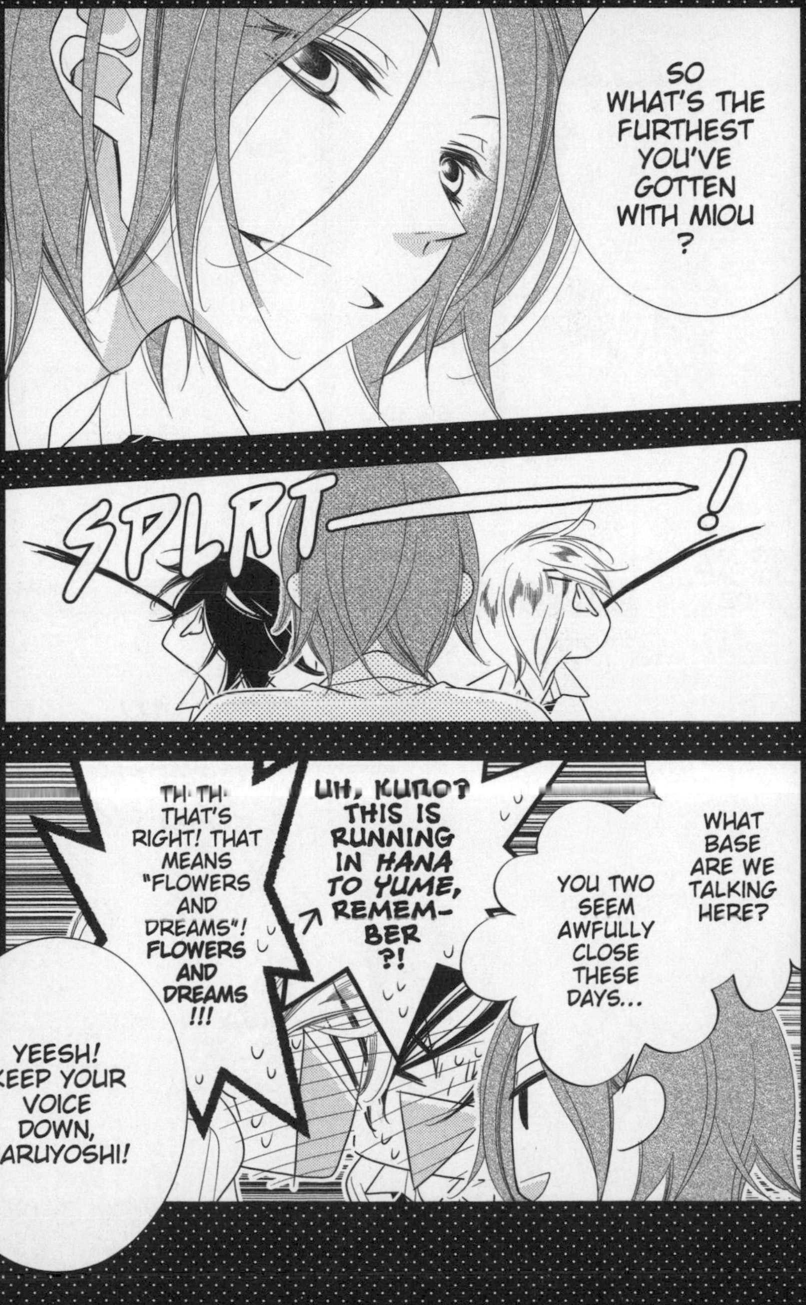
SO WHAT'S THE FURTHEST YOU'VE GOTTEN WITH MIOU ?
SPLRT—!
WHAT BASE ARE WE TALKING HERE?
YOU TWO SEEM AWFULLY CLOSE THESE DAYS...
UH, KURO? THIS IS RUNNING IN HANA TO YUME, REMEMBER?!
TH TH THAT'S RIGHT! THAT MEANS "FLOWERS AND DREAMS"! FLOWERS AND DREAMS!!!
YEESH! KEEP YOUR VOICE DOWN, HARUYOSHI!

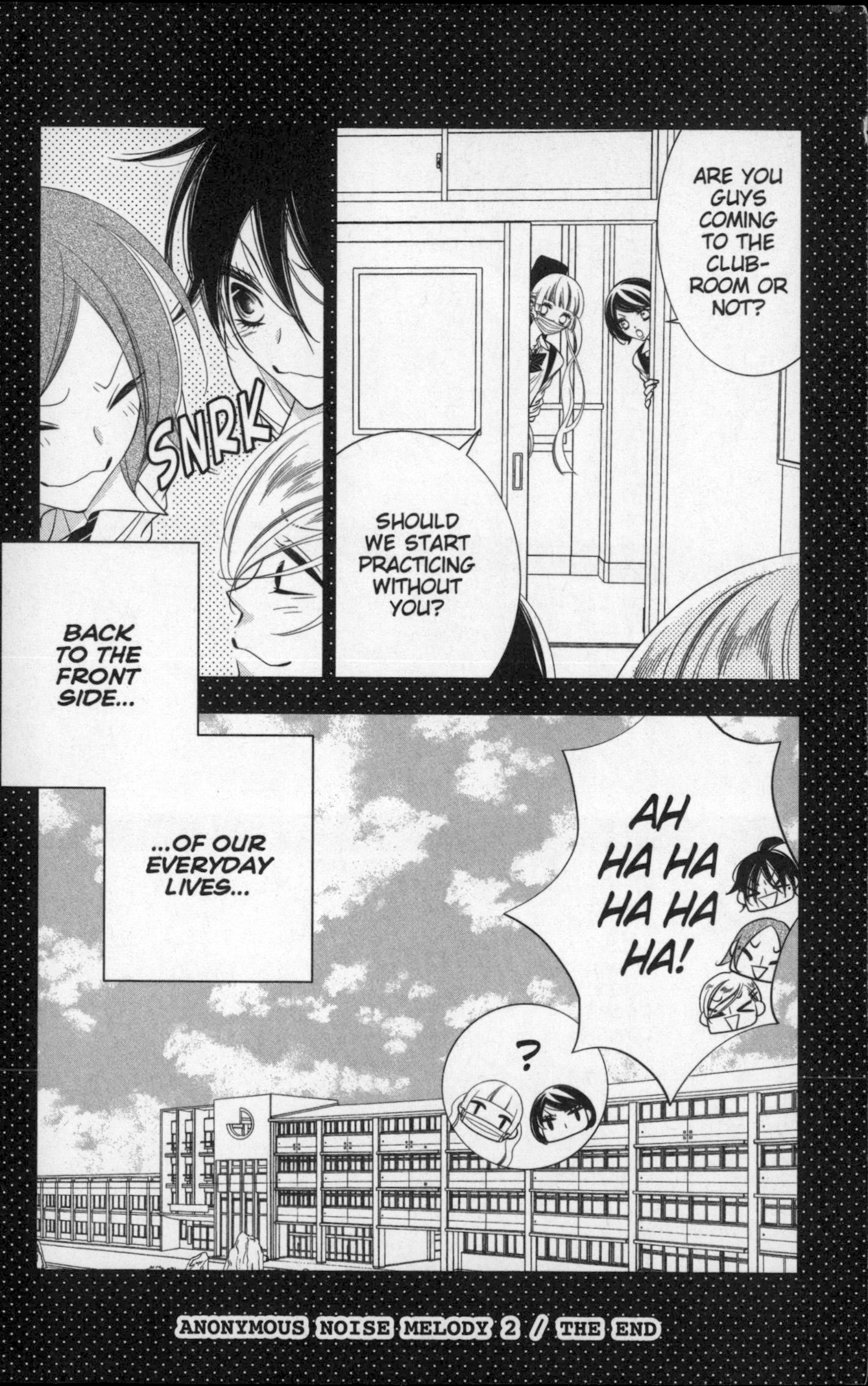
ARE YOU GUYS COMING TO THE CLUB-ROOM OR NOT?
SHOULD WE START PRACTICING WITHOUT YOU?
SNRK
AH HA HA HA HA HA!
?
BACK TO THE FRONT SIDE...
...OF OUR EVERYDAY LIVES...

ANONYMOUS NOISE MELODY 2 / THE END